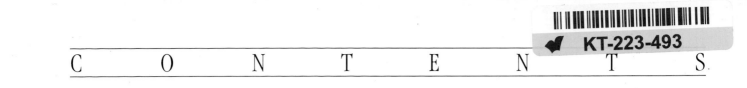
KT-223-493

Like any great cuisine, Italian cooking starts with fresh, local ingredients. Just as outstanding grapes make a fine wine, the best basics become delectable meals.

Italian Cooking

AT • THE • ACADEMY

HALLIE DONNELLY
JANET KESSEL FLETCHER
Writers

SALLY W. SMITH
Editor

KEVIN SANCHEZ
Photographer

SUSAN MASSEY-WEIL
Food Stylist

LIZ ROSS
Photographic Stylist

CALIFORNIA CULINARY ACADEMY

Hallie Donnelly (*left*), a native San Franciscan, has been a chef-caterer for ten years. She holds a degree in music from the University of California, Berkeley, and attended the California Culinary Academy. In France, she studied cooking with Michel Guérard, Roger Vergé, and André Daguin. The author of a book on sushi and sashimi, she has had her own cooking school and television show. She is presently executive chef of the Scottsdale Culinary Institute, a training program for food-industry professionals, and also a consultant for hotels and restaurants. **Janet Kessel Fletcher** (*right*) is a free-lance food and wine writer and editor. She holds a degree in economics from Stanford University and attended the Culinary Institute of America in Hyde Park, N.Y. She has cooked in several west-coast restaurants, including the highly acclaimed Chez Panisse, and now writes a weekly restaurant column for the Oakland *Tribune*. In addition, she writes and produces newsletters, brochures, and promotional literature for clients in the food and wine industry. Ms. Donnelly and Ms. Fletcher are the co-authors of the California Culinary Academy book *Appetizers & Hors d'Oeuvres*.

The California Culinary Academy In the forefront of American institutions leading the culinary renaissance in this country, the California Culinary Academy in San Francisco has gained a reputation as one of the most outstanding professional chef training schools in the world. With a teaching staff recruited from the best restaurants of Western Europe, the Academy educates students from around the world in the preparation of classical cuisine. The recipes in this book were created in consultation with the chefs of the Academy. For information about the Academy, write the Office of the Dean, California Culinary Academy, 625 Polk Street, San Francisco, CA 94102.

Front Cover
The courses of a traditional Italian wine dinner are selected to complement the wines served. This meal features a full-bodied white wine, such as Pinot Grigio, for the pasta and Fried Course, followed by a Chianti for the braised duck (pages 90–91).

Title Page
Italian cooking is a flavorful gathering of regional specialties. Throughout Italy, however, good wine and bread are appreciated.

Back Cover
Upper: Mussels, clams, hot peppers, and toasted bread characterize this Neopolitan shellfish stew, Brodetto alla Neapoletana (page 65).
Lower: For a luscious winter dessert, try Crostata di Frutta alla Panna, a Tuscan tart rich with dried apricots and figs, and topped with Crème Fraîche (page 118).

Special Thanks to Biordi Art Imports; Luciano Creations, supplied by Shears & Window Garden Court; Jeffrey Thomas Fine & Rare Books; Ceramic Showcase; Forrest Jones; Molinari Delicatessen; Debbie Slutsky; Susan White (all San Francisco); Ed and Kaycey Garrone, Monterey, Calif.; David Beckwith, Carmel, Calif.; Derna Passalacqua, Tempe, Ariz.; Maria Zacco, Rome, Italy

Contributors

Illustrator
Edith Allgood

Additional Photographers
Alan Copeland, at the Academy; Marshall Gordon, pages 14,16, 38, 43, 67, and 80; Kit Morris, authors and chefs, at left; Jackson Vereen, page 66

Additional Food Stylists
M. Susan Broussard, page 66; Doug Warne, pages 14,16, 38, 43, 67, and 80

Copy Chief
Melinda E. Levine

Editorial Coordinator
Kate Rider

Copyeditor
Antonio Padial

Proofreader
Andrea Y. Connolly

Indexer
Elinor Lindheimer

Editorial Assistants
Tamara Mallory, Raymond F. Quinton, Leslie Tilley

Composition and Pagination
Linda M. Bouchard, Bob Miller

Series Format Design
Linda Hinrichs, Carol Kramer

Cover Design
Nina Bookbinder

Printed in Hong Kong through Mandarin Offset.

The California Culinary Academy Series is published by the staff of The Cole Group.

Publisher
Brete C. Harrison
Associate Publisher
James Connolly
Director of Operations
Linda Hauck
Director of Production
Steve Lux
Production Assistant
Dotti Hydue

B C D E F G H
3 4 5 6 7 8 9 0

ISBN 1-56426-036-4
Library of Congress Catalog Card Number 92-30274

Address all inquiries to
The Cole Group
4415 Sonoma Highway/ PO Box 4089
Santa Rosa, CA 95402-4089
(707) 538-0492   (800) 959-2717
FAX (707) 538-0497

Distributed to the book trade by Publishers Group West.

Introduction to Italian Cooking

Tomatoes and garlic. Fresh fish and fresh herbs. Hot pasta and vibrant green pesto. These are just some of the many flavors and colors of the lively Italian table. In the following chapters you'll find specialties from every region and corner of Italy, including traditional dishes from fine home cooks and recipes that have made restaurants famous. This first chapter introduces Italian cooking region by region. It also features an explanation of the typical Italian meal and a guide to the ingredients that characterize authentic Italian food. *Buon appetito!*

THE ITALIAN TABLE, REGION BY REGION

Italian cooking is primarily a collection of regional cuisines derived from local ingredients, climate, and geography. The recipes in this book, which are identified by place of origin, are drawn from every corner of Italy.

To appreciate the diversity of Italian cooking, take a closer look at its specialties region by region. From north to south:

Piedmont is wine country, source of some of the best wines of Italy. Barolo, Barbaresco, Nebbiolo d'Alba, Dolcetto, and the sparkling Asti Spumante are among the Piedmontese wines enjoyed worldwide. The region is also renowned for its rare white truffles, for the slender breadsticks of Turin, and for the pungent anchovy-garlic dip, Bagna Cauda (see page 19).

The Valle d'Aosta is a mountainous region known for game and for the rich, nutty fontina cheese. The mountain dwellers of the Valle d'Aosta are big consumers of Polenta (see page 58), potatoes, and bread, all of which are frequently layered with or dipped in melted fontina.

Lombardy is also polenta country. Milan, the urban center of the region, is famous for its cooking—for example, Risotto alla Milanese (see page 61) and a dish of braised veal shanks called Osso Buco (see page 77).

Trentino–Alto Adige features a Germanic style of cooking, not surprising given its proximity to Austria and Switzerland. Fresh pork, smoked pork, and sausages are popular here and may be served with German-style sauerkraut. Many dishes would be equally at home on a German or Austrian table; apple strudel, for example, is a common local dessert. Even some of the white wines of the region are made in the German or Alsatian style.

The Friuli–Venezia Giulia region is not well known for its food, although the ham of San Daniele is highly regarded. The white wines of Friuli, however—especially the Tocai, Pinot Bianco, and Pinot Grigio—are exported to the United States and are delicious with ham and seafood.

The Veneto includes Venice, with its famous scampi from the nearby gulf (see Gamberi del Veneto, page 70), calves' liver with onions, Risi e Bisi (see page 61), and exquisite fish soups. Soave, perhaps the most popular Italian white wine in America, comes from the Veneto.

Emilia-Romagna has a world-renowned cuisine. It is rich, sophisticated cooking more dependent on butter and cream than on olive oil. Bologna produces wonderful sausages and cured meats like mortadella; Parma gives the world Parmesan and prosciutto; Modena produces the sweet-tart balsamic vinegar (*aceto balsamico*) that is increasingly imported to the United States. Bologna is also known for its fresh homemade pasta, used in an endless array of dishes such as *tagliatelle* with Ragù Bolognese (see page 36) and Tortellini in Brodo (see page 38).

Liguria is a coastal region known for its seafood, especially its mussels. Perhaps the most famous Ligurian dish, however, is the aromatic garlic-and-basil sauce called Pesto (see page 35). Tossed with hot pasta and potatoes (see page 41), pesto is a lively reminder of the warmth of the Ligurian sun.

Tuscany is the home of Chianti, of Bistecca alla Fiorentina (see page 76), and of rustic bean soups such as Pasta e Fagioli (see page 28). Tuscan olive oil is prized throughout the world, and its fruity character infuses almost all Tuscan fare. Some of the best cooking in Italy is found in the many *trattorie* (casual restaurants) of Florence and the Tuscan countryside.

The Umbria region is known for black truffles, for pork and pork sausage, and for Orvieto, a light white wine.

The Marches has a varied cuisine, from the *brodetto* (fish soup) of the coast to the *porchetta* (suckling pig) of the interior. It is not a cuisine well known outside its region.

Latium, also known as Lazio, is the region of Rome and is thus one of Italy's gastronomic centers. Roman cooks have given us Saltimbocca (see page 84), Fettuccine Carbonara (see page 41), Carciofi alla Romana (see page 110), and dozens of other popular dishes. Roman restaurants often feature suckling pig or suckling lamb roasted on a spit; vegetables are also served in abundance, from Piselli al Prosciutto (see page 108) to the assertive Cime di Rape alla Romana (see page 110).

Abruzzi is a mountainous region, its cooking hearty but unrefined. Fish, often in the form of Scapece (see page 14), dominates menus near the coast; inland, the diet revolves around pork, a broad variety of vegetables, and the local *scamorze* cheese.

The Campania region includes Naples and Sorrento and boasts a lovely coastline. The cuisine is heavily influenced by what comes from local waters, such as mussels, clams, and squid. The sunny climate yields tomatoes galore for use in salads, in pasta sauce, and on pizza. Neapolitan cooks are not known for their subtle touch; many dishes are aggressively seasoned with garlic, oregano, and olive oil. Pizza alle Vongole (see page 58) and Spaghetti con Aglio e Olio (see page 37) are typical of the assertive flavors of Neapolitan cooking. Among its other distinguishing features is dried pasta, which is much more common here than in the north; fresh pasta is rarely served. The world-renowned mozzarella and provolone cheeses are native to the region; they turn up on pizza, in Calzone (see page 55), and in tomato salads (see Insalata Capricciosa, page 100). Vegetables are used in abundance, especially eggplant, zucchini, spinach, and sweet peppers.

Apulia, in the "heel" of Italy, is surrounded by water. Naturally, the cooking is heavily dependent on seafood. Fish and shellfish fried in the local olive oil (Frutte di Mare Fritti, page 66) are a specialty of the province of Bari. The cooking is similar to that of Naples.

Basilicata is not a region with a strong culinary identity. It is a poor region agriculturally; olive oil is its main product. The cuisine is generally spicy and straightforward.

Calabria, at the tip of the Italian "boot," is also a poor region; its main crops are olives and citrus. The Calabrian diet is a modest one based on dried pasta, tomatoes, eggplant, peppers, and seafood.

Sicily is home to a fascinating array of dishes. The cooking has much in common with that of southern Italy: olive oil, dried pasta, tomatoes, eggplant, peppers, and seafood are used abundantly. Sicilian cooking, however, is more aggressively seasoned—often with hot red peppers. Many dishes, such as Caponatina (see page 23), have a sweet-and-sour component. Sicilians also have a noted sweet tooth, which they assuage with ices, ice cream, and such elaborate creations as Cassata Donna Lugata (see page 122).

A hand-cranked pasta machine makes light work of homemade pasta. Cut by hand or by machine to desired width as shown here (clockwise from left rear): lasagne (see page 42), pappardelle (see page 41) beside uncut dough— both made with Pasta Verde (see page 34), linguine (see page 90) made with Pasta di Herbe (see page 35), and fettuccine (see pages 40–41) made with Pasta di Pomodori (see page 35). Pasta is usually served as a "first course" following the antipasto and preceding the main dish (see page 8).

7

THE ITALIAN TABLE, COURSE BY COURSE

Whether formal or informal, the Italian meal follows a pattern that rarely varies. It isn't built around a main course, as in America; instead, it is a series of small courses, each of relatively equal weight.

In the typical progression, an Italian meal might begin with an *aperitivo* (see page 13), perhaps a glass of sweet or dry vermouth or a Campari and soda. In a private home, the host might offer olives or roasted almonds as an accompaniment.

The first course of an Italian meal is an antipasto, usually an assortment of cured meats, pickled or marinated vegetables, or marinated shellfish. Peperonata (see page 13) and sliced prosciutto, served together, make an appealing and typical antipasto.

Following the antipasto is the "first course" *(primo piatto)*. It may be a risotto, a soup, or a pasta dish. Tortellini in Brodo (see page 38) or Risotto al Limone (see page 61) are both typical first courses.

The second course *(secondo piatto)* may be fish, fowl, or meat. A pork roast seasoned with rosemary (Arrosto di Maiale con Rosmarino, page 84) or a roast chicken stuffed with *porcini* mushrooms (see page 88) would be an appropriate second course. With rare exceptions, vegetables, such as Cime di Rape alla Romana (see page 110) and Piselli al Prosciutto (see page 108), are not served on the same plate as the meat but are offered in separate side dishes.

A salad of raw or very simply cooked greens or vegetables, such as Insalata Mista (see page 100), may follow the second course. If the second course is a grill, the salad sometimes accompanies it in a separate dish; the Roman Insalata dell' Estate (see page 101) is an example.

Italians rarely end a meal with dessert. Instead, meals end with fresh fruit, fruit macerated in wine (Pesche al Vino, page 114), or a wedge of ripe cheese. Espresso, drunk black, is served after the fruit or cheese course; in a home, espresso is served away from the table.

Restaurant Cooking and Home Cooking

The dishes featured in the following chapters are drawn from a variety of sources. Some, such as Pollo con Cavolo al Limone (see page 88), are representative of Italian home cooking and are rarely found in restaurants outside of small, family-run *trattorie*.

Other dishes in this book are rarely made outside of restaurants, although there is no reason they can't be duplicated in the home. Carpaccio (see page 19) is closely associated with Harry's Bar in Venice, where it was invented. Today many restaurants offer it, but the home cook can also prepare it with ease.

In Italy, pizza, bread, and ice cream are rarely made at home. Pizza is a snack food, bought by the slice. Ice cream and fruit ices are enjoyed in caffès or bought from street vendors. Fresh bread is purchased daily from a bakery.

Many American cooks, however, delight in making these items, so the following chapters include recipes for pizza and calzone, traditional breads, and seasonal ice creams.

A LITTLE CULINARY GRAMMAR

For those unfamiliar with Italian, a few tips may help in understanding the terms in this book.

Italian nouns are either masculine *(il pomodoro)* or feminine *(la pera)*. The plural is formed by changing the ending of the word. The preceding articles agree with the nouns.

Examples: *il pomodoro* (the tomato), *i pomodori* (the tomatoes); *la pera* (the pear), *le pere* (the pears); *l'insalata* (the salad), *le insalate* (the salads); *l'antipasto* (the antipasto), *gli antipasti* (the antipastos).

Adjectives, which usually follow nouns, generally agree with the nouns that they modify. Thus: *calamari verdi* (green squid) but *lasagne verde* (green lasagne), *fritto misto* (mixed fry) but *insalata mista* (mixed salad).

These are very general guidelines; for almost every rule there is an exception.

THE ITALIAN KITCHEN IN AMERICA

To reproduce the authentic flavors of the Italian kitchen, stock your pantry and refrigerator with some of the items that Italians use repeatedly. Many of these foods are available in well-supplied supermarkets. If you have difficulty finding them, check specialty stores, Italian markets, and mail-order sources.

Amaretti are crisp almond macaroons sprinkled with coarse sugar. Amaretti are delicious with after-dinner espresso; they can be crumbled and sprinkled over sugared peaches or ice cream sundaes or folded into sweetened whipped cream to make the frozen Biscuit Tortoni (see page 120).

Anchovies are generally available in supermarkets as oil-packed fillets. Far superior are the whole salt-packed anchovies available in some Italian markets and specialty stores. To use whole anchovies, rinse off the salt. Under cold running water, split them open lengthwise with your fingers and lift away the skeleton. Anchovies add a pungent salted-fish flavor to sauces, butters, dressings, pizza, and stuffings.

Arborio rice is the stubby, short-grain polished rice grown in Italy's Po Valley. Its particular starch composition makes it the preferred rice for Italian risotto (see page 61). Italian markets, specialty stores, and some well-stocked supermarkets offer Arborio rice.

Arugula, also known as rocket or roquette, is a salad green that is increasingly cultivated in this country. When young, it has a mild nutty flavor; older leaves develop a peppery pungency. Use young arugula leaves in mixed green salads (Insalata Mista, page 100) or toss them at the last minute with hot pasta. To store arugula, wash and dry, then wrap in paper towels and place in a plastic bag; it will keep in the refrigerator for two to three days.

Balsamic vinegar is an aromatic sweet/tart wood-aged vinegar made from Italian red wine. The best balsamic vinegar is aged for many years and can be very expensive. However, less expensive bottlings are now widely available in this country. The vinegar imparts a distinctive mellow flavor to salads, vegetable dishes, and sauces (see Roasted Balsamic Onions, page 22, and Balsamic Vinaigrette, page 99).

Capers are the unopened buds of a Mediterranean bush; they are generally packed in brine but may occasionally be found packed in salt. Capers add a piquant note to countless Italian dishes, from Agnello con Acciughe e Caperi (see page 82) to Caponatina (see page 23). Choose the tiny nonpareil type rather than the large capers.

Ceci are also known as chick-peas or garbanzo beans. They are widely available canned in supermarkets; some health-food stores and specialty markets carry dried ceci, too. Marinated ceci are often served in Italy as part of an antipasto platter, with sliced meats; they are also added to hearty soups containing vegetables and pasta or rice (see Minestrone Primavera, page 28).

Grappa is a strong, clear Italian brandy made from the distilled remains of pressed grapes. In many Italian homes and restaurants, it is offered after dinner as a digestive.

Italian parsley is a flat-leaf parsley, as opposed to the curly-leaf parsley common in American supermarkets. It has a more pungent flavor and is preferred for Italian cooking. It is fairly widely available; it is also easy to cultivate at home.

Olives are an important ingredient in Italian cooking. They may be served before the meal with an *aperitivo* or as part of a platter of *antipasti* (see Italian Olives, page 15). Olives also impart their pungent flavor to sautéed dishes. For Italian cooking, use imported Mediterranean olives. Among Italian varieties available in specialty markets are the Lugano (a brine-cured, purple-black olive), the Ponentine (a brine-cured, purple-black olive, milder than the Lugano), and the Gaeta (a salt-cured, wrinkled black olive rubbed with oil). French, Greek, or Moroccan varieties are satisfactory substitutes.

Polenta is coarsely ground yellow cornmeal used in a variety of northern Italian dishes (see pages 58–59). Many supermarkets sell polenta; health-food stores and Italian markets often carry it in bulk. It should be stored in a cool, dry place and used within six months.

Porcini are the same wild mushrooms known as *cèpes* in French and as *boletus edulis* in Latin. Fresh *porcini* are fleshy, velvety, and earthy in flavor; the dried porcini are highly aromatic, with an intense woodsy flavor. The recipes in this book call for dried porcini, which are available in Italian markets and specialty stores; they are expensive, but a little goes a long way. To reconstitute, soak them until softened in warm water, about one hour. Lift them out of the soaking liquid with a slotted spoon, strain the liquid through cheesecloth to remove any grit, and save liquid for soups and sauces. Store unused dried porcini in an airtight container in a cool, dry place.

Salt cod is a popular food in southern Italy, even when fresh cod is available. It has a firm, meaty texture that can stand up to hearty treatments (see Baccalà Fritto alla Siciliana, page 44). Salt cod is sold in Italian markets in long slabs; supermarkets occasionally sell it packed in wooden boxes. It must be soaked first in several changes of cold water for about a day to soften it and remove much of the salt. Before soaking, it will keep indefinitely in a cool, dry place.

Semolina is an ivory-colored flour ground from high-protein durum wheat. It is available in both coarse and fine grinds. Semolina is used in most factory-made dried pasta because it makes a sturdy dough that stands up to the kneading and molding. Semolina is also used to make the dumplings known as *gnocchi* (see page 61) and is used in some Italian breads and puddings.

Fresh and canned tomatoes are among the most widely used ingredients in Italian cooking, especially southern Italian cooking. The pear-shaped plum tomatoes are preferred for sauces, as they have a high proportion of meat to seeds and juice. Use fresh plum tomatoes only when they are ripe and fragrant; otherwise, canned plum tomatoes are a better choice. The imported Italian plum tomatoes are generally packed riper than American brands and are preferable.

Sun-dried tomatoes are sometimes available in cellophane packets but are more usually packed in olive oil, which is the form called for in the recipes in this book. Gourmet shops and well-stocked supermarkets carry them. They have a sweet, almost candied tomato flavor and a chewy texture. They are also sometimes extremely salty and should be used in small quantities, to garnish pizza, to flavor pasta dough (see Pasta di Pomodori, page 35), to give a lift to a salad (see Fagioli Bianchi con Peperonata, page 100), or to intensify the flavor of a tomato sauce. Store sun-dried tomatoes, covered with oil, in a capped jar in the refrigerator. They will keep for an indefinite period.

Tomato paste is used to add a concentrated tomato flavor to sauces and stews. Store leftover tomato paste in a nonmetal container covered with a thin film of olive oil; it will keep in the refrigerator for up to two weeks or in the freezer indefinitely. Alternatively, some markets now sell imported Italian tomato paste in tubes, allowing you to use as little as you need and refrigerate the rest indefinitely.

To begin a meal Italians offer savory antipasti such as cured meats, olives, some of the country's famed cheeses, or giardiniera—pickled vegetables.

Antipasti

An Italian meal usually begins with an antipasto, an appetizer course. In this chapter you'll find a representative assortment of antipasti, from the bread-based *crostini* (see page 17) and vegetables with dips (see Legumi in Pinzimonio, page 23) to elegant Carpaccio (see page 19). The chapter also contains an explanation of the Italian before-dinner *aperitivo* (see page 13), step-by-step photographs showing how to roast red peppers (see page 14) and prepare artichoke hearts (see page 16), special features on Italian wines (page 17) and cheeses (page 20), and a description of the tempting cured meats and sausages of Italy (see page 23).

Mixed sweet peppers make tricolored Peperonata, a lively late-summer antipasto. For a more substantial first course, pair the peppers with sliced mozzarella.

ANTIPASTI

The word *antipasto* literally means "before the pasta" and historically refers to any dish served before the pasta course. In actuality, however, even a meal without a pasta course can be launched with a tempting selection of *antipasti*. The portions should be small and the flavors piquant to stimulate the appetite. Popular antipasti include marinated vegetables like Peperonata (see opposite page); marinated fish such as Insalata di Calamari (see page 14) or Scapece (see page 14); thin-sliced salty cheeses and hams, such as Ricotta Salata e Prosciutto (see page 21); olives, marinated or plain; and rustic grilled garlic breads like Bruschetta (opposite page).

ANTIPASTI GRATINATI
Broiled fontina fingers

Fontina melts and browns beautifully over baked eggplant spears in this easy Bolognese appetizer.

> 4 *Japanese eggplants*
> ¼ *cup olive oil*
> ½ *pound fontina cheese*
> *Salt and freshly ground black pepper*
> ¼ *cup minced Italian parsley*

1. Preheat oven to 400° F. Trim ends off eggplants and slice each lengthwise into four "fingers," approximately ¼ inch thick. Brush a baking sheet with 2 tablespoons of the olive oil. Place eggplant slices on sheet and brush with remaining oil. Bake slices until brown (about 12 to 15 minutes). Transfer to paper towels.

2. Preheat broiler 5 minutes. Slice cheese ¼ inch thick and place a slice on each "finger." Put cheese-topped eggplant slices in broiler and brown, watching carefully, until cheese is bubbly. Transfer to a serving platter or individual plates; sprinkle with salt, pepper, and parsley.

Makes 16 fingers, or 8 individual servings.

BRUSCHETTA
Grilled Tuscan garlic bread

Nothing proves the Italians' love of simple food so well as their fondness for *bruschetta*, the Italian version of garlic toast. Made from sturdy country bread grilled (ideally over an open fire), then liberally rubbed with garlic and brushed with the new-crop olive oil, it is an earthy invention, direct and utterly delicious. Because it is so simple, it requires the best olive oil. Serve Bruschetta by itself with a young red wine, or add a platter of olives, prosciutto, and Parmesan. Note that the oil-and-garlic mixture should sit for at least several hours or as long as three days. The longer the oil sits, the better and stronger the garlic flavor. If you're going to keep it more than a few hours, store cooled oil in a covered jar in a cool place.

- *16 slices coarse country-style bread, ⅓ inch thick*
- *¾ cup olive oil*
- *3 tablespoons minced garlic Coarse salt and freshly ground black pepper*

1. Heat olive oil and garlic in a saucepan until a light haze forms. Garlic should not be allowed to brown. Let oil sit for several days, if possible, or at least a few hours.

2. Preheat broiler 5 minutes. Toast bread on both sides until golden (or, even better, toast it over an open fire). Gently reheat garlic-oil mixture. Brush it generously on one side of each bread slice. Sprinkle slices with salt and pepper and serve hot.

Makes 16 pieces.

PEPERONATA
Mixed marinated peppers

Sweet peppers stewed slowly with tomatoes, herbs, and garlic are a popular summer first course in southern Italy. Serve them with crusty bread to mop up the aromatic juices, or offer Peperonata as part of a larger antipasto platter along with Bruschetta (at left), sliced prosciutto, black olives, and a little Insalata di Calamari (see page 14). Select meaty peppers that feel heavy for their size.

- *½ cup olive oil*
- *2 tablespoons minced garlic*
- *½ yellow onion, minced*
- *2 red bell peppers*
- *2 green bell peppers*
- *1 yellow bell pepper (if unavailable, substitute another red or green pepper)*
- *2 tomatoes, peeled, seeded, and coarsely chopped (see page 29)*
- *2 teaspoons salt*
- *¼ cup fresh oregano leaves*
- *½ red onion, in paper-thin slices, for garnish*
- *2 tablespoons minced parsley, for garnish*
- *2 tablespoons fruity olive oil (optional)*

1. In a large skillet over medium heat, heat the ½ cup olive oil until it is hot but not smoking. Add garlic and onion and sauté, stirring until lightly colored (about 3 minutes).

2. Halve peppers; remove seeds and trim away white ribs. Cut lengthwise into strips ½ inch wide. Add all peppers to skillet at one time and stir to blend with garlic-onion mixture. Add tomatoes and salt and mix gently. Place oregano leaves on top. Cover and simmer slowly until peppers are soft (about 12 to 15 minutes). Remove from heat and transfer to serving bowl to cool.

3. Serve peppers at room temperature, garnishing the top with the sliced red onion and minced parsley. If desired, drizzle with the 2 tablespoons fruity olive oil just before serving.

Makes about 3½ cups, or enough for 8 people as part of an antipasto platter.

HOW TO ROAST RED PEPPERS

1. *Hold peppers over an open gas flame or charcoal fire, or place them under a broiler. Turn often until blackened on all sides. Transfer peppers to a paper bag; close and set aside until cool (15 to 20 minutes).*

2. *Peel peppers; halve; remove stem and seeds. Lay halves flat and use dull side of a small knife to scrape away any black bits of skin and stray seeds. Slice into ¼-inch strips.*

Roasted Red Peppers Prepare 2 red bell peppers as directed above. Put sliced peppers in a medium bowl; add 1 clove finely minced garlic, 2 tablespoons extravirgin olive oil, and 1 teaspoon minced fresh oregano. Salt to taste. Toss to blend and let marinate at room temperature for 1 hour before using.

INSALATA DI CALAMARI
Squid salad

Squid are found in abundance all along Italy's lengthy coastline. Because they're so plentiful and inexpensive, they're made into countless different dishes. Southern Italians turn squid into cool, refreshing salads, seasoning them with garlic, hot peppers, and vinegar, then adding sweet peppers and two kinds of onions for color and crunch.

> 2½ pounds squid
> Salt
> ½ red onion, thinly sliced
> 1 green bell pepper, seeded, ribs removed, and sliced in matchsticks
> 1 red bell pepper, seeded, ribs removed, and sliced in matchsticks
> 1 bunch green onions, sliced in half lengthwise, then in 1-inch lengths on the bias
> 2 small carrots, peeled and cut in matchsticks
> ¾ cup olive oil
> 7 tablespoons white wine vinegar
> 1 tablespoon lemon juice
> ½ teaspoon each *dried basil, oregano, and thyme*
> ½ teaspoon freshly ground black pepper
> 1 teaspoon minced garlic
> 1 dash hot sauce or *pinch hot red-pepper flakes*
> 1 tablespoon balsamic vinegar
> 2 dashes Worcestershire sauce

1. Clean squid and slice bodies into ½-inch rings (see page 66). Poach rings and tentacles in plenty of salted water at a low boil just until they turn white (about ½ to 1 minute). Drain; quickly transfer to a bowl of ice water to stop the cooking. When completely cool, drain well and pat dry.

2. In a large bowl combine squid, onions, peppers, green onions, and carrots.

3. In a bowl whisk together olive oil, wine vinegar, lemon juice, dried herbs, pepper, garlic, hot sauce, balsamic vinegar, and Worcestershire sauce. Add salt to taste. Pour over squid and vegetables; taste and adjust seasoning as necessary. Chill at least 30 minutes.

Serves 8 to 10.

Make-Ahead Tip The salad may be made up to 2 days ahead and stored, tightly covered, in the refrigerator. Taste and adjust seasoning before serving.

SCAPECE
Marinated whole fish

Like the Latin American *escabeche*, fish prepared *a scapece* is first floured, then fried, then marinated and served cool. It makes a pretty and piquant first course, surrounded with greens, if desired, or with assorted black and green olives. A crisp and simple white wine—an Italian Verdicchio, for example, or a California Sauvignon Blanc—would be fitting with this Abruzzese appetizer.

> 4 small whole white fish, about 1 pound each, with head and tail intact
> Flour seasoned with salt and pepper, for dredging
> 1 cup olive oil
> ½ cup coarsely chopped onion
> 1½ cups white wine
> ¼ cup lemon juice
> 1½ teaspoons freshly ground black pepper
> 1 teaspoon minced fresh lemon thyme (optional)
> 3 tablespoons grated lemon rind mixed with 3 tablespoons minced parsley
> Lemon wedges, for garnish

1. Clean and scale fish (or have fish merchant do it). Dredge fish in seasoned flour, shaking off excess. Heat oil in a large skillet until a haze forms; do not allow oil to smoke. Fry fish on both sides until well browned (about 5 minutes per side). Transfer fish with a slotted spatula to a glass or enamel dish.

2. In same skillet over medium heat, sauté onions until slightly softened, about 3 minutes. Add wine, 1 tablespoon of the lemon juice, pepper, and lemon thyme (if used). Boil mixture 1 minute, then remove from heat. Cool 2 minutes, then pour over fish. Add remaining lemon juice and half the lemon rind–parsley mixture. Marinate at least 3 hours or up to 1 day. (If you are marinating fish longer than 3 hours, refrigerate it; remove from refrigerator 1 hour before serving.)

3. To serve, lift fish out of marinade and place on serving platter. If desired, fillet fish before serving and arrange fillets on the platter. Garnish fish with remaining lemon rind–parsley mixture and surround with lemon wedges.

Serves 8.

ITALIAN OLIVES

Personalize storebought olives in your own garlicky marinade. Serve them with the makings of little open-faced Italian "sandwiches": good bread, sliced Parmesan or fontina, and a cruet of fruity olive oil.

> 1 *quart cracked black olives in brine*
> ½ *cup olive oil*
> 7 *cloves garlic, peeled and left whole*
> 2 *cups red wine vinegar*
> 2 *tablespoons black peppercorns*
> 2 *roasted red peppers (see opposite page), julienned*
> 1 *cup coarsely chopped fresh fennel*
> *Salt, to taste*

Drain olives, pat dry, and coat lightly with olive oil. In a medium-sized pot combine garlic, vinegar, and peppercorns. Bring to a boil, remove from heat, and cool slightly. Pour over olives. Add peppers and fennel; marinate at room temperature at least 2 hours. Season to taste with salt before serving. Olives keep indefinitely if refrigerated in a clean glass jar.

Serves 6 generously.

Small fried fish soak up a cool lemon marinade in Scapece, a flavorful first course for a warm evening.

15

PREPARING BABY ARTICHOKE HEARTS

When preparing baby artichoke hearts, choose artichokes no larger than 1½ inches in diameter. They should feel crisp and firm and have tightly closed leaves.

1. *Pull off dark green outer leaves to reveal the pale green heart.*

2. *Cut about ⅓ inch off top; trim stems. Rub all over with lemon or soak in acidulated water.*

To cook Prepare baby artichoke hearts as directed above. Place trimmed hearts in a saucepan with acidulated salted water to cover. Boil until just tender, about 5 minutes. Drain, pat thoroughly dry, and put in a clean bowl or jar. Cover completely with olive oil. Oil-covered hearts can be stored, covered, in refrigerator for up to a month.

LEGUMI AL SOTTO
Marinated autumn vegetables

You've heard of speaking *sotto voce* (underneath the voice). Vegetables prepared *al sotto* are "underneath" a marinade—here, an herb-scented blend of lemon, vinegar, and olive oil. The dish is a favorite throughout Italy, served with salami or *coppa* (see page 23) and with bread to soak up the juices. Make it a day or two ahead to allow the flavors to marry.

- 1½ pounds mushrooms
- 1 head cauliflower
- 6 ribs celery
- ¼ cup fresh lemon juice
- ½ cup white wine vinegar
- 5 cups water
- ¼ cup fresh oregano leaves
- ¼ cup fresh basil leaves
- 1 teaspoon salt
- 2 tablespoons dried lemon thyme or ¼ cup fresh lemon verbena leaves (optional)
- 1 cup olive oil
  Salt and pepper
- ½ pound small, oil-cured black olives
  Additional minced basil and oregano, for garnish

1. Trim, clean, and quarter mushrooms. Break cauliflower into bite-sized florets. Trim celery into 3-inch lengths.

2. In a large saucepan combine lemon juice, vinegar, water, oregano, basil, salt, and lemon thyme (if used). Bring to a simmer and simmer gently 5 minutes. Add mushrooms and cook until just tender (about 5 minutes). With a slotted spoon transfer mushrooms to a bowl. Add cauliflower to liquid and cook until crisp-tender. With a slotted spoon, remove to the mushroom bowl.

3. Raise heat to high and reduce liquid to 1½ cups. Remove from heat, strain, and whisk in olive oil. (It may not emulsify completely.) Add salt and pepper to taste. Pour dressing over vegetables in bowl. Add celery and olives and allow to cool completely. Garnish with additional basil and oregano leaves.

Serves 8 generously.

FRITTATA DI CARCIOFI
Open-faced artichoke omelet

To call a frittata an "open-faced omelet" is just the start of a definition. A frittata is thicker than an omelet, for one thing, and it's often served barely warm. But like an omelet, it's the basis for a cook's own inspirations. Butter-steamed asparagus tips, tiny shrimp, minced fresh herbs, spring onions—all are perfectly suitable garnishes for *frittate*. The version below is a Roman classic: tiny artichoke hearts, dusted with Parmesan, baked into the eggs. Serve it as a first course or as a lunch or brunch dish. Then use the basic technique to launch you on your own inventions.

- 8 large eggs
- 1 tablespoon olive oil
- 1 tablespoon butter
- 4 small artichoke hearts in oil, halved (see left)
- 2 tablespoons freshly grated Parmesan
  Salt and freshly ground black pepper
  Thinly sliced sweet red onion, for garnish
  Country-style Italian bread or Bruschetta (see page 13)

1. Preheat oven to 375° F. Beat eggs lightly. Heat oil and butter in a 9- or 10-inch nonstick skillet over moderately high heat. When fats are sizzling, add eggs and reduce heat to low. Arrange artichokes in a pretty pattern on top of eggs. Cook gently, lifting edges of frittata to let uncooked egg run underneath, until it is just set on top. Dust with Parmesan, salt, and pepper. Transfer skillet to oven and bake just until frittata is firm on top; do not overcook or it will be tough.

2. Cool in skillet, then slide onto serving platter and cut into wedges. The frittata can be eaten hot, warm, or at room temperature. Serve with raw onion and bread or Bruschetta.

Serves 4.

CROSTINI DI SALSICCE E POMODORI
Sausage and tomato toasts

Crostini are Italy's version of France's famous canapés: small bread rounds with all manner of savory toppings. They range from earthy to surpassingly elegant, with imagination and good taste the only limiting factors. A hearty sausage-and-ricotta mixture from Rome makes a fine crostini garnish; serve the toasts bubbling hot with cocktails or wine.

½ pound hot Italian sausage, loose or in links
½ cup finely minced onion
1 to 2 teaspoons finely minced garlic (amount depends on garlic in sausage)
½ cup ricotta
1 cup peeled, seeded, and coarsely chopped plum tomatoes (see page 29)
2 tablespoons minced fresh basil
Salt and freshly ground black pepper
1 teaspoon fennel seed
¼ cup freshly grated Parmesan
16 slices baguette-type bread, cut on the diagonal ¼ inch thick
3 tablespoons minced parsley

1. Remove casing from link sausage. In a medium skillet over moderate heat, fry sausage until browned. Transfer sausage to a large bowl, leaving fat in skillet. Sauté onion and garlic until softened in sausage fat, (about 3 minutes). Add to sausage in bowl along with ricotta, tomatoes, basil, salt and pepper to taste, fennel seed, and 2 tablespoons of the Parmesan. Mix lightly but well.

2. Preheat broiler 5 minutes. Mound sausage mixture on bread slices; dust with remaining Parmesan and broil until bubbly. Garnish with minced parsley and serve hot.

Makes 16 rounds, enough to serve 8 with other antipasti.

Make-Ahead Tip Sausage mixture may be made a day ahead and stored in refrigerator. Bring to room temperature before using.

Special Note

ITALIAN WINES FOR EVERY OCCASION

The Italians are the largest per-capita wine consumers in the world, but they are also conscientious consumers. Alcoholism is rare in Italy because wine is always linked to the table. It is respected and regarded like staples such as olive oil, bread, and salt: A meal wouldn't be complete without it.

There are dozens of Italian wines that never make it to this country, but the major varieties are widely represented here. As you might expect in a country with such a broad range of soils and climates, Italian wines are remarkably diverse. For serving purposes, you'll want to know which types are light, fresh, and best served young (apéritif and seafood wines) and which are fuller, richer, and more likely to age well (chicken and red-meat wines).

Once you've learned the broad categories, experiment often to find the producers and varieties you prefer. A good wine merchant can direct you to the best vintages and the most highly regarded producers, but you should always let your palate be the final judge.

The following guidelines should help you choose an Italian wine to suit your meal.

☐ Before dinner: Prosecco, a dry sparkling wine from the Veneto region, is widely available now and makes a refreshing *aperitivo*. A light, crisp white, such as a Soave or an Orvieto, also sharpens the appetite. The most popular Italian aperitivo, however, is vermouth, both sweet and dry. Vermouth is made from wine that has been flavored with roots, herbs, seeds, or other aromatics and given a bitter edge with quinine, then fortified with brandy, sweetened with sugar, and possibly colored with caramel. Vermouths vary a bit from one manufacturer to another; the recipes are closely guarded trade secrets. Martini & Rossi and Cinzano are two of the largest producers. Vermouth should be served chilled, straight up or over ice, with a dash of soda or lemon twist if desired.

☐ With lean white fish and shellfish, simply baked, steamed or grilled; with goat cheeses; with vegetable antipasti: Choose a lean, crisp white wine such as a Cortese di Gavi, a Soave, a Lugana, an Orvieto, or a Verdicchio dei Castelli di Jesi.

☐ With fish in sauce; with richer, oilier fish such as salmon; with seafood pasta or risotto; with Bel Paese cheese: Serve a full-bodied white such as Pinot Bianco, Pinot Grigio, Frascati, Arneis, Vernaccia di San Gimignano, or an Italian Chardonnay.

☐ With picnic food, dry sausages, ham, cold roast chicken, pasta salads, provolone, and antipasti: Serve a light-bodied red or rosé, such as Bardolino, Valpolicella, Grignolino, Lambrusco, or a simple Chianti (not Classico or Riserva).

☐ With chicken in sauce; veal; mushroom dishes; pasta with meat sauce; polenta or risotto with meat components; rabbit and pork; fontina and taleggio cheeses: Serve a medium-bodied red, such as Barbera d'Alba, Barbera d'Asti, Merlot, Nebbiolo d'Alba, Chianti and Chianti Classico, or Dolcetto d'Alba.

☐ With game, lamb, or beef; with Parmesan, Gorgonzola, or aged Asiago cheeses: Choose a full-bodied red wine, such as Barolo, Barbaresco, Gattinara, Spanna, Chianti Classico Riserva, Brunello di Montalcino, Vino Nobile di Montepulciano, Tignanello, or Amarone.

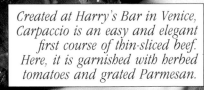

Created at Harry's Bar in Venice, Carpaccio is an easy and elegant first course of thin-sliced beef. Here, it is garnished with herbed tomatoes and grated Parmesan.

CROSTINI DI POLENTA
Polenta crostini with anchovy butter

Crostini (little toasts) are usually based on bread, but northern Italians often replace the bread with polenta. First the polenta is chilled until firm, then it's cut into bite-sized shapes, spread with a seasoned butter, and reheated. The result is a memorable little nibble, open to dozens of variations: Mushroom butter, herb butter, or Gorgonzola butter could take the place of the anchovy butter, for instance. Serve with cocktails or a light red wine.

- 2 tablespoons olive oil
- 1 recipe Basic Polenta (see page 58)
- 8 to 10 anchovy fillets packed in oil, drained
- 8 tablespoons unsalted butter, at room temperature
- 2 tablespoons minced parsley

1. Grease an 11- by 13-inch baking sheet with olive oil. Pour thickened Polenta onto oiled sheet and allow to cool completely.

2. When Polenta has cooled and hardened, cut out triangles, rounds, or squares with a cookie cutter or knife. In a food processor or blender, blend anchovies and butter.

3. Preheat oven to 400° F. Spread a little anchovy butter on each crostino, and arrange on a baking sheet and bake until butter is melted and Polenta is heated through. Dust with minced parsley; serve immediately.

Makes 25 to 32 crostini, depending on size and shape.

Make-Ahead Tip Polenta can be made, chilled, and cut up to 8 hours ahead. Cover with plastic wrap. Bring to room temperature before baking. Anchovy butter can be made several days ahead and stored, covered, in the refrigerator.

BAGNA CAUDA
Oil and garlic dip with bread and vegetables

This "hot bath" is a specialty of Italy's Piedmont region, where it is sometimes garnished with another specialty: shaved white truffles. Even without them, this dip is addictive and highly aromatic. The ingredients are few and simple, but they melt down into a rich bath for bread and vegetables.

- ½ cup olive oil
- 1 tablespoon butter
- ½ tablespoon minced garlic
- 2 ounces anchovy fillets, mashed
  Salt and freshly ground black pepper
- For dipping:
  Cubes of day-old Italian bread
  Whole artichokes, boiled and quartered, chokes removed
  Blanched cauliflower floret
  Raw fennel slices (see page 80)
  Raw carrot sticks
  Raw, sweet red-pepper strips
  Raw celery, pale inner stalks only
  Halved hard-cooked eggs
  Blanched asparagus spears

In a small skillet over moderate heat, heat oil and butter until bubbly. Add garlic. Cook over low heat until fragrant; do not allow garlic to brown. Add anchovies and cook, stirring, for 2 minutes. Remove from heat; add salt and pepper to taste. Transfer dip to a warm serving bowl or, preferably, keep warm in a chafing dish. Serve with a platter of bread and vegetables for dipping.

Makes about ½ cup.

CARPACCIO
Thinly pounded raw beef

To make *carpaccio*, lean raw beef is sliced and pounded tissue-thin, then dressed with Parmesan and a piquant vinaigrette. A popular Venetian restaurant dish, it is also easily made at home. You can slice the beef a couple of hours ahead and keep it between sheets of plastic wrap, but it's best to pound it just before serving. To make slicing easier, put meat in freezer until it is very cold but not frozen.

- 1½ pounds beef tenderloin, trimmed of all fat
- 1½ cups peeled, seeded, and chopped fresh tomato (see page 29)
- ½ cup minced Italian parsley
- ¼ cup minced fresh oregano
- ¼ cup minced fresh basil
- ⅓ cup fresh lemon juice
- 3 to 4 tablespoons olive oil
- 3 tablespoons freshly grated Parmesan
  Salt and freshly ground black pepper
- 2 tablespoons minced fresh chives (optional)

1. Cut beef into 10 thin slices, approximately 2½ ounces each. Put each slice between two sheets of plastic wrap or waxed paper and pound with a mallet or the bottom of a skillet until beef is paper-thin.

2. In a bowl combine tomatoes, parsley, oregano, basil, and 1 tablespoon each of lemon juice and olive oil. Marinate at room temperature for at least 10 minutes or up to 1 hour.

3. To serve, arrange tenderloin slices on individual plates or large platters. Scatter tomatoes around them. Drizzle with remaining olive oil and lemon. Dust with Parmesan. Sprinkle salt and pepper over all and garnish with chives (if used).

Serves 10.

A TREASURY OF ITALIAN CHEESES

It would be impossible to count Italy's cheeses. With diligence, one might compile a list of the cheeses made at the country's many cooperatives. But how could one begin to count the cheeses made of small farms and sold only at local markets? It has been said, albeit jokingly, that there are as many sheep's-milk cheeses in Italy as there are shepherds!

Certainly Italian cheeses form a varied group, reflecting the soil, climate, and geography of the country's vastly different regions. The cheeses also embody methods and traditions handed down for centuries, some of them dating from Etruscan times.

Many of these marvelous cheeses never turn up in the United States because they're highly perishable. Ricotta, for example, must be eaten very fresh and thus is not a good candidate for export. But modern transport has meant that the range of cheeses available here is rapidly expanding. All of the following are obtainable in large cities, and most are carried by well-stocked cheese shops anywhere.

Asiago A cow's-milk cheese, young Asiago is nutty, rich, and slightly piquant. It makes a good table cheese; as it ages, it gets harder and sharper and can be grated. Many shops carry both young and aged Asiago.

Bel Paese A cow's-milk cheese that is creamy and mild, Bel Paese makes a good sandwich or snacking cheese. It melts well and can be used to top casseroles or in sauces. Be sure to buy the imported variety.

Caciocavallo This cow's-milk cheese is made in a pear shape and sometimes lightly smoked. When young, *caciocavallo* is mild but tangy; as it ages, it gets drier and sharper and is sometimes grated.

Caprino *Caprino* is a generic term for goat's-milk cheese. Caprini are usually soft, mild, and spreadable when young, tangier and drier as they age. They are delicious sprinkled with black pepper and olive oil.

Fontina Made from cow's milk, fontina is one of Italy's foremost cheeses. It is creamy and smooth, with tiny holes, a nutty flavor, and an earthy aroma. Fontina is an excellent cooking cheese.

Gorgonzola A cow's-milk cheese, Gorgonzola is undoubtedly Italy's most famous blue-veined cheese. Its texture is creamy and moist, its flavor pungent. It is delicious with pears and peaches, in creamy pasta sauces, and mixed half-and-half with butter as a spread for crackers.

Mascarpone A cow's-milk cheese that must be eaten very fresh, *mascarpone* is luxuriously smooth and creamy, a bit like whipped butter or stiffly whipped cream. It is often sweetened slightly and served for dessert with strawberries, pears, or peaches. Some cheese shops carry a savory *torta* (cake) *di mascarpone* made of layers of the creamy cheese interspersed with layers of provolone, basil, and pine nuts.

Mozzarella Originally made from water-buffalo milk, mozzarella is now primarily a cow's-milk cheese. However, a few shops in major cities import an authentic *mozzarella di bufala*. Both varieties must be eaten very fresh and should be purchased from merchants with a rapid turnover. Mozzarella is perfect for pizza, of course, as well as for sandwiches and salads. Sliced and served with ripe tomatoes, fresh basil, olive oil, salt, and pepper, mozzarella makes a classic summer salad. The packaged domestic varieties bear little resemblance to the real thing.

Parmigiano Reggiano This cow's-milk cheese is one of Italy's most famous exports. Real *Parmigiano* is made within a strictly delimited region and according to strictly controlled methods. It is nutty, golden, and sharp, with a moist texture that gets drier as it ages. Young Parmigiano is a lovely after-dinner cheese with pears or toasted nuts; the aged version is the classic grating cheese for pasta, pizza, soups, and casseroles. Always buy your Parmesan in chunks and grate it just before using. Leftover rinds can be simmered in soups for added flavor. Domestic Parmesan is a poor substitute and not suitable for recipes in this book.

Pecorino Romano The best-known of the *pecorino* (sheep's-milk) cheeses, *Pecorino Romano* is pale, moist, and sliceable when young, becoming sharper and harder as it ages. Older pecorino makes a tangy grating cheese. When young, it is delicious with olive oil, olives, prosciutto, and bread.

Provolone A cow's-milk cheese, provolone is mild, firm, and sliceable. It is good for snacking and melts well on pizza. Smoked provolone makes an especially good ham-and-cheese sandwich.

Ricotta A cow's-milk cheese made from whey, ricotta is mild, creamy, and moist and should be used when very fresh. It is an important ingredient in many dishes, from lasagne and cannelloni to cheesecake, but it is also delightful on its own. Sprinkled with sugar and cinnamon or cocoa and served with seasonal fruits, it makes a lovely dessert.

Ricotta Salata This sheep's-milk cheese has a distinctive, sharp tang. It makes a delicious lunch, sliced and served with sausage, olives, bread, and olive oil.

Robiola This is the name of a family of cheeses made from cow's, goat's or sheep's milk, or a combination. They are generally soft, fresh, and creamy. However, some versions are mild; others are quite pungent. Ask to taste before you buy.

Taleggio A cow's-milk cheese, *taleggio* is one of Italy's best. When well made and ripe, it is soft and creamy with a distinct aroma of truffles. It makes a splendid after-dinner cheese with fruit and bread.

FONTINA FRITTA
Fontina fritters

Golden brown outside and molten within, these Roman fritters are a heavenly mouthful. The batter may be made ahead, but the cheese must be fried at the last minute. Serve with a crisp white wine, such as an Orvieto or a Soave.

- ¾ pound chilled fontina, not too ripe
- ¼ cup dry white wine
- 2 egg yolks
- 1 teaspoon minced garlic
- 1 teaspoon baking powder
- 1½ cups flour
   Salt
- 2½ tablespoons olive oil
- ½ to ⅔ cup ice water
   Vegetable oil, for deep-frying
- 2 egg whites
- ½ cup minced fresh basil

1. Cut cheese into 1-inch cubes. In a bowl whisk together wine, egg yolks, and garlic. Whisk in baking powder, flour, and 1 teaspoon salt. Whisk in olive oil, then add enough ice water to make a thick but pourable batter, about the consistency of pancake batter. Let rest at room temperature for 2 hours.

2. When ready to serve, heat 2 inches of vegetable oil in a frying pan to 360° F. Beat egg whites with a pinch of salt until stiff but not dry. Fold into batter along with basil.

3. Dip cheese cubes into batter. Allow excess batter to drip off; fry chunks in oil until uniformly golden. Drain fritters on paper towels; salt lightly. Serve immediately.

Serves 8 with 2 or 3 other antipasti.

Make-Ahead Tip Batter, minus beaten egg whites, may be mixed a day ahead. Cover and refrigerate; bring to room temperature before adding egg whites and using.

RICOTTA SALATA E PROSCIUTTO
Ricotta salata and prosciutto

Ricotta salata (also known as *ricotta pecorino*) isn't easy to find, but it's worth looking for. Sicilians serve it as an antipasto, with warm bread and a drizzle of olive oil. If necessary, substitute imported feta cheese.

- 1 pound ricotta salata
- ½ pound prosciutto, sliced as thin as possible
- 3 tablespoons (approximately) olive oil
   Freshly ground black pepper
- 2 tablespoons minced parsley
- 2 tablespoons freshly grated Parmesan (optional)
- 8 large or 16 small pieces hot, country-style bread

Slice ricotta salata thinly. (If you use feta, break it into chunks.) Arrange cheese on a rustic serving platter or on individual plates. Surround with slices of prosciutto. Drizzle olive oil and grind pepper over all. Sprinkle with parsley and Parmesan (if used). If feta is very salty, omit Parmesan. Serve with hot bread.

Serves 8.

Dip cubes of fontina cheese in batter, then fry until crisp and brown. The piping-hot Fontina Fritta makes a fine appetizer, served with chilled white wine and herbed olives.

Legumi in Pinzimonio pairs the season's freshest produce with a fine olive oil for a light and brightly colored first course. For a more elaborate antipasto, add a selection of cured meats (see Italy's Cured Meats and Sausages, opposite page) and a loaf of bread.

CIPOLLE AL FORNO
Roasted balsamic onions

Small boiling onions (not pearl onions) are the perfect size for an antipasto. In Modena, they are baked until tender, then glazed with their sweet-and-sour baking juices to make an unusual accompaniment to smoked sliced meats (see opposite page) or fontina. They should be served with a knife and fork and eaten directly from their hard outer skin. Accompany roasted balsamic onions with chunks of warm Italian country bread.

> 2 dozen small boiling onions, about 2 inches in diameter
> ½ to ⅔ cup olive oil
> ⅓ cup balsamic vinegar
> Salt and freshly ground black pepper
> 2 tablespoons minced Italian parsley, for garnish

1. Preheat oven to 350° F. Remove outermost skin of onions, leaving a hard, inedible exterior. Put onions in a bowl. Add enough olive oil to nearly cover them; toss to coat.

2. Transfer onions to a roasting pan, reserving oil. Bake, basting onions occasionally with reserved oil, until onions are tender when pierced with a knife. Baking time depends on onion size, but onions will probably be done in 45 minutes to 1 hour and 15 minutes. Transfer onions to a plate and let cool.

3. Place roasting pan over a medium-hot burner and add vinegar. Reduce liquid to a dark, hazy syrup. Pour syrup over onions. Season to taste with salt and pepper and sprinkle with parsley. Serve cool.

Serves 8.

CAPONATINA
Eggplant relish

Sicily's sweet-and-sour dishes are enjoyed throughout Italy, with *caponatina* a particular favorite. It's an eggplant relish of wonderfully complex flavors and textures, to be scooped up with hearts of lettuce or chunks of bread. Hot and cool, sweet and tart, smooth and crunchy—it's all there in this beguiling dish.

- 3 *large eggplants or 6 small Japanese eggplants*
- 1½ *cups olive oil*
- 3 *cups minced onions*
- ⅓ *cup minced garlic*
- 1 *cup diced celery*
- 2 *cups peeled and seeded tomatoes in ½-inch chunks (see page 29)*
- 3 *tablespoons capers*
- ⅔ *cup minced carrot*
- ½ *cup toasted pine nuts*
- 2 *cups oil-cured black olives*
- ⅓ *cup sugar*
- ⅔ *cup red wine vinegar*
- ½ *teaspoon cayenne pepper, or more to taste*
  Salt
- ⅔ *cup minced parsley*
  Additional olive oil, for garnish
  Additional minced parsley, for garnish

1. Preheat oven to 375° F. Peel eggplants and cut into ½-inch dice. Oil a large baking sheet or roasting pan with 3 tablespoons of the olive oil. Toss eggplant with ¾ cup of the olive oil to coat well, then transfer eggplant to baking sheet or pan. Bake, tossing eggplant frequently, until it is soft and lightly browned (about 20 minutes).

2. While eggplant is baking, heat remaining oil in a large skillet over moderate heat. Add onions and garlic and sauté until soft (7 to 10 minutes); do not allow garlic to brown. Add celery, tomatoes, capers, carrot, pine nuts, olives, sugar, vinegar, and cayenne. Simmer slowly 30 minutes. Add salt to taste. Add eggplant and cook an additional 10 minutes. Add the

⅔ cup parsley and let cool. Taste again and correct seasoning. To serve, transfer to a bowl, drizzle with olive oil and garnish with minced parsley.

Serves 12.

LEGUMI IN PINZIMONIO
Raw vegetables with olive-oil dip

Tuscans show off their finest oil and their freshest vegetables by serving them *in pinzimonio*. You're offered a basket or a platter of crisp and colorful raw vegetables, along with a bowl of the best oil seasoned with nothing but salt and pepper. You "pinch" (*pinzare*) the vegetables and join them in "marriage" (*matrimonio*) with the oil. If the oil is top-notch, there is no finer dip.

- 2 *cups fruity olive oil*
  Coarse salt
  Freshly ground black pepper
  Lemon wedges, for garnish
- *For dipping:*
  Sliced bulb fennel (see page 80)
  Cherry tomatoes
  Carrot sticks
  Innermost celery stalks
  Endive leaves
  Cucumber spears, seeded
  Innermost hearts of baby artichokes (see page 16)
  Hearts of small lettuces
  Spears of young tender zucchini

Season olive oil to taste with salt and pepper. Divide oil among small dipping bowls, one to a person. Arrange vegetables for dipping on a large, rustic platter. Offer each guest a dipping bowl, lemon wedges, and a small salad plate. Or you can pour a little seasoned oil on each salad plate, arrange a bouquet of raw vegetables on top, and garnish the plate with a lemon wedge.

Serves 8.

Basics

ITALY'S CURED MEATS AND SAUSAGES

In Italy cooks avail themselves of a large collection of cured meats for antipasto, sandwiches, and other dishes. Unfortunately, at this writing, American law prohibits importation of these meats. However, domestic versions can be found in delis, specialty shops, and Italian markets. The following are the most widely available. Thinly sliced coppa, mortadella, prosciutto, and salami are all appropriate for an antipasto platter.

Coppa is the cured foreshank of a pig. It has a sweet-salty flavor.

Italian-style link sausage is made from fresh-ground pork highly seasoned with salt, garlic, and wine. "Hot" varieties have a generous lacing of hot red pepper; "sweet" varieties usually include fennel seed instead. They may be grilled and served with peppers or crumbled and used for pizza, pasta sauces, or stuffings.

Mortadella is the original "bologna." It is a large, round, fine-grained sausage studded with fat.

Pancetta is unsmoked bacon made from pork belly. It is seasoned with salt, pepper, and spices, then rolled into a sausage shape and cured. Buy it in slices, uncoil them to make long baconlike strips, then slice as the recipe directs. American bacon, because it is smoked, is not a close substitute.

Prosciutto is a salted and air-cured hind ham. It has a sweet, nutty taste and a velvety texture. Often served as an antipasto with melon, figs, or pears, it may also be used in sandwiches and pasta sauces, on pizzas, in stuffings, and in sautéed dishes.

Salami are air-dried sausages made from seasoned pork or beef. One of the best known is Genoa salami, made with garlic and white peppercorns.

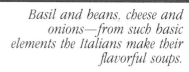

Basil and beans, cheese and onions—from such basic elements the Italians make their flavorful soups.

Soups

Italian soups range from delicate broths, such as Zuppa Pavese (see page 26), to hearty meal-in-a-bowl preparations such as Pasta e Fagioli (see page 28). This chapter offers recipes for some of Italy's most tantalizing soups. They span the seasons, from an autumn Sicilian pumpkin soup (see page 27) to a spring minestrone (see page 28). You'll also find (on page 29) an illustrated step-by-step explanation of how to peel, seed, and chop tomatoes—a technique essential to Italian cooking.

Egg and spinach pastas are the whimsical "straw and hay" of Bologna's famous Paglia e Fieno, traditionally dressed with cream and peas. The colorful noodles can also combine in a meaty broth, as shown here, accompanied by bread and sliced Parmesan in olive oil.

SOUPS

Soups play an important role in the Italians' daily diet, frequently taking the place of pasta as the first course of the main meal and often served as the main course at a light supper. They range from the delicate Zuppa Pavese (below) to the rib-sticking Pasta e Fagioli (see page 28), which is almost more a stew than a soup. In between are the various fish and shellfish soups, such as Zuppa di Vongole con Pomodori (see page 29), and the hearty seasonal minestrones (Minestrone Primavera appears on page 28). The rustic bread-based soups, such as Pappa al Pomodoro (see page 30), are among the most humble and delicious in the Italian repertoire.

ZUPPA PAVESE
Egg soup, Pavia style

This elegant soup can be made in minutes if you have the raw materials at hand: good bread, imported Parmesan, fresh eggs, and rich stock. You simply pour the simmering stock over toast, cheese, and eggs and allow the eggs to cook in the soup. If you prefer your eggs more fully cooked, poach them first before placing them in the soup bowls.

- 10 cups rich unsalted chicken stock
- 16 bread rounds, about 2 inches in diameter and ¼ inch thick, made from dense homemade, country-style bread
- 6 tablespoons (approximately) clarified butter
- 16 eggs
  Salt, to taste
  Freshly grated Parmesan, for garnish

Bring stock to a boil. While stock is heating fry bread rounds in batches in clarified butter until golden and crisp on both sides (about 10 minutes). Put 2 bread rounds in each of 8 warm bowls. Break 2 eggs into each bowl, being careful not to break the yolks. Season with salt; dust lightly with Parmesan. Carefully pour the bubbling stock over eggs. Serve immediately, with extra Parmesan on the side.

Makes about 10 cups, 8 servings.

ZUPPA DI RISO E BIETOLE
Rice and chard soup

This light Bolognese vegetable soup could precede an Arrosto di Maiale con Rosmarino (see page 84), a split grilled chicken, or pan-fried sausages.

- 2 large bunches fresh green or red chard
- ¼ cup olive oil
- ¼ cup minced onion
- 3 cups (approximately) rich chicken stock
- ½ cup Italian Arborio rice
- ⅓ cup fresh basil leaves
  Freshly grated Parmesan

1. Wash chard well. Remove stems and cut them into ¼-inch pieces. Bring a large pot of salted water to a boil and blanch the chard leaves for 10 to 15 seconds. Transfer them with a large slotted spoon to ice water, then drain, squeeze dry, and chop coarsely. Blanch the stems in the same boiling water, refresh them in ice water, then drain and dry.

2. Heat oil in a stockpot over moderate heat. Add onion and sauté until translucent and soft (about 3 to 5 minutes). Add chard stems and stir to coat with oil. Add chicken stock and rice and bring to a simmer. Cover and simmer gently 15 minutes or until rice is just cooked. Add chopped chard and heat through gently. If rice has absorbed most of stock, add a little more, but soup should be thick.

3. To serve, cut the basil into a fine julienne. Divide soup among warm bowls and garnish with julienned basil and Parmesan.

Makes 7 or 8 cups, 6 to 8 servings.

SOPA DI ZUCCA
Sicilian pumpkin soup

For best results, make this soup with small, sweet sugar pumpkins. The big, watery Halloween pumpkins will give inferior results.

- 3 tablespoons olive oil
- 3 small carrots, peeled and diced
- 2½ cups diced red onion
- 1 medium leek, washed and sliced
- 1 parsnip, peeled and diced
- 1 pound small, sweet pumpkin, peeled and cut into approximately 2-inch cubes
- 4 cups rich, homemade chicken stock
- 2 teaspoons grated lemon rind
- 3 tablespoons lemon juice
- 1 teaspoon dried oregano
- ¼ teaspoon hot red-pepper flakes
- 1 cup milk
  Salt and freshly ground black pepper
- 3 tablespoons minced parsley mixed with 1 tablespoon grated lemon rind, for garnish

1. Heat olive oil in a large stockpot over moderate heat. Add carrots, onion, leek, and parsnip; sauté 5 minutes. Add pumpkin, chicken stock, lemon rind, lemon juice, oregano, and pepper flakes. Cover and simmer until pumpkin is tender. Cool slightly.

2. Transfer mixture in batches to a blender and blend, adding milk as necessary to facilitate blending (you should use the entire cup). Return soup to stockpot. Season to taste with salt and pepper. Soup should be peppery. Reheat and serve garnished with parsley–lemon rind mixture.

Makes about 12 cups, 10 generous servings.

PAGLIA E FIENO IN BRODO
"Straw and hay" in broth, Bolognese style

When egg pasta and spinach pasta are tossed in a cream sauce with peas and prosciutto, the result is the *paglia e fieno* ("straw and hay") of Piacenza. The same combination of yellow and green produces a striking first-course soup, the colorful noodles afloat in a rich meat broth. It makes an elegant introduction to almost any main course. For a more casual meal, begin with an *antipasto* assortment and serve the soup as the main event with bread and sliced Parmesan marinated in olive oil.

- 1 quart homemade beef or chicken stock
- 3½ ounces fresh spinach fettuccine (use Pasta Verde, page 34), in 6-inch lengths
- 3½ ounces fresh egg fettuccine (use Pasta Gialla, page 34), in 6-inch lengths
  Salt
- 2 ounces freshly grated Parmesan

1. Bring stock to a simmer in a large stockpot. In a separate pot, bring a large amount of salted water to a boil. Add both spinach and egg fettuccine and cook until just wilted, about 20 to 25 seconds. Drain and run under cold water to remove any starch. Transfer pasta to the simmering stock and simmer until pasta is al dente. Season broth to taste with salt.

2. Ladle soup into warm serving bowls and top each serving with grated Parmesan.

Makes about 7 cups, 4 to 6 servings.

PASTA E FAGIOLI
Pasta and bean soup

Perhaps the only soup that's better than a good *pasta e fagioli* is a pasta e fagioli the second day. This thick, rustic soup is practically a staple in Tuscan homes and a good example of how Italian cooks turn nothing much into something wonderful. If you make it a day ahead, wait to add the pasta until just before you serve it. And if you use homemade pasta, be sure to shake off any excess flour before adding it to the soup.

> 2   cups dried Great Northern white beans or cannellini beans
> ¼   cup olive oil
> 2   ounces pancetta, diced
> 1   cup coarsely chopped onion
> ½   cup diced celery
> ½   cup diced carrot
> 1½ tablespoons sliced garlic
> 9   cups water
> 4½ cups peeled, seeded, and diced tomatoes (see opposite page)
>   Salt and freshly ground black pepper
> 5   ounces pasta, either day-old homemade wide-ribbon noodles or fettuccine (use any of the doughs on pages 34–35) or dried shells or bow ties
>   Freshly grated Parmesan
> ¼   cup (approximately) extravirgin olive oil

1. Soak beans overnight in water to cover (no need to refrigerate). The next day heat the ¼ cup olive oil in a large stockpot over moderate heat. Add pancetta and render slightly (about 3 minutes). Add onion and sauté until soft and translucent (about 3 minutes). Add celery, carrot, and garlic and sauté gently another 5 minutes, stirring occasionally.

2. Drain beans and add to pot along with the 9 cups fresh water and tomatoes. Cover and simmer 1½ hours, or until beans are tender. Season to taste with salt and pepper. If you are using homemade pasta, add it to the soup and cook until tender. If you are using dried pasta, cook it until tender in boiling salted water;

drain it well, add to soup, and heat through. Cool soup slightly before serving. Serve it in warm bowls, topped with a sprinkle of Parmesan and a drizzle of extravirgin olive oil.

Makes 12 to 14 cups, about 12 servings.

MINESTRONE PRIMAVERA
Spring minestrone

A chunky soup chock-full of vegetables often opens an Italian meal, both in homes and in restaurants. It can be made ahead—in fact, it's best made ahead—and it can be served hot, warm, or at room temperature. Put a cruet of extravirgin olive oil on the table for guests to add at will, and follow the soup with a simple roast of lamb or chicken. A hearty minestrone makes a great Sunday supper, with crusty bread, a light red wine, and a fruit dessert. The version that follows is from Bologna.

> 3   tablespoons olive oil
> 1   cup cubed pancetta (½-inch pieces)
> 1   cup minced onion
> 2   small leeks, white part only, well washed and thinly sliced
> 3   cups coarsely shredded inner cabbage leaves
> 4   cups peeled, seeded, and chopped tomatoes (see opposite page)
> 12 small new potatoes, quartered
> 5   cups chicken broth
> 2   cups carrots in ½-inch-thick rounds
> ¾   cup chopped bulb fennel (see page 80)
> 1   cup cooked and drained kidney beans
> 1   cup cooked and drained garbanzo beans (chick-peas)
> 1   cup fresh green beans, preferably Italian beans, in 1-inch pieces
> 2   cups tiny cauliflower florets
> 2   cups cooked and drained small shell pasta or macaroni
> 2   cups fresh shelled peas
>   Salt and freshly ground black pepper
> ½   cup minced Italian parsley
>   Freshly grated Parmesan

1. Heat 2 tablespoons of the olive oil in a large stock pot. Add pancetta and fry gently for 4 minutes. Add onion and leeks and cook 5 minutes, or until onion is soft and translucent but not browned.

2. Add 1 tablespoon oil to the pot and add the cabbage. Stir to coat cabbage with oil, then sauté 1 minute. Add tomatoes, potatoes, and 3 cups of the broth. Bring to a simmer and cook 10 minutes. Add carrots, fennel, and ½ cup more stock. Simmer 10 minutes.

3. Add remaining stock, kidney and garbanzo beans, fresh beans, cauliflower, and pasta. Simmer 10 minutes. Add peas. Continue simmering until potatoes are fully cooked and peas are crisp-tender. Pasta should be cooked slightly beyond al dente.

4. Season to taste with salt and pepper. Stir in half the parsley. Serve soup in warm bowls, garnishing with remaining parsley and Parmesan. Pass additional Parmesan at the table.

Makes about 12 cups, about 8 servings.

ZUPPA DI VONGOLE CON POMODORI
Neapolitan clam soup with tomatoes

To reproduce this soup as it's made on the Naples waterfront, you'll need the tiny Italian clams called *vongole*. Lacking those, choose any small fresh clams and do your best to find fresh Italian parsley. Serve this fragrant soup/stew with plenty of bread to soak up the juices, a bowl for the shells, and a bottle of Verdicchio or Sicilian Corvo.

> 3 to 4 pounds small, fresh clams
> 2 tablespoons cornmeal
> ½ cup olive oil
> ½ cup chopped onion
> ¼ teaspoon hot red-pepper flakes
> 2 tablespoons minced garlic
> 4 large tomatoes, peeled, seeded, and diced (See Step-by-Step at right)
> 2 tablespoons chopped fresh oregano
> 3 tablespoons minced Italian parsley
> Fresh coarsely cracked black pepper

1. Scrub clams well and put in a large pot of salted water along with cornmeal. Refrigerate 3 to 4 hours to purge clams. Drain clams and discard any that have already opened.

2. Heat olive oil in a large stockpot over moderate heat and add onion, pepper flakes, and garlic. Sauté gently until onions are slightly softened, about 3 minutes. Add tomatoes and sauté 7 or 8 minutes, then add oregano and half of the parsley. Add clams, cover, and steam, shaking pan occasionally, until clams are opened, about 5 to 7 minutes.

3. Divide clams and tomato broth among four warm bowls. Garnish with remaining parsley and pass the cracked black pepper.

Serves 4.

PEELING, SEEDING, AND CHOPPING TOMATOES

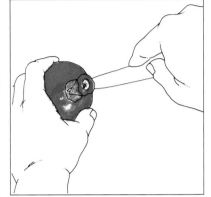

1. *Use a paring knife to core the tomatoes.*

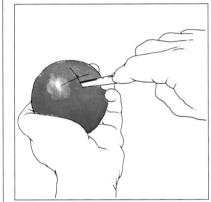

2. *Turn tomatoes over and slit the skin in an X-shaped cut.*

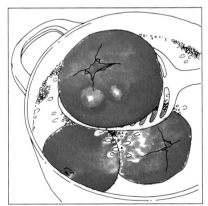

3. *Put the tomatoes in a pan containing enough boiling water to cover them and boil for 15 seconds. Remove them with a slotted spoon and put them in a bowl of cold water. Leave for a few seconds.*

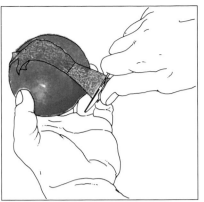

4. *Remove them from the cold water and use a paring knife to pull off the skins.*

5. *Halve the tomatoes horizontally with a chopping knife. Hold each half over a bowl, cut side down, and squeeze to remove the seeds.*

6. *Chop the tomatoes into small pieces.*

MINESTRA DI FUNGHI
Mushroom soup

The dried Italian mushrooms called *porcini* (see page 9) add an earthy flavor to this rustic Piedmontese soup. Save any leftover soaking liquid to flavor other soups, sauces, or stews.

- 1 ounce dried Italian porcini mushrooms
- 1½ cups hot water
- 1½ tablespoons unsalted butter
- 1½ tablespoons minced garlic, plus 1 cut clove
- ¾ cup thinly sliced onion
- 2 teaspoons flour
- 6 tablespoons dry white wine
- 4 cups chicken stock
- 4 ounces fresh mushrooms, cleaned and quartered
  Salt and freshly ground black pepper
- 6 bread rounds, about 2 inches in diameter and ⅓ inch thick, cut from dense, day-old country-style bread
  Olive oil
- ½ cup chopped fresh lemon pulp
- ½ cup minced parsley

1. Soak porcini in the hot water 20 minutes. Carefully lift mushrooms out with a slotted spoon. Strain liquid through cheesecloth and reserve. Pick through porcini carefully to remove any grit. Chop coarsely.

2. Heat butter in a large stockpot over moderate heat. Add the minced garlic and onion; sauté until onion is soft and translucent, about 5 minutes. Add flour and wine; cook gently 5 minutes. Add stock, porcini, and 2 tablespoons of the reserved porcini liquid. Cook 5 minutes. Add fresh mushrooms and cook until they are very tender. Season to taste with salt and pepper.

3. Preheat oven to 350° F. Rub bread rounds with the cut clove of garlic, brush well with olive oil, and toast in oven until browned and fragrant. Add lemon pulp and half of the parsley to the soup; reheat gently. Put a bread round in the bottom of each of 6 warm bowls, ladle soup over, and garnish with remaining parsley.

Makes about 5 cups, about 6 servings.

PAPPA AL POMODORO
Tuscan-style bread soup with greens and tomatoes

Because this soup has so few ingredients, it requires the best: vine-ripened summer tomatoes and dense, chewy, homemade or homestyle bread. It's a popular summer soup in the *trattorie* of Florence, where it often precedes a hefty Bistecca alla Fiorentina (see page 76). It can be served either hot or at room temperature.

- ½ cup plus 2 tablespoons olive oil
- 2 tablespoons thinly sliced garlic
- 4 cups peeled, seeded, and diced tomatoes (see page 29)
- 2 cups arugula, washed, or 1½ cups blanched turnip greens
- 2 cups day-old bread, in 2-inch cubes
- 3 cups water
  Salt and freshly ground black pepper
- *For garnish:*
- 8 one-inch bread cubes (optional; see step 2)
  Olive oil
  Arugula leaves, torn into small pieces

1. Heat ½ cup of the olive oil in a 4-quart pot over moderately low heat. Add garlic and sauté until fragrant. Add tomatoes and cook gently until they begin to exude their liquid (about 7 or 8 minutes). Add arugula and let wilt 3 to 4 minutes. Add remaining 2 tablespoons oil, the 2-inch bread cubes, and the water. Cover the pot and set aside 10 minutes. The bread will absorb most of the water.

2. Season to taste with salt and pepper. *To serve at room temperature:* Garnish with a swirl of olive oil and a few arugula leaves. *To serve hot:* Fry 1-inch bread cubes in olive oil until they are golden and crisp. Divide hot bread cubes among soup bowls and pour soup over them. Garnish with olive oil and arugula.

Makes about 10 cups, 10 to 12 first-course servings, 4 to 6 main-course servings.

ZUPPA DI POMODORO
Sicilian summer tomato soup

Among Italians, only a Sicilian would think to add spices, sugar, and orange to a tomato soup! Make it with sweet, vine-ripened tomatoes and follow it with a grilled or baked fish.

- ¼ cup unsalted butter
- 2 tablespoons olive oil
- 2 red onions, chopped
- 2 yellow onions, chopped
- 1 bunch green onions, minced
- ½ cup minced carrot
- ½ cup minced celery
- ¼ cup minced garlic
- 1 cup coarsely chopped parsley
  Pinch cinnamon
  Pinch nutmeg
- 2 tablespoons tomato paste
- 1½ pounds fresh spinach
- 18 plum tomatoes, peeled and chopped (see page 29)
- 1 teaspoon sugar
  Grated rind of 1 orange
- ¼ cup fresh orange juice
- 4 cups chicken stock
- 1 cup dry white wine
- ½ cup small fresh basil leaves
  Salt, freshly ground black pepper, and cayenne pepper

1. Heat butter and olive oil in a large pot over moderate heat. Add red and yellow onions; sauté about 5 minutes, until soft and translucent. Add green onions, carrot, celery, garlic, parsley, cinnamon, nutmeg, and tomato paste. Stir and cook 5 minutes.

2. Wash spinach and remove stems. Blanch leaves briefly in boiling water. Shock leaves in ice water to stop the cooking. Drain well; chop coarsely.

3. Add chopped tomatoes, spinach, sugar, orange rind, and orange juice to pot. Add stock and wine. Bring to a simmer and cook 10 to 15 minutes. Stir in basil and remove from heat. Purée soup in a blender in batches. Return to pot; season to taste with salt, pepper, and cayenne. Reheat and divide among warm bowls to serve.

Makes about 9 cups, 8 to 10 first-course servings, 4 main-course servings.

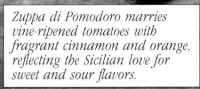

Zuppa di Pomodoro marries vine-ripened tomatoes with fragrant cinnamon and orange, reflecting the Sicilian love for sweet and sour flavors.

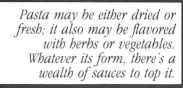

Pasta may be either dried or fresh; it also may be flavored with herbs or vegetables. Whatever its form, there's a wealth of sauces to top it.

Pasta & Sauces

To many Americans, the heart of Italian cooking is pasta in all its forms. Spaghetti, lasagne, cannelloni, ravioli, fettuccine—these are the dishes we love. This chapter presents the basics— pasta doughs and sauces—and the dishes made from them. The familiar favorites are all here, with some interesting new twists, such as dried-mushroom sauce in lasagne (see page 42) and potatoes mixed with pesto and *pappardelle* (see page 41). There are helpful step-by-step photographs showing how to form tortellini (page 38) and ravioli (page 43). A menu for a hearty Sicilian country dinner completes the chapter.

PASTA, FRESH AND DRIED

Pasta has graced the Italian table since before Marco Polo, and it is now eaten from one end of "the boot" to the other. Northern Italian pasta dishes are usually based on a fresh Pasta Gialla (at right); southern Italians eat considerably more dried pasta, made with only durum (hard wheat) flour and water. The south is historically a poor region, and possibly families couldn't afford the luxury of eggs in their pasta dough. In any case, the best dried pasta today is made in the factories of southern Italy and exported all over the world.

The variety of pasta shapes (see page 7) is surpassed only by the variety of sauces. And the Italian cook is very careful to match the right shape to the right sauce! Hearty meat sauces are best with a sturdy dried pasta, especially a shape—like a shell or a ridged tube—that can trap bits of the sauce. Soft fresh noodles are the choice for delicate cream sauces and butter-based sauces and for floating in soups.

A food processor makes the job of mixing fresh dough much faster, although the dough can easily be mixed and kneaded by hand. Rolling out the dough, however, is a tedious task by hand. If you plan to make pasta regularly, a hand-cranked pasta machine is a practical investment.

DOUGHS FOR HOMEMADE PASTA

Fresh homemade pasta doughs are made with eggs for easy handling. The egg provides the only moisture and makes the dough softer and easier to knead than a flour-and-water dough. Pasta Gialla (Basic Egg Dough) is probably the one you will use most often. However, the dough can also be varied with the addition of cooked spinach, fresh herbs, grated lemon rind, or puréed sun-dried tomatoes. The flavored doughs are a fun twist, but take care to serve them with complementary sauces. Suggestions precede each recipe.

Each of the following recipes yields about 1¼ pounds of pasta. If the dish you are making calls for less, don't throw away the leftover dough. Consider these possibilities:

☐ Wrap it and freeze for later use; it will keep indefinitely.

☐ Roll it out and cut into shapes for soup that day or the next.

☐ Roll it out, cut into uniform shapes, allow to dry on racks, and then store in an airtight container. Use it as you would any dried pasta.

☐ Roll, cut, and cook the leftovers immediately; use them in a cold pasta salad.

PASTA GIALLA
Basic egg dough

    1½ cups unbleached flour
    1   teaspoon coarse salt
    1½ large eggs (see Note) or
        2 medium eggs,
        lightly beaten

To mix by hand: Put flour and salt in a bowl. Stir to blend. Make a well in the center and add the eggs. With a fork or with your fingertips, gradually incorporate all the flour to form a mass. Knead lightly to form a smooth ball. Cover with plastic wrap and let rest 20 minutes or overnight before rolling and cutting. *To mix in a food processor:* Put flour and salt in work bowl of processor fitted with steel blade. Begin processing. With the machine running, add eggs through the feed tube in a slow, steady stream. Process until mixture begins to come together but has not formed a ball. Stop machine and press a bit of

dough between thumb and first finger. If it holds together, remove dough from bowl and knead by hand to form a smooth ball. If it doesn't hold together, process another 5 seconds, then knead by hand to form a smooth ball. Cover with plastic wrap and let rest 20 minutes or overnight before rolling and cutting.

Makes 1¼ pounds pasta.

Note Break 2 large eggs into a bowl. Whisk with a fork to blend. Measure volume and pour off one quarter.

PASTA VERDE
Spinach pasta

Be sure to squeeze as much moisture as possible out of the spinach or the dough will be too wet. Serve spinach fettuccine with Ragù Bolognese (see page 36) or use it to make a colorful lasagne.

    1   recipe Pasta Gialla (at left)
    ¾   pound fresh spinach, leaves
        and stems, blanched, drained,
        squeezed dry, and finely
        minced

To mix by hand: Combine flour and salt as directed for Pasta Gialla. Combine spinach and eggs. Make a well in the flour and add spinach-egg mixture. Continue as directed for Pasta Gialla. *To mix in a food processor:* Place spinach in work bowl of food processor along with flour and salt. Process until blended, then add eggs and continue as directed for Pasta Gialla.

Makes 1¼ pounds pasta.

PASTA DI HERBE
Fresh herb pasta

Fresh herbs from your garden or market can turn Pasta Gialla into a fragrant pasta that's delicious with just butter and cheese. Or use buttered herb pasta as a bed for a saucy stew, such as Osso Buco (see page 77). Be careful with strong herbs like rosemary and oregano; use them in small quantities, rounding out the cup of herbs called for with mild parsley.

- 1 recipe Pasta Gialla (opposite page)
- 1 cup mixed fresh herbs (basil, chives, parsley, chervil), loosely packed

To mix by hand: Combine flour and salt as directed for Pasta Gialla. Mince herbs and combine with beaten egg. Make a well in the center of the flour and add the herb-egg mixture. Continue as directed for Pasta Gialla. *To mix in a food processor:* Mince herbs and place in work bowl of food processor fitted with the steel blade. Add flour and salt. Process until blended, then add eggs and continue as directed for Pasta Gialla.

Makes 1¼ pounds pasta.

PASTA DI LIMONE
Lemon pasta

Serve this zesty pasta with steamed mussels or seafood sauces. Dressed with olive oil and parsley, it could partner a simple roast chicken or a veal stew. Use only the bright yellow part of the lemon rind; the white part is bitter.

- 1 recipe Pasta Gialla (opposite page)
- 1½ tablespoons grated lemon rind
- ½ teaspoon lemon juice

To mix by hand: Combine flour and salt as directed for Pasta Gialla. Combine lemon rind and juice with eggs, then make a well in the center of the flour and add the egg-lemon mixture. Continue as directed for Pasta Gialla. *To mix in a food processor:* Place lemon rind in work bowl of food processor along with flour and salt. Process until blended. Combine lemon juice with eggs, then add to flour and continue as directed for Pasta Gialla.

Makes 1¼ pounds pasta.

PASTA DI POMODORI
Sun-dried–tomato pasta

Garlic warmed in olive oil, shredded basil, and Parmesan are all that's needed to turn this pasta into a splendid first course.

- 1½ cups unbleached flour
- ½ teaspoon coarse salt
- 2 sun-dried tomatoes, plus 1 teaspoon tomato oil from jar
- 1 large egg

To mix by hand: Combine flour and salt as directed for Pasta Gialla (opposite page). Mince tomatoes almost to a paste. Combine tomatoes and tomato oil with egg, then make a well in the center of the flour and add the egg-tomato mixture. Continue as directed for Pasta Gialla. *To mix in a food processor:* Put flour and salt in work bowl of processor fitted with the steel blade. Process 3 seconds to blend. Add tomatoes and process until they are blended. Add egg and tomato oil and continue as directed for Pasta Gialla.

Makes 1¼ pounds pasta.

SAUCES

The sauces suitable for pasta are as numerous and varied as the cook can imagine. However, a few basics should be mastered by anyone who wants to perfect a repertoire of pasta dishes. A northern-style cooked-tomato sauce, an uncooked tomato sauce, a tomato-meat sauce, a cream sauce, and pesto are not only useful on their own but also important building blocks for other dishes.

PESTO GENOVESE
Garlic and basil sauce with pine nuts

Pesto is a summer sauce, to make when basil is abundant and inexpensive. Its pungent aroma is unforgettable, whether it's tossed with hot linguine or stirred into a steaming minestrone. For Genoese sailors long at sea, a fragrant *pasta al pesto* is the traditional welcome home.

- 2 cups fresh basil leaves, loosely packed
- ½ cup light olive oil
- 2 tablespoons pine nuts, toasted
- 4 large cloves garlic, minced
- 1 teaspoon coarse salt
- ½ cup freshly grated Parmesan
- 2 tablespoons freshly grated Pecorino Romano cheese
- 3 tablespoons unsalted butter, softened

Put basil, olive oil, pine nuts, garlic, and salt in a blender or food processor. Blend or process until smooth. Transfer to a bowl and stir in Parmesan, Pecorino Romano, and butter.

Makes 1 cup.

Make-Ahead Tip Pesto may be made up to 1 week ahead, covered with a thin film of olive oil, and refrigerated in an airtight container. It may frozen for up to 1 month, covered with a thin film of olive oil. If you plan to freeze it, make Pesto without the garlic; stir minced garlic in just before using. Or freeze Pesto in ice-cube trays, then unmold and store cubes in plastic bag. Each cube will sauce one portion of pasta. In this case, wait to incorporate Parmesan, butter, and garlic until ready to serve.

SUGO DI POMODORO
Northern-style tomato sauce

Cooks in northern Italy often enrich sauces with butter. They add vegetables and herbs for depth, then simmer the sauce slowly to marry the flavors. Their basic tomato sauce is a building block for dozens of other dishes: lasagne, cannelloni, and ravioli; baked vegetable casseroles; and braised entrées. If you can't get sweet, vine-ripened tomatoes, use the best available canned variety.

- 2 teaspoons olive oil
- 4 teaspoons butter
- 1 large carrot, peeled and diced
- 2 ribs celery, diced
- 1 onion, diced
- 2 tablespoons minced garlic
- 1 teaspoon flour
- 3 pounds ripe tomatoes, peeled, seeded, and chopped, or one 28-ounce can plum tomatoes, whirled briefly in a blender
- 1 tablespoon tomato paste
  Pinch sugar
- ¼ cup fresh chopped basil or 1 teaspoon dried basil
- 4 sprigs fresh parsley
- 2 sprigs fresh oregano
- 1 bay leaf
  Salt and freshly ground black pepper

Heat oil and butter in a large, heavy saucepan over moderate heat. When butter foams, add carrot, celery, onion, and garlic and stew gently for 10 minutes. Stir in flour and continue cooking 5 minutes. Add tomatoes, tomato paste, sugar, basil, parsley, oregano, and bay leaf. Simmer, partly covered, for 1 hour. Remove bay leaf and herb stems. Pass sauce through a food mill if you prefer a smoother texture. Adjust seasoning to taste with salt and pepper.

Makes 4 cups.

Make-Ahead Tip Sauce may be made up to 1 week ahead and refrigerated. It may be frozen for up to 1 month.

SALSA DI CREMA E FORMAGGIO
Parmesan cream sauce

Use this delicate sauce from northern Italy to dress up almost any pasta, fresh or dried. Bathe fettuccine in it and you've made a classic Fettuccine Alfredo.

- 2 tablespoons olive oil
- 1 tablespoon butter
- 3 tablespoons minced shallots
- ½ cup heavy cream
- ½ cup freshly grated Parmesan

Heat olive oil and butter in a skillet over moderate heat. Add shallots; cook gently until soft. Add cream; cook over low heat 3 to 4 minutes more, whisking to incorporate cream. Add Parmesan and remove from heat.

Makes about 1 cup, 4 to 6 servings.

Make-Ahead Tip Sauce may be made up to 4 hours ahead and refrigerated. Reheat gently before serving.

SUGO DI POMODORI FRESCHI
Uncooked fresh-tomato and herb sauce

Only fresh, vine-ripened, height-of-season tomatoes will do for the uncooked sauce found throughout Italy. When hot pasta hits cool tomatoes and fresh herbs, the aroma explodes!

- 3 pounds fresh, ripe tomatoes, peeled, seeded, and diced (see page 29)
- 2 tablespoons garlic, finely minced
- ½ cup olive oil
- ¼ cup chopped fresh basil or 1 tablespoon minced fresh oregano
- 2 tablespoons minced fresh parsley
- ½ teaspoon hot red-pepper flakes
  Freshly ground black pepper, to taste
- 1 tablespoon balsamic vinegar
- 1 teaspoon coarse salt

Combine all ingredients but salt in a large nonaluminum bowl. Stir to blend well, then let sit at room temperature for 30 minutes. Just before serving, add salt.

Makes slightly over 2 cups, 4 servings.

RAGÙ BOLOGNESE
Classic Bolognese sauce

The cooking of Bologna is widely considered the richest in Italy. No dainty herbs and textures for the Bolognese: They add body to their tomato sauce with meat, lots of vegetables, and milk or cream. Bolognese sauce is especially good with sturdy pasta—like shells or rigatoni—that have holes or ridges to trap the sauce.

- ½ cup olive oil
- ½ cup unsalted butter
- 1½ cups diced onion
- 1 cup diced celery
- 1 cup peeled and diced carrot
- 2 pounds extra-lean ground beef
- 1¾ cups dry white wine
- 1 cup milk
- 5 pounds ripe tomatoes, peeled, seeded, and chopped (see page 29), or two 28-ounce cans plum tomatoes, whirled briefly in a blender
- 1 teaspoon coarse salt
- ⅛ teaspoon freshly grated nutmeg
- 1 teaspoon freshly ground black pepper

Heat oil and butter in a medium stockpot over moderate heat. When butter foams, add onions, celery, and carrots and cook for 10 minutes. Add beef, breaking it up with a wooden spoon; cook until meat is lightly browned. Add wine and simmer until wine has been completely absorbed. Add milk and simmer until milk has been completely absorbed. Add tomatoes, salt, nutmeg, and pepper and simmer gently, uncovered, until mixture is reduced to a rich sauce, about 2 hours and 30 minutes. Taste and adjust seasoning. Serve immediately over egg noodles or cool and refrigerate.

Makes about 4 cups.

Make-Ahead Tip Sauce may be made up to 1 week ahead and refrigerated. It may be frozen for up to 2 months.

PASTA FAVORITES, NORTH AND SOUTH

Italian pasta dishes differ from north to south. The rich, elaborate northern dishes are usually made with fresh pasta and often contain butter, meat, and cream. Lasagne con Sugo di Funghi Secchi and Cannelloni are typical of the north.

In the south, dried pasta takes the place of fresh, and the dishes become simpler and more aggressively seasoned. Along the southern coasts, fish and shellfish appear frequently. Maccheroni al Tonno bears a distinctly southern stamp.

The following recipes give just a brief glimpse of this vast repertoire.

SPAGHETTI CON AGLIO E OLIO
Spaghetti with garlic and oil

A straightforward garlic-and-oil sauce (found throughout Italy) is delightful when made with young garlic. Choose heads with firm, pale ivory cloves that have a fresh, sweet flavor. Cloves that are sprouting or hot and bitter will ruin the dish.

1 *large head young garlic*
½ *cup olive oil*
1 *tablespoon unsalted butter*
1 *pound dried spaghetti*
Pinch hot red-pepper flakes (optional)
2 *tablespoons minced anchovies (optional)*
Salt and freshly ground black pepper

1. Separate head of garlic into cloves. Peel and chop cloves. Heat oil and butter in a skillet over moderate heat. Add garlic and sauté until fragrant. Remove from heat and let stand 20 minutes.

2. Cook spaghetti in plenty of boiling salted water until just done. Drain thoroughly, then transfer to a warm serving bowl. Reheat garlic and oil mixture, stirring in pepper flakes or anchovies (if used). Add sauce to pasta and toss well. Season to taste with salt and pepper. Serve immediately.

Serves 4 generously.

A robust Sugo di Pomodoro—a basic tomato sauce—is important to countless Italian dishes, from lasagne and cannelloni to braised meats and vegetables.

MAKING TORTELLINI

Tortellini can be made with a variety of fillings. In the photographs here the Pumpkin Filling from the recipe at right is used.

The pasta should be quite thin. For greatest ease of preparation, use a pasta machine.

Once cooked, tortellini may be added to beef or chicken broth, as in Tortellini in Brodo, at right. They may also be simply sauced with butter or bathed in a sauce of butter, cream, and cheese (see Salsa di Crema e Formaggio, page 36).

Tortellini can be formed a few hours ahead and spread on lightly floured baking sheets. Make sure they do not touch. Cover and refrigerate.

Tortellini can also be frozen before cooking. Follow directions for freezing ravioli on page 43.

2. *Fold circle in half to enclose filling; press edges together firmly to seal.*

3. *With sealed edge out, place folded circle over index finger. Bring ends toward each other under the finger, turning sealed outer edge up to form a cuff.*

1. *Cut 2-inch circles from pasta dough. Put a scant teaspoon of filling in center of each. Brush edges lightly with cold water.*

4. *Pinch ends together firmly. Let tortellini dry for a few minutes on a lightly floured surface before cooking.*

TORTELLINI IN BRODO
Tortellini in broth

It is said that tortellini are the inspiration of a lovesick cook, who shaped them to resemble the navel of his beloved. Conjectures aside, they're delicious in soup and are commonly served that way as a first course in Italy. They are often stuffed with ground veal and prosciutto, but the Modenese pumpkin filling below is popular, too. Use them in soups, as in this recipe, or toss them with butter and serve them with your Thanksgiving turkey.

- 2 recipes Pasta Gialla or other pasta dough (see pages 34–35) or 1 recipe each of two different kinds
- 6 cups chicken stock, preferably homemade

Pumpkin Filling

- ½ cup cooked, puréed pumpkin or winter squash
- 5 ounces freshly grated Parmesan
- ¼ cup ricotta
- 2 eggs plus 1 egg yolk
- 1 tablespoon brandy
- 1 teaspoon powdered sage
  Salt and freshly ground black pepper
  Pinch nutmeg

1. Make filling.

2. Roll out pasta and form tortellini as shown at left, using a teaspoon of filling for each one. You will have 36 to 40 tortellini. Bring stock to a boil in a saucepan. Add tortellini. They will sink, then float. After they float to the surface, cook 2 minutes. Remove one and taste for doneness. Transfer tortellini as they are cooked to warm soup plates. Ladle hot chicken stock over each portion.

Serves 5 or 6.

Pumpkin Filling Combine pumpkin, Parmesan, ricotta, eggs, egg yolk, brandy, and sage in a bowl. Season to taste with salt, pepper, and nutmeg.

CANNELLONI
Stuffed pasta rolls

Made from neat rectangles of pasta rolled around a savory filling, cannelloni can be a main course or, in small portions, a first course. In this dish from Abruzzi, both herb and egg doughs are filled with a spinach-and-cheese mixture, then topped with a creamy *balsamella* and a meaty Bolognese sauce.

    1   recipe Pasta Gialla
        (see page 34)
    1   recipe Pasta di Herbe
        (see page 35)
    1   recipe Salsa Balsamella
        (see page 42)
    1   recipe Ragù Bolognese
        (see page 36)
    ¼   cup freshly grated Parmesan
    3   tablespoons unsalted butter,
        at room temperature

Spinach and Cheese Filling

    2   tablespoons olive oil
    2   tablespoons minced shallot
    2   tablespoons minced carrot
    4   bunches fresh spinach,
        stemmed, leaves blanched,
        squeezed dry, and chopped
    ⅓   pound prosciutto, sliced
        paper-thin and shredded
    ¾   pound whole-milk ricotta
    1   cup freshly grated Parmesan
    ¼   cup grated mozzarella
    2   eggs plus 1 egg yolk
        Salt and freshly ground
        black pepper
        Pinch nutmeg

1. Roll pasta into sheets. Cut into 16 rectangles approximately 3 by 4 inches. Bring a large pot of salted water to a boil. Parboil pasta in batches for 10 seconds. Remove with a slotted spoon and refresh under ice water. Drain and dry thoroughly. Arrange atop clean dish towels. Top with clean dish towels and set aside.

2. Preheat oven to 350° F. Spoon 3 tablespoons of filling on each pasta rectangle. Roll up into a neat tube. Spread 1 cup of Salsa Balsamella over bottom of an ovenproof casserole, approximately 11 by 14 inches. Arrange cannelloni in the

casserole side by side, alternating egg and herb rolls. Top with Ragù Bolognese and remaining Balsamella. Dust with Parmesan, dot with butter, cover with foil, and bake 10 minutes. Uncover; bake 10 minutes more to brown the top. Serve immediately.

Serves 8 as a main course, 16 as a first course.

Spinach and Cheese Filling Heat olive oil in a large skillet over moderate heat. Add shallot and carrot; sauté 3 minutes. Remove from heat. Stir in spinach, prosciutto, ricotta, Parmesan, mozzarella, eggs, and egg yolk. Season to taste with salt, pepper, and nutmeg.

PASTA PUTTANESCA
Harlot's pasta

Legend has it that we owe this dish to Rome's "ladies of the night," who favored it because it was so quickly made. It's a spicy, sassy dish that calls for lots of crisp white wine.

    ¼   cup plus 1 tablespoon olive oil
    2   tablespoons butter
    ½   cup minced onion
    2   tablespoons minced garlic
    2½ cups peeled, seeded,
        and chopped tomatoes
    2   ounces anchovies, minced
    ½   teaspoon hot red-pepper flakes
    1   tablespoon capers
    1   cup unpitted Calamata olives
    ¼   cup julienned prosciutto
        (optional)
    1   pound dried spaghetti
    2   tablespoons minced parsley

1. Heat ¼ cup olive oil and the butter in a large skillet over low heat. When butter foams, add onion and garlic; sauté slowly until very soft, about 10 minutes. Add tomatoes; simmer 10 minutes. Add anchovies and pepper flakes; cook 1 minute. Stir in capers, olives, and prosciutto (if used).

2. Bring a large pot of salted water to a boil. Add remaining tablespoon olive oil and spaghetti and cook until pasta is just tender. Drain thoroughly and add to sauce in skillet. Toss together well and serve immediately, garnished with minced parsley.

Serves 4.

MACCHERONI AL TONNO
Pasta with fresh tuna

This brassy Sicilian sauce is not for delicate palates. Garlic, anchovies, capers, and olives enliven its fresh-tomato base; strips of tuna are tossed in at the last minute. This is a summer dish, to precede grilled fish or grilled shrimp.

    4   cup fresh bread crumbs
    ¼   cup minced parsley
    ¼   cup freshly grated Romano
    8   ounces fresh tuna fillet,
        cut into strips approximately
        ¼ by ¼ by 2½ inches long
        Freshly ground black pepper
    3   tablespoons olive oil
    ½   cup minced yellow onion
    1   tablespoon minced garlic
    3   anchovy fillets, minced
    1   pound plum tomatoes, peeled,
        seeded, and chopped
    1   tablespoon capers
    ¼   cup pitted green olives
    1   pound dried elbow-shaped
        macaroni

1. Combine bread crumbs, parsley, and cheese in a small bowl. Set aside. Season tuna lightly with pepper.

2. Heat olive oil in a large skillet over moderate heat. Add onion and garlic and sauté 3 minutes. Add anchovies and mash them with a wooden spoon until they "melt" into the garlic and onions. Add tomatoes. Cover partially and simmer 15 minutes. Turn heat to medium-high, add tuna, and toss quickly, cooking just until tuna is barely done. Stir in capers and olives, cook 30 seconds, cover, and remove from heat. Taste and adjust seasoning as necessary.

3. Bring a large pot of salted water to a boil. Add pasta and cook until just tender. Drain thoroughly and transfer to a warm serving bowl. Add half the bread-crumb mixture and toss well. Ladle the sauce over the top, then garnish with the remaining bread-crumb mixture.

Serves 4.

A bouquet of spring vegetables makes Pasta Primavera one of the lightest and liveliest Italian pasta dishes.

FETTUCCINE CON COZZE
Fettuccine with mussels and greens

The nutty-flavored green that Italians call arugula (also known as rocket or roquette) works particularly well in this Neapolitan dish, but other greens may be substituted. Take care not to overcook the mussels; the greens should be just barely wilted.

 ¼ *cup olive oil*
 ¼ *cup minced onion*
 2 *tablespoons minced garlic*
 ½ *cup dry white wine*
 1 *tablespoon grated lemon rind*
 1 *sweet red pepper, diced*
 6 *pounds fresh mussels, scrubbed clean and debearded (see page 67)*
 1 *tablespoon grappa (optional)*
 1 *pound fresh spinach, stems removed, leaves washed and dried*
 2½ *cups loosely packed arugula or other bitter greens (watercress, dandelion greens, collard greens, turnip greens)*
 1 *pound homemade fettuccine (use Pasta Gialla, page 34, or Pasta di Herbe, page 35)*
  Freshly ground black pepper

1. Heat olive oil in a large saucepan over medium heat. Add onion and garlic and sauté slowly until soft, about 3 to 5 minutes. Add wine, lemon rind, and red pepper; raise heat to high and add mussels. Cover and steam mussels until they open, about 3 minutes. Lift the lid and check them occasionally, removing those mussels that have opened. Discard any that refuse to open. Remove all mussels to a warm bowl. If you wish, add grappa to pan and flame; when flames die down, add spinach and greens. Or just add spinach and greens to still-hot pan. Cook greens about 10 seconds, until they are just wilted. Remove from heat.

2. Bring a large pot of salted water to a boil. Add pasta and cook until just done. Drain noodles well and transfer to pan with sauce. Return pan to low heat and toss noodles to coat well with sauce. Add mussels and toss again, then divide pasta among warm serving plates. Top each portion with freshly ground black pepper and serve immediately.

Serves 4.

PASTA PRIMAVERA
Spring vegetable pasta

The typical *pasta primavera* is a veritable garden on a plate—the most tender young vegetables tossed with herbs and thin pasta. You can readily substitute whatever is freshest in your market, but remember to aim for lively colors and contrasting textures. This is a Bolognese recipe.

- 1 pound sugar snap peas, strings removed, or 1 cup shelled fresh peas
- 1 pound fresh asparagus
- 1 cup sliced slender green beans, in 2-inch lengths
- ½ cup thin carrot strips
- 3 tablespoons olive oil plus 1 tablespoon if using dried pasta
- 2 tablespoons unsalted butter
- ½ cup diced sweet red pepper
- ½ cup diced sweet yellow pepper (optional)
- 2 tablespoons pine nuts, toasted
- 1 recipe Pasta di Herbe (see page 35) or ¾ pound dried spaghettini or cappelletti pasta
- 1 cup thinly shredded romaine lettuce
- 2 tablespoons minced fresh chives
  Salt
- 4 tablespoons minced fresh parsley, for garnish
  Freshly grated Parmesan

1. Bring a large pot of salted water to a boil. Blanch peas, asparagus, beans, and carrots separately, removing each batch to ice water as it is crisp but still tender, to stop the cooking. Drain well and pat dry. Save the cooking water.

2. Heat the 3 tablespoons olive oil and the butter in a large, heavy skillet over moderate heat. When butter foams, add red and yellow peppers (if used) and sauté one minute. Add pine nuts and sauté one more minute. Add blanched and dried peas, asparagus, beans, and carrots and toss until coated with oil and warmed through.

3. To cook pasta, bring the reserved vegetable water to a rolling boil. If you are using dried pasta, add 1 tablespoon oil; if you are using fresh pasta, there is no need to add oil. Add pasta and cook until just done. Drain well and transfer to a warm serving bowl. Add hot vegetables to pasta with romaine and chives. Toss well, add salt to taste, then toss again. Divide pasta among warm serving plates. Garnish each portion with minced parsley and pass grated Parmesan separately.

Serves 4.

FETTUCCINE CARBONARA
Pasta with bacon and eggs

In this popular Roman dish, the heat of the pasta cooks the eggs to yield a sauce made right in the serving bowl. Carbonara is a rich first course; follow it with a simple veal or chicken dish.

- 2 tablespoons olive oil
- 1 tablespoon unsalted butter
- 2 tablespoons finely minced garlic
- 8 ounces pancetta, in small dice
- ⅓ cup dry white wine
- 2 large eggs
- ⅓ cup freshly grated Pecorino Romano cheese
- ⅓ cup freshly grated Parmesan
- 1 recipe Pasta Gialla (see page 34)
  Salt and freshly ground black pepper, to taste

1. Heat oil and butter in a skillet over moderate heat. When butter foams, add garlic and sauté until garlic is fragrant. Add pancetta and fry until it is lightly browned. Add wine and simmer until wine is almost completely evaporated. Remove skillet from heat.

2. Break eggs into a large serving bowl and beat lightly. Stir in Pecorino Romano and Parmesan.

3. Cook pasta in plenty of boiling salted water until just done. Drain thoroughly; add to egg-cheese mixture. Toss well, then add hot pancetta mixture and toss again. Season with salt and plenty of pepper.

Serves 4.

PAPPARDELLE CON PESTO E PATATE
Broad noodles with pesto and potatoes

If you order pasta with pesto along the Italian Ligurian coast, you'll probably spot potato slices among the noodles. To Americans unaccustomed to starch-upon-starch, the combination surprises, but the first taste invariably wins converts. A crisp Italian Orvieto or Frascati is a fine accompaniment.

- 1 pound new red potatoes, scrubbed
- 2 tablespoons olive oil, plus 1 tablespoon if using dried pasta
- 1 tablespoon coarse salt
- 1 recipe Pasta Gialla (see page 34) or 1 pound broad noodles, storebought
- 1 recipe Pesto Genovese (see page 35), at room temperature
- 2 tablespoons toasted pine nuts, for garnish
- 2 tablespoons minced parsley, for garnish
  Freshly grated Parmesan

1. In a vegetable steamer, steam potatoes until just tender. Dry well, slice ¼ inch thick, then toss in a bowl with the 2 tablespoons olive oil and the salt.

2. Bring a large pot of salted water to a boil. If you are using dried pasta, add 1 tablespoon oil. Add pasta and cook until just done. Drain well and transfer to a warm serving bowl. Add potatoes and pesto and toss thoroughly, making sure that potatoes are coated with pesto, too. Garnish with pine nuts and parsley. Divide pasta among warm serving plates and pass the Parmesan separately.

Serves 4.

RAVIOLI DI SCAROLE E FORMAGGI
Spinach ravioli stuffed with cheese and escarole

These plump little pillows from Bologna have an unusual savory filling that's complemented by either tomato sauce or a light Salsa di Crema e Formaggio. They're quite rich and should be followed with a simple main course.

- 2 recipes Pasta Verde (see page 34)
- 1 recipe Sugo di Pomodoro or 1 recipe Salsa di Crema e Formaggio (both, page 36)
- 3 tablespoons minced parsley, for garnish
- ¼ cup freshly grated Parmesan, for garnish

Cheese and Escarole Filling

- 3 tablespoons olive oil
- 1 tablespoon butter
- 3 tablespoons minced leek or onion
- ½ tablespoon minced garlic
- 1 large bunch escarole, washed and finely shredded
- 1 teaspooon dried oregano
- 2 tablespoons Marsala
- 2 tablespoons whipping cream
- ¼ cup whole-milk ricotta
- ¼ cup grated Bel Paese or grated fresh mozzarella
  Salt and freshly ground black pepper
  Pinch nutmeg

1. Roll pasta dough out into sheets. Place ¾ teaspoon filling at regular intervals the length of the pasta (opposite page). Place another sheet of pasta over the first and use your fingers to press sheets together between the mounds of filling. Cut ravioli with a pizza cutter or pastry wheel. Use a fork to crimp the edges.

2. Bring a large pot of salted water to a boil. Add ravioli to boiling water a few at a time; do not crowd the pot.

Ravioli will sink, then float. After they begin to float, cook 2½ minutes. Remove one and taste for doneness. With a slotted spoon, remove cooked ravioli to a warm platter and keep warm in a low oven. Add remaining ravioli to boiling water in batches until all are cooked.

3. Meanwhile, reheat sauce. When all ravioli are on the platter, top with hot sauce. Garnish with parsley and Parmesan.

Serves 4 to 6.

Cheese and Escarole Filling Heat oil and butter in a skillet over moderate heat. When butter foams, add leek and garlic. Sauté gently until leek is very soft, about 15 minutes. Add escarole and oregano and sauté 2 minutes. Add Marsala, turn heat up to high, and cook until Marsala is almost completely evaporated. Reduce heat to medium and add cream. Stir to combine; simmer until cream thickens into a sauce, about 2 to 3 minutes. Remove from heat and cool slightly. Stir in cheeses; season to taste with salt, pepper, and nutmeg.

LASAGNE CON SUGO DI FUNGHI SECCHI
Lasagne with dried-mushroom sauce

The dried Italian mushrooms called *porcini* add a rich, woodsy flavor to any sauce or dish. Here they lend their fragrance to a rustic meatless lasagne from Piedmont (substitute water for the chicken stock if you prefer a vegetarian version). Serve it in cool weather as a main course with a salad, or in small portions as a first course followed by a chicken or veal roast.

- 1½ recipes Pasta Gialla (see page 34) or Pasta di Herbe (see page 35) or 1 pound dried lasagne noodles
  Olive oil
- 1 cup ricotta
- ½ cup minced parsley plus 3 tablespoons, for garnish
- ¼ cup freshly grated Parmesan

Sugo di Funghi Secchi

- 1 cup chicken stock
- 2 ounces dried porcini mushrooms
- 3 tablespoons olive oil
- 1 tablespoon butter
- 1 onion, minced
- 2 tablespoons finely minced garlic
- 2¾ cups tomato sauce (preferably Sugo di Pomodoro, page 36, but storebought will do) or puréed and strained fresh tomatoes
  Grated rind of 1 lemon
- ½ cup small fresh basil leaves, loosely packed
- 2 sprigs fresh oregano
- ¼ cup parsley sprigs
- 1 bay leaf
- 1¼ cups dry red wine
  Salt and freshly ground black pepper
- 3 tablespoons shredded basil

Salsa Balsamella

- 6 tablespoons unsalted butter
- 1½ tablespoons flour
- 3 cups milk
- ⅓ to ½ cup half-and-half
- 1 tablespoon sweet vermouth
  Pinch nutmeg
  Salt and white pepper

1. If you are using fresh pasta, roll out dough and cut it into lasagne shape (see page 7). Bring a large pot of salted water to a boil. Add lasagne noodles and cook until almost tender. Drain and refresh under cold water. Drain thoroughly and dry. Moisten noodles with olive oil and spread out on clean kitchen towels.

2. Preheat oven to 350° F. Coat bottom and sides of a casserole pan (approximately 13 by 11 by 2 inches) with 2 tablespoons olive oil. Spread 1 cup Sugo di Funghi Secchi over the bottom of the pan. Top with a layer of one third of the lasagne noodles. Combine ricotta, ½ cup minced parsley, and half of the Salsa Balsamella. Spread this mixture over the noodle layer. Top with another layer of one third of the noodles, then 1½ cups of the mushroom sauce, the remaining balsamella, a final layer of noodles, and the remaining mushroom sauce. Dust the top with Parmesan.

3. Cover pan with foil and bake 15 minutes. Uncover and bake until lasagne bubbles around the edges. Do not overcook. Let rest 10 minutes before serving.

Serves 6.

Sugo di Funghi Secchi

1. In a small saucepan bring stock to a boil. Add dried mushrooms and simmer 20 minutes. Carefully lift mushrooms out with a slotted spoon. Strain liquid through cheesecloth and reserve. Pick through porcini carefully to remove any grit. Chop coarsely.

2. Heat oil and butter in a large skillet over moderate heat. When butter foams, add onion and sauté 3 minutes. Add garlic and sauté until onion softens and begins to color, an additional 5 to 7 minutes. Add tomato sauce, lemon rind, basil leaves, oregano, parsley, and bay leaf. Stir well, then add strained stock, mushrooms, wine, and salt and pepper to taste. Simmer until liquid is reduced to a rich, dark sauce, about 45 to 50 minutes. Remove bay leaf and herb sprigs. Taste and adjust seasoning. Stir in shredded basil and remove from heat.

Makes about 4 cups.

Salsa Balsamella In a 1½-quart saucepan over moderate heat, melt 4 tablespoons of the butter. Add flour and cook, stirring, for 5 minutes. Gradually add milk in a slow, steady stream, whisking constantly. Cook over medium heat 20 minutes, stirring occasionally. Stir in ⅓ cup of the half-and-half, vermouth, nutmeg, and salt and pepper to taste. Continue cooking about 15 minutes, or until sauce is thick and smooth. If sauce thickens too much, add a little more half-and-half. Whisk in remaining butter. Taste and adjust seasoning. Set aside to cool.

Makes about 3 cups.

Step·by·Step

PREPARING RAVIOLI

Ravioli can be made with a variety of fillings. In the photographs here, Pasta Verde (spinach pasta) is used with a filling of escarole and cheese (see recipe on facing page). You could also use the pumpkin filling from the recipe for Tortellini in Brodo, page 38, or the spinach and cheese filling from the recipe for Cannelloni, page 39. Other pasta doughs can also be used. See pages 34 and 35 for Pasta Gialla (basic egg dough) and its variations. Be careful to match the dough and filling to make a compatible combination.

The pasta dough should be quite thin. For greatest ease of preparation, use a pasta machine.

Once they have been cooked, ravioli can be added to beef or chicken broth. They can also be sauced with Sugo di Pomodori Freschi (see page 36) or Salsa di Crema e Formaggio (see page 36).

Ravioli can be prepared a few hours ahead of serving time and spread on lightly floured baking sheets. Make sure they do not touch. Cover and refrigerate.

Ravioli can also be frozen after they have been formed (and before cooking). Arrange ravioli in a single layer on a baking sheet or tray, being sure they are not touching. Place tray in freezer. When ravioli are frozen solid, remove them from tray and place in a freezer-weight plastic bag or other freezer container. They can be stored in the freezer up to three months.

1. *Roll pasta dough into sheets. Place mounds of filling, about ¾ teaspoon each, at regular intervals the length of the pasta. Brush lightly with cold water between the mounds.*

2. *Place another sheet of pasta over the first and use your fingers to press sheets together between the mounds of filling.*

3. *Cut ravioli with a pizza cutter or pastry wheel. Use a fork to crimp and seal the edges.*

A SICILIAN COUNTRY DINNER

Pomodori dell' Estate
(see page 109)

Minestra all' Aglio

Baccalà Fritto alla Siciliana

Focaccia
(see page 52)

Caciocavallo
(see page 20)

Mele ed Uve
(Apples and Grapes)

Dolci della Festa

This menu is sensible for company because so much of the meal may be made ahead. Assemble the tomato casserole in the morning, bake it just before guests arrive, and serve it at room temperature. The soup, too, may be made in the morning, except for the final addition of cheese. The sauce for the salt cod is made ahead, but the fish is fried at the last minute. The Focaccia can be made in the morning and warmed through before serving; offer it along with the first two courses. Drink a crisp Italian white wine throughout the dinner, and pour espresso or strong coffee with the party cookies.

MINESTRA ALL' AGLIO
Chicken broth with garlic

Potatoes, cheese, and cream enrich this quickly made chicken soup. A healthy dose of garlic and hot red-pepper flakes brand it as Sicilian.

    5 cups chicken stock
    1 cup peeled and diced
       raw potato
    3 tablespoons olive oil
    ¼ cup sliced garlic
    ½ cup minced onion
    ½ cup whipping cream
    ½ cup milk
    ½ teaspoon hot red-pepper flakes
    2 ounces fontina, grated
       Coarse salt

1. Combine stock and potato in a large saucepan. Bring to a boil over high heat, reduce heat to maintain a simmer, and cook 10 minutes.

2. While stock is simmering heat olive oil in a large saucepan over moderately low heat. Add garlic and onion and sauté gently for 10 minutes; do not let garlic and onion brown. Add stock and potato and simmer 20 minutes, covered. Transfer mixture to a blender in batches along with cream, milk, and red-pepper flakes. Blend until smooth.

3. Put mixture in a clean large saucepan. Add 2 tablespoons of the fontina and reheat, stirring until cheese melts and mixture is almost boiling. Add salt to taste. Serve immediately, garnishing each portion with some of the remaining fontina.

Serves 4.

Make-Ahead Tip The soup may be made through step 2 several hours ahead and refrigerated.

BACCALÀ FRITTO
ALLA SICILIANA
Fried salt cod Sicilian style

A day-long soaking rids dried salt cod of its excess salt and restores its meaty, firm texture. Briefly marinated with lemon juice and hot red-pepper flakes, then breaded and deep-fried, it is as sweet and succulent as any fresh-caught fish. Serve it as the Sicilians do, with a pungent olive-and-anchovy sauce, and accompany it with a bone-dry Verdicchio or Sicilian Corvo. Note that the sauce must stand for at least 12 hours and can be made as much as a week in advance.

    1½ pounds boneless salt cod
     2 cups milk
     ¼ cup olive oil
     ¼ cup lemon juice
     2 tablespoons minced parsley
     ½ onion, minced
     ½ teaspoon hot red-pepper flakes
        Flour, for dredging
     ¼ cup dry white wine
     2 eggs
     2 cups soft bread crumbs
     2 tablespoons corn oil

Olive Sauce

    1½ cups green pimiento-stuffed
        olives
     ⅔ cup olive oil
     ½ cup minced parsley
     1 sweet red bell pepper, seeded,
        with ribs removed, and
        minced
    1½ ounces anchovy fillets, mashed
     ¼ cup capers
     1 tablespoon minced garlic
     1 tablespoon minced fresh
        oregano
     1 teaspoon black pepper

1. Put salt cod in a baking dish and cover with cold water. Refrigerate 24 hours, changing the water 3 times. On the final change, add the milk to the water.

2. Drain salt cod and pat dry. Cut into 12 pieces. In a large bowl, combine olive oil, lemon juice, parsley, onion, and red-pepper flakes. Put fish pieces in the bowl and marinate 45 minutes at room temperature.

3. Put flour on a plate or a sheet of waxed paper. Combine wine and egg in a small bowl; whisk to blend. Have bread crumbs ready on a plate. Drain fish. Dredge each piece lightly in flour. Dip fish in egg mixture, letting excess drip off, then coat with bread crumbs. Transfer breaded salt cod to a plate or baking sheet.

4. Heat corn oil in a large skillet over moderately high heat. Fry fish on both sides until nicely browned, about 3 to 4 minutes on each side depending on thickness. Drain on paper towels and arrange on a warm serving platter. Spoon Olive Sauce over cod and serve immediately.

Serves 4.

Olive Sauce Chop olives coarsely. Put in a ceramic, stainless steel, or glass bowl along with olive oil, parsley, bell pepper, anchovies, capers, garlic, oregano, and black pepper. Stir to blend. Cover and refrigerate for at least 12 hours or up to 1 week. Serve at room temperature.

DOLCI DELLA FESTA
Party cookies

These chocolate macaroons are traditionally eaten at All Souls' Day parties.

> 2 *egg whites*
> ½ *cup sugar*
> *Pinch of salt*
> 6 *ounces milk chocolate, melted*
> 2 *teaspoons vanilla extract*
> ½ *teaspoon ground cinnamon*
> 1 *cup unsweetened shredded coconut*

1. Preheat oven to 325° F. Beat egg whites until frothy. Add sugar and salt and beat until stiff but not dry.

2. In a medium bowl combine chocolate, vanilla, cinnamon, and coconut. Gently fold in egg whites.

3. Drop batter by teaspoons onto a lightly greased baking sheet. Bake 15 minutes. Cool on a rack and store in airtight containers (cookies can be stored for 2 to 3 weeks).

Makes 3 dozen cookies.

This country dinner reflects the Sicilian taste for bold flavors: garlic and peppers, anchovies and capers. There is nothing refined about dishes like Minestra all' Aglio or Baccalà Fritto alla Siciliana. They are the creations of good home cooks: The presentations are simple; the flavors, direct. The soup and fish are accompanied by a tomato casserole and crusty Focaccia; fresh fruit and cookies complete the meal.

Starting with corn, rice, and wheat, Italian cooks make such favorite foods as polenta, risotto, a multitude of breads, and pizzas by the dozen.

Breads, Pizza & Grains

Many of the earthy basics of Italian cooking are presented in this chapter. Virtually every meal includes bread, whether a sweet slice for breakfast (see Pane di Mattina alla Siciliana, page 50), a savory accompaniment to a soup lunch (see Pane per la Zuppa, page 49), or a crusty loaf with dinner (see Pane Toscano, page 48). In the north polenta (see page 58) and risotto (see page 61) are age-old traditions; from the south comes the much-beloved pizza (see page 53). A special feature of the chapter is a Pizza Party menu (see page 55).

Like French toast, Pane per la Zuppa is dipped in egg and then cooked to a golden finish. This Italian version, however, is savory—seasoned with garlic, fennel, and pepper and dusted with Parmesan—and it's baked. Serve Pane per la Zuppa with soup for a filling lunch or light dinner.

BREADS, PIZZA & GRAINS

Whole grains and grain derivatives are a large part of the Italian diet. Indeed, corn and rice in the north and wheat in the south are the foundation of many of Italy's best-known dishes. Corn is made into polenta (see page 58) and a variety of corn breads; short-grain rice becomes creamy risotto (see page 61); wheat, of course, is the basis of Italy's huge repertoire of breads, ranging from Pane Toscano (at right) to Focaccia (see page 52) to pizza (see page 53).

The beauty of pizza, breads, and grains is their versatility. Master the basic techniques, and then let your imagination and the state of your larder suggest variations. The recipes that follow merely hint at the enormous range of Italian pizzas, breads, and grains.

BREADS

The most basic sort of bread—nothing but flour, yeast, and water—plays a fundamental role in the Italian diet. In fact, many Italians consider good bread, good oil, and salt, and perhaps a vine-ripened tomato, enough to make them perfectly happy at lunch. But more often the basic bread is used to soak up juices from other dishes or to accompany Italy's famous cheeses (see page 20).

More elaborate breads play other roles. The sweet Pane di Mattina alla Siciliana (see page 50) is a foil for the bitter morning espresso. Pane Rustico (see page 50), packed with pancetta and cheese, is a perfect picnic bread, and Focaccia and Merenda Fiorentina (see page 49) are popular snacks. And a Focaccia di Palermo stuffed with sausage and cheese (see page 53) or a bubbling Pizza del Norte made with fontina and provolone (see page 53) can be enjoyed as a meal in itself.

Although most Italians buy their breads from the local *panetteria* (bakery), there is no denying the appeal of a homemade loaf. The interested home baker will want to try the following recipes and should find the results immensely satisfying.

PANE TOSCANO
Basic Tuscan bread

This rustic bread requires some patience but little actual working time. Begin the Starter four days ahead and you'll get a chewy, full-flavored loaf that is absolutely authentic. Its basic goodness is the perfect foil for antipasti, salads, soups, cheeses, and sauces of all sorts. Such wonderful bread can become an antipasto or a lunch in minutes: Just toast and rub with garlic, brush well with extravirgin olive oil, sprinkle with coarse salt, and top it with a crushed ripe tomato.

- 2 cups warm (105° F) water
- 6 cups (approximately) unbleached flour
- 1 teaspoon active dry yeast

Starter

1½ cups unbleached flour
1 teaspoon sugar
½ cup warm (105° F) water

1. Put half the Starter in a bowl; cover with cool water and soak 3 hours. Gently pour off the water, taking care not to lose any moist bits of dough at the bottom of the bowl. Add ½ cup of the warm water and 1 cup flour. Stir well, then cover and set aside for 3 hours. Add remaining warm water and as much of the remaining flour as necessary to make a dough firm enough to knead.

2. Turn out dough onto a lightly floured board and knead 15 minutes, adding more flour as necessary to make a firm, smooth dough. Form dough into 2 round loaves and place on a lightly oiled baking sheet. Snip tops of loaves with scissors at 2-inch intervals. Cover and let rise until doubled in bulk, about 2 hours.

3. When dough has almost doubled, preheat oven to 450° F and place a pan of hot water on the lowest rack. Bake bread 12 minutes at 450° F, then reduce heat to 375° F and continue baking until bread sounds hollow when tapped. Cool on racks before slicing.

Makes two 1-pound loaves.

Starter Combine flour, sugar, and the water in a bowl and mix to form a rough ball. Dough will be stiff and coarse. Dust with a little additional flour, cover, and set aside 4 days. Starter will become quite hard. On the fourth day, divide starter in half. Put half in a bowl covered with plastic wrap, at room temperature, to make dough; wrap remaining half and refrigerate it for up to 2 months.

Makes enough starter for 4 loaves.

MERENDA FIORENTINA
Florentine snack bread

This flat "pizza" bread is scented with rosemary, oil, and garlic, which fill the house with tantalizing aromas when it's baked. Cut it into "fingers" and serve it as a snack with a glass of red wine, or tuck it into your picnic basket along with roast chicken and Roasted Red Peppers (see page 14).

1 package active dry yeast
1 teaspoon salt
3 cups unbleached flour
1 cup warm (105° F) water
3 tablespoons olive oil plus olive oil for brushing crust
1 tablespoon minced garlic Cornmeal, for dusting Coarse salt
1 teaspoon minced fresh rosemary (optional)

1. Combine yeast, salt, and flour in a large bowl. Combine the water and oil in a small bowl. Add liquid to dry ingredients and mix until they form a rough mass. Knead mixture in the bowl with your hands until it holds together, then turn it out onto a lightly floured surface and knead in the garlic. Continue kneading until dough is smooth and elastic, about 8 minutes. Form into a ball and let rest on a lightly floured surface, covered, for 1 hour.

2. Preheat oven to 375° F. Roll dough into a 12- by 14-inch rectangle and transfer to a baking sheet sprinkled with cornmeal. Use your fingertips to make indentations in the dough at 2-inch intervals. Sprinkle dough lightly with coarse salt and drizzle olive oil over the top. Sprinkle with rosemary (if used). Bake until golden, about 25 minutes. Remove from the oven and brush with a little more olive oil. Cool slightly on a rack; serve warm.

Makes one 12- by 14-inch rectangle.

PANE PER LA ZUPPA
Bread for soup

This Neapolitan version of French toast is an excellent complement to a soup or stew. Thick slices of egg-dipped bread are seasoned with garlic, pepper, and fennel, then topped with Parmesan and baked until golden.

1 teaspoon minced garlic
1 tablespoon fennel seed, lightly crushed in a mortar
1 tablespoon freshly ground black pepper
1 teaspoon salt
5 or 6 eggs
3 or 4 tablespoons olive oil
1 loaf Pane Toscano (opposite page), cut in ¾-inch slices
2 tablespoons freshly grated Parmesan

1. Preheat oven to 350° F. Lightly oil a large baking sheet. Combine garlic, fennel seed, pepper, and salt in a small bowl and set aside.

2. Whisk together 5 eggs and 3 tablespoons olive oil. Dip bread slices in egg mixture one at a time and let them soak briefly to absorb some egg. Arrange bread slices on baking sheet. If bread is slightly stale, you may need an additional egg and a little extra oil.

3. Dust bread slices with half the fennel mixture. Bake 10 minutes. Turn slices, dust with remaining fennel mixture, and bake 10 minutes. Sprinkle with Parmesan and bake an additional 5 minutes or until bread is golden. Serve hot with soup or stew.

Makes 12 slices.

PANE RUSTICO
Country bacon-and-cheese bread

These round Roman loaves are practically a lunch in themselves, especially with a green salad and a bottle of red wine. They make delicious toast to accompany a chicken broth or a tomato soup, and when toasted and properly filled, they make the ultimate BLT.

- 2 packages active dry yeast
- 2 cups warm (105° F) water
- 4½ cups (approximately) unbleached flour
- ½ cup whole wheat flour
- 1 tablespoon coarse salt
- ½ cup coarse cornmeal
- 4 ounces pancetta, sliced thin
- 8 ounces whole-milk mozzarella, cut in ⅓-inch cubes
  Cornmeal, for dusting

1. Combine yeast and ½ cup of the water in a small bowl and stir to dissolve. Set aside 15 minutes.

2. In a large bowl, combine 4½ cups unbleached flour, whole wheat flour, salt, and the coarse cornmeal. Add the remaining warm water and mix well. Dough will be sticky. Add additional unbleached flour as necessary to make a dough firm enough to knead. Turn out onto a lightly floured board and knead until dough is shiny, elastic, and smooth, about 15 minutes.

3. Put dough in a lightly oiled bowl and turn to coat with oil. Cover and let rise until doubled in bulk, about 1½ hours. Punch down and let rise, covered, an additional hour.

4. Render pancetta in a skillet over moderate heat until crisp. Drain, cool, and crumble coarsely. Punch dough down and knead in pancetta and mozzarella. Form into 1 large round or 2 smaller loaves. Place on a baking sheet dusted with fine cornmeal. Cover and let rise until doubled in bulk, about 1 hour.

5. Preheat oven to 425° F. Brush tops of loaves with water. Let dry 5 minutes, then brush again. Bake 10 minutes at 425° F, then reduce heat to 350° F. Bake until bread is golden brown and sounds hollow when tapped, an additional 25 to 30 minutes. Cool on racks before slicing.

Makes 1 large or 2 small loaves.

PANE DI MATTINA ALLA SICILIANA
Sicilian morning bread

Sicily's alternative to the morning Danish is a subtly sweet egg bread fragrant with lemon, Marsala, and fennel. The dough has a long, slow rising to ensure its good flavor and texture; to have it for breakfast, make it a day ahead and rewarm it the following morning.

- 1 teaspoon olive oil
- 1 package active dry yeast
- ½ cup plus 1 teaspoon sugar
- 1⅓ cups scalded milk, cooled to 100° F
- 6½ cups (approximately) unbleached flour
- ¼ cup dried currants
- ⅓ cup golden raisins
- ⅓ cup Marsala
- ½ cup unsalted butter
- 3 tablespoons shortening
- 1½ teaspoons fennel seed
- 4 eggs
- 1 tablespoon grated lemon rind
- ½ teaspoon salt

Egg Wash
- 1 tablespoon whipping cream
- 1 egg yolk
- ½ tablespoon Marsala

1. Brush olive oil over surface of a large stainless steel bowl. Put yeast and 1 teaspoon of the sugar in bottom of bowl. Add 1 cup of the scalded milk and stir to dissolve yeast. Set aside for 10 minutes, then add 1½ cups of the flour and the remaining milk. Knead by hand or with a mixer and dough hook until dough is soft and silky, about 7 or 8 minutes. Cover and let rise 5 hours.

2. While dough rises, soak currants and raisins in Marsala for at least 1 hour. In a small saucepan over low heat, melt butter and 2 tablespoons of the shortening. Add fennel seed, remove from heat, and let stand until cool. Add eggs to fennel-seed mixture one at a time, blending well after each addition, then add lemon rind and the remaining sugar. Set aside.

3. When dough has risen 5 hours, add fennel-seed mixture and mix well. Add salt and begin adding the remaining flour, ½ cup at a time. When dough is firm enough to knead, turn out onto a lightly floured board and knead until smooth and soft, about 10 to 15 minutes, adding as much additional flour as necessary to keep it from sticking. During the final 5 minutes, knead in raisins and currants.

4. Form dough into 2 loaves. Use remaining shortening to grease two 9-inch loaf pans. Place dough in pans, cover and let rise until doubled in bulk. This may take as long as 3 hours. (Dough may also be formed into 1 large round loaf and baked free-form.)

5. Preheat oven to 375° F. Brush Egg Wash on loaves 5 minutes before baking. Brush again immediately before baking. Bake until loaves are golden brown and sound hollow when tapped, about 35 minutes. Cool on racks.

Makes two 9-inch loaves or one large round loaf.

Egg Wash Combine cream, yolk, and Marsala in a small bowl.

PANE GIALLO
Polenta bread

This cornbread from northern Italy
bears a strong resemblance to American spoon bread: It's lightened with
egg whites and baked to an almost
pudding-like texture. Red peppers and
garlic mark it as distinctly Italian,
however, and it is served in the same
contexts as its cousin, polenta: with
grilled chicken or chops, roast quail,
or pan-fried sausages.

    5   tablespoons unsalted butter
    2   tablespoons minced garlic
    1   cup polenta (coarse yellow
        cornmeal)
  1½   teaspoons salt
    1   teaspoon freshly ground black
        pepper
    3   eggs, separated
    2   cups milk
    ½   cup half-and-half
    1   cup Roasted Red Peppers
        (see page 14), minced
        Olive oil

1. In a small skillet over moderately
low heat, melt 2 tablespoons of the
butter. Add garlic and sauté until
fragrant. Remove from heat. Combine
polenta, salt, and pepper in a bowl
and set aside.

2. Put egg yolks, milk, and half-and-
half in a saucepan and whisk well.
Bring to a boil, whisking constantly.
Add cornmeal mixture gradually,
then add garlic and red peppers.
Cook 2 minutes, stirring constantly
with a wooden spoon. Add the
remaining butter and cook an additional 2 minutes.

3. Preheat oven to 375° F. Brush an
8-cup soufflé dish or casserole with
olive oil. Place dish in oven 5 minutes to warm it. Beat egg whites with
a pinch of salt until stiff peaks
form. Gently fold whites into thickened cornmeal. Pour mixture into hot
soufflé dish. Bake until puffed and
golden, about 30 minutes. Serve
immediately.

Serves 8.

*A richly scented call to
rise and shine, Pane di
Mattina alla Siciliana
is flavored with lemon,
Marsala, and fennel. With
caffè latte (see page 118),
it's a very Italian way to
start the day.*

The flat bread called focaccia is a popular children's snack but it can also accompany a meal. Serve this onion-and-herb version with soup or salad for a casual lunch.

1¼ cups warm (105° F) water
¾ teaspoon sugar
1 package active dry yeast
2¾ cups unbleached flour
3 tablespoons unsalted butter
½ cup minced onion
⅓ cup minced fresh basil
1½ teaspoons coarse salt
½ teaspoon freshly ground black pepper
2 tablespoons olive oil plus olive oil for drizzling
Cornmeal, for dusting

1. Combine ½ cup of the water, the sugar, and yeast in a large bowl. Set aside 10 minutes. Stir in ¾ cup of the flour, cover, and let rise 2½ hours.

2. While dough is rising, heat butter in a skillet over low heat. Add onion and sauté until onion is soft but not browned, about 15 minutes. Remove from heat and stir in basil, ½ teaspoon of the salt, and pepper.

3. Add the remaining flour to dough and beat well. Combine the 2 tablespoons olive oil and remaining warm water, then add to dough. Beat until dough forms a mass. Turn out onto a lightly floured surface and knead until dough is shiny and smooth, 8 to 10 minutes. Transfer dough to a lightly oiled bowl and turn to coat all sides with oil. Cover and let rise until doubled in bulk, about 1½ hours.

4. Preheat oven to 450° F. Punch dough down and roll into a 13- by 15-inch rectangle. Transfer to a baking sheet sprinkled with cornmeal. Spread top with onion mixture. Drizzle with additional olive oil. Sprinkle with the remaining coarse salt and bake until golden, about 15 minutes. Cool slightly on a rack; serve warm.

Makes one 13- by 15-inch rectangle.

FOCACCIA
Italian flatbread

By most accounts, *focaccia* is reckoned to be Italy's oldest bread—a simple yeast dough flattened and baked on a stone slab in a wood-fired hearth. Quite likely, it's the grandfather of the famous Neapolitan pizza. Today's cooks can easily make this versatile country bread at home, even without the stone and the hearth. Garnished as you like—here, with sautéed onions and basil—it can partner salads and soups, sliced tomatoes and cheese, or cocktails.

FOCACCIA DI PALERMO
Stuffed focaccia with sausage

The Sicilian cooks of Palermo have their own version of *focaccia:* a stuffed rendition that's rather like a sandwich. Any pizza topping will work. Here, a stuffing of garlicky sausage and cheese makes this a hearty luncheon dish.

   1 recipe Focaccia (opposite page); see instructions below
   ½ pound sweet Italian sausage, casings removed, cooked, and crumbled
   ½ cup ricotta
   ¼ cup freshly grated Parmesan
   ⅓ cup minced Italian parsley
   3 tablespoons minced onion
   1 teaspoon minced garlic
      Salt
      Cornmeal, for dusting
   ¼ cup grated mozzarella, provolone, or jack cheese
      Olive oil

1. Prepare step 1 of Focaccia recipe.

2. While dough is rising, combine sausage, ricotta, Parmesan, parsley, onion, and garlic. Taste; add salt if desired. Refrigerate while dough rises.

3. Complete step 3 of recipe for Focaccia.

4. When dough has doubled in bulk, divide it in half. Roll into 2 rectangles of equal size.

5. Preheat oven to 450° F. Dust a baking sheet with cornmeal and transfer one of the rectangles to the baking sheet. Spread filling over the top, leaving a ½-inch border. Sprinkle with grated cheese. Top with second rectangle and crimp the edges. Brush top with olive oil and sprinkle with salt. Bake until golden, about 15 to 20 minutes. Transfer to a rack to cool 10 minutes, then serve.

Serves 4.

PIZZA

Probably no Italian dish is as familiar to Americans as pizza. In fact we tend to think of it as our own invention, although it almost certainly originated in Naples. The basic dough, rolled thin, can be topped with whatever is best and freshest. In Naples that usually means fresh mozzarella and vine-ripened tomatoes. In your house it can mean the best from your garden (see page 54) or a freshly made Pesto Genovese (see page 55). For a delicious switch, fold the pizza in half before baking to make a Calzone (see page 55).

BASIC PIZZA DOUGH

A little rye flour adds distinctive flavor to this basic dough. The recipe can be doubled. For toppings, see the recipes that follow.

   ½ cup warm (105° F) water
   ½ teaspoon sugar
   ½ package active dry yeast
   2 cups plus 2 tablespoons unbleached white flour
   2 tablespoons rye flour
   ½ teaspoon salt
   1 tablespoon olive oil
      Cornmeal, for dusting

1. Combine the water and sugar in a small bowl; sprinkle yeast over it, stir to dissolve, then set aside 10 minutes.

2. Set aside ½ cup unbleached flour. Combine the remaining unbleached flour with rye flour and salt in a large bowl. Stir in yeast mixture and olive oil. Put reserved ½ cup flour on a flat work surface. Turn out dough onto floured surface and knead, slowly incorporating the additional flour. Knead until smooth, about 10 minutes. Transfer dough to a bowl brushed with olive oil; turn dough to coat all sides with oil. Cover and let rise 30 minutes.

3. Punch dough down and divide in half. Roll each half into an 8-inch round; transfer rounds to a baking sheet dusted with cornmeal. Dough is now ready to be topped and baked.

Makes enough dough for two 8-inch pizzas.

PIZZA DEL NORTE
Fontina and provolone pizza alla Valle d'Aosta

The mountainous northern region of Italy known as the Valle d'Aosta is the source of one of the country's finest cheeses: fontina. An excellent melting cheese with a buttery, nutty flavor, it is used in *fonduta*, the Italian version of fondue; here, it transforms a tomato-and-cheese pizza into a memorable dish.

   1 recipe Basic Pizza Dough (at left)
      Olive oil
   1½ cups peeled, seeded, and chopped fresh tomato (see page 29)
   6 ounces Italian fontina, in thin slices
   3 tablespoons paper-thin garlic slices
   ¼ cup diced provolone
   ¼ cup coarsely chopped parsley, preferably Italian parsley
   4 ounces Parmesan
      Additional minced parsley, for garnish (optional)

Preheat oven to 425° F. Roll dough out into two rounds according to instructions in Basic Pizza Dough and transfer to baking sheet. Brush surface with olive oil. Divide tomatoes among the two rounds. Top with fontina, garlic, provolone, and parsley. Use a cheese slicer to shave thin sheets of Parmesan over tops of pizzas. Drizzle with olive oil. Bake until the edges are browned and the top is bubbly, about 12 to 15 minutes. Garnish with additional parsley, if desired.

Makes two 8-inch pizzas.

What's a calzone? In short, a folded-over pizza. This one reveals its filling of spinach, prosciutto, and molten cheeses.

PIZZA DELL' ESTATE
Summer garden pizza

This simple pizza from Palermo is a fine way to show off your garden tomatoes. Non-gardeners should buy the best vine-ripened tomatoes available. A fruity olive oil and the best-quality whole-milk mozzarella are other musts.

> 1 large, ripe tomato, peeled, seeded, and chopped
> 3 tablespoons minced fresh basil
> 4 tablespoons olive oil
> 2 tablespoons minced shallot or green onion
> 1 recipe Basic Pizza Dough (see page 53)
> 3 tablespoons minced garlic
> ½ cup paper-thin red onion slices
> 6 ounces whole-milk mozzarella, grated
> 6 tablespoons freshly grated Parmesan
> 2 anchovy fillets, julienned (optional)
> Additional olive oil

1. Combine tomato, basil, 2 tablespoons of the olive oil, and shallots; set aside to marinate for at least 30 minutes or up to 8 hours. Combine garlic and the remaining olive oil in a small bowl and set aside for 30 minutes.

2. Preheat oven to 425° F. Roll dough out according to instructions in Basic Pizza Dough and transfer to baking sheet. Combine garlic and tomato mixtures and divide between the two rounds. Top with onion slices, mozzarella, and Parmesan. Arrange anchovies (if used) on top. Drizzle surface with a little additional olive oil. Bake until the edges are browned and the top is bubbly, about 12 to 15 minutes. Serve immediately.

Makes two 8-inch pizzas.

CALZONE
Stuffed pizza turnover

A calzone is a pizza by another name: Mound the filling on half the dough and fold the other half over to form the bulging half-moon shape of this clever creation from Venice. Small ones are eaten out of hand, as a snack or a quick lunch; large ones are served with a knife and fork. Cutting into a hot calzone and releasing the molten filling is part of the pleasure of this fragrant dish, but small ones should be cooled slightly to firm the filling and avoid burning fingers.

- 1½ cups cooked fresh spinach, squeezed dry
- 1¼ cups ricotta
- 3 tablespoons freshly grated Parmesan
- ¼ cup pitted and chopped Greek Calamata olives
- ¼ cup minced parsley
- 1 recipe Basic Pizza Dough (see page 53)
- ½ cup shredded prosciutto
- ½ cup grated whole-milk mozzarella
- 1 egg mixed with 1 tablespoon water
  Olive oil

Preheat oven to 475° F. Combine spinach, ricotta, Parmesan, olives, and parsley. Roll dough out on a lightly floured surface into 1 large or 2 small rounds, ¼ inch thick. Place spinach mixture on bottom half of the dough, leaving a ⅝-inch border. Top spinach with prosciutto and mozzarella. Brush border with egg mixture, then fold top half over the bottom and seal the edges. Brush top with olive oil. Bake until golden, about 12 to 15 minutes. Brush again with olive oil. If calzone will be eaten out of hand, let cool slightly before serving.

Makes two 4-inch or one 8-inch calzone.

A PIZZA PARTY

*Bagna Cauda
(see page 19)*

Pizza al Pesto

Pizza alle Vongole

Pizza Rossa

Amaretti Sundaes

Wine and Coffee

What better way to ring in the New Year or fete that monumental fortieth birthday than with a lighthearted pizza party for adults only? Begin with cocktails or white wine and a grand Bagna Cauda, then bring on the Chianti Classico and the pizzas. For dessert, set out vanilla ice cream, crushed amaretti cookies, whipped cream, and hot fudge sauce, and let guests invent their own little bit of heaven.

NEAPOLITAN PIZZA DOUGH

The classic Neapolitan pizza dough has no oil in it. It yields a drier crust that can support a moist topping.

- 2 tablespoons dry yeast
- 1 cup warm (105° F) water
- 4½ cups (approximately) flour
- 1 teaspoon salt

Dissolve yeast in the water in a medium bowl. Add 2 cups of the flour, mix well to make a sponge, cover, and let rise 45 minutes. In a large bowl, combine 2 cups of the remaining flour and the salt. Add risen sponge and mix well. Turn out onto a lightly floured surface and knead until smooth and silky, about 5 minutes, adding flour as necessary. Put dough in a lightly oiled bowl, turn to coat all sides with oil, cover and let rise 2 hours. Punch down dough and divide in halves, quarters, or eighths, depending on desired pizza size. Roll and top as desired.

Makes enough dough for 8 small, 4 medium, or 2 large pizzas.

PIZZA AL PESTO
Pizza with fresh basil sauce

Despite the simplicity of its ingredients, this pizza is rich and satisfying; don't be tempted to gussy it up with other garnishes. The brilliant green of the pesto is the perfect counterpoint to an all-red Pizza Rossa.

- 1 recipe Neapolitan Pizza Dough (above)
  Cornmeal, for dusting
- 4 ounces mozzarella, sliced
- 1 recipe Pesto Genovese (see page 35)
- ¼ cup pine nuts

Preheat oven to 475° F. Divide dough into 2, 4, or 8 portions, as desired. Roll out on a lightly floured surface into rounds ⅓ inch thick. Transfer to a baking sheet dusted with cornmeal. Arrange mozzarella over dough; brush each round with a thin layer of pesto. Garnish with pine nuts and bake until browned and bubbly, 12 to 18 minutes depending on size.

Makes 8 small, 4 medium, or 2 large pizzas.

Begin a Pizza Party with a basket of colorful vegetables and an anchovy-garlic dip: follow with three rustic, crusty pizzas. Recipes begin on page 55.

PIZZA ALLE VONGOLE
Pizza with fresh clams

Rubbery, canned clams and over-cooked tomato sauce are the norm on restaurant clam pizzas. You can make a far better version at home with fresh, chopped tomatoes and freshly steamed clams. To keep the clams from toughening, add them just as the pizza comes out of the oven.

    2½ cups seeded and chopped
        tomatoes (see page 29)
    ⅓ cup plus 2 tablespoons
        olive oil
    2 tablespoons minced fresh
        oregano
    1 recipe Neapolitan Pizza Dough
        (see page 55)
        Cornmeal, for dusting
    2 tablespoons minced garlic
    1 cup dry white wine
    3½ pounds small clams
    2 tablespoons coarsely chopped
        Italian parsley

1. Preheat oven to 475° F. In a small bowl, combine tomatoes, ⅓ cup of the olive oil, and the oregano; let stand 15 minutes.

2. Divide dough into 2, 4, or 8 portions, as desired. Roll out dough on a lightly floured surface into rounds ⅓ inch thick. Transfer to a baking sheet dusted with cornmeal. Brush dough rounds with 2 table-spoons of the liquid from the toma-toes. Divide tomatoes among the dough rounds and brush with oil remaining in the tomato bowl. Bake until browned and puffy, 12 to 18 minutes depending on size.

3. While pizza is baking, heat re-maining oil over moderately low heat in a kettle or skillet large enough to hold all the clams. Add garlic and sauté until fragrant but not browned, about 2 minutes. Add wine, raise heat to high, and bring to a boil. Add clams, cover, and steam until they open, about 3 to 5 minutes. Shake kettle occasionally and check clams, removing any that have opened. Dis-card any that haven't opened after 5 minutes.

4. Remove clams from shells; return clams to kettle. Add parsley and remove from heat. Remove pizza from oven when it is done. Scatter clams over the surface. Serve immediately.

Makes 8 small, 4 medium, or 2 large pizzas.

PIZZA ROSSA
All-red pizza

Sun-dried tomatoes have a sweet in-tensity that's almost candylike. Just a few, cut in strips, will enrich and enliven fresh tomatoes. Add some sweet height-of-summer red peppers and you have a brassy, bright-red topping for a warm-weather pizza.

    3 tablespoons olive oil
    3 tablespoons minced garlic
    2½ cups seeded and chopped
        tomatoes (see page 29)
    ¼ cup chopped fresh basil
    1 recipe Neapolitan Pizza Dough
        (see page 55)
        Cornmeal, for dusting baking
        sheet
        Additional olive oil
    1 recipe Roasted Red Peppers
        (see page 14)
    ¼ cup julienned sun-dried
        tomatoes (from jar)
    2 tablespoons oil from
        sun-dried tomatoes
    ¼ cup coarsely grated Parmesan

1. Heat olive oil over moderately low heat in a large skillet. Add garlic and sauté gently until fragrant but not browned, about 3 minutes. Add fresh tomatoes and basil; stir to mix and remove from heat.

2. Preheat oven to 475° F. Divide pizza dough in 2, 4, or 8 portions, as desired. Roll out dough on a lightly floured surface into rounds ⅓ inch thick. Transfer to a baking sheet dusted with cornmeal. Brush rounds lightly with olive oil. Divide fresh tomato mixture among rounds. Top with Roasted Red Peppers; garnish with sun-dried tomato. Drizzle with tomato oil and dust with Parmesan. Bake until browned and bubbly, 12 to 18 minutes depending on size.

Makes 8 small, 4 medium, or 2 large pizzas.

GRAINS

Because grains are inexpensive, nutri-tious, and easily stored, they've long dominated the cooking of Italian peasants. Today these frugal cooks' creations are favorites among even the well-heeled, although admittedly the dishes have been refined from their humble beginnings. Polenta is now on restaurant menus all over the north, served with game birds or with melted fontina cheese and shaved truffles. Hardly humble!

The famous Arborio rice from the Po Valley can also be served plain or fancy. At its simplest it's cooked with stock to make a modest risotto (see page 61), but when the pocketbook allows, it's dressed up with shrimp, saffron, or wild mushrooms.

Italy's grain-based dishes change with the whim of the cook and the season. The following recipes are only a glimpse of the possibilities.

BASIC POLENTA
Cornmeal mush

Polenta must be watched and stirred continuously as it cooks, but diligence yields delicious results: a thick, creamy, golden pudding that has inspired cooks to countless variations. Common throughout northern Italy, polenta can be eaten hot, or it can be poured into a pan, cooled until firm, and sliced. In that form it can be layered with meat sauces, or mush-rooms and cheese, and baked until bubbly. Serve the following recipe hot from the pan, to partner grilled sau-sages, chicken, or chops.

    4 cups water
    1½ teaspoons coarse salt
    1 cup polenta (see page 9)
    4 tablespoons unsalted butter
    ¼ cup freshly grated Parmesan

In a heavy saucepan bring water and salt to a boil. Gradually add polenta, whisking constantly. Stir in half of the butter. Cook over low heat, stir-ring continuously with a wood spoon, for 20 minutes. Mixture will become quite thick. Stir in remaining butter and Parmesan and serve immediately.

Serves 4.

POLENTA CON GORGONZOLA
Polenta with Gorgonzola

With a simple green salad, this delectable Venetian dish is a meal in itself. Use only best-quality imported Gorgonzola.

   1 recipe Basic Polenta
     (opposite page)
   6 ounces Gorgonzola, crumbled
   ¼ cup whipping cream

1. Preheat oven to 350° F. Prepare polenta. Stir half the Gorgonzola into hot polenta. Pour it into an 11- by 13-inch baking dish. Cool slightly to firm the polenta.

2. Pour cream over the top and dot with the remaining cheese. Bake about 15 minutes, until cream is absorbed and cheese melts.

Serves 4.

POLENTA ALLA GRIGLIA
Grilled polenta

When cooled until firm, then sliced and grilled, polenta makes a great companion to "saucy" dishes. Serve it with braised rabbit or veal stew, with Ragù Bolognese (see page 36), or with fat sausages sautéed with peppers.

   1 recipe Basic Polenta
     (opposite page)

1. Oil an 8- or 9-inch loaf pan or a 1-inch-deep cake pan. Pour hot polenta into prepared pan. Cool, then chill until firm.

2. Prepare a medium-hot charcoal fire. Oil the grilling rack. Slice polenta ½ inch thick. Grill on both sides until hot throughout. The polenta may also be successfully cooked on an indoor griddle. Serve immediately.

Serves 4.

There are probably as many ways to cook polenta as there are cooks. Here, a creamy version both mixed and topped with Gorgonzola contrasts with Polenta alla Griglia, which has been cooled till firm, then grilled.

The classic Risotto alla Milanese is made with saffron and the short, plump Italian Arborio rice. Shown here is a Roman version flavored with lemon juice and rind. It makes a good first course before Gamberi con Peperoni e Prosciutto (see page 69), grilled salmon or tuna, or a brochette of swordfish and artichokes.

RISO CON GAMBERI
Rice with Venetian shrimp

Whether this dish can be called authentic without the splendid Venetian scampi is a question for nitpickers only. Americans can make it with medium shrimp, what the Italians call *gamberi*, and it will still be an exquisite first course.

> 1 tablespoon olive oil
> 2 tablespoons butter
> 2 tablespoons minced shallot
> 1 cup raw Arborio rice
> 2 cups fish stock
> ¼ cup tomato purée
> 16 to 18 medium shrimp (about 1¼ lb), shelled and deveined
> Salt and freshly ground black pepper
> 2 tablespoons minced parsley

1. Heat olive oil and butter in a saucepan over moderately low heat. Add shallot and sauté gently until softened, about 5 minutes. Add rice and cook, stirring, for 1 minute. Add fish stock and tomato purée. Bring to a boil. Cover, reduce heat to low, and cook 8 minutes.

2. Arrange shrimp on top of rice, recover, and cook until shrimp are just done, about 7 minutes more. Add salt and pepper to taste. Pour rice into a warm serving platter and arrange shrimp on top. Dust with parsley and serve immediately in warm bowls.

Serves 4.

RISI E BISI
Italian rice with fresh peas

The first spring peas prompt Venetian cooks to make Risi e Bisi. It is a popular first course, usually thin enough to require a bowl and spoon.

- 1 tablespoon olive oil
- 4 tablespoons unsalted butter
- 3 tablespoons minced shallot
- 1 cup Arborio rice, uncooked
- 3 cups chicken stock
- ¾ pound shelled fresh peas
- 6 tablespoons freshly grated Parmesan
- 3 tablespoons minced fresh basil
- 1 tablespoon minced parsley
  Coarse salt

Heat olive oil and 3 tablespoons of the butter in a saucepan over moderately low heat. Add shallots; sauté gently until softened, about 5 minutes. Add rice; cook, stirring, for 1 minute. Add stock, bring to a boil, cover, and reduce heat to low. Cook 2 minutes. Add peas and remaining butter. Cook until rice and peas are just tender, 8 to 10 minutes more. Stir in Parmesan, basil, and parsley. Salt to taste. Serve immediately.

Serves 4.

RISOTTO AL LIMONE
Lemon risotto

Serve this sprightly Roman risotto before a fish main course.

- 2 tablespoons plus 2 teaspoons unsalted butter
- 2 tablespoons olive oil
- ¼ cup minced onion
  Grated rind of 1 lemon
- 1½ cups Arborio rice, uncooked
- 4½ cups hot chicken stock
- ¼ cup plus 2 teaspoons lemon juice
- ½ cup freshly grated Parmesan

1. In a heavy saucepan over moderately low heat, melt 2 tablespoons of the butter and the olive oil. Add onion and lemon rind; sauté slowly for 5 minutes. Add rice; stir to coat with oil. Turn up heat to high; toast rice, stirring, for 30 seconds. Immediately add ½ cup of the stock; reduce

heat to medium-low and stir until stock is absorbed. Add more, ½ cup at a time, stirring constantly and adding more only when previous portion has been absorbed. When all stock is absorbed (about 20 to 25 minutes), stir in ¼ cup of the lemon juice. The rice should be tender. If not, add warm water bit by bit until rice is tender yet firm.

2. Stir in Parmesan and remaining butter. Cook briefly to blend and melt cheese. Season to taste with salt and pepper. Add remaining lemon juice; serve immediately in warm bowls.

Serves 4.

Risotto alla Milanese Omit lemon rind and lemon juice. Increase chicken stock to 4¾ cups. Add ¼ teaspoon saffron threads or ⅛ teaspoon powdered saffron to hot chicken stock.

RISO DELL' AUTUNNO
Italian rice with autumn vegetables

A trio of late-harvest vegetables—eggplant, celery, and mushrooms—added to a traditional Milanese risotto yields a filling dish for a simple autumn dinner.

- 1 recipe Risotto al Limone (at left)
- ½ cup olive oil
- 2 tablespoons unsalted butter
- ¼ cup minced onion
- 2 tablespoons minced garlic
- 1 large eggplant (about 1 to 1¼ lb), peeled and cut into ½-inch dice
- ½ teaspoon hot red-pepper flakes
- ½ cup minced celery
- 1 cup cooked garbanzo or kidney beans (rinsed and drained, if canned)
- ½ cup quartered mushrooms
- 1 teaspoon minced fresh rosemary (optional)
- ¼ cup minced parsley
  Salt and freshly ground black pepper
- 2 tablespoons freshly grated Parmesan

1. Make Risotto al Limone and set aside. Heat oil and butter in a large

skillet over moderate heat. Add onion and garlic and sauté until fragrant and slightly softened, about 3 minutes. Add eggplant and brown on all sides. Add hot-pepper flakes and celery and cook an additional 3 minutes. Remove from heat.

2. Preheat oven to 375° F. Stir beans, mushrooms, rosemary (if used), and half of the parsley into eggplant mixture. Combine vegetables and risotto. Season to taste with salt and pepper. Transfer to a buttered 2-quart casserole, cover, and bake until heated through, about 20 minutes. Serve from casserole, topped with remaining parsley and Parmesan.

Serves 4.

GNOCCHI ALLA ROMANA
Baked semolina gnocchi

Cooked semolina enriched with butter, cheese, and eggs is the basis for the classic Roman *gnocchi*.

- ½ cup butter
- 2 egg yolks
- 1 tablespoon kosher salt
- 1 cup grated Parmesan
- 4¼ cups milk
- 1 cup plus 1 tablespoon semolina

1. Combine 3 tablespoons of the butter, the egg yolks and salt, and ¾ cup of the Parmesan. Set aside.

2. Put milk in large saucepan and bring to a simmer over medium heat. Pour in semolina in a steady stream, whisking constantly. Cook, stirring occasionally, until thickened and smooth. Remove from heat; immediately stir in cheese mixture. Pour onto an oiled baking sheet, spread ¼ inch thick, and cool ½ hour.

3. Preheat oven to 400° F. Cut cooled mixture into diamonds or rounds. Spread 2 tablespoons of the butter in an ovenproof 8-inch dish. Place gnocchi in dish in a single layer, slightly overlapping. Dot remaining butter over top; sprinkle with remaining Parmesan. Bake 10 minutes. Place under broiler until crust forms (1 to 2 minutes). Serve piping hot.

Makes about 20, serves 4 to 5.

Surrounded by water, Italy boasts a wealth of seafood. From scampi to swordfish to salt cod, fish and shellfish are fundamental to Italian cuisine.

Fish & Shellfish

Increasingly, Americans are cooking and eating fish and shellfish; Italians always have. In this chapter you'll find recipes for preparing seafood in a wide variety of ways, from grilling (see Gamberi del Veneto, page 70) and frying (see Frutte di Mare Fritti, page 66) to braising (see Calamari Verdi, page 65) and roasting (see Cozze al Forno, page 66). Step-by-step photographs show how to clean squid (see page 66) and open clams, oysters, and mussels (page 67). A highlight of the chapter is a menu for a Lakeside Picnic (see page 70).

Offer bibs and finger bowls when you serve Brodetto alla Napoletana, the spicy southern Italian version of shellfish stew.

FISH AND SHELLFISH

As you might expect in a country bordered by water on three sides, fish and shellfish figure prominently in the Italian diet. From tiny anchovies to giant Sicilian swordfish, there are few sea creatures that Italians don't eat. Neapolitan clams, Sardinian tuna, Genoese eels, and Venetian scampi have reputations that extend far beyond their regions.

The Adriatic yields red mullet and sole, sardines and squid, spiny lobster and shrimp of all sizes. From the lakes of Lombardy and the mountain streams of Piedmont come trout, carp, and fresh-water eels. Some observers find it ironic that a country so rich in fresh fish should have developed an abiding passion for salt cod. But once you taste Baccalà Fritto alla Siciliana (see page 44) or Baccalà del Venerdì (see page 69), you'll understand what good cooking can do to a "poor man's fish."

The good cooking extends to recipes such as Brodetto alla Napoletana (opposite page), Calamari Fritti (see page 66), and Gamberi del Veneto (see page 70), to name only a few of the seafood dishes that form an integral part of Italian fare.

OSTRICHE TREVISIANE
Grilled oysters Treviso style

A warm, grilled-oyster salad makes an unusual first course, served with sparkling wine or an Italian Verdicchio. The smoky juices from the oysters are whisked into the vinaigrette just before it's drizzled over the salad. For best results, choose sturdy, colorful lettuces with a slightly bitter edge, like curly endive and red radicchio.

> 2 tablespoons lemon juice
> ½ cup olive oil
> 1 teaspoon grated lemon rind
> 2 tablespoons minced parsley
> 2 tablespoons minced green onion
> ½ teaspoon salt
> ½ teaspoon freshly ground black pepper
> 1 small head curly endive
> 1 small head radicchio
> 30 fresh oysters
> Freshly ground black pepper

1. Prepare a medium-hot charcoal fire in grill.

2. To make dressing: Combine lemon juice, olive oil, lemon rind, parsley, green onion, salt, and pepper. Whisk well and set aside.

3. Separate lettuces into individual leaves; wash well and dry thoroughly. Tear large leaves into small pieces. Arrange on a serving platter.

4. When charcoal fire is ready, position rack above the coals and set oysters directly on the rack. After about 2½ minutes, they will begin to open. They should be fully open and hot after about 3½ minutes. Be careful not to overcook. Discard any that don't open.

5. Remove oysters as they open. Pour oyster liquor into a small bowl. Remove oysters from shells and arrange them atop the lettuce. Add reserved oyster liquor to dressing and whisk well. Taste and adjust salt if necessary; pour dressing over oysters. Grind some black pepper over the top and serve immediately.

Serves 6 as an appetizer.

BRODETTO ALLA NAPOLETANA
Neapolitan shellfish stew

Shellfish soup as made in Naples is usually loaded with mussels and clams, invariably spiked with hot peppers, and often served atop toasted bread. It's a gutsy soup to eat with gusto, accompanied by a rough white wine. You can add saffron, prawns, and crab to dress it up a bit for company, but it's still a dish for guests who don't mind getting their fingers messy. Bibs and finger bowls are a good idea.

12 small, fresh clams
1 quart water
2 tablespoons cornmeal
12 fresh mussels
1 cup dry white wine
1 onion, coarsely chopped
3 cloves garlic, peeled and smashed (not minced)
½ teaspoon hot red-pepper flakes
1 tablespoon butter
3 tablespoons olive oil
½ cup minced carrot
½ cup minced celery
½ cup minced red or yellow bell pepper
½ pound white potatoes, peeled and cut into ½-inch cubes
2 cups peeled, seeded, and chopped tomatoes (see page 29)
¾ teaspoon saffron threads dissolved in 2 tablespoons hot fish stock
3½ cups fish stock, preferably homemade, or bottled clam juice
8 jumbo shrimp or prawns in shells
½ pound shelled crabmeat or 1 cooked Dungeness crab, broken into manageable sections and cracked
Coarse salt
½ cup minced green onion
3 tablespoons minced parsley
Bruschetta (see page 13)

1. Scrub clams and put them in a bowl with water and cornmeal. Soak 2 hours to rid clams of any grit. Drain and set aside. Scrub mussels and remove beards (see page 67). Set aside.

2. Combine wine, onion, garlic, and red-pepper flakes in a large, lidded pot and bring to a boil over high heat. Add clams and mussels and cover. Reduce heat to medium and steam covered, 3 to 7 minutes. After 3 minutes, begin checking clams and mussels, removing any that have opened. Discard any that haven't opened after 7 minutes.

3. Heat butter and oil in a large pot over moderate heat. Add carrot, celery, bell pepper, and potatoes. Sauté vegetables gently for 7 minutes. Add tomatoes and cook another 5 minutes. Remove clams and mussels from broth and set aside. Strain the broth through a double thickness of cheesecloth and reserve. Add saffron, stock, and reserved steaming liquid and simmer 10 minutes. The vegetables should be thoroughly tender. Add prawns, cover, and simmer until prawns turn bright pink. Add crab and heat about 30 seconds. Add clams and mussels and heat through gently. Taste and add salt if necessary. Stir in green onions and remove from heat.

4. Ladle soup into warmed tureen or into warmed soup bowls. Garnish with parsley and serve with a basket of Bruschetta. Pass the pepper mill at the table.

Serves 4 to 5.

CALAMARI VERDI
Braised spinach-stuffed squid

Whole squid lend themselves perfectly to savory stuffings of all kinds. Here, in a Florentine dish, they're plumped with spinach, basil, and rice, then braised with garlic, more spinach, and wine. The result is tender squid in a delicious green sauce, to serve as is or on a bed of lemony rice.

4 pounds fresh squid
½ cup cooked rice, preferably short-grain Arborio
8 cups chopped fresh spinach leaves
¼ cup chopped fresh basil
½ cup minced onion
½ tablespoon minced garlic
¼ cup olive oil
½ cup white wine
2 teaspoons white wine vinegar
2 teaspoons tomato paste
1 teaspoon coarse salt
Lemon wedges, for garnish
3 tablespoons minced parsley, for garnish

1. Clean squid, removing tentacles (see page 66). Chop tentacles coarsely; leave bodies whole. In a bowl, combine chopped tentacles, rice, 4 cups of the spinach, 1 tablespoon of the basil, 1 tablespoon of the onion, and a pinch of the garlic. Moisten with a little of the olive oil and 1 tablespoon of the wine.

2. In a large saucepan or stockpot, heat 1 tablespoon olive oil over high heat; add rice-spinach mixture. Sauté, stirring constantly, until spinach just wilts. Remove from heat and let cool. Stuff squid bodies loosely with cooled mixture, saving any extra stuffing for the sauce.

3. In a Dutch oven, heat remaining olive oil over moderate heat. Add remaining onion and garlic; sauté until softened. Add stuffed squid bodies; sauté about 12 minutes. They should color slightly. Add remaining wine and the vinegar; cook gently until wine evaporates. Add tomato paste and remaining spinach, remaining basil, the salt, and any leftover stuffing. Cover; cook slowly for 15 to 20 minutes. Squid should be quite tender; most of liquid in pan will have evaporated. Transfer to a serving platter and surround with lemon wedges. Garnish with parsley.

Serves 4.

CLEANING SQUID

1. *Rinse squid in cold water. Cut off tentacles just above eye. Squeeze thick center part of tentacles, pushing out the hard beak. Discard beak.*

2. *Squeeze the entrails from the body by running fingers from the closed to the cut end. Pull out the transparent quill that protrudes from body.*

3. *Slip a finger under the skin; peel it off. Pull off edible fins and skin them.*

COZZE AL FORNO
Roasted mussels

Roasting mussels in the dry heat of an oven *(il forno)* seems to intensify their flavor. Simple Italian pizza restaurants often offer mussels this way, baking them in the searing-hot, wood-fired oven and serving them in the baking dish so that diners can mop up the fragrant juices with bread. To approximate this Genoese dish at home, preheat your oven to its highest setting 30 minutes ahead.

> 2 tablespoons minced fresh basil
> ½ tablespoon minced fresh oregano
> 2 teaspoons minced garlic
> 1 teaspoon coarse salt
> ¾ cup olive oil
> 3 dozen fresh mussels
> Freshly ground black pepper
> Lemon wedges

1. Combine basil, oregano, garlic, salt, and oil in a pitcher. Stir to blend and set aside for up to 6 hours.

2. Preheat oven to 500° F. Scrub mussels and remove their beards (see opposite page). Put mussels on a baking sheet in one layer. Bake 4 to 8 minutes. After about 3 minutes, begin checking mussels, removing any open ones to a warmed serving dish. Drizzle the herb-flavored oil over the mussels as you add them to the serving dish. Discard any mussels that have not opened after 8 minutes. When all of the mussels are in the serving dish, grind some black pepper over the top and serve immediately with lemon wedges and any remaining oil.

Serves 4.

CALAMARI FRITTI
Fried squid

For perfect fried squid, choose the smallest you can find, flour them lightly, and monitor the temperature of your oil closely. Fry in small batches to keep the oil at an even 375° F. Fried squid are enjoyed throughout Italy, served hot in a napkin-lined basket with cocktails or a crisp white wine.

> 2 pounds small, fresh squid
> 1½ cups flour
> 1½ teaspoons coarse salt
> 1 teaspoon freshly ground black pepper
> Oil, for deep-frying (1 part olive oil, 3 parts corn oil)
> Lemon wedges

1. Clean squid (at left), remove tentacles, and cut bodies into ¼-inch rings. Combine flour, salt, and pepper in a bag. Dredge squid rings and tentacles in flour, shaking off excess. Transfer floured squid to a plate.

2. Heat about 3 inches of oil in a wok or deep-fryer to 375° F. Use a thermometer to check the oil temperature and to maintain it during frying. Fry squid in batches until golden and crisp, about 1 minute. Transfer with a slotted spoon to a warm baking sheet lined with paper towels. Keep warm in a low oven while you fry the remaining batches. Pile fried squid on a serving platter and surround with lemon wedges.

Serves 4 as an appetizer.

FRUTTE DI MARE FRITTI
Mixed fried shellfish

When freshly shucked, lightly breaded, and quickly fried, these fruits of the sea retain their clean ocean flavors. For easy shucking, invest in a specially designed oyster or clam knife (see opposite page for instructions on opening clams and oysters and cleaning mussels). A cooperative fishmonger will shuck them for you, but you should use them shortly thereafter. Pan-fry them as they do in the southern Italian seaport of Bari and serve with warm anchovy sauce or lemon wedges.

3 slices (approximately 3 oz)
  firm-textured, homemade-type
  white bread, 2 to 3 days old
1 teaspoon coarse salt
¼ teaspoon hot-pepper flakes
½ teaspoon freshly ground
  black pepper
3 eggs
1½ cups flour, for dredging
16 oysters, freshly shucked
  and liquor reserved
16 clams, freshly shucked
16 mussels, freshly shucked
  Bagna Cauda (sauce only;
  see page 19), or lemon wedges
  Olive oil, for frying

1. Grind bread in a food processor or blender to make fine crumbs. You should have about 2½ cups. Stir in salt, pepper flakes, and black pepper. Put in a bowl and set aside.

2. Beat eggs lightly to blend. Put flour in a small bowl. Dredge shellfish lightly in flour, shaking off excess. Dip in eggs, letting excess egg drip off. Dip in bread crumbs and transfer to a plate.

3. If you are using Bagna Cauda, heat it in a small saucepan, add reserved oyster liquor, and keep warm. Have a tray lined with a double thickness of paper towels beside the stove. Set a large skillet over high heat; when it is hot, add just enough olive oil to coat the pan. When oil is almost smoking, add shellfish a few at a time and fry quickly on both sides until golden, adding additional olive oil as necessary. Transfer to paper towels as they are done. To serve, either put a little warm sauce on each of four warm plates and top with shellfish, or garnish shellfish with lemon wedges.

Serves 4.

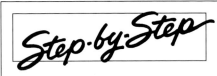

OPENING BIVALVES

Refrigerate oysters, clams, and mussels, for a few hours or freeze for 30 minutes to relax muscles; they will be easier to open. Then scrub shells thoroughly with a stiff brush under cold water. Soft-shell clams are fragile; take care not to break them.

Oysters

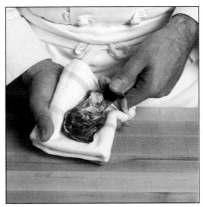

1. *Wearing work gloves or using a heavy cloth, anchor the oyster in the palm of one hand, with the deep cup of the oyster down. Insert tip of oyster knife into hinge and lift up to open shell.*

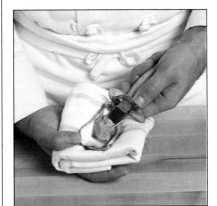

2. *Slide knife along inside of upper shell to sever the muscle that attaches the shell to the flesh. Discard upper shell. Keep oyster level to avoid spilling juices. Slide knife under flesh, being careful not to pierce it, and sever bottom muscle. Remove any bits of broken shell.*

Clams

1. *Slide the blade of a clam knife into the seam between the two shells. Work knife between shells toward the hinge until you can pry the shells apart. Keep clam level to avoid spilling juices, or work over a bowl.*

2. *Slide blade along inside of one shell to sever muscles and under clam to dislodge it from shell.*

Mussels

"Debeard" mussel by removing the byssus, the threads of tissue that protrude from the shell. Mussels die soon after debearding, so cook them promptly. Open a mussel as you would a clam.

Swordfish, tomato, and fennel make a tantalizing trio, as in the Sicilian Pesce Spada al Forno con Finocchi. Serve the dish with a crisp white wine.

TONNO DELL' ESTATE
Tuna for the summertime

Grilled tuna, barely cooked, makes a refreshing summer salad when it's dressed with lemon and oil and tossed with tomatoes, peppers, and capers in the style of Genoa. Let it marinate at room temperature for an hour to blend the flavors, or make it a day ahead and refrigerate. Serve the tuna as a first course on a bed of soft lettuce; pass warm bread and a cruet of olive oil. For a stand-up cocktail party, nestle small portions of tuna in tender butter lettuce "cups" so guests can eat them taco-style.

> 2 pounds fresh tuna fillet, in one or two pieces
> ¼ cup balsamic vinegar
> 2 pounds tomatoes, peeled, seeded, and chopped (see page 29)
> 1 cup olive oil
> ¼ cup lemon juice
>   Pulp of 2 lemons, seeded and cut into ⅓-inch dice
> ¼ cup capers
> 1 cup minced parsley
> 1 cup pitted and chopped Calamata olives
> 1 cup diced red bell pepper
> ½ cup diced green bell pepper
> ¼ cup minced green onion
> ½ cup thinly sliced red onion
>   Salt and freshly ground black pepper
>   Additional olive oil

1. Prepare a hot charcoal fire. When fire is ready, sear tuna quickly on all sides until outside changes color but inside is still nearly raw. Transfer fish to a baking sheet and pour vinegar over it. When fish is cool, cut it into 1-inch chunks and transfer to a large serving bowl.

2. In a small bowl, combine tomatoes, olive oil, lemon juice, lemon pulp, and capers. Mix well, then add to fish. Add parsley, olives, bell peppers, green onion, and red onion. Stir gently to blend. Let marinate 1 hour at room temperature, or cover and marinate overnight in refrigerator, bringing to room temperature before serving. Season to taste with salt and pepper before serving; add a little more olive oil if salad seems dry.

Serves 4.

GAMBERI CON PEPERONI E PROSCIUTTO
Shrimp with peppers and prosciutto

This Tuscan dish can be made in minutes and served as an appetizer or a main course. The shrimp are steamed with prosciutto and peppers, then glazed with an Italian sweet-and-sour sauce—rich, mellow Marsala balanced by lemon and balsamic vinegar.

- ¼ cup olive oil
- 1 cup diced onion
- 1 tablespoon minced garlic
- ½ cup diced red bell pepper
- ½ cup diced green bell pepper
- ½ cup diced yellow bell pepper
  Pinch hot red-pepper flakes
- 4 ounces prosciutto, thinly sliced
- ¼ cup Marsala
- 16 jumbo shrimp or 24 large shrimp or 32 medium shrimp, shelled
- 1 tablespoon balsamic vinegar
  Salt
- 1 tablespoon minced parsley
- 1 tablespoon minced fresh basil
- 1 teaspoon grated lemon rind

1. Heat olive oil in a large sauté pan over moderate heat. Add onion, garlic, all bell peppers, and pepper flakes. Sauté 3 minutes. Add prosciutto and cook 1 minute longer. Add Marsala and cook 20 seconds.

2. Add shrimp and vinegar, cover, and cook until shrimp turn pink, 4 to 7 minutes, depending on size of shrimp. Be careful not to overcook. Remove shrimp from pan and arrange on a warmed serving platter. Taste the juices in the pan and add salt, if necessary. Spoon peppers and pan juices over shrimp. Combine parsley, basil, and lemon; sprinkle over shrimp. Serve immediately.

Serves 4.

PESCE SPADA AL FORNO CON FINOCCHI
Roasted swordfish with fennel

Sicilian cooks know dozens of ways to prepare their prized swordfish. Here, in a classic dish, it is baked with tomato sauce, fennel, and herbs, bold flavors that might overpower a more delicate fish. Precede it with Spaghetti con Aglio e Olio (see page 37), and follow it with ripe summer peaches in wine (see page 114).

- 3 tablespoons olive oil
- 1 onion, diced
- 1 tablespoon minced garlic
- ¼ cup dry white wine
- ½ cup chopped fresh basil
- ½ cup chopped fresh parsley
- 8 small (2-inch dia) whole bulbs fennel or 4 larger ones cut in half lengthwise (see page 80)
- 2 cups homemade Sugo di Pomodoro (see page 36)
- 2 pounds swordfish steaks
- ¼ cup lemon juice
  Salt and freshly ground black pepper

1. Preheat oven to 400° F. Heat oil in a large sauté pan over moderate heat. Add onion and garlic and sauté until slightly wilted, about 5 minutes. Add wine, basil, parsley, and fennel. Bring to a boil, reduce heat, and simmer, covered, until the fennel begins to soften, about 10 minutes. Transfer mixture to an ovenproof casserole large enough to hold the fish steaks in one layer.

2. Add tomato sauce to casserole and stir to blend. Arrange fish steaks atop the sauce and pour the lemon juice over. Bake until fish just flakes and fennel is tender, about 20 minutes. Remove fish and fennel to a warmed serving platter. Taste sauce and adjust seasoning with salt and pepper. Spoon sauce over fish and serve immediately.

Serves 4.

BACCALÀ DEL VENERDI
Friday's salt cod

A day-long soaking rids the cod of much of its salt and yields a firm-fleshed, deliciously flavored fish. Fry it quickly, then bake it slowly with tomatoes, capers, hot peppers, and lemon for a one-dish winter meal, Neapolitan style.

- 1 pound boneless salt cod
- 1 cup milk
- ⅓ cup olive oil
- 1 cup chopped onion
- 1 tablespoon minced garlic
- ½ cup flour, for dredging
- 4 cups peeled, seeded, and diced tomatoes (see page 29)
- 2 tablespoons capers
- 2 tablespoons lemon juice
- 2 tablespoons fresh oregano leaves
- ½ teaspoon hot red-pepper flakes
- 1½ pounds new red or white potatoes, in ½-inch dice
- ¼ cup freshly grated Parmesan

1. Soak cod in water to cover for 24 hours, changing water 3 or 4 times. Drain and pour milk over fish. Marinate 45 minutes. Drain and discard milk. Cut fish into four 4-ounce portions. Pat dry.

2. Heat olive oil in a heavy, stove-to-table casserole over moderate heat. Add onion and garlic and sauté 5 minutes. Dredge fish lightly in flour, shaking off excess. Brown fish on both sides in oil, about 2½ minutes on each side, and remove to a warm plate. Add tomatoes, capers, lemon juice, oregano, and pepper flakes to casserole. Simmer 5 minutes. Add fish and potatoes and simmer about 25 minutes, or until fish is very soft and potatoes are tender. Dust with Parmesan and place under a broiler to brown for 1 to 2 minutes. Serve from the dish if possible, or transfer to a warm serving bowl.

Serves 4.

GAMBERI DEL VENETO
Venetian grilled rosemary shrimp

These succulent shrimp absorb the flavors of both pre- and post-grilling marinades, emerging full of the essence of lemon, garlic, and rosemary. Serve them warm or cool, atop lettuce as a salad, or in bowls as a first course with chunks of bread to soak up the sauce.

24 large fresh shrimp, in the shell
 1 cup black Calamata olives

Wine Marinade

1 cup olive oil
2 large sprigs fresh rosemary
½ cup lemon juice
2 tablespoons minced lemon rind
3 tablespoons minced garlic
¼ cup dry white wine
1 teaspoon coarse salt
1 teaspoon freshly ground black pepper

Parsley Marinade

¼ cup olive oil
2 tablespoons lemon juice
½ teaspoon coarse salt
½ teaspoon freshly ground black pepper
1 large sprig fresh rosemary
½ cup minced parsley

1. Place shrimp in a stainless steel, glass, or earthenware bowl and add Wine Marinade ingredients. Stir to blend, then cover and refrigerate 4 hours.

2. Prepare a medium-hot charcoal fire. Thread shrimp on metal skewers or on wooden skewers (soaked 1 hour in water to keep them from burning). Reserve the marinade. Grill shrimp until bright pink and barely cooked throughout. Return shrimp to bowl and add reserved Wine Marinade and all the ingredients of the Parsley Marinade. Add olives and stir well. Serve barely warm, or chill and serve the next day.

Serves 4 as a first course.

A LAKESIDE PICNIC

Scapece
(see page 14)

Gamberi del Veneto
(at left)

Legumi al Sotto
(see page 16)

Pollo alla Griglia con Aceto

Pizzette

Insalata di Patate e Cozze

Frutta e Formaggio con Dolci di Polenta

An assortment of marinated dishes makes refreshing picnic fare, especially in Indian summer weather. And all but the Little Pizzas (pizzette) can be made the night before. Bake the pizzette an hour or so before leaving; they don't need to be hot from the oven. Wrapped in plastic, they become soft and chewy and imbued with the flavor of their garnish. A chilled Verdicchio or other crisp white wine would stand up to the various marinades, but you might also want to provide some good cold beer.

POLLO ALLA GRIGLIA CON ACETO
Vinegar-marinated grilled chicken

In contrast to the usual method, this Tuscan preparation calls for the chickens to be grilled first and then marinated. As the chicken cools, it readily absorbs the tangy flavors of the marinade. Juices from the chicken and marinade will run onto a bed of lettuce, making the leaves a delectable finale.

4 chicken breast halves
   Salt and freshly ground black pepper
1 head soft-leaf lettuce (butter lettuce or red leaf, for example), washed, dried, and separated into whole leaves

Vinegar Marinade

1 tablespoon grated lemon rind
2 tablespoons lemon juice
2 tablespoons dry white wine
3 tablespoons balsamic vinegar
¾ cup olive oil

1. Prepare a medium-hot charcoal fire. Season chicken with salt and pepper, then place over coals, skin side up. Brush lightly with Vinegar Marinade and grill until chicken is just done, 8 to 10 minutes on a side. Do not overcook.

2. Let chicken cool 5 minutes. If desired, remove breast bones, leaving breast halves in one piece. Put chicken in bowl along with Vinegar Marinade and continue cooling in the marinade.

3. Pack lettuce leaves and chicken in separate containers, pouring all the marinade over the chicken. Serve chicken in the center of a mound of lettuce leaves and spoon some marinade on top. Serve unboned chicken with a knife and fork. To eat boned chicken, tear off pieces of the chicken and wrap them taco-style in lettuce leaves.

Serves 4.

Vinegar Marinade In a large bowl, whisk together lemon rind, lemon juice, wine, and vinegar. Whisk in oil until thoroughly combined.

PIZZETTE
Little pizzas

A pizza topped with mozzarella or another good melting cheese should be eaten hot, before the cheese turns gummy. But a pizza that has no cheese makes a perfect snack for a picnic because it's as tasty cool as hot. By the time you've unpacked your picnic, the crust will be infused with the flavors of basil, tomato, and garlic.

> 1 recipe Basic Pizza Dough (see page 53)
> 1 tablespoon unsalted butter
> 6 tablespoons olive oil
> 1 tablespoon minced garlic
> ¾ cup minced onion
> ½ cup chopped mushrooms (optional)
> 2 tablespoons balsamic vinegar
> ¼ cup julienned fresh basil leaves
>   Cornmeal
> 1 cup seeded and diced fresh plum tomatoes (see page 29)
> 4 tablespoons freshly grated Parmesan
> 4 anchovy fillets, cut lengthwise into 4 strips each

1. Make the pizza dough through step 2 according to the directions on page 53. While dough is rising heat butter and 2 tablespoons of the oil in a medium skillet over low heat. Add garlic and onion and sauté until they are fragrant and slightly softened, about 10 minutes. If you are using mushrooms, add them to skillet after 5 minutes.

2. Turn heat to high and, when mixture begins to sizzle, add vinegar. Whisk 10 seconds and remove from heat. Stir in basil.

3. Preheat oven to 450° F. When pizza dough has doubled in volume, divide it into quarters. Roll each quarter into a small circle, about 4 to 5 inches in diameter. Dust a large, heavy baking sheet with cornmeal and transfer rounds to baking sheet. Divide onion mixture among the rounds, spreading it evenly over the surface. Garnish each round with a quarter of the tomatoes and dust each with 1 tablespoon Parmesan. Arrange anchovy strips neatly over each round. Drizzle each with one tablespoon of the remaining olive oil. Bake until bubbly, browned, and fragrant, about 12 to 16 minutes. Cool on racks, then wrap in plastic wrap.

Makes 4 little pizzas.

INSALATA DI PATATE E COZZE
Potato salad with mussels

Saffron-steamed mussels are a delicious addition to potato salad, as the cooks of Brindisi, on the "heel" of Italy, well know. They cook potatoes and mussels separately, then base the vinaigrette on the mussel cooking liquid. Sweet red peppers are a colorful but optional addition.

> 2 pounds new red potatoes
> 3 tablespoons lemon juice
> ½ cup olive oil
> 1 tablespoon coarse salt
> 6 tablespoons unsalted butter
> ½ cup minced red onion
> ½ cup dry white wine
>   Several sprigs fresh parsley
> 1 bay leaf
> 1 sprig fresh thyme
> 1 loosely packed teaspoon saffron threads
> 3 dozen mussels, well scrubbed and with beards removed (see page 67)
>   Salt and freshly ground black pepper
> ⅓ cup toasted pine nuts
> ½ cup minced green onions
> 1 bunch chives, minced
> ½ recipe Peperonata (see page 13), optional

1. Wash potatoes and put them in a large, heavy pot. Add cold salted water to come at least 2 inches above potatoes and bring to a boil over high heat. Simmer uncovered until potatoes are barely tender. Drain well. When potatoes are cool enough to handle, cut into ¾-inch dice and put them in a large bowl.

2. In a small bowl, whisk together lemon juice, olive oil, and salt until salt dissolves. Add half the mixture to the potatoes while they're still warm and toss gently to distribute dressing.

3. Melt butter in a large pot over moderate heat. Add red onion and sauté until softened, about 3 to 5 minutes. Add wine, parsley, bay leaf, thyme, and saffron. Raise heat to high and bring to a boil. Add mussels, cover, and steam until shells open, about 3 minutes, shaking pan often. Check occasionally and remove any mussels that have opened. Discard any mussels that are unopened after 3 minutes. Reserve the liquid.

4. Remove mussels from shells and discard shells. Put mussels in a small bowl and moisten with 3 tablespoons of the lemon-oil mixture. Remove parsley, bay leaf, and thyme sprig from mussel steaming liquid. Put liquid in a clean saucepan (pouring carefully to leave behind any grit) and bring to a boil over high heat. Reduce to 2 tablespoons, then remove from heat. Cool slightly, then whisk in remaining lemon-oil mixture. Season to taste with salt and pepper.

5. To the potatoes, add mussels, pine nuts, green onions, half the chives, and all remaining dressing. If using Peperonata, mix in ⅓ cup. Toss gently to blend. Taste and adjust seasoning. At the picnic site, arrange the salad in a serving bowl and garnish with the remaining chives and strips of Peperonata, if desired.

Serves 4 to 6.

FRUTTA E FORMAGGIO CON DOLCI DI POLENTA
Almond-scented fruit and ricotta with cornmeal biscuits

Juicy berries, creamy ricotta, and crisp cornmeal biscuits contrast memorably in this Piedmontese dessert. Note that the fruit must marinate at least 4 hours, and biscuit dough must chill at least 1 hour.

- 2 large oranges
- 3 tablespoons almond liqueur
- 5 large leaves fresh mint
- 1 pint raspberries
- ¼ cup blanched whole almonds
- 8 ounces whole-milk ricotta
- 1 tablespoon honey
- 1½ tablespoons sugar
- ¼ teaspoon almond extract
  Grated rind of 1 lemon
- 1 tablespoon lemon juice
- 1 pint strawberries, washed, dried, cored, and halved

Dolci di Polenta

- 1 cup cornmeal
- 1¾ cups flour
- ½ teaspoon baking powder
  Pinch salt
- 6 tablespoons mascarpone or natural cream cheese
- 10 tablespoons unsalted butter, softened
- ½ cup sugar
- 1 egg
- ½ teaspoon almond extract
- ½ teaspoon vanilla extract
- ½ cup dried currants soaked in 2 tablespoons Marsala for 1 hour

1. Grate rind of one orange and set aside. Peel both oranges and remove all white skin with a small sharp knife. Section oranges and put them in a ceramic, glass, or stainless steel bowl. Add grated orange rind, liqueur, mint, and half of the raspberries. Cover and marinate, refrigerated, at least 4 hours or overnight.

2. Preheat oven to 300° F. Toast almonds on a baking sheet until lightly browned and fragrant, about 10 minutes. Cool.

3. Put ricotta, honey, sugar, almond extract, lemon rind, lemon juice, and almonds in a food processor fitted with metal blade. Process until almonds are coarsely chopped. *Or,* chop almonds coarsely by hand, then put them in a bowl with ricotta, honey, sugar, almond extract, lemon rind, and lemon juice and stir well. Transfer mixture to a plastic container and refrigerate until departure.

4. Just before leaving for the picnic, stir strawberries and remaining raspberries into orange mixture. Transfer to a plastic container.

5. To serve, put a dollop of seasoned ricotta on each of 4 plates. Surround with marinated fruit and pass the Cornmeal Biscuits.

Serves 4.

Dolci di Polenta

1. Sift together cornmeal, flour, baking powder, and salt. Set aside.

2. *To prepare in food processor:* Put cheese and butter in processor workbowl. Process until well blended, about 5 to 8 seconds. Add sugar and process 3 seconds. Add egg, almond extract, and vanilla. Process 3 seconds. Add currants and process 3 seconds. Add flour mixture and process with on-off pulses until just mixed. *To prepare in electric mixer:* Cream the cheese and butter until blended. Add sugar and beat until light. Add egg, almond extract, and vanilla and beat until well blended. Add currants and mix to incorporate. Add flour and mix just to blend.

3. Remove dough from processor or mixer and, handling it as little as possible, form it into 2 cylinders, each 2 inches in diameter. Wrap each cylinder in plastic wrap or foil and freeze 1 hour or chill 4 to 5 hours.

4. Preheat oven to 350° F. Cut cylinders into slices ⅜ inch thick and place on greased baking sheets, leaving ½ inch between them. Bake until lightly colored, about 16 to 18 minutes. Cool on racks and store in airtight containers (biscuits will keep about a week; if they get soft, recrisp in 400° F oven for 5 minutes).

Makes about 4 dozen biscuits.

A Lakeside Picnic features grilled shrimp and chicken, marinated vegetables, mini-pizzas, potato salad, fruit, cheese, and cookies. Recipes start on page 70.

Start with a roast or a bird, combine it with the distinctive seasonings of Italy, and the result is a superb "second course" for the dinner table.

Meat & Poultry

W hat's for dinner? How about steak (see Bistecca alla Fiorentina, page 76), veal scaloppine (see Scaloppini di Vitello, pages 78–79), or a stew of lamb and fennel (see Spezzatino d'Agnello e Finocchi, page 81)? Or perhaps some poultry— elegant little quail in polenta nests (see Quaglie in Nidi di Polenta, page 87) or Pollo alla Diavola (see page 93)? Dishes both hearty and fancy abound in this chapter; there is also a menu for a Dinner to Honor a Fine Old Chianti (see page 90) plus instructions for preparing fennel (see page 80).

Serve Osso Buco with buttered fettuccine and a tiny spoon for scooping the soft marrow out of the veal shank bones. The hollow bone gives the dish its name.

MEAT

Italian cooks are frugal and practical connoisseurs of meat. Whether the subject is beef, veal, pork, or lamb, they know how to use every part, from the head to the tail. They braise veal shanks slowly until tender for Osso Buco (opposite page), slice expensive leg of veal into thin scallops and cook it dozens of ways (see page 78), and bring out the best in the best cuts by cooking them simply.

Simplicity and seasonality are the hallmarks of Italian meat cookery. The same basic lamb stew will incorporate tomatoes in summer, fennel in autumn, and artichokes in spring. And when the budget allows a fine piece of meat—such as a thick steak from Italy's famous Chianina beef or some young and tender lamb chops— the Italian cook's instinct is to season it simply and grill it. Dishes like Bistecca alla Fiorentina (at right) and Cotolette alla Griglia con Aglio Dolce (see page 81) reflect this innate appreciation for the simple and seasonal.

BISTECCA ALLA FIORENTINA
Florentine-style steak

The most popular dish in Florence's casual *trattorie* is a beefsteak from the local Chianina cattle. At places like Sostanza in Florence, patrons gather at long tables to enjoy what many consider the finest grilled steak in the world. A first course of minestrone and a bottle of Chianti are an important part of the ceremony.

> *Freshly ground black pepper*
> 2 *T-bone steaks (1 lb each)*
> *Kosher salt*
> *Extravirgin olive oil*
> *Cipolle al Forno (see page 22), for garnish*
> *Lemon wedges, for garnish*

Prepare a hot charcoal fire. Press ground pepper into both sides of steaks, then cook about 5 to 7 minutes per side for a rare steak, as Bistecca alla Fiorentina is traditionally served. When meat is done, salt lightly and brush with olive oil. Place on a warm serving platter and garnish with onions and lemon wedges.

Serves 4.

BRACIOLE
Rolled beef with prosciutto

Braciole is the Italian word for boneless meat cutlets, which are almost invariably stuffed, rolled, and tied. Here, in a Roman version, the cutlets are wrapped around a filling of prosciutto and celery, then gently braised with tomatoes and aromatic Italian mushrooms. Serve with a robust Italian red wine, such as a Nebbiolo d'Alba.

> 1 pound bottom round of beef
> ⅓ pound prosciutto, sliced paper-thin
> 1 cup coarsely chopped celery leaves
> 3 to 4 tablespoons olive oil
> 1 tablespoon minced garlic
> 1 cup minced onion
> 1½ ounces dried Italian porcini mushrooms, soaked in hot water to cover for 1 hour
> 2 cups peeled, seeded, and diced tomatoes, fresh or canned (see page 29)
> Salt and freshly ground black pepper

1. Have butcher slice meat into eight 2-ounce slices, or freeze it briefly and slice it yourself with a sharp knife. Place slices between two sheets of lightly oiled waxed paper and pound with a mallet or the bottom of a skillet until they are paper-thin.

2. Place beef slices on a flat surface. Divide prosciutto slices evenly among them and sprinkle chopped celery leaves over prosciutto. Roll each beef slice into a neat bundle and tie securely with kitchen string.

3. Heat 3 tablespoons oil in a heavy skillet over medium-high heat until a light haze forms. Brown beef rolls on all sides, in batches if necessary, then set aside. If necessary, add a little more oil to coat the surface of the pan, then add garlic and onion and sauté over moderate heat until softened but not browned.

4. With a slotted spoon, remove mushrooms from soaking liquid and squeeze them dry. Strain the liquid through cheesecloth to remove any grit or sand. Add mushrooms, tomatoes, and reserved soaking liquid to skillet. Season with salt and pepper to taste. Return meat to skillet and bring sauce to a simmer. Cover, reduce heat to maintain a slow simmer, and cook two hours. Check meat after 1 hour, adding a little water if sauce has reduced too much. When meat is quite tender, transfer rolls to a warm serving plate, cut the strings carefully with a small knife, and cover with the sauce.

Serves 4.

OSSO BUCO
Braised veal shanks with marrow

Meaty veal shanks turn fork-tender when braised slowly with wine and vegetables, and they yield a delectable dividend: a nugget of marrow in each "hollow bone" *(osso buco)*. Serve this Milanese classic with Risotto alla Milanese (page 61) or surrounded by lightly buttered fettuccine.

> 3 veal shanks, each sawed into 6 to 8 pieces about 2½ inches long
> Salt and freshly ground black pepper
> 2 cups flour, for dredging
> ½ to ¾ cup safflower oil
> 1¼ cups dry white wine
> 2 cups veal stock or beef stock (if using canned beef stock, dilute with water to taste, to reduce strength and saltiness)
> 4 sprigs fresh thyme
> ½ cup parsley sprigs and stems
> 3 bay leaves
> 1 cup whole fresh basil leaves
> 5 tablespoons butter
> 1½ cups chopped onion
> 1 cup diced celery
> 1 cup diced carrot
> 1 tablespoon minced garlic
> 2 cups peeled, seeded, and chopped tomatoes (see page 29)

Gremolata

> 2 tablespoons finely minced Italian parsley
> 1 tablespoon grated lemon rind
> 1 teaspoon finely minced garlic

1. Salt and pepper the shanks well, then dredge them lightly in flour and shake off excess. In a large Dutch oven over medium-high heat, heat oil. Add shanks and brown them well on all sides, in batches if necessary. Transfer shanks to a plate as they are browned.

2. When all the shanks have been browned, add wine to Dutch oven and bring to a boil. With a wooden spoon, scrape up any browned bits clinging to the bottom of pot. Add stock and simmer 2 minutes.

3. Place thyme, parsley, and bay leaves in a cheesecloth bag. Add to pot along with basil. Return shanks to pot and set aside.

4. In a large skillet over moderate heat, melt butter. Add onion, celery, carrot, and garlic and cook until vegetables are slightly softened, about 5 minutes. Add tomatoes and simmer 5 minutes. Transfer mixture to Dutch oven, cover tightly, and bring to a simmer over moderately high heat. Reduce heat to maintain simmer and cook gently for at least 2 hours. (The dish may also be baked in a 325° F oven for 2½ to 3 hours; bring it to a simmer on top of stove first.) Check occasionally to make sure liquid has not reduced too much; add a little wine, stock, or water if necessary.

5. When meat is fork-tender, transfer the shanks to a warm serving platter. Place the pot briefly over high heat to reduce sauce slightly. Add Gremolata during final 30 seconds, then spoon the sauce over the meat.

Serves 8.

Gremolata Combine parsley, lemon rind, and garlic in a small bowl.

MAIALE CON FAVE, CIPOLLE, E POMODORI
Tenderloin of pork with fava beans, onions, and tomatoes

For this Umbrian dish, season pork medallions in a lemon marinade overnight, then grill them quickly over charcoal for informal summer parties. Accompany with grilled onions and a relish made from vine-ripened tomatoes; if your grill is large enough, include a platter of Polenta alla Griglia (see page 59).

    2½ pounds pork loin
    ½   cup olive oil
    2   tablespoons lemon juice
    1   tablespoon grated lemon rind
    2   tablespoons minced garlic
    ¼   cup fresh basil leaves
    3   cups onion, slices, ¼ inch
        thick (do not separate into
        rings)
    2   cups peeled, seeded,
        and chopped fresh tomatoes
        (see page 29)
    ⅓   cup minced parsley
    2   tablespoons minced shallot
    2   tablespoons minced chives
    2   tablespoons balsamic vinegar
        Salt, to taste

1. Have butcher cut loin into 12 medallions about ½ inch thick (or cut them yourself). Pound them lightly with a mallet or the back of skillet.

2. Whisk together ¼ cup olive oil, the lemon juice, lemon rind, garlic, and basil. Put pork medallions and onion slices in a glass, ceramic, or stainless steel container; pour olive oil mixture over them. Cover and marinate, refrigerated, at least 4 hours or up to 12 hours.

3. Prepare relish by combining tomatoes, the remaining olive oil, the parsley, shallot, chives, and vinegar, and salt to taste. Set aside.

4. Remove meat from refrigerator about 1 hour before grilling. Prepare a medium-hot charcoal fire. Remove onions from marinade, pat dry, and grill briefly, until charred but still crunchy. Set aside and spoon some of the marinade over them. Grill the pork quickly on both sides, until just cooked through. Serve the pork hot off the grill, with a spoonful of tomato relish on top and grilled onions alongside.

Serves 6.

Make-Ahead Tip The tomato relish may be made a day ahead, covered, and refrigerated, but wait to add salt until just before serving. Bring relish to room temperature before serving.

SCALOPPINE DI VITELLO
Veal scaloppine

Use milk-fed veal from the leg for these quick sautés. When pounded to an even ⅛-inch thickness, the little scallops (scaloppine) cook through quickly and remain tender. You probably won't want to attempt scaloppine for large parties; even dinner for four requires two skillets and two burners. However, the technique is easy and quick, and many garnishes can be prepared ahead. Veal scaloppine are extremely versatile and can be prepared with dozens of different sauces and garnishes; three possibilities are given here. The lemon-sauce recipe is from Venice, the *porcini*-and-Marsala from Piedmont, and the basil-butter version from Genoa.

    ¾   pound leg of veal, cut into
        six 2-ounce scallops
        Salt and freshly ground
        black pepper
    ½   cup flour for dredging
    2   tablespoons unsalted butter
    2   tablespoons olive oil

Salt and pepper veal lightly. Dredge veal lightly in flour, shaking off excess. Arrange veal slices on a plate near your stove top. In each of two large skillets, heat 1 tablespoon of the butter and 1 tablespoon of the oil over moderately high heat. When mixture foams add three scallops to each pan. Do not crowd scallops. Brown meat quickly on both sides (about 30 seconds per side), then transfer to warmed plates and serve immediately.

Serves 2 to 3.

Scaloppine al Limone
Sweet-and-sour lemon sauce

    ¼   cup dry white wine
    1   tablespoon water
    1½ tablespoons sugar
    1   teaspoon honey
    1   lemon, seeded and sliced
        paper-thin
    2   tablespoons minced shallots
    3   tablespoons lemon juice plus
        additional to taste
    4   tablespoons unsalted butter,
        softened
    1   tablespoon minced parsley
        Freshly ground black pepper

1. Place wine, water, sugar, and honey in a nonaluminum saucepan and bring to a boil. Add lemon slices and simmer gently for 10 minutes, or until slices are translucent. Remove lemons from syrup and continue cooking until syrup is reduced to about ½ cup. Return lemon slices to syrup and set aside.

2. Sauté veal as directed above, reducing cooking time to 15 to 20 seconds on each side (they will finish cooking in the sauce). Use at least one nonaluminum skillet. Transfer cooked veal to a plate. Consolidate any juices and browned bits in nonaluminum skillet, add shallots, and sauté until almost golden, about 3 minutes. Add lemon juice, then swirl in butter to thicken. Add 2 tablespoons reduced lemon syrup.

Taste and add up to 2 teaspoons more lemon juice, if desired. Return veal to skillet just to heat through, then divide scallops and sauce among warmed dinner plates. Arrange two slices of cooked lemon on each plate and sprinkle veal with parsley and black pepper.

Make-Ahead Tip Sweet-and-sour lemon sauce may be made up to 3 hours ahead and stored, covered, in refrigerator. Warm sauce before placing scallops in it.

Scaloppine con Porcini e Marsala
Porcini and Marsala sauce

> 1 ounce dried Italian
>   porcini mushrooms
> 1 cup warm water
> 4 tablespoons unsalted butter
> 2 tablespoons finely minced
>   garlic
> ¼ cup Marsala
>   Salt and freshly ground
>   black pepper
>   Minced parsley

1. Soak porcini in the warm water for 30 minutes. Drain, reserving liquid. Strain liquid through a double thickness of cheesecloth to remove any sand or dirt. Dry mushrooms, inspecting them closely for dirt or grit, and slice thinly.

2. Sauté veal as directed on opposite page, reducing cooking time to 15 to 20 seconds on each side (they will finish cooking in the sauce). Transfer cooked veal to a plate. To one of the skillets used to sauté veal, add 1 tablespoon butter and the garlic. Sauté until fragrant, then add mushrooms, Marsala, and ½ cup reserved mushroom liquid. Bring to a boil and reduce until about ½ cup remains. Remove pan from heat and swirl in remaining butter, cut into small pieces. Season to taste with salt and pepper. Return veal to pan briefly just to warm through. Divide scallops and sauce among warmed dinner plates. Garnish with minced parsley.

Scaloppine alla Genovese
Basil butter with pine nuts

> 4 tablespoons unsalted butter,
>   softened
> 1 tablespoon olive oil
> ½ cup fresh basil leaves
> 1 teaspoon finely minced garlic
>   Salt and freshly ground
>   black pepper
> 2 tablespoons pine nuts
> 2 tablespoons freshly grated
>   Parmesan

1. Preheat oven to 375° F. In a blender or food processor, combine butter, oil, basil, garlic, and salt and pepper to taste. Blend until smooth; set aside. Toast pine nuts in oven on a rimmed baking sheet, shaking it often, until fragrant and lightly colored, about 7 minutes.

2. Sauté veal as directed above. Transfer veal to warmed dinner plates. Top each portion with a dollop of basil butter, a few toasted pine nuts, and a dusting of Parmesan.

Scaloppine alla Genovese shows fork-tender scaloppine at its simplest and best, with a fragrant basil butter and pine nuts.

PREPARING FENNEL

1. *Cut off and discard fennel tops; remove bruised or discolored outer ribs; trim base.*

2. *Halve bulbs and core them.*

3. *Slice thinly lengthwise.*

SPEZZATINO DI CONIGLIO CON POLENTA
Rabbit stew with baked polenta

Slow braising with wine and herbs brings out the best in storebought rabbit. Here it's simmered until fork-tender, then sauced with capers, anchovies, and cream. Baked Polenta is served alongside to absorb the sauce. Serve this full-flavored Venetian dish in the fall or winter with a similarly full-flavored wine—a Barbaresco or an Italian Merlot.

- 3 *tablespoons butter*
- 3 *tablespoons (approximately) olive oil*
- 2 *large rabbits (about 3 lb each), cut into serving pieces*
- 1½ *cups (approximately) flour, for dredging*
- ¼ *cup brandy*
- 1 *cup diced pancetta*
- 4 *cups sliced onion*
- 2 *tablespoons minced garlic*
- 2 *tablespoons flour*
- 1 *small sprig fresh rosemary or 1 teaspoon dried rosemary*
- *A few fresh sage leaves*
- 1 *teaspoon fresh tarragon leaves or ½ teaspoon dried tarragon*
- 6 *fresh oregano sprigs*
- 2 *cups dry white wine*
- 1 *cup cream*
- 2 *anchovy fillets, mashed to a paste*
- 1 *tablespoon capers*
- *Salt and freshly ground black pepper*
- *Fresh parsley sprigs, for garnish*

Baked Polenta

- 1 *cup water*
- 3 *cups milk*
- 1 *teaspoon salt*
- 12 *tablespoons unsalted butter*
- 1 *cup polenta*
- ¼ *cup flour*
- 1¼ *cups freshly grated Parmesan*
- 2 *egg yolks*

1. Preheat oven to 350° F. Heat butter and oil in an ovenproof skillet over moderately high heat. Dredge rabbit pieces lightly in flour, shaking off excess. Brown well on all sides, in batches if necessary. Add brandy to last batch and carefully flame with a long match. When flames die down, remove rabbit to a plate.

2. Add pancetta, onions, and garlic to fat in skillet. Sauté gently until onions are golden and pancetta is crisp, about 15 minutes. (Add more olive oil if necessary to keep pancetta from sticking.) Add flour and cook, stirring, 5 minutes. Add rosemary, sage, tarragon, oregano, and wine. Stir with a wooden spoon to loosen browned bits from bottom of skillet. Return rabbit pieces to skillet. Bring to a simmer, cover with lid or foil, and transfer to oven. Cook 1¼ to 1½ hours, or until fork-tender.

3. Remove rabbit to a warmed serving platter and cover with foil to keep warm. Pour sauce into a cup and let fat rise to the top. Spoon off fat, then return liquid to a small clean saucepan. Reduce liquid by half over high heat. Whisk in cream, anchovy paste, and capers. Taste and adjust seasoning as necessary.

4. Pour anchovy sauce over rabbit pieces on serving platter, surround with Baked Polenta, and serve immediately.

Serves 8.

Baked Polenta

1. In a heavy, medium saucepan over moderate heat, combine water and milk with salt and 2 tablespoons of the butter. Bring to a boil, then gradually whisk in polenta and flour. Continue whisking until mixture thickens slightly, then switch to a wooden spoon and cook, stirring constantly, until mixture is smooth and thick, about 20 minutes. Stir in 6 tablespoons more butter and cook an additional 5 minutes, stirring often. Remove polenta from heat and stir in half the cheese and the two egg yolks. Pour polenta onto a buttered 9- by 11- by 1½-inch roasting pan. Cool.

2. Twenty-five minutes before the rabbit is done, cut cooled polenta into desired shapes (rounds, hearts, diamonds, squares, for example). Place on a buttered baking sheet. Dot with remaining butter; sprinkle with remaining cheese. Place in oven alongside the rabbit and cook 15 minutes. After removing rabbit from the oven, turn heat up to 450° F and brown the polenta.

Serves 8.

COTOLETTE ALLA GRIGLIA CON AGLIO DOLCE
Grilled lamb chops with sweet garlic

To grill the most aromatic lamb chops ever, toss lemon branches or leaves or fresh rosemary sprigs on top of the hot coals. A lemon marinade adds even more character to this Tuscan lamb; sweet stewed garlic and hot tomato-topped bread are the perfect accompaniments. Serve with a cool Italian Merlot, and end the meal with homemade ice cream.

- 12 small loin lamb chops
- 1 small white onion, minced
- ¼ cup dry white wine
- ¼ cup lemon juice
- 1 tablespoon finely minced lemon rind
- 1 pound whole garlic cloves, unpeeled
- 11 tablespoons olive oil
  One 10-inch round loaf (or equivalent) of day-old, country-style bread, preferably homemade
- 2 cups peeled, seeded, and chopped tomatoes (see page 29)
  Salt and freshly ground black pepper
  Lemon branches or leaves or fresh rosemary sprigs
- 2 tablespoons melted butter mixed with 1 tablespoon olive oil
- ¼ cup minced parsley
  Freshly grated Parmesan

1. Put lamb chops in a glass, ceramic, or stainless steel container. Make a marinade by combining onion, white wine, lemon juice, and lemon rind in a bowl. Pour over chops and marinate 2 hours at room temperature.

2. Put garlic and 3 tablespoons olive oil in a saucepan. Add water just to cover. Bring to a simmer, reduce heat, cover, and simmer until garlic is very soft (45 minutes to 1 hour). Drain and reserve garlic.

3. Cut bread into slices about ½ inch thick. Combine tomatoes, remaining olive oil, and salt and pepper to taste and let steep 30 minutes. Spread a little tomato mixture on each slice of bread, stacking bread slices as you go. Wrap slices, re-formed in loaf shape, in foil and set aside.

4. Prepare a medium-hot charcoal fire. When coals are ready, place lemon branches or leaves or rosemary sprigs on them. When flames die down, grill chops to desired doneness. Brush garlic cloves with butter-oil mixture, wrap in foil, and reheat on top of the grill. If you have room underneath the grate, tuck foil-wrapped bread in with the coals to reheat. Otherwise, preheat oven to 350° F and reheat bread for 15 minutes.

5. To serve, arrange chops in the center of a large platter. Surround with slices of tomato-scented bread sprinkled with parsley. Salt the garlic cloves and scatter them around the platter. Pass Parmesan at the table to sprinkle on the bread.

Serves 6.

SPEZZATINO D'AGNELLO E FINOCCHI
Lamb and fennel stew

Look for fennel in autumn and winter and enjoy its licorice flavor as the Italians do: in soups and salads, with fish and pork, and in lamb stews like this Roman one. Like most stews, it can easily be made ahead and re-heated. If fennel is unobtainable, choose another lamb dish, such as Agnello con Carciofi or Agnello con Acciughe e Caperi (both on page 82).

- ¾ cup olive oil
- 2½ pounds lamb shoulder, in 2-inch cubes
- 1 cup thinly sliced red onion
- 1 tablespoon coarse salt
- 2 teaspoons freshly ground black pepper
- ¾ cup dry white wine
- 6 small fennel bulbs, well trimmed and halved, or 3 large bulbs, quartered (opposite page)
- 2 tablespoons minced garlic
- 2 tablespoons balsamic vinegar

1. Preheat oven to 350° F. Heat ½ cup of the oil in a large skillet and brown lamb on all sides, in batches if necessary. Transfer browned lamb to a large, flameproof casserole.

2. Add onions to skillet and sauté until softened, about 5 minutes. Add to lamb in casserole along with salt and pepper. Add wine to the skillet and bring to a boil. Use a wooden spoon to scrape up any browned bits clinging to the bottom. Add wine to casserole. Bring contents of casserole to a simmer on top of the stove, then cover and place in oven.

3. Heat remaining olive oil in a large skillet until hot but not smoking. Add fennel and brown on all sides. Transfer browned fennel to a plate and add garlic to skillet. Sauté just until fragrant. Pour vinegar into skillet and bring to a boil, stirring with a wooden spoon to scrape up any browned bits. Pour over fennel. If fennel is large, add fennel-garlic mixture to casserole when lamb has cooked 1 hour. If it is young and small, add it when lamb has cooked 1½ hours. Continue braising until lamb is fork-tender, a total of about 2 to 2½ hours.

4. When meat tests done, transfer meat and fennel pieces to a warmed serving platter with a slotted spoon. If braising juices are too thin, reduce them over high heat, then spoon them over the stew.

Serves 6.

AGNELLO CON ACCIUGHE E CAPERI
Leg of lamb with anchovies and capers

Easy to carve, a boned and butterflied leg of lamb cooks quickly on a charcoal grill (it can also be roasted in the oven). This recipe features both a marinade of anchovies, garlic, and wine, which adds a southern Italian flavor, and a tangy anchovy-caper sauce. Leftovers make memorable sandwiches.

    2 tins (2 oz each) anchovy
       fillets
    2 tablespoons minced garlic
    1 leg of lamb, boned and
       butterflied
    ¼ cup olive oil
    ¾ cup red wine
    ¼ cup lemon juice
    3 sprigs fresh rosemary
    1 cup mixed fresh herbs (basil,
       thyme, oregano)
       Salt and freshly ground
       black pepper
    4 ounces unsalted butter
    ½ cup capers
    2 tablespoons lemon juice

1. Purée 2 ounces of the anchovies with garlic in a food processor or mortar. Lay butterflied lamb out flat and spread anchovy paste over the underside. Whisk together olive oil, wine, and lemon juice. Put lamb, paste side up, in a glass, ceramic, or stainless steel container along with rosemary and mixed herbs, and pour the olive oil mixture over. Cover and marinate overnight. Bring the lamb to room temperature before continuing.

2. *To grill:* Prepare a medium-hot charcoal fire. Season lamb with salt and pepper. Place lamb paste side down on grill; grill, covered, until internal temperature reaches 120° F to 125° F for rare, 25 to 30 minutes. If fire is very hot, check lamb after about 15 minutes; it will cook quickly. *To roast in oven:* Preheat oven to 350° F. Season lamb with salt and pepper. Roast lamb paste side down until internal temperature reaches 120° F to 125° F for rare, 25 to 30 minutes. Let rest 10 minutes before slicing.

3. To make caper sauce: Heat butter in a skillet. Add the remaining anchovies and mash with the back of a wooden spoon. Heat through gently, then add capers and lemon juice.

4. To serve, slice lamb thinly against the grain and transfer to warmed platter. Spoon caper sauce over lamb or serve it on the side.

Serves 6.

AGNELLO CON CARCIOFI
Lamb with artichokes

This rustic dish from Empoli is best presented family-style: Arrange the sage-scented chops in the center of a large platter and surround with braised artichokes and prosciutto on toast. Fresh sage and a good, dense bread are essential ingredients.

    1 lemon
    3 small fresh artichokes,
       no larger than 1½ inches
       in diameter
    ¼ pound prosciutto, in one piece
    3 tablespoons olive oil (more
       if necessary)
    2 tablespoons unsalted butter
    6 loin lamb chops, thick-cut
    ⅓ cup fresh whole sage leaves
    ⅓ cup Marsala
    6 thick slices toasted
       country-style bread,
       preferably homemade
    3 tablespoons minced parsley,
       for garnish

1. Squeeze juice from lemon into a small bowl filled with water. Prepare artichokes according to the directions on page 16. Quarter artichokes and remove any fuzzy chokes. Drop artichokes into the bowl of lemon juice and water.

2. Cut prosciutto into small dice. Heat 1 tablespoon olive oil in a skillet over medium-low heat, add prosciutto, and sauté until brown. Drain and dry artichokes; add to skillet and sauté over medium-low heat until tender, 10 to 15 minutes, adding more oil if necessary. Transfer prosciutto and artichokes to a plate; keep warm.

3. Put 1 tablespoon oil and 1 tablespoon butter in each of two skillets. Brown chops quickly on both sides over high heat. Add half the sage leaves and half the Marsala to each skillet and cook until lamb is done to your liking, adjusting heat to keep Marsala from boiling away. Remove chops to a warm serving platter and surround them with toasts. Put all the juices in one skillet along with the artichokes and prosciutto. Reduce slightly over high heat to glaze artichokes, then arrange them over toast and garnish with parsley.

Serves 3 to 4.

SALSICCE CON PEPERONI MISTI E POLENTA
Sausage with mixed peppers and polenta

Plump sausage and golden polenta make a rib-sticking family supper or a colorful dish for casual entertaining. If you have a large platter, serve this Venetian dish family-style: Make a foundation of polenta, then arrange the browned sausages and sautéed peppers on top. To complete the meal, add a Barbera or a simple Chianti and a light fruit dessert.

    4 hot Italian pork sausages
    4 sweet Italian pork sausages
       with fennel
    ½ cup dry white wine
    ½ cup olive oil
    3 tablespoons minced garlic
    1 cup coarsely chopped green
       bell pepper
    1 cup coarsely chopped red
       bell pepper
    1 cup coarsely chopped yellow
       bell pepper (or substitute an
       additional ½ cup each green
       and red pepper)
    ½ cup thinly sliced red onion
    ¼ cup fresh oregano leaves
       Salt, to taste

Creamy Polenta

    4 cups water
    1 tablespoon salt
    3 tablespoons unsalted butter
    1 cup polenta
    ¾ cup whipping cream
    ½ cup freshly grated Parmesan

1. Prick sausages all over with a fork and place in a lidded sauté pan (no fat or liquid is needed). Brown over high heat on all sides. Turn down heat and add wine carefully (it will sputter). Cover pan, and poach sausages gently until done, about 10 minutes.

2. While sausages are cooking, heat olive oil in a separate skillet over moderate heat. Add garlic and sauté until fragrant. Add peppers, onions, and oregano and sauté, stirring often, until slightly softened, about 5 minutes. Add salt to taste.

3. To serve, divide polenta among warm serving plates. Top with sautéed peppers and place one of each kind of sausage alongside.

Serves 4.

Creamy Polenta In a large saucepan with a heavy bottom over high heat, bring water, salt, and 1 tablespoon butter to a boil. Slowly whisk in polenta in a steady stream until mixture is smooth. Cook, stirring often with a wooden spoon, for 10 minutes. Add cream and cook, stirring often, until mixture is thick and creamy and tastes fully cooked, about 10 minutes more. Stir in remaining butter and cheese and keep warm until ready to serve.

Serves 4.

Salsicce con Peperoni Misti e Polenta combines sausage with peppers and polenta in a Venetian dish for hearty appetites. Its vivid colors and rustic flavors would suit an informal dinner for friends. Steamed greens, such as the red chard shown here, would make a good side dish.

Garlic, rosemary, and hot-pepper flakes add zest to a Sicilian-style pork roast. Serve Arrosto di Maiale con Rosmarino with sautéed greens and a light red wine.

SALTIMBOCCA
Veal scallops with prosciutto and sage

This Roman dish is a good example of the Italian penchant for whimsical food names; it is so succulent it almost leaps into your mouth *(salta in bocca)*. The success of the dish depends on tender, milk-fed veal and fresh sage. Serve with a light red wine or a rich Italian Chardonnay.

    1¼   pounds leg of veal, cut into
          12 scallops
          Salt and freshly ground
          black pepper
    12   fresh sage leaves
    12   paper-thin slices prosciutto
    2   tablespoons unsalted butter
    3   tablespoons dry white wine
    1½   tablespoons minced parsley

1. Place each scallop between pieces of oiled waxed paper and, using a mallet or the bottom of a skillet, pound to a uniform ⅛-inch thickness. Salt and pepper scallops lightly. Put a sage leaf on each and cover with a slice of prosciutto. Secure prosciutto to scallop with toothpicks.

2. Melt 1 tablespoon of the butter in each of two large skillets. Add scal-

lops and brown quickly on both sides. When scallops are just barely cooked, transfer them to a warmed serving platter; remove toothpicks. Scrape juices and browned bits from one skillet to the other. Add the wine to the skillet with the juices and reduce slightly over high heat. Pour sauce over scallops; garnish with parsley.

Serves 4.

ARROSTO DI MAIALE CON ROSMARINO
Sicilian-style pork roast with rosemary

This well-seasoned pork roast appears on Sunday lunch tables all over Italy, usually preceded by a soup or pasta and accompanied by sautéed greens. In Florence it's rubbed with rosemary or fennel and called *arista* (the best); Sicilian cooks add garlic and hot-pepper flakes.

    2   tablespoons minced garlic
    1   tablespoon grated lemon rind
    1   teaspoon hot red-pepper flakes
    2   teaspoons salt
    5   pounds boneless pork rib
          roast, untied
    3   tablespoons olive oil
    1   tablespoon freshly ground
          black pepper
    5   sprigs fresh rosemary

1. Preheat oven to 350° F. Put garlic, lemon rind, hot-pepper flakes, and 1 teaspoon salt in food processor or blender. Process to a paste. Set aside 1½ teaspoons paste and rub the remainder into the underside of the meat. Tie the roast neatly with string. Using a small, sharp knife, make four incisions, about ½ inch long and ½ inch deep, in the roast. Stuff the incisions with the remaining paste. Rub roast all over with olive oil, then with black pepper and remaining teaspoon of salt. Tie the rosemary sprigs onto the roast with string.

2. Place roast on a rack in a roasting pan and roast 2 to 2½ hours, or until a meat thermometer registers 145° F. Remove and let rest 10 minutes before slicing.

Serves 8.

ARROSTO DI MAIALE AL LATTE
Pork loin in milk

The idea may sound odd to Americans, but pork pot-roasted in milk is a much-loved Tuscan dish. The milk cooks down into rich, nutty clumps that are what the Italians call *bruti ma buoni* (ugly but good). Serve the roast with wilted chard or spinach and a light Chianti.

> 1 tablespoon unsalted butter
>
> 2 tablespoons olive oil
>
> 1½ pounds boneless pork loin, neatly tied to hold its shape
>
> 2 cups milk
>
> ½ cup half-and-half
> Salt and freshly ground black pepper
>
> 2 sprigs fresh rosemary (optional)
>
> 1 bay leaf
>
> ½ pound pearl onions, peeled and parboiled 5 minutes
>
> 2 tablespoons minced parsley

1. In a Dutch oven just large enough to hold the pork, melt butter and oil over moderately high heat. Add meat and brown well on all sides.

2. In a separate pot, scald milk and half-and-half. Add to browned meat along with salt and pepper to taste, rosemary (if used), and bay leaf. Bring to a simmer, cover, and reduce heat to maintain a steady simmer. Braise 1½ hours, or until meat is tender when pierced with a knife. Add onions about 15 minutes before meat is done. If milk is still runny, remove meat and keep warm; put Dutch oven over high heat and reduce milk till brown clumps form, whisking occasionally.

3. After meat has rested 10 minutes, remove string and slice with a long, sharp knife. Arrange slices on a warmed serving platter and scatter the onions around. Spoon the sauce over the meat and garnish with minced parsley.

Serves 4.

POULTRY

"Poultry" in Italy means quite a bit more than just the ubiquitous chicken. Italians are enthusiastic eaters of duck, squab, quail, and other wild birds large and small. They love them grilled or spit-roasted (especially popular in restaurants), braised in the oven, stewed in sauce, or simply baked with garden herbs. The collection that follows is just a hint of this extensive repertoire. Pollo alla Griglia con Salsa d'Aglio (see page 95) and Gambe d'Anitra alla Griglia (see page 93) are typical of dishes suited to casual, warm-weather dinners; more formal, sit-down meals might feature Pollo Novello alla Cacciatora (see page 89) or Quaglie in Nidi di Polenta (see page 87). For best results, buy freshly killed poultry that has not been frozen.

FETE DI POLLO CON PIGNOLI E LIMONE
Grilled chicken "steaks" with pine nut and lemon sauce

Boned and flattened chicken breasts can be quickly pan-fried and served with any of the sauces or garnishes used for Scallopine di Vitello (see pages 78–79). In this Tuscan dish, a light and lemony sauce enriched with ground pine nuts is made in minutes with a chicken stock reduction. Barely wilted spinach or chard is a good accompaniment.

> 4 whole chicken breasts, split and boned
>
> 3 cups chicken stock
>
> 1 cup dry white wine
>
> ½ cup minced carrot
>
> ½ cup minced onion
>
> 2 tablespoons white wine vinegar
> Pinch hot red-pepper flakes
> Grated rind of 1 lemon
> Salt
>
> 3 tablespoons butter
>
> 3 tablespoons olive oil
>
> ¼ cup toasted and finely ground pine nuts

> 2 tablespoons lemon juice
>
> 2 tablespoons minced Italian parsley
>
> 2 tablespoons toasted pine nuts, for garnish

1. Pound chicken breasts between two pieces of oiled waxed paper to ¼-inch thickness. Put stock, wine, carrot, onion, vinegar, pepper flakes, and lemon rind in a nonaluminum saucepan and bring to a boil. Simmer uncovered until sauce is reduced to about 2 cups (about 1 hour). Strain through a sieve; taste and add salt if necessary.

2. Heat two large skillets over moderately high heat. Divide butter and oil between them; when butter foams, add chicken and sauté quickly, about 45 to 60 seconds per side. Remove chicken to a warm serving platter and keep in a warm oven while you finish the sauce.

3. Bring chicken stock mixture to a boil and whisk in ground pine nuts, lemon juice, and 1 tablespoon parsley. Pour sauce over chicken and garnish with whole pine nuts and remaining parsley.

Serves 8.

Plump sausage-stuffed quail in polenta "nests" are a dish for a fancy dinner party. Accompany Quaglie in Nidi di Polenta with a fine red wine.

ALI DI POLLO CON PANCETTA
Chicken wings with pancetta

Knives and forks can't possibly get to the good parts on chicken wings. Fingers are the best utensils, and big napkins or bibs are a must. If you have a stove-to-table casserole, serve this colorful Modenese dish country-style, with some good, crusty bread to soak up the tomato and saffron sauce.

- ¼ pound pancetta, in one piece
- ¾ cup unbleached flour
- 1 teaspoon freshly ground black pepper
- 2 teaspoons salt
- 2 pounds chicken wings, wing tips removed
- 2 tablespoons butter
- 1½ teaspoons olive oil
- ½ cup minced onion
- 2 tablespoons minced green onion
- 1½ teaspoons minced garlic
- 2 sprigs fresh oregano, leaves only, or 1 teaspoon dried oregano
- ½ cup dry white wine
- ½ teaspoon saffron threads softened in 2 teaspoons warm water; reserve liquid
- 2 cups coarsely chopped mushrooms
- 1 cup peeled, seeded, and chopped fresh tomatoes (see page 29) or ½ cup Sugo di Pomodoro (see page 36)
- ½ cup chicken stock
  Salt and freshly ground black pepper
- 2 tablespoons minced parsley, for garnish

1. Dice pancetta, then render slowly in a large frying pan until crisp. Transfer with a slotted spoon to paper towels to drain, leaving fat in pan.

2. Combine flour, black pepper, and salt in a paper bag. Dredge wings lightly in flour mixture, shaking off excess. Add butter and olive oil to pancetta fat in skillet. Brown wings in fat over moderately high heat. Remove them to a plate when they are brown all over.

3. Add onion, green onion, garlic, and oregano to skillet and cook slowly for 10 minutes. Return wings to skillet; add wine, saffron, and saffron-soaking liquid to skillet. Cook 5 minutes over medium heat. The mixture should reduce slightly.

4. Add mushrooms, tomatoes, and stock to skillet. Cover and simmer 25 minutes or until wings are tender. Add rendered pancetta and cook uncovered for about 5 minutes to reduce the sauce slightly. Season to taste with salt and pepper. Transfer to a warmed serving bowl or platter and garnish with minced parsley.

Serves 3 to 4.

QUAGLIE IN NIDI DI POLENTA
Stuffed quail in polenta cups

Cut into these tender quail to reveal a juicy sausage stuffing, made in minutes using storebought fennel sausage. The dark-breasted birds make a rich autumn entrée that stands up to a Gattinara or a stately Chianti Classico Riserva. Surround the quail with hot polenta (see page 58) if you prefer, but the nestlike cups make a particularly charming presentation. The recipe is from Venice.

- ⅔ pound fresh sweet Italian pork sausages with fennel, casing removed
- ¼ cup freshly grated Romano
- 2 tablespoons lemon juice
- 1 tablespoon minced garlic (optional)
- 8 quail
  Salt and freshly ground black pepper
- 3 tablespoons unsalted butter
- 1 tablespoon olive oil
- 2 tablespoons white wine

Polenta Cups

- 1 recipe Basic Polenta (see page 58)
  Butter, to grease dishes

1. Make stuffing by crumbling sausage and frying it slowly in a skillet until it is no longer pink. Remove with slotted spoon to a bowl and cool slightly. Stir cheese and lemon juice into sausage. If sausage is not already highly seasoned with garlic, add the 1 tablespoon minced garlic. Set stuffing aside.

2. Preheat oven to 450° F. Season quail generously with salt and pepper. Place half the butter and half the oil in a large skillet over medium-high heat; heat until butter melts. Brown birds quickly, in batches if necessary. Transfer to a plate and cool slightly. Stuff birds loosely with stuffing mixture. Reserve any remaining stuffing.

3. Place remaining oil and butter in a small skillet over low heat; heat until butter melts. Remove from heat and add wine. Brush quail all over with this mixture. Transfer quail to a roasting pan and roast breast side up, basting occasionally with wine-butter mixture, for 10 to 12 minutes. Quail should be nicely browned, and legs should move freely. Arrange each quail in a Polenta Cup, on top of any extra stuffing. Serve immediately.

Serves 8 as a first course or 4 as a main course.

Polenta Cups Preheat oven to 400° F. Spoon still-warm polenta into buttered 1½-cup soufflé dishes, custard cups, or 3-inch tartlet pans with removable bottoms. As polenta cools, push it up the sides of the dish to form a cup shape. Cool completely. Bake cups 10 minutes. Cool and remove from dishes.

POLLO CON PORCINI
Porcini roast chicken

Stuff a plump chicken with aromatic *porcini* mushrooms, then use the mushroom stuffing to make a simple, last-minute sauce. Serve this Parma-style chicken with Creamy Polenta (see page 82) and a Nebbiolo d'Alba.

- 1½ ounces dried Italian porcini mushrooms
- 1 tablespoon rendered chicken fat
- 2 tablespoons olive oil
- 3 tablespoons butter
- 1 tablespoon minced garlic
  Chicken liver and heart, minced
- ½ pound mushrooms, minced
- 1 tablespoon Marsala
  Salt and freshly ground black pepper
- 1 roasting chicken (about 4 lb)
- 1 lemon
- 1 cup less 2 tablespoons chicken stock
  Fresh parsley sprigs or watercress, for garnish

1. Soak porcini in warm water to cover for 30 minutes. Lift them out with a slotted spoon and check them carefully for grit. Slice thinly. Strain liquid through a double thickness of cheesecloth and set aside.

2. Heat chicken fat, olive oil, and butter in a large skillet over moderately low heat. Add garlic and sauté slowly for 3 minutes. Add chicken liver and heart and sauté 3 minutes. Add mushrooms and porcini and cook an additional 3 minutes. Add Marsala and cook 2 minutes. Remove from heat and season to taste with salt and pepper.

3. Preheat oven to 325° F. Dry chicken thoroughly inside and out. Stuff cavity with mushroom mixture. Truss the chicken. Squeeze the lemon over the top and lightly salt and pepper the outside. Place on a rack in a roasting pan and roast breast side down for 45 minutes, basting occasionally with drippings. Turn chicken

over and roast until the juices run clear. When chicken is done, place it under broiler for 1 to 2 minutes, or until the skin is crisp and golden. Remove from broiler and let rest 5 minutes.

4. While chicken is resting, bring chicken stock and 2 tablespoons porcini liquid to a boil in a saucepan and reduce to ½ cup. Turn heat to low while chicken is being carved. Add stuffing to the sauce, blend well, and pour over chicken. Garnish platter with parsley or watercress.

Serves 3 to 4.

FAGOTINI DI POLLO CON CIPOLLE BALSAMICHE
Chicken livers with balsamic onions

Grilled sage-scented poultry livers served with sweet-and-sour onions are a delightful variation on the liver-and-onions theme. With chunks of country bread, guests can make their own *crostini*, piling livers and onions on top to make a juicy mouthful. In smaller portions, this dish from Modena makes a fine appetizer.

- 1 tablespoon sweet Italian vermouth
- ¼ cup olive oil
- 1 tablespoon fresh sage leaves or *pinch dried sage*
- 1 teaspoon minced fresh oregano
  Salt and freshly ground black pepper
- 1 pound chicken or duck livers, trimmed of all fat
- 1 recipe Cipolle al Forno (see page 22)
- 2 tablespoons minced fresh chives or parsley, for garnish

1. Put vermouth, olive oil, sage, oregano, and salt and pepper to taste in a stainless steel, glass, or ceramic bowl. Add livers, toss to coat well, and let marinate, refrigerated, 12 hours or overnight.

2. Prepare a medium-hot charcoal fire. Soak 8 wooden or bamboo skewers in water to cover for 30 minutes. Thread livers on skewers. Grill quickly to brown livers well outside but keep them pink within. Transfer skewers to a serving platter and surround with Cipolle al Forno. Garnish with minced chives or parsley.

Serves 4 as a main course or 8 as a first course.

POLLO CON CAVOLO AL LIMONE
Lemon chicken with lemon cabbage

This lemon-scented chicken is first roasted in the oven, then finished by braising on a bed of shredded cabbage. The cabbage absorbs the roasting juices, the chicken becomes tender, and the finished dish far surpasses its modest ingredients. A bottle of Pinot Grigio is an excellent complement. The dish comes from The Marches.

- 1 roasting chicken (about 4 lb)
  Salt and freshly ground black pepper
- 1 lemon
- ½ cup plus 1 tablespoon unsalted butter
- ¼ cup plus 2 tablespoons lemon juice
- ¼ cup olive oil
  Grated rind of 1 lemon
- 2 pounds green cabbage, finely shredded
- ½ cup dry white wine
- 2 tablespoons white wine vinegar
- 1 teaspoon sugar

1. Preheat oven to 425° F. Season chicken inside and out with salt and pepper. Grate rind of lemon; halve lemon. Place rind and lemon in chicken cavity. Melt ¼ cup of the butter; add ¼ cup of the lemon juice and 1 tablespoon of the olive oil. Brush mixture all over chicken. Put chicken on a rack in a roasting pan breast side up; roast 25 minutes.

2. Place remaining butter and remaining oil in a Dutch oven over moderate heat; heat until butter melts. Add lemon rind and sauté

1 minute. Add cabbage and toss to coat with butter and oil. Turn up heat and add remaining lemon juice, the wine, vinegar, and sugar, and salt and pepper to taste. When mixture bubbles and sizzles, turn heat to low, cover and cook 20 minutes.

3. Remove chicken from oven and place on top of cabbage. Cover and continue cooking over moderately low heat until chicken tests done, 25 to 30 minutes. Remove chicken to cutting board. Taste cabbage and add more lemon, salt, or pepper as necessary. Carve chicken and arrange it in the center of a large warmed platter. Surround with cabbage. Pour pan juices over chicken and serve.

Serves 4.

POLLO NOVELLO ALLA CACCIATORA
Cornish hens, hunter's style

Pollo alla cacciatora turns up on Italian restaurant menus all over the United States because it can easily be made ahead and reheated. Unfortunately, it sometimes tastes as if it's been steadily reheating for months. The version below, from Tuscany, is lively and light, for the birds are first roasted and then topped with a sauce made at the last minute from pan juices, mushrooms, and tomatoes. An elegant party dish, it can also be made with split baby chickens.

    6   Rock Cornish game hens,
        split down the back and
        backbone removed
        Salt and freshly ground
        black pepper
    3   tablespoons olive oil
    4   tablespoons butter
    3   cups thinly sliced mushrooms
    2   shallots, minced
    ½   cup dry white wine
    1¼ cups chicken stock
    3   tablespoons brandy
    1   pound tomatoes (canned or
        fresh), peeled, seeded, and
        chopped (see page 29)
        Parsley sprigs, for garnish

1. Preheat oven to 350° F. Season game hens well with salt and pepper. Heat olive oil and 2 tablespoons of

the butter in a large skillet over medium-high heat. Brown hens well, in batches if necessary, transferring them to a roasting pan when they are browned. Cover pan and roast until hens are fork-tender, about 50 minutes. Transfer hens to a plate, cover with foil, and keep warm in a low oven. Pour off and reserve any juices in the roasting pan.

2. In a large skillet over medium heat, melt remaining butter. Add mushrooms and sauté until softened. With a slotted spoon remove mushrooms; set aside. Spoon off any fat accumulated on top of reserved roasting juices, then add juices to skillet. Add shallots and cook 4 minutes. Add wine and cook over moderately high heat until wine evaporates. Add stock and reduce by one half. Add brandy and carefully flame with a long match. When flames die down, add tomatoes and cook until heated through. Return mushrooms to skillet. Season to taste with salt and pepper.

3. Transfer game hens to a warmed serving platter. Spoon sauce over them. Garnish platter with parsley sprigs and serve immediately.

Serves 6.

Tender young Cornish hens prepared alla cacciatora are a pleasing variation on the usual chicken dish. Authentic Italian bread, such as the twisted baguette shown here, is always a good addition to the meal.

A DINNER TO HONOR
A FINE OLD CHIANTI

Pasta con Funghi

Zucchine, Cipolle, e Carciofi Fritti

Anitra al Chianti

*Spinaci con Pignoli
(see page 108)*

Parmigiano Reggiano

*Pesche al Vino
(see page 114)*

Biscotti per il Vino

The traditional scheme of a wine dinner is to progress from white to red, from young to old, from light to heavy. The creamy mushroom sauce on the pasta suggests a fragrant, full-bodied white, such as a Pinot Grigio or a Tocai. The same wine can also accompany the small Fried Course, but switch to a fruity, medium-bodied red for the duck. The same young Chianti that you use in the marinade is a suitable choice. Save the wine of honor for the cheese course: a moist Parmigiano Reggiano, sliced thin.

PASTA CON FUNGHI
Linguine with field and wild mushrooms

Unless you collect them yourself, wild mushrooms can be expensive, but their flavor far surpasses that of the common cultivated variety. Mix wild and cultivated types to hold down the cost of this Piedmontese dish, and be sure you buy the wild mushrooms from a knowledgeable source that can positively identify them as edible. Clean mushrooms carefully with a soft toothbrush or a mushroom brush. The wild varieties in particular are usually too delicate to wash.

- 4 quarts lightly salted water
- 4 tablespoons unsalted butter
- 1 tablespoon olive oil
- 1 shallot, minced
- 2½ tablespoons minced garlic
- ½ pound medium cultivated field mushrooms, cleaned and quartered
- ½ pound fresh porcini or other wild mushrooms, cleaned and halved
- 3 tablespoons Chianti or other dry red wine
- 3 tablespoons whipping cream
  Salt
  Freshly ground black pepper
- ⅓ cup minced fresh chives
- 1 pound fresh linguine (use Pasta Gialla, page 34)

1. In a large pot over high heat, bring the water to a boil. While water is heating melt butter and oil in a large skillet over moderately low heat. Add shallots and garlic; cook gently 3 minutes. Add mushrooms, raise heat to high, and cook briskly 3 minutes. Add wine and let evaporate over high heat. Add cream and reduce slightly. Remove from heat; add salt and black pepper to taste. Gently stir in half of the minced chives.

2. Add pasta to rapidly boiling water and cook until just done. Drain well in a colander and transfer to a warm serving bowl. Add sauce and toss well. Garnish with remaining minced chives and serve hot.

Serves 4.

In front are pasta and the Fried Course. Braised duck, spinach, and the cheese flank the honored Chianti. Dessert is marinated peaches with wine rusks.

ZUCCHINE, CIPOLLE, E CARCIOFI FRITTI
The Fried Course: zucchini, onions, and artichokes

Florentine cooks are expert at deep-frying; in fact, the traditional Florentine meal includes a separate fried course. The batter and vegetables are prepared ahead, leaving only the whipping of egg whites and the frying for the last minute. Use a thermometer to keep oil temperature constant.

- 2 cups cake flour
- 1 teaspoon coarse salt
- ¼ cup olive oil
- 3 eggs, separated
- 1⅓ cups cold water
- 3 tablespoons dry red wine
- 1 teaspoon freshly ground black pepper
- 2 medium zucchini
- 4 small onions, about 2 inches in diameter
- 4 small artichokes, no larger than 1½ inches in diameter
- Corn or peanut oil, for deep-frying
- Gremolata (see page 77)

1. In a large bowl stir flour and salt together. In a small bowl whisk together olive oil and egg yolks. Slowly add oil-egg mixture to flour. Whisk in water, wine, and pepper. Set aside at room temperature for 2 hours.

2. Trim ends of zucchini. Cut zucchini in half lengthwise, then cut each half crosswise into thirds. Peel onions and halve them. When you are ready to cook, prepare artichoke hearts according to the directions on page 16. Halve them (top to bottom) and remove any fuzzy inner choke.

3. Heat at least 4 inches of oil in a large kettle or deep fryer to 375° F. While oil is heating, whip egg whites with a pinch of salt until stiff but not dry. Fold into batter. Dip vegetables, a few at a time, in batter; fry until golden brown. As they brown, remove with a slotted spoon to paper towels to drain, then keep warm in low oven. When all are fried, arrange on a warm serving platter or on individual plates; garnish with Gremolata.

Serves 4.

ANITRA AL CHIANTI
Duck braised in young Chianti

The fruitiness of a young Chianti flatters the sweet flavor of duck. For this Tuscan dish, marinate the duck overnight in Chianti, then braise it slowly in the same wine with herbs and aromatic vegetables. The finished bird will be fork-tender, the resultant sauce rich and mellow.

- 2 ducks (about 4 lb each), preferably fresh
- 2 carrots, coarsely chopped
- 2 large onions, peeled and cut into eighths
- 1 celery stalk, coarsely chopped
- 1 bay leaf
- 1 sprig fresh thyme or 1 teaspoon ground thyme
- 6 garlic cloves, unpeeled
- 1 bottle (750 ml) young Chianti
- ¼ cup flour
- 2 to 2½ cups duck or chicken stock

1. Wash ducks inside and out and dry thoroughly with paper towels. Remove any visible fat (reserve for another use). Cut ducks into quarters. Put duck into a ceramic, stainless steel, or glass bowl and add carrots, onion, celery, bay leaf, and thyme. Smash garlic lightly with the side of a knife and add to bowl along with wine. Cover bowl with plastic wrap and let marinate at room temperature for about 12 hours (refrigerate in very hot weather). Remove duck pieces from marinade and pat dry. Strain marinade and reserve both strained wine and vegetables.

2. Heat a large, heavy skillet over moderately high heat. Add duck pieces and brown well on all sides. The duck will render considerable fat. Pour fat off as it accumulates; save it for browning potatoes or cooking omelets. When duck is well browned, transfer it to a plate and pour off all but 2 tablespoons fat.

3. Preheat oven to 350° F. Add marinade vegetables to fat in skillet and sauté over moderate heat until somewhat tender, about 5 minutes. Add flour and sauté an additional 3 minutes, stirring. Transfer vegetables to a baking dish just large enough to hold the duck in 1 layer and arrange duck pieces on top. Add reserved wine and about 2 cups stock. The liquid should come about halfway up the sides of the duck. Cover with foil and braise ducks in oven until fork-tender and richly colored, about 1½ hours. Check occasionally and add more liquid if necessary to maintain the same level.

4. When duck is done, transfer pieces to a serving platter and keep warm. Strain the sauce through a sieve, let settle briefly, then carefully remove as much fat as possible with a spoon. Put the degreased sauce in a saucepan and reduce over high heat to 1¼ cups. Pour sauce over duck and serve immediately.

Serves 4.

BISCOTTI PER IL VINO
Wine rusks

Almost every Italian bakery sells several varieties of dry *biscotti*, twice-baked *(bis cotto)* cookies that are meant to be dunked in either coffee or wine. To bring your dinner to an authentic Tuscan end, serve these along with the Pesche al Vino (see page 114) and encourage guests to soften the rusks in the wine syrup. They keep for weeks in an airtight container; offer them with afternoon tea or coffee or with a late-night glass of sweet wine. Note that the dough must chill at least 1 night.

- ¼ cup dried currants
- 2 tablespoons Marsala
- ½ pound unsalted butter, softened
- 2 cups sugar
- 4 eggs
- 1 teaspoon vanilla extract
- 1 tablespoon anise-flavored apéritif

4 cups flour
1 teaspoon baking powder
1 teaspoon baking soda
½ teaspoon salt
2 teaspoons grated lemon rind
1 teaspoon aniseed
½ cup half-and-half
1 cup coarsely chopped toasted walnuts
1 cup coarsely chopped toasted hazelnuts

1. Put currants in a bowl with Marsala; soak for 20 minutes.

2. Cream butter; add sugar gradually and beat until light. Add eggs one at a time, beating until light and fluffy. Add vanilla, apéritif, and currants with their soaking liquid.

3. Sift together flour, baking powder, baking soda, and salt. Stir in lemon rind and aniseed. Add to creamed mixture alternately with half-and-half. Stir in walnuts and hazelnuts by hand. Cover and chill dough for at least 2 hours or overnight.

4. Divide dough into quarters and place each quarter on a length of waxed paper. Form into a roll about 15 inches long and 1½ inches thick. Wrap in waxed paper, then in foil. Chill overnight (dough can be frozen at this point for up to 1 month; bring frozen dough to refrigerator temperature before proceeding).

5. Preheat oven to 350° F. Unwrap rolls and place them on ungreased baking sheets. Bake until very lightly browned, about 20 to 25 minutes. Carefully transfer rolls to a cutting board and cut on a 45° angle into slices about ½ inch thick. Place slices cut side up on the baking sheets and return to oven. Bake until golden, about 8 to 12 minutes. Cool rusks thoroughly on racks. Store in airtight containers.

Makes about 4 dozen rusks.

GAMBE D'ANITRA ALLA GRIGLIA
Grilled duck legs with garlic and balsamic vinegar

A purée of garlic stuffed under the skin perfumes these grilled duck legs, with balsamic vinegar adding its sweet-tart flavor. Roasting the legs first releases most of the fat; they can then be quickly finished on the grill. Serve the duck legs with Bruschetta (see page 13) and an assortment of grilled vegetables, or offer a salad of shredded romaine dressed with olive oil, balsamic vinegar, and Parmesan. The recipe comes from the town of Maremma, near Grosseto in Tuscany.

2 tablespoons unsalted butter
½ cup olive oil
3 heads garlic, cloves separated and peeled but left whole
6 fresh oregano sprigs
Salt and freshly ground black pepper
4 tablespoons dry white wine
12 duck legs and thighs, in one piece
½ cup balsamic vinegar
10 tablespoons olive oil

1. In a medium skillet over moderate heat, melt butter with oil. Add garlic, oregano, and salt and pepper to taste. Cook gently 30 minutes. Garlic cloves should be very soft. Add wine, reduce by half over high heat, then remove skillet from heat. Remove oregano sprigs. Purée the garlic in a food processor or blender.

2. Using 1½ teaspoons garlic purée per duck piece, spread purée between the skin and the flesh. Combine vinegar, olive oil, and any remaining purée. Put duck in a stainless steel, enamel, or glass bowl or baking dish and cover with vinegar mixture. Marinate 2 hours at room temperature (or in refrigerator if weather is warm).

3. Preheat oven to 350° F. Prepare a medium-hot charcoal fire. Remove duck from marinade and place on a rack in a roasting pan. Roast 30 minutes in preheated oven, basting with marinade twice. Finish cooking duck on the grill to crisp the skin.

Serves 6 to 8.

POLLO ALLA DIAVOLA
Deviled chicken

For this Roman dish, brush flattened broiler halves with a peppery lemon and mustard mixture, then broil slowly and baste until the skin crisps and browns. The result is a devilishly good *diavola*, to serve with wilted greens and a basket of crunchy toast topped with fennel seed and pepper.

2 broiling chickens (about 3 lb each)
1 shallot, minced
1 teaspoon grated lemon rind
2 teaspoons lemon juice
½ teaspoon hot red-pepper flakes
2 tablespoons olive oil
1 tablespoon red wine vinegar
1 tablespoon Dijon-style mustard
¼ cup dry white wine
¼ cup unsalted butter, melted
1 recipe Pane per la Zuppa (see page 49)

1. Halve the chickens lengthwise and remove any fatty deposits. Place halves between sheets of waxed paper or parchment paper. Using the flat side of a large cleaver or a mallet, pound the chickens flat. (It doesn't matter if the bones crack.)

2. Whisk together shallot, lemon rind, lemon juice, red-pepper flakes, olive oil, vinegar, and mustard. Combine wine and butter in a small bowl.

3. Preheat broiler. Coat chickens well with olive oil mixture and place on a broiler rack, skin side down. Position rack at least 6 inches from heat and broil about 12 minutes, basting occasionally with wine-butter mixture. Turn chicken and continue broiling and basting for about 10 minutes more. When chicken is done, remove to a heated platter and pour any leftover olive oil mixture over it. Serve immediately with a basket of Pane per la Zuppa.

Serves 6.

Pollo alla Griglia con Salsa d'Aglio makes a perfect patio meal. The chicken, marinated in garlic, olive oil, rosemary, and wine, cooks on the grill while the accompanying potato slices bake. Serve with garlic mayonnaise and a lightly chilled Grignolino. A salad of sliced tomatoes, mozzarella, and basil can open the meal.

POLLO TOSCANO CON PEPERONI E CARCIOFI
Tuscan chicken with peppers and artichokes

American southerners aren't the only cooks who use cornmeal in frying. The practice is popular in Tuscany, too. Tuscan cooks coat chicken with cornmeal, then brown it quickly, braise it in wine, and smother it with sweet peppers and artichokes. The multicolored dish needs no garnish or accompaniment other than a bottle of hearty red wine.

     ¾ cup flour
     ¼ cup cornmeal
     1 teaspoon dried oregano
     1 teaspoon dried basil
     1 teaspoon salt
    14 chicken legs
     4 tablespoons olive oil
     4 tablespoons butter
     1 cup chopped onion
     3 tablespoons minced garlic
     ¾ cup dry white wine
     2 cups chicken stock
     ¼ cup cream
     ½ cup fresh basil leaves,
        roughly torn

Pepper and Artichoke Garnish

     6 baby artichokes
     1 lemon, halved
     ⅓ cup olive oil
     1 tablespoon minced garlic
     1 cup thinly sliced green
        bell pepper
     1 cup thinly sliced yellow
        bell pepper
     1 cup thinly sliced red
        bell pepper
     4 sprigs fresh oregano,
        leaves only
        Coarse salt

1. Combine flour, cornmeal, oregano, basil, and salt. Dredge chicken legs in mixture, shaking off excess. In a large skillet over moderate heat, melt oil and butter. Add legs and brown, in batches if necessary. Transfer legs to a plate as they finish browning.

2. Add onion and garlic to the skillet and sauté gently 10 to 12 minutes. Add wine, stock, and browned chicken legs (if necessary, transfer half the mixture and half the legs to another skillet). Cover and simmer gently 30 minutes.

3. Test chicken legs for doneness. When juices run clear, transfer chicken legs to a warmed serving platter and keep warm. Strain the chicken liquid through a fine sieve into a clean skillet. Add cream and reduce by one third. Add Pepper and Artichoke Garnish. Taste and adjust seasoning as necessary. Add basil leaves and chicken. Turn to coat chicken with sauce, then transfer to serving dish.

Serves 6.

Pepper and Artichoke Garnish

1. Peel away tough, dark green outer leaves of artichokes until you reach the pale green heart. Trim stem ends. Cut about ½ inch off the tip with a sharp knife. Put hearts in a bowl of water acidulated with the juice of half a lemon (to prevent browning). Bring a medium pot of salted water to a boil over high heat. Add juice and pulp of remaining half lemon. Drain artichoke hearts and add them to boiling water. Cook until just tender when pierced with the tip of a knife. Drain well and dry. (Preparation of baby artichoke hearts is illustrated on page 16.)

2. Heat olive oil in a skillet over moderately low heat. Add garlic and sauté 1 minute. Add peppers and oregano, raise heat to medium, and cook, covered, for 15 minutes. Taste and add salt if necessary. Add artichokes, stir to blend, and cook just until they are hot.

POLLO ALLA GRIGLIA CON SALSA D'AGLIO
Grilled chicken with garlic sauce

Spread out the red-and-white cloth, open some cool Grignolino, and serve this casual Tuscan dinner for patio parties. The creamy garlic mayonnaise can be slathered on chicken hot off the grill or on herbed, oven-baked potatoes. Leftover mayonnaise is great on tomato salads, cold chicken, or an egg salad sandwich.

      ½ cup olive oil
      2 tablespoons minced garlic
      3 sprigs fresh rosemary
      ¼ cup dry white wine
         Salt and freshly ground
         black pepper
      1 roasting chicken (about 4 lb),
         in 8 pieces
      3 baking potatoes
      2 tablespoons minced shallots
      ¼ cup unsalted butter, melted
      1 tablespoon lemon juice
      4 sprigs fresh thyme

Garlic Sauce

      4 tablespoons olive oil
      2 tablespoons peanut oil
      1 egg yolk
         Juice of ½ lemon
   1½ teaspoons minced garlic
      2 tablespoons cream
      1 tablespoon freshly grated
         Parmesan
         Salt and freshly ground
         black pepper

1. To marinate the chicken: Heat olive oil in a saucepan over moderately low heat. Add garlic and sauté gently 5 minutes; do not let garlic brown. Remove from heat and add rosemary and wine. Cool slightly. Salt and pepper chicken pieces and put them in a stainless steel, glass, or ceramic bowl or baking dish. Cover with wine mixture and marinate, refrigerated, 3 to 12 hours.

2. About 30 minutes before serving, prepare potatoes as follows: If potatoes are russets, peel them; there's no need to peel thin-skinned potatoes. Slice them into rounds ¼ inch thick and arrange them in a single layer on a large baking sheet. Combine shallots, butter, and lemon juice and pour over the potatoes. Arrange thyme sprigs on top.

3. Prepare a medium-hot charcoal fire. Preheat oven to 450° F. Remove chicken from marinade and place on grill. Grill chicken, turning occasionally and basting with marinade, until it is done to your liking, about 20 to 25 minutes. Fifteen minutes (approximately) before chicken is done, put potatoes in oven. Roast 10 to 15 minutes, turning them over as they brown. When potatoes are done, season them with salt and pepper, turn off the oven, and leave them in the oven with the door ajar until the chicken is ready. Serve chicken and potatoes family-style with Garlic Sauce on the side.

Serves 3 to 4.

Garlic Sauce Combine the two oils and set aside. Put egg yolk, lemon juice, and garlic in workbowl of food processor fitted with steel blade or in blender. Process until yolk is pale yellow. With the machine running, slowly add the oil through the feed tube to make a mayonnaise, then slowly add the cream. When sauce is thick, transfer it to a bowl and stir in Parmesan by hand. Season to taste with salt and pepper. If you are not going to use the sauce immediately, it can be stored, covered, in the refrigerator. Before serving it, be sure to bring it to room temperature.

95

Vegetables shine in Italian salads and side dishes. Salad dressings are often very simple, showcasing the fine vinegars and olive oils for which Italy is renowned.

Salads & Vegetables

I talian salads and vegetable dishes generally reflect the seasons. In this chapter you'll find a salad based on the tender, young vegetables of spring (see Una Piccola Insalata di Primavera, page 100), one that uses summer's wealth of tomatoes and zucchini (see Insalata dell' Estate, page 101), and a winter salad of beets and turnips (see Insalata dell' Inverno, page 102). There is a recipe for spring's asparagus and new onions (see Asparagi di Primavera, page 106), one for June's peas (see Piselli al Prosciutto, page 108), and one for a summer tomato casserole (see Pomodori dell' Estate, page 109). The chapter also includes a menu for a Cold Supper (see page 104).

Tuscan cooks take advantage of day-old bread to make Panzanella, a lively summer salad that can be a one-dish lunch.

SALADS

The most common Italian salad is made of raw greens alone, lightly dressed with olive oil and vinegar. But Italians also love to make salads out of tender, young seasonal vegetables. In spring they combine carrots and radishes in a light mustard dressing or serve the first fava beans and asparagus with oil and lemon. In summer, squash and tomatoes are bathed in an herb marinade. Autumn brings eggplant, fried and layered with garlic and vinegar. Winter salads of beets and their greens are often supplemented with turnips and dressed with anchovy, lemon, and oil.

The broad-minded cook can find salad makings in every season's harvest. Italian cooks do, and you'll find a few of their best ideas in the collection that follows.

VINAIGRETTE

The simplest and possibly the best vinaigrette is made at the table. Offer a cruet of light virgin olive oil, a cruet of fine red wine vinegar, a dish of coarse salt, and a pepper mill and let guests dress their own salad to taste.

Vinaigrettes may be made several hours ahead. They may be stored, covered, in the refrigerator for up to one week with only slight loss of flavor. Bring to room temperature, taste, and reseason before reusing.

The basic vinaigrette, below, is excellent for salads made with heartier greens, such as romaine, dandelion greens, and chicory.

> *Juice of 1 lemon*
> 4 *tablespoons red wine vinegar*
> *Coarse salt to taste*
> ¾ *cup olive oil*
> 1 *teaspoon freshly ground black pepper*

In a small bowl, combine lemon, vinegar, and salt. Stir to dissolve salt. Whisk in olive oil. Let sit 10 minutes. Add pepper, taste, and add more salt if needed.

Makes about 1 cup.

Balsamic Vinaigrette Substitute balsamic vinegar for the red wine vinegar.

Lemon Vinaigrette Substitute lemon juice for the red wine vinegar. This is an excellent vinaigrette for salads with a fruit or fish component.

Anchovy Vinaigrette

This lively dressing is particularly good on a salad served before a rustic main course, such as pizza or calzone.

- *3 anchovy fillets, minced*
- *4 tablespoons red wine vinegar*
- *Juice of 1 lemon*
- *¾ cup olive oil*
- *2 tablespoons freshly grated Parmesan*
- *1 teaspoon freshly ground black pepper*

In a small bowl, whisk together anchovy, vinegar, and lemon juice. Whisk in olive oil, then stir in Parmesan and pepper.

Makes about 1 cup.

PANZANELLA
Tuscan bread salad

This colorful salad owes a debt to some resourceful cook who couldn't bear to throw away the day-old bread. Many of Florence's *trattorie* have this cool salad on the menu all summer. Note that the cubed bread must sit out overnight and the vegetables must marinate at least 2 hours.

- *½ loaf day-old dense country-style bread*
- *3 medium tomatoes, peeled, seeded, and chopped*
- *1 cucumber, peeled, seeded, and diced*
- *1 red bell pepper, seeded and diced*

- *1 small red onion, in paper-thin rings*
- *¼ cup diced giardiniera (Italian pickles)*
- *3 tablespoons drained small capers*
- *½ cup minced parsley*
- *¼ cup red wine vinegar*
- *¼ cup Dijon mustard*
- *1 ounce anchovy fillets, minced (optional)*
- *2 teaspoons minced fresh oregano*
- *1 cup olive oil*
- *Salt and freshly ground black pepper*
- *Additional red onion slices, for garnish*
- *Imported unpitted black olives, for garnish (optional)*
- *Additional anchovy fillets, for garnish (optional)*
- *3 tablespoons minced parsley, for garnish*

1. Cut bread into 1-inch cubes. Spread cubes out on a tray and let sit overnight to harden.

2. Combine tomatoes, cucumber, red pepper, onion, pickles, capers, and parsley in a large nonreactive bowl; mix gently but well. Set aside.

3. In a small bowl, combine vinegar, mustard, minced anchovies (if used), and oregano. Whisk in olive oil. Add salt and pepper to taste. Pour over mixed vegetables, stir to blend, and let sit at room temperature at least 2 hours or overnight, covered, in a cool place.

4. About 20 minutes before serving, combine 2 cups of the bread cubes with the marinated vegetables. Taste and adjust salt and pepper as needed. Add additional red onion slices, and olives, if used. Just before serving, stir in remaining bread cubes, pile salad onto a serving platter and top with anchovy fillets (if used) and parsley.

Serves 4 generously.

OLIVE OIL

Some of the world's best olive oil comes from Italy. Although some northern dishes are made with butter, it is olive oil that gives most Italian cooking its characteristic flavor.

The flavor of the oil varies according to the type of olives it is pressed from, the region where the olives are grown, and the method of pressing. The best oils have a clean, fruity aroma, a full but not heavy body, and a fruity or peppery flavor.

Olive oils are categorized according to their acidity and the procedure used to make them. To merit one of the top four categories, the oil must be pressed from olives that have not been subjected to chemical treatments of any kind.

Extravirgin olive oil contains no more than 1 percent oleic acid.

Superfine virgin olive oil contains no more than 1½ percent oleic acid.

Fine virgin olive oil contains no more than 3 percent oleic acid.

Virgin olive oil contains no more than 4 percent oleic acid.

Olive oil that contains more than 4 percent oleic acid is considered unfit for human consumption. Many large olive oil manufacturers treat such oil with chemical solvents to reduce the acid below 4 percent, then add some virgin olive oil to improve the flavor. The result may be called pure olive oil or *olio d'oliva*.

Heat changes the character of an olive oil. For frying or sautéing, it makes little sense to use an expensive extravirgin oil, whose character would change in the process. Use a good-tasting affordable olive oil and save your best oils for uncooked dishes or for drizzling on cooked dishes at the end of the cooking time.

Store all olive oils in a cool, dark place—they go rancid when exposed to heat and light. Use within a year.

FAGIOLI BIANCHI CON PEPERONATA
White bean salad with peppers

White beans and red peppers are a happy match that's found all over Italy—as a picnic salad, as an antipasto, or as a side dish to cold roast lamb. Dress them while they're warm so that they absorb the flavors of lemon, oil, and onion. Note that beans must soak for an hour.

    2   cups dried white beans
    ½   white onion, stuck with
        2 cloves
    1   bay leaf
    1   large sprig thyme
    2   sprigs parsley
    2   teaspoons salt
    ⅓   cup olive oil
    ½   cup peeled, seeded, and
        diced tomatoes (see page 29)
    2   green onions, minced
    2   sun-dried tomatoes (from
        jar), slivered
    2   tablespoons oil from sun-dried
        tomatoes
    2   tablespoons lemon juice
    1   tablespoon white wine vinegar
    1   recipe Peperonata (see
        page 13)
        Lettuce leaves (optional)
    4   thick slices of Pane Toscano
        (see page 48), brushed well
        with olive oil and grilled or
        toasted

1. Cover beans with cold water and soak 1 hour. Drain; place beans in a large kettle. Add onion, bay leaf, thyme, parsley, and salt. Cover with water; bring to a boil. Reduce heat; simmer until beans are just tender, about 45 minutes. Drain; discard onion, bay leaf, thyme, and parsley.

2. Cool beans slightly; place in a stainless steel, glass, or ceramic bowl. Add olive oil, tomatoes, green onions, sun-dried tomatoes and their oil, lemon juice, and vinegar. Cool to room temperature; taste and add salt if needed.

3. Stir in Peperonata, then serve salad as is or atop lettuce leaves. Accompany with warm grilled bread.

Serves 4.

UNA PICCOLA INSALATA DI PRIMAVERA
A little salad of spring vegetables

In early spring the Bologna markets are filled with tiny golden carrots and sweet young radishes, red and white. Grated and tossed with a mustard dressing, they make a light and refreshing spring salad to precede Arrosto di Maiale con Rosmarino (see page 84) or a baked Easter ham.

    4   to 6 small carrots
    12 radishes
    2   heads romaine
    1   bunch arugula or radish
        sprouts (optional)
    2   teaspoons Dijon mustard
    ¼   cup red wine vinegar
        Grated rind of ½ lemon
    ½   cup full-flavored olive oil
        Salt and freshly ground
        black pepper
        Lemon juice
    12 slices Bruschetta (see page 13)
    2   tablespoons coarsely grated
        Parmesan (optional)

1. Wash and scrub carrots and radishes. Grate them coarsely by hand or in the food processor. Wash and dry romaine; remove outer leaves and reserve for another use. Wrap hearts in damp paper towels and refrigerate until ready to use. If you are using arugula, wash and dry it; wrap in damp paper towels and refrigerate.

2. In a medium bowl whisk together mustard and vinegar. Add lemon rind and slowly whisk in olive oil. Add salt, pepper, and lemon juice (up to 1 tablespoon) to taste. Add carrots and radishes to bowl and toss to coat with dressing. Marinate at room temperature for about 20 minutes.

3. To serve, arrange romaine hearts, Bruschetta, and arugula (if used) on individual plates. Top with vegetables, spooning some of vegetables and dressing over bread rounds. Garnish, if desired, with Parmesan.

Serves 4.

INSALATA CAPRICCIOSA
Classic "capricious" salad

This classic is a salad for summer, when the tomatoes and basil are at their best. Use only sweet, vine-ripened tomatoes, and visit a cheese merchant for the finest whole-milk mozzarella. A hot loaf of crusty Pane Toscano (see page 48) should be on the table, too.

    8   ounces fresh whole-milk moz-
        zarella or imported buffalo-
        milk mozzarella, at room
        temperature
    4   tomatoes, at room tempera-
        ture, cored and thinly sliced
    ½   cup extravirgin olive oil
        Juice of 1½ large or 2 small
        lemons
    ¼   cup shredded fresh basil leaves
        Coarse salt and freshly
        ground black pepper
        Additional basil sprigs,
        for garnish

1. Slice cheese into rounds about ⅛ inch thick. On a large serving platter or on individual salad plates, arrange alternate slices of cheese and tomato in a concentric pattern.

2. In a small bowl combine olive oil, lemon juice, and basil. Whisk well. Spoon dressing over salad. Season with salt and pepper. Garnish with basil sprigs and serve immediately.

Serves 4 as a first course.

INSALATA MISTA
Wild and gathered greens

The typical Italian green salad is simply the freshest seasonal greens in a light oil-and-vinegar dressing. But the range of salad greens used in Italy astounds many American visitors. who may be familiar with only a couple of the varieties. Fortunately, more big-city markets are stocking an assortment of greens and herbs. Look for a market that takes care of its greens, then make your salad with whatever is freshest and dress it lightly with a vinaigrette. When you toss the salad, use wooden utensils if possible; metal utensils bruise the leaves, and the heat of one's hands can wilt this delicate salad.

Mixed greens: Choose from hearts of romaine, butter lettuce, red-leaf lettuce, limestone lettuce, Belgian endive, arugula, radicchio, purple kale, dandelion greens, tender radish tops, young sorrel leaves, fresh oregano, whole small basil leaves, thyme flowers, chive flowers
Vinaigrette (see pages 98–99)

1. Carefully wash greens; dry thoroughly. Do not break up or chop them. Wrap in damp paper towels; refrigerate until serving time. Chill salad plates and bowl slightly.

2. To serve, toss greens with vinaigrette. Divide among salad plates or serve from the bowl. Offer a pepper mill at the table.

INSALATA DELL' ESTATE
Summer salad of zucchini and tomatoes

Italian cooks turn squash and tomatoes into a sprightly summer salad by adding oil, vinegar, and lots of fresh herbs. Mint marks this version as a Roman dish; in Rome, diners spoon it into the hollows of hard, crusty rolls.

½ *pound* each *small, firm green zucchini and yellow crookneck squash*
2 *tablespoons white wine vinegar*
½ *cup olive oil*
3 *tablespoons minced parsley*
1 *tablespoon* each *minced fresh chives and mint*
4 *tomatoes, peeled, seeded, and diced*
1 *head* each *butter and red-leaf lettuce*
⅓ *cup minced prosciutto*
   Salt
1 *teaspoon freshly ground black pepper*
   Additional mint leaves, for garnish

1. Grate zucchini and squash coarsely. In a large bowl whisk together vinegar, oil, parsley, chives, and mint. Add zucchini, squash, and tomatoes; stir gently and set aside.

2. Wash and dry lettuces; tear into bite-sized pieces. Arrange on a large serving platter. Just before serving, mix prosciutto into vegetables. Salt to taste; add pepper. Pile vegetables onto platter; garnish with mint leaves.

Serves 4.

Use the freshest young greens that you can find for an Insalata Mista— shown here are endive, butter lettuce, dandelion, purple kale, arugula, and romaine, garnished with chive blossoms—and dress it simply with fine olive oil and vinegar.

Beets with their greens and young turnips make a distinctive winter salad. Serve Insalata dell' Inverno before Arrosto di Maiale con Rosmarino (see page 84), a Sicilian-style pork roast with rosemary.

INSALATA DELL' INVERNO
Winter salad of beets and turnips

Most Italians are as fond of the beet greens and stems as they are of the sweet round beets. The greens are blanched, dressed, and served alone as a salad; or, as here, they're mixed with beets and turnips for a heartier first course. Note that beets must bake for 1½ hours.

> *3 or 4 medium beets with greens attached*
> *7 or 8 small turnips*
> *2 tablespoons each lemon juice and red wine vinegar*
> *1 tablespoon Dijon mustard*
> *½ tablespoon anchovy paste*
> *½ cup plus 2 tablespoons olive oil*
> *3 tablespoons freshly grated Parmesan*
> *Salt and freshly ground black pepper*
> *½ head each green-leaf and romaine lettuce, washed and dried*
> *2 tablespoons minced parsley*

1. Preheat oven to 375° F. Remove beet greens and stems and set aside. Wash beets and put them in an ovenproof bowl or baking dish. Add water to come halfway up the sides of the beets, then cover tightly with a lid or aluminum foil and bake until beets can be easily pierced with a knife, about 1½ hours. Remove from oven and let cool. While beets are still warm, peel them and slice into rounds, then into thin matchsticks.

2. Wash beet stems and greens, then separate stems from greens. Bring a large pot of salted water to a boil and blanch greens 30 seconds. Transfer greens with a slotted spoon to a bowl of ice water. Drain and pat thoroughly dry. Boil stems 1 minute in same water; transfer to ice water and, when cool, drain and dry them. Chop both beet greens and stems coarsely.

3. In a large bowl, combine lemon juice, vinegar, mustard, and anchovy paste. Whisk in the ½ cup olive oil. Stir in 1 tablespoon of the Parmesan. Add beet greens and stems and marinate 15 minutes.

4. Bring another large pot of salted water to a boil. Wash turnips, then boil under tender. Very small turnips may take only 10 minutes, larger turnips up to 45 minutes. Drain and dry. While still warm, peel turnips, slice into rounds, then into thin matchsticks. Very small turnips may be left whole or halved.

5. Add beets, turnips, and remaining 2 tablespoons oil to marinating beet greens; let marinate 20 minutes. Add salt and pepper to taste. Line a serving platter with lettuce and romaine leaves. Top with salad. Combine remaining Parmesan and the parsley and sprinkle over salad.

Serves 4.

INSALATA DI FAVE
Fresh fava bean salad

Meaty fava beans are an Italian favorite from north to south: in soups and stews, as a hot first course with olive oil and salt, or as a cool spring salad. Sicilian cooks often add a pinch of hot red-pepper flakes to their beans. To make a lunch or a more substantial first course, they might serve the salad on a large platter surrounded with tomatoes, sliced prosciutto, hard-cooked eggs, and *pecorino* cheese.

- 2 pounds fresh unshelled fava beans
- 2 tablespoons lemon juice
- 1 tablespoon white wine vinegar
  Coarse salt
  Freshly ground black pepper
  Large pinch hot red-pepper flakes
- ½ cup olive oil
- ½ cup finely minced red onion
- 8 tender butter-lettuce cups
- 2 tablespoons minced fresh chives
- 2 tablespoons coarsely chopped parsley

1. Bring a large pot of water to a boil. Shell beans, add to boiling water, and boil for 2 minutes. Drain, refresh under cold running water, and pat dry.

2. In a small bowl, combine lemon juice and vinegar; add salt, black pepper, and red-pepper flakes to taste. Stir and set aside for 5 minutes to dissolve salt. Whisk in olive oil.

3. Combine beans and dressing in a serving bowl. Add onion and mix well. Set aside to marinate at least 30 minutes or up to 8 hours in a cool place. Divide lettuce cups among four salad plates. Spoon beans into lettuce cups. Garnish with chives and parsley.

Serves 4.

INSALATA DI PATATE CON CIPOLLE
Roman potato and onion salad

Dress potatoes while they're still warm and they will absorb the maximum flavor. Serve at room temperature, at picnics or patio meals, with anything from cold sliced Italian sausages to American hamburgers.

- 3 tablespoons white wine vinegar
- 1 tablespoon lemon juice
  Grated rind of 1 lemon
- 2 tablespoons finely minced fresh oregano
- 2 tablespoons drained small capers
- 1 tablespoon coarse salt
- 1½ teaspoons freshly ground black pepper
- ¾ cup extravirgin olive oil
- 2 large white onions, sliced in ¼-inch rounds
- 1½ pounds small red potatoes
- 3 tablespoons minced parsley mixed with ½ tablespoon grated lemon rind, for garnish

1. In a large bowl, combine vinegar, lemon juice, lemon rind, oregano, capers, salt, and pepper. Whisk in olive oil. Add onion slices and mix thoroughly.

2. Bring a large pot of salted water to a boil. Add potatoes and boil until barely tender. Drain, and when cool enough to handle, slice potatoes ¼ inch thick. Immediately add potatoes to dressing and toss with hands to coat well. Cool to room temperature, then taste and adjust seasoning. Garnish with minced parsley and lemon rind.

Serves 4.

INSALATA DI FINOCCHI E CARCIOFI
Fennel and artichoke salad

The first spring artichokes are a delicious partner to the last of the fennel. Marinated in oil and lemon, then served with toasts and Parmesan, the pair flatter each other and harmonize with almost any main course: Grilled fish, roast lamb, or chicken are all fine choices.

- 1 large or 2 small fennel bulbs
- 3 lemons
- ¾ cup olive oil
  Coarse salt and freshly ground black pepper
- 4 small artichokes, about 2 to 3 inches in diameter
- 12 slices Bruschetta (see page 13)
- 4 ounces Parmesan, in long, thin slabs
  Additional olive oil

1. Wash fennel bulbs and remove any tough outer stalks (see page 80). Halve and core them, and slice thinly lengthwise. Put fennel slices in a stainless steel, glass, or ceramic bowl. Add juice of 2 lemons, the olive oil, and salt and pepper to taste. Toss to blend and set aside to marinate.

2. Remove dark green outer leaves of artichokes; cut off the top third of the artichokes with a serrated knife. Rub all cut surfaces with lemon. Cook in boiling salted water until just tender, about 12 to 15 minutes. Drain and refresh under cold running water, then drain thoroughly and pat dry. Cut artichokes in half. Add to fennel in bowl and stir to coat with oil. Marinate an additional 30 to 45 minutes. Taste and add more salt or lemon if necessary.

3. To serve, spoon a little of the marinade onto individual salad plates. Arrange fennel atop marinade. Surround with slices of Bruschetta. Top bread with artichoke hearts. Place Parmesan slices between bread slices and drizzle salad with a little additional olive oil. Serve immediately and pass the pepper mill.

Serves 4.

A COLD SUPPER

Panzanella (see page 99)

Bistecca con Salsa Cruda

Funghi alla Griglia

Granita di Melone

On a balmy summer evening, tempt guests with a cold meal of Tuscan specialties. The Florentines know how to beat the heat: with a cool, vinegar-laced salad of bread and vegetables; a platter of their famous grilled beef, sliced and served cold; and a bowl of marinated mushrooms. Granita di Melone makes a fitting dessert. Do as the Florentines do and wash it down with a fresh, young Chianti that's been chilled about 20 minutes before serving. Apart from toasting the sandwich bread, the entire meal can be made well in advance.

BISTECCA CON SALSA CRUDA
Skirt steak with fresh tomato sauce

Steak sandwiches don't get any better than this Florentine version, made with marinated and grilled skirt steak, grilled bread, and a fresh (uncooked) tomato and herb sauce. A mushroom or two from the accompanying Funghi alla Griglia would make a fine addition to each sandwich. Note that the steak needs to marinate overnight and to cool after it is cooked.

- ½ bottle (375 ml) young Chianti
- 3 cloves minced garlic
- 2 tablespoons balsamic vinegar
- 1 tablespoon freshly ground black pepper
- 2 large sprigs fresh rosemary
- ½ red onion, minced
- 2 pounds skirt steak, lightly pounded
- 8 large slices Pane Toscano (see page 48), about ⅓ inch thick Olive oil
- 1 recipe Sugo di Pomodori Freschi (see page 36)

1. In a large bowl combine wine, garlic, vinegar, pepper, rosemary, and onion. Add meat, cover bowl with plastic wrap, refrigerate, and marinate overnight.

2. Prepare a medium-hot charcoal fire. Bring meat to room temperature. When coals have burned down to a gray ash, sear meat quickly on both sides, basting with marinade. It should be browned outside but still pink within. Set aside and let rest 10 minutes before carving.

3. Put marinade in a small saucepan and bring to a boil over high heat. Reduce to ½ cup. Remove rosemary sprigs; reserve marinade.

4. Carve meat into long thin strips across the grain. Moisten with ¼ cup of the reduced marinade. Set aside at room temperature for 1 hour or refrigerate for several hours, but bring to room temperature before serving.

5. Preheat oven to 375° F. Brush bread slices lightly with olive oil and with remaining marinade. Toast on a

baking sheet until lightly colored, about 5 to 8 minutes. Pile toasts on a platter. Pile sliced steak on another platter and spoon the tomato sauce over it. Serve while toasts are warm.

Serves 4.

FUNGHI ALLA GRIGLIA
Grilled and marinated mushrooms

Mushrooms are like sponges: They readily absorb liquids, and if that liquid is a tangy marinade, it's all to the good. In the recipe below, the mushrooms are marinated briefly, then grilled in a foil pan over coals. After grilling, they're returned to the marinade to cool and reabsorb its flavors. Serve the mushrooms at room temperature.

- 2 pounds whole mushrooms, cultivated and/or wild
- ½ cup olive oil
- 2 tablespoons unsalted butter, melted
- ½ teaspoon hot red-pepper flakes
- 2 teaspoons minced garlic
- ¼ cup dry white wine
- 1 teaspoon grated lemon rind
- ¼ cup minced green onions

1. Clean mushrooms with a brush or a damp paper towel; do not wash. In a large bowl whisk together oil, butter, red-pepper flakes, garlic, wine, and lemon rind. Add mushrooms, toss to coat well, and marinate 15 minutes at room temperature.

2. After removing skirt steak from the grill (see Bistecca recipe at left), arrange a large piece of heavy-duty foil atop the grate, turning up the edges to make a sort of pan. Remove mushrooms from their marinade, reserving marinade, and place them in foil pan. Cover grill and cook until hot throughout, 5 to 8 minutes. Remove foil and put mushrooms in a serving bowl with reserved marinade. Let cool to room temperature. Stir in green onions just before serving.

Serves 4.

Beat the summer heat with chilled Chianti and a Cold Supper: steak with fresh tomato sauce, grilled marinated mushrooms, salad, and a refreshing melon ice.

GRANITA DI MELONE
Melon ice

A typical Sicilian breakfast includes thick slices of golden brioche (see Pane di Mattina alla Siciliana, page 50), inky espresso—and melon ice! Americans might find it more suitable as a summer dessert, however, especially refreshing after a clambake or barbecue. Note that the melon must marinate at least 2 hours, and the blended mixture must chill for another 2 hours.

>   2 *pounds ripe melon (honeydew, cantaloupe, or Persian)*
> ⅓ *cup sugar*
> 1½ *tablespoons lemon juice*
>   *Grated rind of 1 lemon*
> ¼ *teaspoon ground allspice*
> ¼ *teaspoon freshly ground black pepper (optional)*
>   *Pinch of nutmeg*
> ½ *cup diced melon sprinkled with 2 tablespoons lemon juice or sweet white wine, for garnish*
>   *Fresh mint sprigs, for garnish*

1. Peel melons, halve, and seed. Cut into chunks and put in stainless steel, glass, or ceramic bowl. Add sugar, lemon juice, lemon rind, allspice, pepper (if used), and nutmeg. Cover and marinate at room temperature for 2 hours, or refrigerate up to 12 hours.

2. Strain the accumulated juices into a small saucepan. Bring to a boil over high heat and cook 1 minute. Remove from heat and let cool. Combine marinated melon and reduced juices in a food processor or blender and blend until smooth. Chill for 2 hours.

3. Pour mixture into container of an ice cream freezer and freeze according to manufacturer's directions. Serve garnished with diced melon and fresh mint.

Serves 6 or 7.

VEGETABLES

Italians rarely serve vegetables on the same plate with meat, as Americans do. In an Italian meal the vegetable appears as a separate dish or as a separate course. Asparagi di Primavera (at right), for example, or Piselli al Prosciutto (see page 108) would certainly be served on their own before the main course. Even such a dish as Funghi Saltati (opposite page), although it goes wonderfully with red meats and game, might occasionally appear as a first course.

Among vegetable dishes that do usually accompany meat or fish are Spinaci con Pignoli (page 108) and Patate al Forno (below). A dish such as Melanzane alla Parmigiana (page 110) would probably be served separately in Italy, but in the context of an American meal it goes well as a side to roast chicken or lamb.

The dozen vegetable dishes that follow include both first-course and side-dish selections. Serving suggestions have been made with American dining habits in mind.

PATATE AL FORNO
Tuscan-style roasted potatoes

Crusty baked potato wedges get the royal Tuscan treatment: a basting of olive oil and a dusting of garlic and Parmesan. They're as divine with an American burger as they are with the traditional Bistecca alla Fiorentina (see page 76).

>   3 *large baking potatoes*
> ¾ *cup (approximately) olive oil*
>   *Coarse salt*
>   1 *tablespoon minced garlic*
>   2 *tablespoons freshly grated Parmesan*

1. Preheat oven to 375° F. Wash potatoes, dry well, and quarter lengthwise. Coat a heavy baking sheet with oil; arrange potatoes on sheet. Rub them well all over with olive oil, then dust with salt. Bake, basting every 15 minutes with oil, until well browned and cooked through.

2. When potatoes are almost tender, heat ¼ cup olive oil in a small saucepan or skillet over moderately low heat. Add garlic and cook 1 minute, stirring constantly. Strain, setting garlic aside and reserving oil for another use.

3. Transfer potatoes to a warm serving platter; sprinkle with garlic and Parmesan. Serve immediately.

Serves 4.

ASPARAGI DI PRIMAVERA
Asparagus with lemon, tomato, and onions

When asparagus and the new onions turn up in the markets at the same time, the chefs of Bologna prepare this dish and put it in their windows.

> 1½ *pounds medium asparagus*
>   2 *small, sweet new onions or 4 green onions, minced*
>   2 *tablespoons lemon juice*
> ½ *cup extravirgin olive oil*
>   *Grated rind of 1 lemon*
>   2 *tablespoons minced fresh chives*
>   2 *tomatoes, peeled, seeded, and diced (see page 29)*
>   *Salt and freshly ground black pepper*

1. Bring a large pot of salted water to a boil. Add asparagus and cook until barely tender (about 5 minutes). Transfer with tongs to a bowl of ice water. When cool, drain and dry well. Transfer to a serving platter with all tips facing the same direction.

2. Combine onion, lemon juice, olive oil, lemon rind, and half of the chives. Whisk well, then stir in tomatoes. Season to taste with salt and pepper. Spoon sauce over asparagus, then garnish with remaining chives. Serve at room temperature.

Serves 4.

FUNGHI SALTATI
Mixed mushroom sauté

Northern Italians are avid stalkers of wild mushrooms, which their woods and mountains yield in abundance. Braised with garlic, cream, and herbs, mushrooms are the partner par excellence for roasted red meats, game, and fine wines.

> 1½ pounds fresh wild mushrooms (porcini, chanterelles, morels, or oyster mushrooms)
> 1 pound small cultivated button mushrooms
> ½ cup butter
> 1 tablespoon olive oil
> 3 tablespoons minced garlic
> 2 tablespoons whipping cream
> Salt and freshly ground black pepper
> ⅓ cup minced mixed herbs (parsley, basil, chives, oregano)

1. Clean mushrooms well with a mushroom brush or soft toothbrush; do not wash. Cut wild mushrooms into rough chunks about the size of the button mushrooms; leave button mushrooms whole.

2. Heat butter and olive oil in a large skillet over low heat. Add garlic and sauté one minute, stirring; do not allow garlic to color. Raise heat to high, add mushrooms and toss to coat with butter. Sauté quickly until mushrooms have softened, about 2 minutes. Add cream and cook until it is absorbed. Season to taste with salt and pepper. Add herbs, remove from heat, and transfer to a warm serving platter. Serve immediately.

Serves 4.

Potatoes Italian style: Cut them in wedges, bake with olive oil, then sprinkle with garlic and Parmesan. The resulting golden Patate al Forno can accompany any sturdy meat dish.

1. Pick over spinach carefully and discard any large, tough outer leaves or bruised leaves. Leave inner leaves attached to their tender stems. Wash well and dry.

2. Heat olive oil in a large sauté pan over moderately low heat. Add garlic and sauté about 30 seconds, stirring constantly. Raise heat to medium-high. Add spinach and salt to taste. Sauté, turning spinach over constantly with tongs, for about 25 seconds or until spinach just wilts. Reduce heat to low, add pine nuts and raisins. Cook an additional 15 seconds. Drizzle lemon juice over dish and season to taste with pepper. Taste and add more salt if needed. Serve immediately.

Serves 4.

PISELLI AL PROSCIUTTO
Peas with prosciutto

The first June peas usually turn up in Roman restaurants stewed with butter, prosciutto, and green onions. They're always served as a separate first course, with bread to mop up the buttery juices.

> 5 pounds fresh peas
> 6 tablespoons butter
> ½ cup green onions, in pea-size dice
> 1 cup unsalted homemade chicken stock
> 1 cup paper-thin julienned prosciutto
> 2 tablespoons minced green onions, white part only, for garnish

Shell peas. Melt butter in a sauté pan over moderately low heat. Add diced green onions and cook 2 minutes. Add peas and stock; cook until peas are just tender, about 8 to 10 minutes. Stir in prosciutto and remove from heat. Top with minced green onions and serve immediately.

Serves 6.

Braise the first June peas the Roman way—with scallions and sliced prosciutto—and serve as a first course before a roast spring lamb.

SPINACI CON PIGNOLI
Wilted spinach with pine nuts and raisins

Barely wilted spinach seasoned with garlic, pine nuts, and lemon is a side dish that fits in just about anywhere. Sicilian cooks add golden raisins and serve it with grilled tuna or swordfish; you might also serve it with Pollo alla Diavola (see page 93), Fagotini di Pollo con Cipolle Balsamiche (see page 88), Saltimbocca (see page 84), or Arrosto di Maiale al Latte (see page 85).

> 3 bunches spinach
> 3 tablespoons olive oil
> 2 teaspoons minced garlic
> Coarse salt
> ¼ cup toasted pine nuts
> 2 tablespoons golden raisins
> 2 tablespoons lemon juice
> Freshly ground black pepper

POMODORI DELL' ESTATE
Summer tomato casserole

If you drive through Italy in the height of summer, you might think you're seeing more tomatoes than the world can consume. The country seems to be bursting with them, but they all eventually get used, some in simple, rustic concoctions like this one. The dish depends on great tomatoes and good oil for its success. Serve it with herbed roast chicken, grilled fish, or lamb.

- ⅓ cup extravirgin olive oil
- ½ large red onion, sliced in ⅓-inch rounds
- 1½ large tomatoes, sliced ⅓ inch thick
  - Salt and freshly ground black pepper
- ⅓ cup chopped fresh basil
- 4 garlic cloves, thinly slivered
- 2 small green zucchini, cut in ¼-inch dice
- 1 small yellow zucchini, cut in ¼-inch dice
- 3 tablespoons freshly grated Parmesan

1. Preheat oven to 350° F. Using 2 tablespoons of the oil, coat the bottom and sides of a small baking dish, about 8 by 6 inches. Line bottom with onion slices; do not let slices overlap. Top with half of the tomato slices, a little salt and pepper, and half of the basil. Insert half of the garlic slivers in tomatoes. Drizzle with half of the remaining oil.

2. Repeat with another layer of tomato slices, salt and pepper, basil, and garlic. Combine the diced squashes and strew over the top. Drizzle with remaining oil and dust with Parmesan. Cover and bake 35 minutes. Cool slightly before serving directly from the casserole.

Serves 4.

MELANZANE FRITTE
Deep-fried eggplant

One of the charms of eggplant is how readily it absorbs other flavors. Layer it with garlic, vinegar, and basil, and it will be heavenly in a matter of hours. The slender Japanese eggplants sliced into fans make a clever, if nontraditional, presentation. Serve the dish as a summer first course with Bruschetta (see page 13), or offer it as a side dish with grilled lamb or poultry.

- 8 small, long Japanese eggplants
  - Olive oil and safflower oil, for deep-frying
  - Coarse salt
- ¼ cup minced garlic
- ½ cup minced fresh basil
- ¼ cup red wine vinegar

1. Wash and dry eggplants; do not peel. Cut eggplants into "fans": Starting at broad end, cut them lengthwise into slices about ⅓ inch thick, being careful not to cut through the stem.

2. Heat oil in a large deep kettle or deep-fryer. Use 1 part olive oil to 3 parts safflower oil. When oil reaches 350° F, add half the eggplants and fry until they float and are soft, about 4 to 6 minutes. Remove immediately with a slotted spoon to a stainless steel, glass, or ceramic bowl. Dust with salt and sprinkle with half of the garlic and half of the basil.

3. Repeat with remaining eggplants, transferring them to the same bowl as they are done and sprinkling them with salt and the remaining garlic and basil. Sprinkle vinegar over top and let vegetables cool to room temperature. Cover and refrigerate 6 to 8 hours or overnight.

4. To serve, bring eggplants to room temperature. Transfer to a serving platter with a lip and pour any marinade over them.

Serves 4.

CARCIOFI FRITTI CON CIPOLLE
Artichoke and onion sauté

This northern Italian dish is quickly made and great with veal and lamb. Use leftover artichokes in a frittata or as a simple topping for pasta.

- 3 medium artichokes
- 1 lemon, halved
- 2 tablespoons butter
- 2 tablespoons olive oil
- ½ cup minced onion
- 2 tablespoons chopped fresh oregano
- ½ cup white wine
- 2 tablespoons drained small capers
  - Coarse salt and freshly ground black pepper
  - Additional lemon (optional)

1. Remove the tough, dark green outer leaves of the artichokes. Trim the stems and cut off the top third of the artichokes with a serrated knife. Quarter the artichokes and remove the fuzzy choke. Rub all cut surfaces with a lemon half. Transfer to a bowl of cold water acidulated with the juice of half a lemon.

2. In a large sauté pan, heat butter and olive oil over moderately low heat. Add onion and cook gently until softened but not browned. Drain artichokes in a colander, then add to sauté pan. Turn heat to high to sear them quickly, shaking pan constantly. Add oregano, wine, capers, and salt and pepper to taste. Reduce heat to low, cover partially, and simmer 8 minutes. Uncover and cook until almost all the liquid has evaporated and artichokes are tender. Taste and add more salt or pepper if needed. Add a squeeze of lemon juice if desired. Transfer to a serving bowl and serve immediately.

Serves 4.

CARCIOFI ALLA ROMANA
Herb-steamed artichokes, Roman style

In Rome artichokes are bathed in oil, then baked with garlic, herbs, and wine until fragrant and tender. They are a delicious first course on their own, with sturdy bread to soak up the juices, but they're equally good as a buffet dish or as part of an antipasto.

    4   medium artichokes
    1   lemon, halved
    4   large cloves garlic, minced
    ¼   cup chopped fresh basil
    2   tablespoons minced parsley
    2   teaspoons coarse salt
    1½ teaspoons freshly ground
        black pepper
    ½   cup plus 2 tablespoons
        olive oil
    ¼   cup white wine
        Additional 2 tablespoons
        minced mixed basil and
        parsley, for garnish

1. Remove the tough, dark green outer leaves of the artichokes. Trim the stems and cut off the top third of the artichokes with a serrated knife. Quarter the artichokes and remove the fuzzy choke. Rub all cut surfaces with a lemon half. Transfer to a bowl of cold water acidulated with the juice of half a lemon.

2. Preheat oven to 350° F. In a bowl, combine garlic, basil, parsley, salt, and pepper. Whisk in the ½ cup oil. Drain artichokes, pat them dry, and add to the bowl. Turn to coat well with oil.

3. Transfer artichokes and their marinade to a baking dish, overlapping the pieces slightly. Sprinkle wine around the corners of the dish. Drizzle with the remaining oil. Cover dish tightly with aluminum foil and bake 30 minutes. Check artichokes for tenderness. When they are done, a small, sharp knife will pierce them easily. Continue cooking until tender. Remove to a serving platter and garnish with additional basil-parsley mixture. Serve hot or at room temperature.

Serves 4.

CAVOLO DI VENEZIA CON PANCETTA
Cabbage with pancetta, Venetian style

Venetians braise cabbage with *pancetta* and garlic, then spike it with wine vinegar. With a bowl of steaming polenta (see page 58), this dish makes a humble but wonderful supper. Any leftovers can be the beginning of a delicious frittata.

    6   ounces pancetta, cut in
        small cubes
    1   tablespoon olive oil
    4   tablespoons butter
    ¾   cup minced onion
    1   tablespoon minced garlic
    8   cups shredded cabbage
        Salt and freshly ground
        black pepper
    3   tablespoons red or white wine
        vinegar
    2   tablespoons minced Italian
        parsley, for garnish

1. In a large saucepan or small stockpot over moderately low heat, fry pancetta cubes slowly until crisp. Transfer with a slotted spoon to a small bowl. Pour off all but 1 tablespoon of fat. Add olive oil and 2 tablespoons of the butter to the pan. When butter has melted and fats are hot, add onion and garlic. Sauté gently over low heat until softened but not browned, about 5 minutes.

2. Add cabbage to pan and turn to coat well with oil. Add rendered pancetta, salt and pepper to taste, and vinegar. Top with remaining butter, cut in small pieces. Cover and cook over moderately low heat until cabbage is almost "melted," about 1 hour. Taste and add more salt or pepper if needed. Garnish with parsley and serve immediately.

Serves 4.

CIME DI RAPE ALLA ROMANA
Roman-style broccoli raab

The flavorful broccoli raab (sometimes called *rape* or *broccoletti di rape*), loved and served all over Italy, can be found in this country as well. Its full flavor stands up to garlic and cheese and is an excellent foil for pork or tomato-sauce dishes. Substitute Swiss chard if it is unavailable.

    2   pounds broccoli raab
    ¼   cup olive oil
    ½   tablespoon minced garlic
        Coarse salt and freshly
        ground black pepper
    3   tablespoons lemon juice
    2   tablespoons grated Romano
        cheese

1. Wash broccoli raab and trim away any woody stems. Bring a large pot of salted water to a boil. Blanch broccoli raab 2 minutes. Drain and refresh in a bowl of ice water. Drain again and gently towel-dry.

2. Heat olive oil in a large skillet over moderate heat. Add garlic and sauté, stirring constantly, 1 minute. Add broccoli and cook, turning often with tongs, until greens are coated with oil, hot throughout, and tender, about 2 minutes. Season to taste with salt and pepper; add lemon juice. Transfer to a warm serving platter. Dust with cheese and serve at once.

Serves 4.

MELANZANE ALLA PARMIGIANA
Eggplant Parma style

An elegant eggplant Parmigiana is definitely not a contradiction in terms. When the eggplant is fried without breading and layered with a lively sauce, prosciutto, and peppers, the result is a vibrant dish that's appropriate for company meals. It's equally tasty at room temperature and is thus well suited to buffets. For a more formal, dinner-party presentation, bake the dish in individual ramekins. Note that the eggplant must stand 2 hours.

110

2 large eggplants (about 1 to
    1¼ lb each)
    Coarse salt

1 cup light olive oil

6 ounces prosciutto, sliced
    paper-thin

1 large red onion, sliced
    paper-thin

1 recipe Roasted Red Peppers
    (see page 14)

⅓ cup freshly grated Parmesan
    plus ¼ cup for garnish

1 teaspoon freshly ground
    black pepper

1½ cups Sugo di Pomodoro
    (see page 36)

3 tablespoons minced parsley,
    for garnish

1. Wash and dry eggplants; slice into rounds about ½ inch thick. Place rounds on baking sheets lined with paper towels. Sprinkle with salt and let stand 2 hours to draw out the bitter juices. Pat dry.

2. Preheat oven to 350° F. Using ¼ cup olive oil at a time, fry eggplant slices on both sides in a large skillet over moderately high heat. Blot them lightly on paper towels and set aside.

3. Using an 11- by 13-inch baking pan, make layers as follows: eggplant slices, then prosciutto, then onion, then a few red pepper strips, then a light dusting of Parmesan and a sprinkling of pepper, then one third of the tomato sauce. Repeat two times, ending with tomato sauce. Bake 35 minutes, or until bubbling hot throughout. Dust top with additional Parmesan and parsley. Cool slightly before serving directly from the baking dish.

Serves 4 generously.

Make-Ahead Tip The dish can be assembled a day in advance, then covered and refrigerated. Bring to room temperature before baking.

Melanzane alla Parmigiana can be a fit-for-company dish when made with roasted red peppers and prosciutto. The eggplant is fried without breading to keep the flavors and textures light.

Succulent fruit, sweet chocolate, crunchy nuts, spicy cinnamon—Italians combine such ingredients in toothsome desserts to bring a meal to a close.

Desserts

Although the most common Italian
dessert is fruit, such as wine-
marinated peaches (see Pesche
al Vino, page 114), luscious cakes and other
sweets are not unknown. In this chapter
you'll find the familiar Zabaglione (see page
119) and Biscuit Tortoni (see page 120),
a fig tart (see Crostata di Frutta alla
Panna, page 118), rich Torta di Ricotta
(see page 114), and Italian ices (see
page 117). A special note on *caffè*
(see page 118) explains the many forms
in which Italians drink this beverage,
and the chapter concludes with a
magnificent dessert buffet (see page 120).

DESSERTS

Except on holidays and other special occasions, Italian meals rarely end with a rich dessert. Fresh fruit, fruit and cheese, or desserts based on fruit—like Pesche al Vino (at right) or Fichi al Forno (see page 118)— are far more common than elaborate pastries or cakes. Ice cream (*gelato*) is a popular midafternoon pick-me-up, usually purchased by the cup from a street vendor. Cakes such as Torta di Ricotta (at right) or Torta del Re (see page 119) might be offered in the late afternoon with a glass of sweet wine.

TORTA DI POLENTA
Polenta pound cake

Use this golden loaf cake as the basis of a delectable strawberry shortcake: Slice it and toast it, then top it with berries and cream. Sugar the berries an hour or so before serving to draw out their juices. The use of polenta marks this as a northern Italian dish.

> 6 ounces unsalted butter, softened
> ⅔ cup sugar
> 2 eggs
> 1½ cups flour
> ½ cup semolina
> ⅔ cup polenta
> 2 teaspoons baking powder
> 1 teaspoon baking soda
> ½ teaspoon salt
> 1 cup buttermilk
> Sugar, for dusting pan
> Fresh raspberries, sliced strawberries, or sliced figs
> Lightly whipped and sweetened cream

1. Preheat oven to 375° F. In a large mixing bowl, cream butter until light. Add sugar gradually and beat until light and fluffy. Beat in eggs one at a time and mix thoroughly.

2. Sift together flour, semolina, polenta, baking powder, baking soda, and salt. Add to creamed mixture in three parts, alternating with buttermilk. Beat just to blend.

3. Butter a 9-inch loaf pan; sprinkle bottom and sides with sugar, shaking out excess. Pour in batter and bake until a tester inserted in the center comes out clean, about 1 hour. Cool completely on a rack before serving. Slice and serve with fruit and whipped cream.

Makes one 9-inch loaf.

PESCHE AL VINO
Peaches in Chianti

In Tuscany the local red wine is used to marinate thick-sliced peaches, producing a simple and supremely refreshing summer dessert. Choose a young and inexpensive Chianti and peaches that are fragrant but not overly soft.

> 8 medium to large freestone peaches, ripe but firm
> 2 tablespoons lemon juice
> 3 tablespoons sugar
> 1 bottle (750 ml) Chianti Biscotti per il Vino (see page 92)

Peel peaches and cut into eighths. Place in a stainless steel, glass, or ceramic bowl. Add lemon and sugar and mix gently but well. Let stand 5 minutes. Pour wine over peaches and cover. Refrigerate 8 hours or overnight. To serve arrange peach segments in wine glasses or wide-mouthed dessert glasses and spoon a little wine into each glass. Serve with *biscotti*.

Serves 8.

TORTA DI RICOTTA
Ricotta cheesecake

Cheesecakes in southern Italy are made with ricotta, raisins, and pine nuts and are commonly flecked with chocolate and flavored with rum. The version below incorporates crunchy pine-nut brittle, a delicious candy to savor on its own. Offer this rich *torta* in the afternoon with a glass of Marsala, or serve it as the luscious finish to a light meal.

> 1 cup superfine sugar
> 3 tablespoons water
> 5 tablespoons pine nuts
> 4 tablespoons golden raisins
> 2 tablespoons rum
> 3¼ cups flour
> 1 tablespoon baking powder
> ½ cup dark brown sugar
> 1¼ cups ground almonds
> 8 ounces chilled, unsalted butter, in small pieces
> 1 egg
> 1 teaspoon vanilla extract
> 1½ pounds whole-milk ricotta
> 1 teaspoon grated lemon rind
> 2 ounces milk chocolate, coarsely chopped

1. In a 1-quart saucepan, heat ¼ cup of the superfine sugar and the water over high heat. When mixture boils and sugar dissolves, add pine nuts. Continue cooking, swirling pan often, until sugar turns a light brown. Turn out mixture onto an oiled baking sheet and let cool. Break up into small chunks.

2. Combine raisins and rum in a small bowl and set aside for 1 hour.

3. *To make dough in a food processor:* Combine flour, baking powder, brown sugar, and almonds in workbowl of food processor. Process 5 seconds. Add butter and process until mixture resembles coarse meal, about 10 seconds. Whisk egg and vanilla together, then add to food processor with motor running. Process just until dough nearly holds

together. Turn out dough onto a board and gather into a ball; do not knead or work the dough, even if it doesn't hold together well. Wrap in plastic and refrigerate at least 1 hour. *To make dough by hand:* Stir together flour, baking powder, brown sugar, and almonds. Cut in butter with two knives or a pastry blender until mixture resembles coarse meal. Whisk egg and vanilla together, then add to flour mixture. Toss lightly with a fork, just until dough holds together. Gather into a ball; do not knead or work the dough, even if it doesn't hold together well. Wrap in plastic and refrigerate at least 1 hour.

4. In a large bowl, combine ricotta, the remaining superfine sugar, lemon rind, raisins, and rum. Add chocolate pieces and pine-nut brittle; mix well.

5. Preheat oven to 350° F. Line bottom and sides of a 10-inch spring-form baking pan with foil. Place a little more than half of the dough on the bottom of the pan, patting it into place and pushing it partway up the sides. Spoon in ricotta filling; roll out remaining pastry into a 10-inch round and lay it over the top of the filling. Bake 50 to 55 minutes; top will color slightly.

6. Transfer cheesecake to a rack and cool in the pan. Release sides of springform pan and gently peel back the foil from the sides. Lift the bottom of the cake gently with a spatula and pull out the foil. Serve barely warm or at room temperature.

Makes one 10-inch cheesecake.

Make-Ahead Tip Pastry dough may be made a day ahead and refrigerated.

Torta di Ricotta is cheesecake made the southern Italian way, with a ricotta filling encased in pastry. Raisins, pine nuts, almonds, and a hint of chocolate enrich the filling.

Make creamy Gelato d'Albicocca with dried apricots and apricot brandy for a winter reminder of a favorite summer fruit. Cookies and espresso partner it well.

GELATO DI CAFFÈ
Espresso ice cream

The dark-roasted beans that make such strong, rich coffee are often used to flavor ice cream, too. In fact, Gelato di Caffè is a favorite of all Italians who like ice cream—which is to say, it's a favorite of all Italians.

- ¼ cup very finely ground (espresso grind) espresso coffee beans
- 1 cup half-and-half
- ½ cup milk
- 1½ cups whipping cream (preferably not ultrapasteurized)
- 5 egg yolks
- 1 cup sugar
  Cocoa powder or ground cinnamon, for garnish (optional)
- 8 chocolate-coated espresso beans, for garnish (optional)

1. Put ground coffee in paper-lined coffee filter as if making drip coffee. Set filter over a bowl. Combine half-and-half and milk in a small saucepan and scald. Pour milk mixture over coffee grounds and let drip; it may take up to 15 minutes to drip through. Pour filtered milk-coffee mixture back into saucepan, add whipping cream, and set pan over low heat.

2. Combine egg yolks and sugar in a bowl and whisk until they form a "ribbon" when the whisk is lifted. Add warm cream to egg yolks in a steady stream and whisk to blend. Pour mixture back into saucepan and set over low heat. Cook, stirring constantly with a wooden spoon, until mixture thickens slightly and coats the spoon. Do not allow to boil. Remove from heat and let cool to room temperature.

3. Transfer mixture to an ice cream freezer and freeze according to manufacturer's directions. Serve as is or with a dust with sifted cocoa powder or cinnamon. If desired, garnish each serving with a chocolate-coated espresso bean.

Serves 8.

GELATO D'ALBICOCCA
Apricot ice cream

This creamy dessert from Rome is extremely rich and should be proffered in small portions. A dainty demitasse makes an elegant serving dish. Note that the mixture needs to chill for a day before freezing.

- 8 egg yolks
- 1 tablespoon sugar
  Grated rind of 1 lemon
- 2¼ cups whipping cream
- ¼ teaspoon almond extract
- 1½ teaspoons ground cinnamon
- 1¾ cups minced dried apricots
- ¼ cup apricot brandy
- ½ cup water
- 8 ounces thick apricot preserves
- 1 tablespoon lemon juice

1. Combine egg yolks and sugar in top of double boiler. Set over, but not in, simmering water and whisk well. Add lemon rind and cream, then cook, whisking constantly, until mixture is slightly thickened and has reached 180° F. Remove from heat. Add almond extract and cinnamon.

2. Combine apricots, brandy, and water in a small saucepan. Bring to a boil over high heat and boil until no liquid remains and apricots are very soft. Add apricots to cream mixture.

3. Combine preserves and lemon juice in a small saucepan. Cook, stirring, over moderately low heat until preserves become thin and runny. Remove from heat, cool slightly, and add to cream mixture. Cool to room temperature, then cover and refrigerate 24 hours. Transfer mixture to an ice cream freezer and freeze according to manufacturer's directions. Store ice cream in freezer for at least 1 hour before serving.

Makes about 6 cups, 12 to 14 small servings.

Make-Ahead Tip The ice cream keeps up to 1 week.

TORTA DI RISO
Italian rice cake

The stubby, short-grain, Arborio rice that makes the creamy *risotti* of Piedmont (see page 61) is also turned into sweet rice puddings. Enriched with dried fruits and nuts and enlivened with citrus peel, a warm Torta di Riso is a winter dessert best accompanied by Asti Spumante.

- ½ cup hazelnut- or almond-flavored liqueur
- 4¼ cups water
- ½ cup each *golden raisins, dried currants, minced dried figs, and Italian Arborio rice*
- 4 cups milk
  Grated rind of 1 lemon
  Grated rind of ½ orange
- ¾ cup sugar plus sugar for dusting pan
- 6 eggs
- ¾ cup chopped almonds
- 1 teaspoon almond extract
  Butter, for greasing pan

1. Combine liqueur, ¼ cup of the water, raisins, currants, and figs in a small saucepan. Bring to a simmer over medium heat and let simmer 5 minutes. Set aside until all liquid is absorbed (this may take a few hours).

2. In a medium saucepan over high heat, bring the remaining water to a boil. Add rice and cook 3 minutes. Drain, then return rice to a clean saucepan with milk, lemon rind, and orange rind. Bring to a simmer over moderately high heat, then reduce heat to low, cover, and cook 1 hour. Remove from heat, cool, and add sugar. Add eggs one at a time, blending well, then stir in nuts, almond extract, and fruit mixture.

3. Preheat oven to 325° F. Butter bottom and sides of a 9-inch round cake pan, then coat with sugar, shaking out excess. Pour batter into prepared pan. Bake until a knife inserted in center comes out clean, about 1 hour. Remove cake to a rack; cool in pan. To serve, turn cake out of pan and cut into wedges. Serve warm, at room temperature, or cold.

Serves 8.

COFFEE, ITALIAN STYLE

The bittersweet flavor of strong Italian coffee is an acquired taste for many Americans. For most Italians, however, it is a pleasure indulged in daily, sometimes several times a day.

Inky-dark espresso, served in small cups, is always offered at the end of a restaurant meal. Espresso is made by forcing water under considerable pressure through dark-roasted, tightly packed coffee grounds. The resulting brew is bitter and rich, a welcome jolt that prepares one for the rest of the day's or evening's activities. Some hardy souls request a *doppio* (double) or an added splash of grappa or anisette.

Few Italian homes are equipped with the powerful steam-generating machines required to make a true espresso. At home, the after-dinner coffee is usually made in a *napole-tana*, a three-part coffeepot that sits on the stove burner. Water goes into the bottom part, and coffee into a basket in the middle. The top part, which has a spout, is screwed on spout side down. When the water in the bottom begins to steam, the whole contraption is turned upside down to allow the hot water to drip through. The coffee is dark, rich, and less bitter than a steam-made espresso.

Coffee is not reserved for the end of a meal, however. Most Italians begin their morning with a cup of coffee, too. And in the middle of the afternoon, when a pause or a pick-me-up is desired, Italians gather in caffès for coffee, conversation, and a little something sweet.

Although everyone drinks espresso after meals, in the morning and mid-afternoon many Italians prefer a gentler brew. *Caffè latte*—one part espresso to three parts steamed milk—is a particularly soothing morning beverage. Cappuccino—one part espresso to two parts steamed milk, the top sometimes dusted with chocolate—makes a delicious and satisfying afternoon treat.

CROSTATA DI FRUTTA ALLA PANNA
Fruit tart with cream

This Tuscan tart is easy to make and as humble as an apple dumpling. Dried fruits are stewed with Marsala and grappa, then puréed, spread in a tart shell, and topped with soft Crème Fraîche. Wedges of ripe fresh figs make a handsome garnish. For best results, fill and garnish tart shell just before serving.

    1 cup flour
       Pinch of salt
    5 tablespoons chilled, unsalted
       butter
    3 tablespoons ice water
    6 ounces dried figs, stems
       removed
    2 ounces dried apricots
    2 tablespoons Marsala
    1 tablespoon grappa or brandy
    1 tablespoon honey
    2 tablespoons water
    ¼ cup Crème Fraîche
       (see page 123)
    2 large fresh figs, for garnish

1. Stir together flour and salt. Cut in butter until mixture resembles coarse crumbs. Add ice water and toss with a fork until mixture begins to come together. Quickly form it into a smooth ball, wrap in waxed paper, and chill 15 minutes.

2. In a saucepan combine figs, apricots, Marsala, grappa, honey, and 2 tablespoons water. Bring to a boil, reduce heat to maintain a simmer, and cook 15 minutes to soften the fruit. Set aside to cool.

3. Preheat oven to 375° F. Roll out dough on a lightly floured surface to a round ⅛ inch thick. Transfer to a 10-inch tart pan and press dough onto the bottom and sides. Trim away any excess. Prick well all over with

a fork. Cover surface with foil and weight with rice or beans. Bake 10 minutes, then remove foil and rice and bake until golden and crisp, another 12 to 15 minutes. Cool tart shell on a rack.

4. Put cooled fruit mixture into food processor or blender and blend until smooth. Lightly whip the Crème Fraîche. Put puréed fruit mixture in cooled tart shell. Spread a thin layer of Crème Fraîche over the purée. Cut fresh figs into thin wedges and arrange attractively atop the tart.

Makes one 10-inch tart.

FICHI AL FORNO
Roasted figs

Ripe, fresh figs baked with butter, lemon, and honey are one of the easiest and most delectable of summer desserts. They are a specialty of Agropoli, an ancient Greek settlement on Italy's Amalfi coast. Serve with a pitcher of heavy cream or a small scoop of vanilla ice cream.

     3 tablespoons butter
     2 tablespoons honey
     8 fresh figs, halved through
        the stem end
     4 tablespoons bitter lemon
        marmalade
     1 tablespoon brown sugar
     1 teaspoon ground cinnamon
    16 perfect walnut halves
     2 tablespoons grated lemon
        rind, for garnish

1. Preheat oven to 350° F. Coat bottom of a 13- by 9-inch glass baking dish with 1 tablespoon of the butter. Pour in honey and spread it over the bottom of the dish with a spatula. Place dish in oven to melt the honey, about 10 minutes.

2. Add figs to baking dish, skin side down. Dot with the remaining butter and top each half with a dollop of marmalade. Combine brown sugar and cinnamon and sprinkle over figs. Top each with a walnut half. Bake until figs are hot and honey begins to caramelize, about 12 minutes. Serve warm, garnished with lemon rind.

Serves 8.

TORTA DEL RE
King's cake

Serve this sweet with small cups of steaming espresso. For a more elaborate dessert, add seasonal fruit and a bowl of fresh ricotta. Torta del Re comes from Friuli, a region in northern Italy adjacent to Yugoslavia.

- 1 cup unsalted butter, at room temperature
- ⅔ cup honey
- 2 eggs
- 1 cup flour
- ½ cup coarsely chopped dried figs
- ½ cup toasted pine nuts

Preheat oven to 325° F. In a large mixing bowl, cream butter. Add honey and beat until light. Beat in eggs one at a time, mixing well. Add flour gradually, beating until smooth. Stir in figs and nuts. Place dough in a 9-inch square baking dish and bake until tester inserted in center comes out clean, about 40 minutes. Cool on a rack; serve warm or at room temperature, in small squares.

Makes one 9-inch square cake.

ZABAGLIONE
Italian wine custard

The strong arm of a professional chef can whip eggs and wine to an airy foam in less than a minute. The confident home cook can do the same, but less experienced whisk-wielders may want to use electric beaters. Serve the frothy warm custard with crunchy Biscotti per il Vino (see page 92) for textural contrast, or spoon it over sliced strawberries. Although Zabaglione is made only with the Marsala wine of Sicily, it is enjoyed all over Italy.

- 4 egg yolks
- 3 tablespoons superfine sugar
- ½ cup Marsala

In the bottom of a double boiler over high heat, bring water to a boil. Reduce heat to maintain a bare simmer. Put egg yolks and sugar in top of double boiler and set over, but not in, simmering water. Whisk by hand or with electric beaters until mixture thickens slightly and begins to turn pale. Add Marsala and continue whisking until mixture doubles in volume and is very smooth and fluffy. Serve immediately.

Serves 5 or 6.

Dried apricots and figs make a sweet, smooth filling for a winter Crostata di Frutta alla Panna. Top with silky Crème Fraîche and a dried fig cut in half.

119

A DESSERT BUFFET

Torta di Pere

Biscuit Tortoni

Budino di Mascarpone

Cassata Donna Lugata

Panini di Gelato

Gelato di Limone

For a bridal shower, an afternoon tea, or an end to an evening of theater, consider offering your guests an elaborate dessert buffet. Set the ice cream container in a wine bucket surrounded by ice and let guests serve themselves; all the other desserts can be arranged individually on trays. To give guests a chance to try everything, you might want to reduce portion sizes from those indicated in the recipes. The Cassata, for example, may be made in thirty-six 1½-inch miniature cupcake tins. Offer coffee, tea, and an Italian sweet wine or a chilled Asti Spumante.

TORTA DI PERE
Tuscan pear cake

This rustic country cake can be on the table within an hour and is best shortly after it's made. Bosc pears are recommended as they hold their shape when baked, but other pears or even apples could be substituted.

> 2 tablespoons butter
> ⅓ cup fine amaretti crumbs or stale cake or cookie crumbs
> 1 pound ripe Bosc pears
> ⅓ cup dark rum
> 4 eggs
> 1½ cups granulated sugar
> 3 cups flour
> 2 teaspoons baking powder
> ½ teaspoon salt
> ¼ cup confectioners' sugar

1. Preheat oven to 350° F. Grease an 8-inch springform pan with butter; dust all over with *amaretti* crumbs.

2. Quarter unpeeled pears; core them and cut them into slices ⅛ inch thick. Put slices in a ceramic, glass, or stainless steel bowl and add rum. Toss gently to blend and set aside for a few minutes.

3. Beat eggs and granulated sugar in an electric mixer on high speed until light and fluffy. Sift together flour, baking powder, and salt. Fold flour mixture into egg mixture by hand. Place half the pear slices on the bottom of the prepared pan; cover with batter and arrange the remaining pear slices on top. Bake 20 minutes; quickly dust top with confectioners' sugar and return to oven until cake is well browned and a tester inserted in the center comes out clean, about another 20 minutes. Serve warm.

Serves 4 to 6.

BISCUIT TORTONI
Frozen almond cream

The original Biscuit Tortoni debuted in 1798, the creation of a Neapolitan (Signor Tortoni) who owned a Parisian ice cream shop. The clever Tortoni used crushed *amaretti* (almond macaroons) to flavor a frozen cream. It delighted Parisians and even today is probably better known outside than within Italy. Restaurants and dinner-party hosts love it because it's elegant and easy, and because it must be made ahead. Use the commercially available amaretti to make crumbs.

> ¾ cup half-and-half
> ¾ cup medium-fine amaretti crumbs
> 2 tablespoons confectioners' sugar
> Grated rind of 1 orange
> 3 tablespoons golden raisins
> Pinch of salt
> ½ cup whipping cream
> ½ cup Crème Fraîche (see page 123)
> ½ teaspoon almond extract
> ¼ cup slivered blanched almonds, for garnish
> Fresh mint leaves, for garnish

1. In a large bowl, combine half-and-half, amaretti crumbs, sugar, orange rind, raisins, and salt. Let stand at room temperature 1 hour.

2. In a large bowl, whip cream lightly to soft peaks; fold in Crème Fraîche and almond extract, then fold in amaretti mixture. Divide mixture among four goblets or ramekins and freeze for 3 to 4 hours.

3. Preheat oven to 350° F. Toast almonds until lightly browned and fragrant. Just before serving, garnish each Biscuit Tortoni with hot toasted almonds and a mint leaf.

Serves 4.

A sampling of Italy's sweet
specialties (top to bottom): Biscuit
Tortoni, Budino di Mascarpone,
Panini di Gelato, Torta di Pere,
and Cassata Donna Lugata.

BUDINO DI MASCARPONE
Mascarpone pudding

Cream cheese will work in this souf-fléed pudding, but look hard for *mascarpone* (see page 20); it has a buttery, nutty richness that cream cheese doesn't match. Serve this northern Italian dessert with espresso or sweet wine and offer a plate of Dolci di Polenta (see page 72) or some far-from-Italian ginger snaps.

- 2 tablespoons unsalted butter, melted
  Sugar, for dusting
- 2 tablespoons dried currants
- 2 tablespoons golden raisins
- 2 moist dried figs, coarsely chopped
- 3 tablespoons light rum
- 1 cup whole-milk ricotta, well drained
- 5 ounces mascarpone or natural cream cheese
- 4 eggs, separated
- ¼ cup flour
- ½ cup sugar
- 1 teaspoon cinnamon
  Pinch of nutmeg
- ½ teaspoon salt
- 3 tablespoons dark rum

1. Brush melted butter on bottom and sides of a 2-quart soufflé dish or four 1½-cup individual soufflé dishes. Dust bottom and sides with sugar, shaking out excess. Set aside.

2. Preheat oven to 350° F. In a small bowl, combine currants, raisins, figs, and light rum. Stir to blend and set aside to marinate for at least 15 minutes.

3. In a large bowl, combine ricotta and mascarpone. Beat well; add egg yolks one at a time, beating well after each addition. Sift together flour, sugar, cinnamon, nutmeg, and salt. Add to cheese mixture and beat well. Fold in marinated fruit mixture.

4. Beat egg whites until stiff but not dry and gently fold into cheese mixture. Transfer mixture to soufflé dish(es); bake until nicely risen and firm to the touch, but not stiff. A 2-quart soufflé takes about 30 minutes; smaller soufflés cook faster. Quickly and gently brush the tops with dark rum. Serve hot or at room temperature. Pudding will deflate slightly as it cools.

Serves 4.

CASSATA DONNA LUGATA
Individual Sicilian cheesecakes

Lemon, cinnamon, and sweet Marsala flavor these miniature cheesecakes, with a drizzle of dark chocolate on top. Dress them up with paper-lined silver foil muffin cups.

- 1½ pounds whole-milk ricotta or baker's cheese
- 8 ounces natural cream cheese
- ½ cup sugar
- 2 eggs
- 1 teaspoon grated lemon rind
- 1 teaspoon ground cinnamon
  Pinch of nutmeg
- 2 tablespoons Marsala
- 4½ ounces extra-bittersweet chocolate, melted and cooled slightly

Sweet Dough

- 1¾ cups flour
- ½ cup sugar
- ¾ teaspoon baking powder
  Pinch of salt
- 6 tablespoons chilled unsalted butter
- 1 egg, lightly beaten
- 1 teaspoon vanilla extract

1. Preheat oven to 400° F. In a mixer or food processor, combine ricotta, cream cheese, sugar, and eggs. Beat well or process until well blended. Add lemon rind, cinnamon, nutmeg, and Marsala and beat or process until combined. Refrigerate mixture while making Sweet Dough.

2. Form Sweet Dough into a ball, then divide ball in half. Divide each half into 9 pieces, then roll each piece on a lightly floured surface into a 3-inch round. Line 18 muffin tins with paper cups, then press a dough round into each cup, pressing dough about a quarter of the way up the sides. Spoon chilled filling into dough cups.

3. Drizzle ½ tablespoon of melted chocolate over each cupcake and bake until well-browned and slightly puffed, about 20 minutes. Cool cakes on a rack and serve from their paper holders, either at room temperature or chilled.

Makes 18 little cakes.

Sweet Dough Sift together flour, sugar, baking powder, and salt. Cut in butter until mixture resembles coarse crumbs. Combine egg and vanilla, then add to dry mixture and toss with a fork until dough begins to hold together.

PANINI DI GELATO
Ice cream sandwiches

You may never find this creation in Italy, although its basic parts are Italian. California chef David Beckwith provided the original inspiration; fine cook Derna Passalacqua supplied the *pizzelle* recipe. Everything but the final assembly of this whimsical sandwich can be done ahead of time. Pizzelle irons are available in specialty cookware stores and gourmet shops, or by mail order. Note that the Crème Fraîche must sit for 1 or 2 days.

Gelato di Limone (at right)

Pizzelle

4 eggs
1 cup sugar
1 cup vegetable oil
2 cups plus 2 tablespoons flour
1¼ teaspoons baking powder
½ teaspoon salt
1 teaspoon anise-flavored apéritif
1 teaspoon grated lemon rind
1 teaspoon lemon juice

Strawberry Sauce

2 pints fresh strawberries
Juice of ½ lemon
1 tablespoon orange-flavored liqueur
2 tablespoons brown sugar

Crème Fraîche

1 cup whipping cream, preferably not ultrapasteurized
1 tablespoon buttermilk

Cut a Pizzelle in half. Place one half on the bottom of a large dinner plate. Place two small scoops Gelato di Limone on top. Top with other Pizzelle half. Put a dollop of Crème Fraîche on top and a little Strawberry Sauce on the side.

Makes about 1 dozen sandwiches.

Pizzelle Put eggs and sugar in a large bowl and whisk until light. Add oil and whisk well. Sift together flour, baking powder, and salt. Add to egg mixture with liqueur, lemon rind, and lemon juice. Beat just until blended. Bake in a pizzelle iron according to manufacturer's directions. Extra portions may be cooled and frozen.

Makes about 3 dozen small pizzelle.

Strawberry Sauce Wash, dry, and hull the berries, reserving eight of the largest ones. Put the rest in a processor or blender along with lemon juice, liqueur, and sugar. Process or blend until smooth. Strain through a fine sieve. Cut the reserved berries in thick slices and stir them into the sauce. Chill sauce until ready to serve.

Makes about 2 cups.

Crème Fraîche Combine cream and buttermilk in a clean glass jar with a lid; shake well. Set aside at room temperature until thickened, 24 to 48 hours. (Crème Fraîche will keep, refrigerated, for up to 1 week.)

Makes about 1 cup.

GELATO DI LIMONE
Lemon ice cream

Most Italians buy their ice cream from street vendors, but it is easily made at home with an ice cream freezer. With diced fresh lemon and orange liqueur, this homemade version far outshines commercial products.

1 small lemon
1 tablespoon honey
1 tablespoon orange-flavored liqueur
⅓ cup sugar
¾ cup half-and-half
1 vanilla bean
  Pinch salt
3 egg yolks
½ cup whipping cream
½ cup Crème Fraîche (at left)

1. Grate rind from lemon and reserve. Using a small sharp knife, remove all the remaining white pith. Section lemon and cut flesh into ¼-inch dice. In a small bowl combine honey and liqueur. Add diced lemon and let marinate 2 hours at room temperature.

2. Put lemon rind and sugar in a food processor or blender and process or blend until sugar almost begins to melt. Set aside. Put half-and-half in a medium saucepan. Cut vanilla bean in half crosswise, then split one piece in half lengthwise. Scrape seeds from the two split quarters into the half-and-half, then add the split quarter-pods to the half-and-half as well. Save remaining vanilla-bean piece for another use. Bring half-and-half to a simmer over moderate heat, then add sugar-lemon mixture and salt. Whisk well to combine and remove from heat.

3. Whisk yolks in a small bowl; add ½ cup of the hot half-and-half mixture, whisk well, and mix back into the rest of the half-and-half. Return saucepan to low heat and cook, stirring constantly, until mixture reaches 175° F. Do not allow to boil. Remove from heat and strain mixture through a sieve into a stainless steel bowl. Cool; then stir in cream and Crème Fraîche. Chill mixture 2 hours, then stir in marinated diced lemon and freeze in an ice cream machine according to manufacturer's directions. Do not serve ice cream directly from the freezer; let it soften 5 minutes in the refrigerator before serving.

Makes 3 cups, serves 6.

INDEX

*Note: Page numbers in italics refer to
photos separated from recipe text.*

126

U.S. MEASURE AND METRIC MEASURE CONVERSION CHART

Formulas for Exact Measures

Rounded Measures for Quick Reference

	Symbol	When you know:	Multiply by:	To find:			
Mass (Weight)	oz	ounces	28.35	grams	1 oz		= 30 g
	lb	pounds	0.45	kilograms	4 oz		= 115 g
	g	grams	0.035	ounces	8 oz		= 225 g
	kg	kilograms	2.2	pounds	16 oz	= 1 lb	= 450 g
					32 oz	= 2 lb	= 900 g
					36 oz	= 2¼ lb	= 1,000 g (1 kg)
Volume	tsp	teaspoons	5.0	milliliters	¼ tsp	= ⅟₂₄ oz	= 1 ml
	tbsp	tablespoons	15.0	milliliters	½ tsp	= ⅟₁₂ oz	= 2 ml
	fl oz	fluid ounces	29.57	milliliters	1 tsp	= ⅙ oz	= 5 ml
	c	cups	0.24	liters	1 tbsp	= ½ oz	= 15 ml
	pt	pints	0.47	liters	1 c	= 8 oz	= 250 ml
	qt	quarts	0.95	liters	2 c (1 pt)	= 16 oz	= 500 ml
	gal	gallons	3.785	liters	4 c (1 qt)	= 32 oz	= 1 liter
	ml	milliliters	0.034	fluid ounces	4 qt (1 gal)	= 128 oz	= 3¾ liters
Temperature	°F	Fahrenheit	5/9 (after subtracting 32)	Celsius	32° F		= 0° C
					68° F		= 20° C
	°C	Celsius	9/5 (then add 32)	Fahrenheit	212° F		= 100° C

PATHWAYS

SECOND EDITION

Listening, Speaking, and Critical Thinking

PAUL MACINTYRE

NATIONAL GEOGRAPHIC
L E A R N I N G

Australia • Brazil • Mexico • Singapore • United Kingdom • United States

Pathways 4: Listening, Speaking, and Critical Thinking, 2nd Edition

Paul MacIntyre

Publisher: Sherrise Roehr

Executive Editor: Laura Le Dréan

Managing Editor: Jennifer Monaghan

Associate Development Editor: Lisl Bove

Director of Global and U.S. Marketing: Ian Martin

Product Marketing Manager: Tracy Bailie

Media Research: Leila Hishmeh

Senior Director, Production: Michael Burggren

Manager, Production: Daisy Sosa

Content Project Manager: Mark Rzeszutek

Senior Digital Product Manager: Scott Rule

Manufacturing Planner: Mary Beth Hennebury

Interior and Cover Design: Brenda Carmichael

Art Director: Brenda Carmichael

Composition: MPS North America LLC

© 2018 National Geographic Learning, a Cengage Learning Company

ALL RIGHTS RESERVED. No part of this work covered by the copyright herein may be reproduced or distributed in any form or by any means, except as permitted by U.S. copyright law, without the prior written permission of the copyright owner.

"National Geographic", "National Geographic Society" and the Yellow Border Design are registered trademarks of the National Geographic Society ® Marcas Registradas

For product information and technology assistance, contact us at
Cengage Learning Customer & Sales Support, cengage.com/contact
For permission to use material from this text or product,
submit all requests online at **cengage.com/permissions**
Further permissions questions can be emailed to
permissionrequest@cengage.com

Student Edition: 978-1-337-40774-8
SE + Online Workbook: 978-1-337-56254-6

National Geographic Learning
20 Channel Center Street
Boston, MA 02210
USA

National Geographic Learning, a Cengage Learning Company, has a mission to bring the world to the classroom and the classroom to life. With our English language programs, students learn about their world by experiencing it. Through our partnerships with National Geographic and TED Talks, they develop the language and skills they need to be successful global citizens and leaders.

Locate your local office at **international.cengage.com/region**

Visit National Geographic Learning online at **NGL.Cengage.com/ELT**
Visit our corporate website at **www.cengage.com**

Printed in China
Print Number: 06   Print Year: 2021

Contents

Scope and Sequence

Speaking & Presentation	Vocabulary	Grammar & Pronunciation	Critical Thinking
• Signaling Additional Aspects of a Topic • Presenting in Pairs **Lesson Task** Evaluating the Impact of Tourism **Final Task** Presenting a Problem and Solutions	Word Families: Suffixes	• Passive Voice • Linking with Word-Final *t*	**Focus:** Predicting Analyzing Visuals, Applying, Evaluating, Making Inferences, Organizing Ideas, Reflecting
• Responding to an Argument **Lesson Task** Discussing Environmental Impact **Final Task** A Debate on Wild Animals in Zoos	Two-Part Verbs with *Out*	• Essential Adjective Clauses • Saying and Linking *–s* Endings	**Focus:** Evaluating Arguments in a Debate Analyzing, Analyzing a Chart, Applying, Evaluating, Making Inferences, Predicting, Reflecting
• Paraphrasing • Preparing Visuals for Display **Lesson Task** Conducting a Survey **Final Task** A Presentation about Fashion Trends	Suffix *-ive*	• Tag Questions • Intonation for Clarification	**Focus:** Interpreting a Bar Graph Analyzing, Applying, Evaluating, Interpreting, Organizing Ideas, Predicting, Reflecting
• Defining Terms • Managing Nervousness **Lesson Task** Role-Playing a Job Interview **Final Task** Evaluating a Social Media Platform	Using Collocations	• Gerund Phrases • Saying Parentheticals	**Focus:** Evaluating Analyzing, Applying, Interpreting a Graph, Interpreting a Map, Interpreting Visuals, Organizing Ideas, Ranking, Reflecting
• Approximating • Handling Audience Questions **Lesson Task** Discussing Family Origins **Final Task** A Pair Presentation on Animal Migration	Suffixes *–ant* and *–ist*	• Modals of Past Possibility • Linking with *You* or *Your*	**Focus:** Distinguishing Fact from Theory Applying, Evaluating, Interpreting a Map, Making Inferences, Organizing Ideas, Reflecting, Synthesizing

Scope and Sequence

 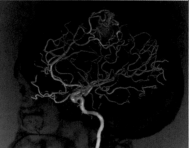

Introduction to *Pathways*

Pathways Listening, Speaking, and Critical Thinking, Second Edition

uses compelling National Geographic stories, photos, video, and infographics to bring the world to the classroom. Authentic, relevant content and carefully sequenced lessons engage learners while equipping them with the skills needed for academic success.

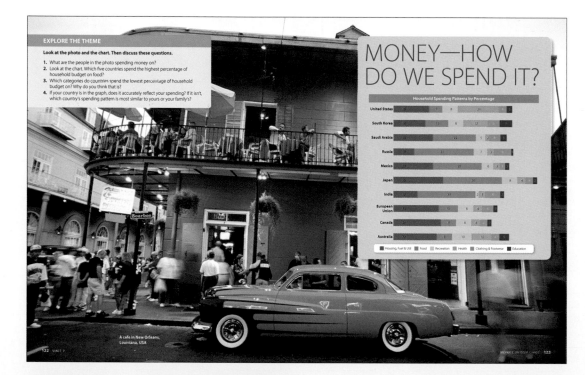

Explore the Theme provides a visual introduction to the unit, engaging learners academically and encouraging them to share ideas about the unit theme.

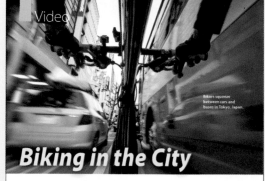

LISTENING FOR MAIN IDEAS **B** **2.7** Listen to a podcast about augmented reality (AR). Check (✓) the two main ideas the speakers discuss.

1. ☐ AR is a useful technology with many different applications.
2. ☐ AR's popularity has contributed to the widespread use of portable devices.
3. ☐ AR is useful when deciding which pieces of furniture to purchase.
4. ☐ AR facilitates the globalization of culture through popular games.
5. ☐ Pokémon Go's popularity has unquestionably benefited local economies.

NEW Integrated listening and speaking activities help **prepare students for standardized tests** such as IELTS and TOEFL.

UPDATED *Video* sections use relevant National Geographic **video clips** to give learners another perspective on the unit theme and further practice of listening and critical thinking skills.

Listening Skills

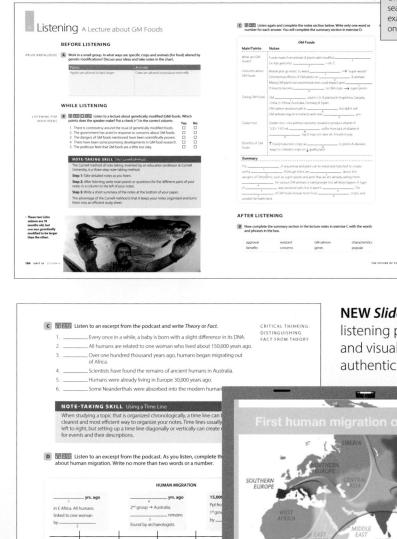

NEW *Vocabulary Skills* help students develop essential word building tools such as understanding collocations, word forms, and connotation.

Listening passages incorporate a variety of listening types such as podcasts, lectures, interviews, and conversations.

NEW *Slide shows* for selected listening passages integrate text and visuals to give learners a more authentic listening experience.

UPDATED Explicit listening and note-taking skill instruction and practice prepares students to listen and take notes in academic settings.

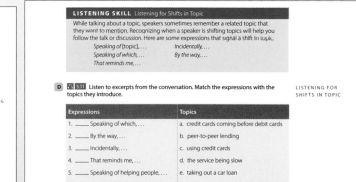

Speaking and Presentation Skills

Speaking lessons guide learners from controlled practice to a final speaking task while reinforcing speaking skills, grammar for speaking, and key pronunciation points.

Presentation skills such as starting strong, using specific details, making eye contact, pausing, and summarizing, help learners develop confidence and fluency in communicating ideas.

A **_Final Task_** allows learners to consolidate their understanding of content, language and skills as they collaborate on an academic presentation.

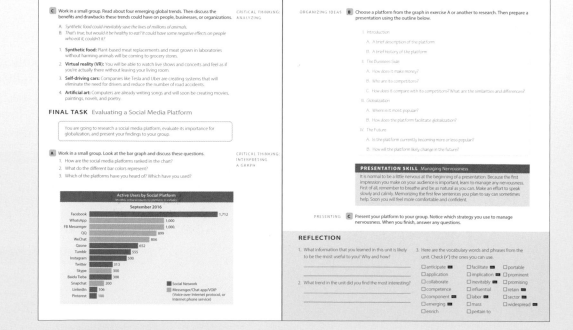

URBAN CHALLENGES 1

A worker in Washington, D.C., installs a triple-glazed window in a building designed to meet strict "green-building" standards.

ACADEMIC SKILLS

LISTENING	Understanding the Introduction to a Lecture
	Using Abbreviations
SPEAKING	Signaling Additional Aspects of a Topic
	Linking with Word-Final *t*
CRITICAL THINKING	Predicting

THINK AND DISCUSS

1 What challenge are green buildings intended to solve? In addition to windows, in what other ways can buildings be made "green"?

2 Would you move to a city that is dealing with challenges such as overcrowding? Explain.

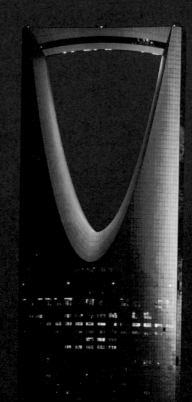

EXPLORE THE THEME

Look at the map and read the information. Then answer the questions.

1. In your own words, what is a *cosmopolitan hotspot? A tourism hotspot?*

2. Have you visited any of the hotspots on the map? If so, what were your impressions? If not, which would you like to visit?

3. What other cities not on the map do you think are cosmopolitan or tourism hotspots? Why?

4. What potential challenges could residents of cosmopolitan hotspots face? Of tourism hotspots?

Skyline of Riyadh, Saudi Arabia

WORLD CITIES: HOTSPOTS

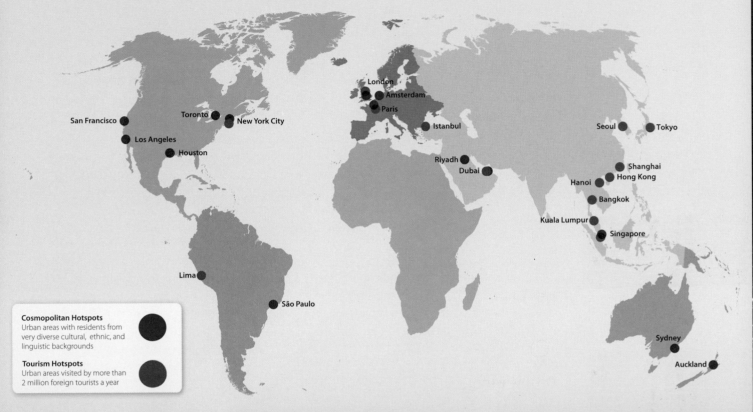

Cosmopolitan Hotspots
Urban areas with residents from very diverse cultural, ethnic, and linguistic backgrounds

Tourism Hotspots
Urban areas visited by more than 2 million foreign tourists a year

Map labels:
- San Francisco
- Los Angeles
- Houston
- Toronto
- New York City
- Lima
- São Paulo
- London
- Amsterdam
- Paris
- Istanbul
- Riyadh
- Dubai
- Seoul
- Tokyo
- Shanghai
- Hong Kong
- Hanoi
- Bangkok
- Kuala Lumpur
- Singapore
- Sydney
- Auckland

A Vocabulary

A 🎧 1.2 Read and listen to the information. Notice each word in **blue** and think about its meaning.

URBAN CHALLENGES

Today's urban areas face a variety of challenges. One challenge is a **scarcity** of land for housing. To address this problem, some residents of Tokyo, Japan, have found a unique solution: they are having homes constructed on pieces of land as small as 344 square feet (32 square meters). These "micro-homes" allow residents to live close to central Tokyo and are much more **affordable** than traditional homes in that area. Despite their size, many micro-homes have several floors and big windows that **maximize** sunlight.

Many urban areas also suffer from poor air quality due to pollution and smog.[1] What can these cities do to **regulate** the amount of chemicals from cars and factories? One **innovative** solution has been developed by an Italian company: smog-eating cement. The cement contains a substance that converts pollution into harmless chemicals that are then washed off roadways when it rains. The smog-eating material has also been effectively used in roof tiles in Los Angeles, California, where air-pollution control is **prioritized**.

Another urban challenge is finding creative ways to build public parks, gardens, and outdoor areas when space is limited. In 2002, the city of New York, for example, **authorized** a project to transform the High Line, an unused railroad line, into an elevated urban park. The **funds** necessary for this **renovation** project were provided through donations, and it was money well spent. The High Line has become one of the most inviting public spaces in the city. Visitors can **stroll** through the gardens, relax on the sundeck, or attend public art exhibits and special events.

---

[1]**smog** (n): a combination of smoke and fog that can damage the health of humans, plants, and animals

---

B Match each sentence beginning to its ending to complete the definitions of the words in **blue** from exercise A.

1. When there is a **scarcity** of something, _____
2. Something that is **affordable** _____
3. If you **maximize** something, _____
4. To **regulate** something means _____
5. An **innovative** idea is _____
6. If a project is **prioritized**, _____
7. If a project is **authorized**, _____
8. To provide **funds** to a project means _____
9. If a building is in need of **renovation**, _____
10. To **stroll** means _____

a. it requires repairs or improvements.
b. to walk slowly in a relaxed way.
c. there isn't enough of it.
d. it is given special importance.
e. it is given official approval.
f. you increase it as much as possible.
g. new and creative.
h. can be bought at a reasonable price.
i. to control it.
j. to give it money.

VOCABULARY SKILL Word Families: Suffixes

Knowing a word means learning its different forms, or its "family". Keep a log of different word forms. Here are examples of word families.

Noun	Verb	Adjective
creator/creation	*create*	*creative*
classification	*classify*	*classified*

Often the different forms of a word have different endings, or suffixes. Here are some common suffixes.

Noun	Verb	Adjective
-or/-er, -ity, -tion	*-ate, -ify, -ize*	*-d/-ed, -able, -ing, -ive*

C Complete the chart with the correct forms of each word. Use a dictionary to help you.

	Noun	Verb	Adjective
1.		afford	affordable
2.	authorization		
3.			innovative
4.	maximum		
5.	priority		
6.		regulate	
7.		renovate	

D Work with a partner. What other challenges do cities face? What are some solutions? Discuss your ideas. Then list them in a T-chart in your notebook.

◀ **People strolling through the High Line park in New York City, USA**

Listening A Lecture about Venice, Italy

BEFORE LISTENING

PREDICTING **A** Look at the photo. Can you guess how many tourists visit Venice each year? How do you think tourists help the city? How do they hurt it? Discuss your ideas with a partner.

WHILE LISTENING

> **LISTENING SKILL** Understanding the Introduction to a Lecture
>
> Lecture introductions often have two parts:
>
> - In the first part, the speaker provides background information about the topic or reviews what was covered in earlier lectures.
>
> - In the second part, the speaker announces the specific topic to be discussed and explains how the information will be presented.
>
> Understanding the structure of the introduction can improve your listening comprehension and help you organize your lecture notes.

B 🎧 **1.3** Listen to the lecture introduction. Then answer the questions.

① First Part
1. What topic did the lecturer previously speak about?
   a. how tourism has affected waterway repairs
   b. difficulties Venice faces related to flooding
   c. where Venice finds funds for large projects

② second part
2. Which *specific* topic is today's lecture going to be about?
   a. the problem of flooding
   b. the effects of the MOSE project
   c. the effects of tourism in Venice

Venice, Italy

Tourists enjoy a gondola ride in Venice.

C 🎧 1.4 ▶ 1.1 Listen to the entire lecture. Check (✓) the three main ideas.

increase in garbage collection.

1. ✓ the (impact) of tourism on (city services) *impact → result, effect*
2. ___ how (tourists) could change their behavior *change → alter behavior → attitude*
3. ___ the (causes) of increased tourism in Venice *causes → reasons, factors increased → rising*
4. ✓ the (effects) of tourism on residents of Venice *residents → local, citizens*
5. ___ the (drawbacks) of visiting Venice as a tourist *drawbacks → cons, disadvantages*
6. ✓ the (benefits) of tourism for Venice *benefits → advantages.*

2 Billion revenue, MOSE project, jobs related to tourism.

NOTE-TAKING SKILL Using Abbreviations

There is no right way to abbreviate words. The important thing is to remember what the abbreviation means when you review your notes. Good note takers create their own abbreviations and use them consistently. Here are some examples of abbreviations.

about/around	~	less/more than	</>	number	#	thousand	K
billion	B/bil	million	M/mil	positive	pos/+	with	w/
is/is called/ means	=	negative	neg/-	problem	prob	without	w/o

---

D 🎧 1.5 Listen to an excerpt from the lecture. Complete the notes with abbreviations from the skill box above.

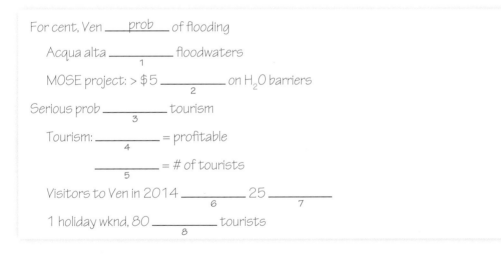

For cent, Ven ___prob___ of flooding

   Acqua alta _____1_____ floodwaters

   MOSE project: > $5 _____2_____ on H_2O barriers

Serious prob _____3_____ tourism

   Tourism: _____4_____ = profitable

   _____5_____ = # of tourists

Visitors to Ven in 2014 _____6_____ 25 _____7_____

1 holiday wknd, 80 _____8_____ tourists

E Work with a partner. What other forms of abbreviations do you see in the notes above? What are some examples of abbreviations you use in your notes?

AFTER LISTENING

F Discuss these questions with a partner.

1. Based on the lecture, what is the attitude of Venetian residents toward tourists? Use information from the lecture to support your answer.
2. What is the lecturer's attitude about Venice's future? Explain.

A Speaking

A 🎧 1.6 Listen to an excerpt from the lecture. Complete the T-chart below.

Negative Side of Tourism	Positive Side of Tourism
Trash left behind	Generates a lot of money
_____ is crowded 1	Tourism pays for city _____ 4
_____ in parts of the 2 economy	People have _____ related 5 to it
Serious _____ 3	

CRITICAL THINKING: **B** Work with a partner. Take turns answering the following question: What urban
APPLYING challenges does a city you know face? Take one minute to prepare and two minutes to present your answer. Use signal phrases to introduce additional aspects of the topic.

C Work with a partner. Look at the visuals below, and complete the conversation about the main features of the MOSE project. Use the correct form of the verb in the active or passive voice.

A: According to the photo and diagram, the MOSE flood barrier project _____consists_____ (consist) of three barriers.

B: Right, and the barriers _____ (locate) in three places: in the Lido, Malamocco, and Chioggia inlets.
1

A: It looks like the barriers usually _____ (stay) on the seabed.
2

B: Yes, they _____ (raise) when high tides and storms
3
_____ (forecast).
4

A: In those cases, air _____ (pump) into the hollow gates to make the
5
barriers rise.

B: Each barrier has 78 gates, which _____ (move) independently of each
6
other, so they can _____ (adjust) as needed.
7

A: And when the threat of flooding is gone, the barriers _____ (lower)
8
into the seabed.

D Work with a partner. Summarize the most important features of the MOSE flood barrier project in Venice. Include information not mentioned in the conversation above. Use the passive voice to emphasize the object of the action.

> *The gates can be raised in 30 minutes.*

E Work with a partner. Do you think the MOSE barrier will stop floods? Explain. What other defenses can cities use to prevent flooding?

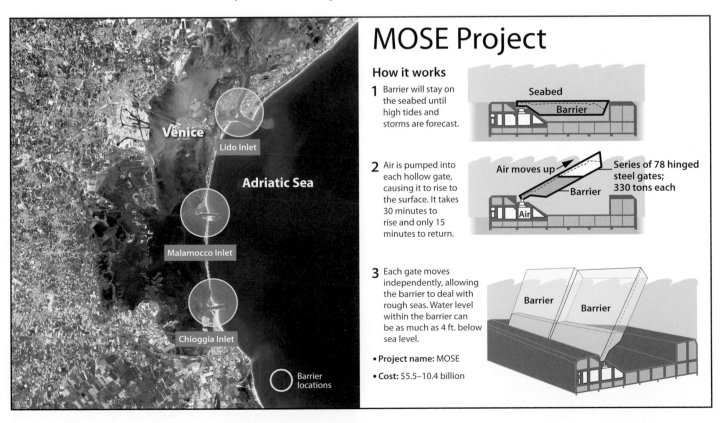

F Work in a small group. Imagine that you live by the ocean and your city was hit by a powerful hurricane. Describe the disaster using the verbs below. Use the passive voice when appropriate.

blow off	damage	destroy	flood	hit
injure	lose	rescue	trap	wash away

A: *What a terrible storm! My dog ran off, but luckily he was rescued by some neighbors. My house is OK. It wasn't damaged too much.*

B: *You're lucky! My car was hit by a tree. It's destroyed! Luckily, no one in my family was injured.*

LESSON TASK Evaluating the Impact of Tourism

CRITICAL THINKING:
EVALUATING

A Work in a small group. Look at the list of topics. How does tourism impact these aspects of urban life? Discuss your ideas with your group. Add your own topic(s) to the list.

public transportation	job opportunities for residents
culture (arts, restaurants, and museums)	the cost of living
historical sites	the city's reputation
cleanliness	other: _____

Over two million international tourists visit Rio de Janeiro, Brazil, each year.

B Choose a tourist city that you know. What are the pros and cons of tourism there? Write your notes in the chart.

City: _____

Pros	Cons

EVERYDAY LANGUAGE Turn Taking

Why don't I/you start?   *Who wants to go first/next?*
I'll start.   *Does anyone want to go first/next?*
I'll go first/next.   *Does anyone mind if I go first/next/last?*

C Rejoin your group. Use your chart from exercise B to tell your group about the impact of tourism on the city you chose. Explain your ideas and answer questions from the group. Use phrases for turn taking.

A: *Who wants to go first?*
B: *I'll start. I chose Muscat. Muscat is the capital of Oman. It is a beautiful city, and tourists from all over the world visit. Tourists bring lots of advantages but also some problems.*

Video

Urban Solution: Farming on Rooftops

Aerial view of rooftop garden on a parking lot in Chengdu, China

BEFORE VIEWING

> **CRITICAL THINKING** Predicting
>
> Before listening to a lecture or watching a video, look at the title and any accompanying visuals, and predict what you will learn about. Thinking about the topic in advance will make you a more active listener and increase your comprehension.

CRITICAL THINKING: PREDICTING

A The video is about Brooklyn Grange, a company working to solve some of the problems of urban life. Look at the title and photo. Then discuss the questions with a partner.

1. What benefits do you think there are to growing vegetables on a rooftop?
2. Farming includes more than just growing vegetables. What other types of farming could be done on a rooftop?

B Match each word from the video with its meaning. Use a dictionary to help you.

1. _____ (n) momentum   a. to do something first
2. _____ (v) pioneer   b. main, central
3. _____ (adj) core   c. income produced by a business or government
4. _____ (n) revenue   d. separated, disconnected
5. _____ (adj) alienated   e. increased speed of development or progress

WHILE VIEWING

C ▶ 1.2 Watch the video. Check (✓) the points that the speakers make.

UNDERSTANDING MAIN IDEAS

1. ☐ Rooftop farming is having an enormous effect on cities everywhere.
2. ☐ Ben Flanner discovered his passion for farming when he came to New York City.
3. ☐ The farmers have given consideration to the soil and water.
4. ☐ Rooftop farms connect the community with the production of its food.
5. ☐ The farmers' objective is to provide most of New York City's vegetables.

D ▶ 1.2 Read the questions. Then watch the video again. Take notes as you watch. Write no more than three words or a number to answer each question.

UNDERSTANDING DETAILS

1. Is rooftop farming practiced on a large scale or a small scale? _____

2. What type of creatures does their apiary business involve? _____

3. How long did it take to move the soil up onto the roof? _____

4. How do the stones in the soil compare to a typical rock?

    _____

5. About how much storm water a year does each farm manage?

    _____

6. What influence do the farms have on "urban heat island effect"?

    _____

E Look back at your predictions in exercise A. Were they correct? Tell a partner.

CHECKING PREDICTIONS

AFTER VIEWING

F With your partner, discuss the questions.

PERSONALIZING

1. What experience do you have with growing vegetables or raising animals?
2. Do you feel connected to the production of your food? Explain.
3. If you were given funds to set up a farm to raise crops and animals within your city or town, where would you put it? How could you involve your community?

Vocabulary

A Match each word or phrase with its definition. Use a dictionary to help you.

1. _____ **affluent** (adj)
2. _____ **be unique to** (v phr)
3. _____ **conform** (v)
4. _____ **debatable** (adj)
5. _____ **dominant** (adj)
6. _____ **enforce** (v)
7. _____ **ethnic** (adj)
8. _____ **internalize** (v)
9. _____ **rank** (v)
10. _____ **restrict** (v)

a. relating to people with the same culture, race, and traditions
b. to occupy a position in a list or in relation to other people or things
c. to make sure that a rule is obeyed
d. to exist only in one place or situation
e. having a strong influence
f. to make a belief part of your way of thinking
g. to limit, often by official rules or laws
h. not certain; questionable
i. wealthy
j. to behave in the same way as other people

B 🎧 1.7 Complete the article with the correct form of a word from exercise A. Then listen and check your answers.

SINGAPORE

Singapore is one of Asia's most interesting countries. Among all the nations of the world, Singapore _____ only 176th in size; nevertheless, it is among the most _____ , with an average income of about US$61,000. Many believe that Singapore's economic success is due to the leadership of Lee Kuan Yew, Singapore's first Prime Minister. His ideas have been _____ in Singapore for decades.

Singapore's model of success is unlike that of any other country. The model is a combination of two ideas: the encouragement of business and strict laws that regulate many aspects of life. To follow this model, the people of Singapore have learned to live and work together in an orderly way. There are laws that encourage cooperation between _____ 4 groups, and like all laws in Singapore, they are strictly _____ by the authorities.

Things such as selling chewing gum, littering, and even spitting are all _____ by law. While these laws, some of which _____ Singapore, may surprise first-time visitors, most Singaporeans have _____ them, and for the most part, they follow the rules and laws without thinking about them.

Most Singaporeans believe that strict laws are necessary for an orderly and secure society. They are willing to _____ to the system if it makes life in Singapore more pleasant. However, for some Singaporeans and people from other countries, the issue is _____ . They argue that the laws are too restrictive.

C Complete the chart with the correct form of each word. Then complete each sentence below with the correct form of one of the words. Use a dictionary to help you.

	Noun	Verb	Adjective
1.			debatable
2.		enforce	
3.			ranked
4.		restrict	

1. Dogs are _____ on public beaches and in many parks.

2. The two candidates for president held a public _____ .

3. In the United States, a law against chewing gum wouldn't be easy to _____ .

4. In the 2016 World Happiness Report, Singaporeans _____ 22nd in happiness.

D Read the statements about Singapore. Guess if they are true or false. Choose T for *True* or F for *False*. Then check your answers at the bottom of the page.

1. The cream-colored giant squirrel is an animal that is unique   T   F
    to Singapore.

2. The largest ethnic group in Singapore is Malay.   T   F

3. In Singapore, where you can eat ice cream is restricted by law.   T   F

4. Singapore has a special government agency that enforces   T   F
    anticorruption laws.

E Work in a small group. Discuss the questions.   PERSONALIZING

1. What is a tradition that is unique to your family? To your culture?
2. What is an important value you have internalized? Explain how it impacts you.
3. Describe a time when you chose to conform to what others were doing. Do you think
    you made the right choice, or did you regret it later?

ANSWERS: 1. T; 2. F (The largest ethnic group in Singapore is Chinese.); 3. F (It is not restricted.); 4. T

B Listening A Conversation about Singapore

BEFORE LISTENING

A With a partner, predict the answers to these questions about Singapore.

1. What do you think Singapore is famous for?
2. Singapore is a city-state. What do you think *city-state* means?
3. Look at the photo. Why do you think the Merlion was chosen as the symbol of Singapore?

WHILE LISTENING

B 🎧 1.8 Read the statements. Then listen to the conversation about Singapore. Choose T for *True* or F for *False*.

1. The name *Singapura* means "lion city."	T	F
2. Singapore is rich in natural resources.	T	F
3. Nearly all the people of Singapore belong to one ethnic group.	T	F
4. The spirit of *kiasu* is about enjoying life every minute.	T	F
5. Nick thinks the laws of Singapore are too strict.	T	F
6. Sofia believes strict laws are a positive thing.	T	F

C Compare your answers to exercise B with a partner. Revise the false statements to make them true.

The Merlion, a statue that is half lion, half fish, is the symbol of Singapore.

D 🎧 1.8 Listen again. Complete the notes with no more than two words or a number.

1. Sing. started off as a _____ .

2. Modern Sing. founded in _____ .

3. Sing. is ~ _____ sq. miles.

4. Sing. = _____ % urbanized.

5. Sing. econ. ranked the _____ most innovative in the wrld.

6. Lee Kuan Yew's ideas = dominant in _____ for 50 yrs.

7. *Kiasu* = "afraid _____ ."

AFTER LISTENING

E With your partner, discuss these questions.

PERSONALIZING

1. Do you have the spirit of *kiasu*? Explain.
2. Do you think that Singapore's laws are too strict or that they're beneficial? Explain.
3. What annoying behaviors that you see in public would you like to be restricted or made illegal?

F Look at this list of regulations in Singapore and the maximum fines and penalties they carry. Take notes on what you think the purpose of each regulation is.

CRITICAL THINKING: EVALUATING

Regulations and Penalties	Purpose
1. Selling chewing gum ($100,000 or two years in prison)	_____
2. Spitting in public ($1,000)	_____
3. Annoying people by playing a musical instrument in public ($1,000)	_____
4. Connecting to another person's Wi-Fi ($10,000 or three years in prison)	_____
5. Forgetting to flush a public toilet (around $150)	_____
6. Allowing mosquitoes to breed in your empty flower pots ($200)	_____
7. Feeding pigeons ($500)	_____

G Work in a small group. Discuss whether you think the regulations in exercise F would be a good idea where you live.

PERSONALIZING

> *I guess gum can cause problems when people don't throw it away properly. Still, I don't think I'd want it outlawed around here.*

B Speaking

PRONUNCIATION Linking with Word-Final *t*

🎧 **1.9** The letter *t* at the end of a word links with the next word in these ways.

1. When *t* is followed by an unstressed word that begins with a vowel, the *t* is pronounced like a quick *d* sound.

   state of sounds like *sta dof*   *what about* sounds like *wha dabout*

2. When *t* is followed by a word that begins with a consonant (other than *t* or *d*), hold your teeth and tongue in a *t* position, but do not release air.

   right now sounds like *right now*   *street can* sounds like *street can*

3. When *t* is followed by *you* or *your*, the *t* becomes soft, like *ch*.

   what you sounds like *wha chyu*   *don't you* sounds like *don chyu*

A Look at the following pairs of words. How is the final *t* of the first word pronounced? Write the phrase in the correct column below.

1. at you	3. hit us	5. thought your	7. eight o'clock
2. upset about	4. what now	6. not you	8. not really

Like a quick *d*	No air	Soft *t*, like *ch*

B 🎧 **1.10** Listen and check your answers to exercise A. Then listen again and repeat the phrases.

C 🎧 **1.11** Listen to the conversations. Pay attention to the pronunciation of each word-final -*t*. Then take turns practicing the dialogs with a partner.

1. A: I didn't hear what you said about which plan we'll prioritize.
   B: I'm sorry. I'll say it again.
2. A: Do you want some tips on planning the renovation?
   B: Yes, I would. And how about some help with building regulations?
3. A: About that budget I submitted. Has it been authorized yet?
   B: Not yet.
4. A: What are you going to do to maximize rentals?
   B: See that ad? We're going to put it everywhere online.
5. A: What are you so upset about?
   B: Haven't you heard? There are no funds for that project!

Customers play with a cat at "Café des Chats", the first cat cafe in Paris.

D Work with a partner. Read the statements related to different urban issues. Do you agree or disagree with each? Explain why to your partner.

CRITICAL THINKING: EVALUATING

> *I agree that smoking should be prohibited in all public places. Second-hand smoke is unhealthy.*

1. It's impossible for people from different ethnic groups to live together in peace.
2. It's the government's responsibility to provide housing for homeless people.
3. Billboards beside the road are ugly and distracting. They should be illegal.
4. In crowded cities, the government should limit the number of cars a family can have.
5. Smoking should be prohibited in all public places, both indoors and outdoors.
6. Pets should be allowed in restaurants, shops, and movie theaters.

FINAL TASK Presenting a Problem and Solutions

> You and your partner will present a problem affecting a city and propose solutions to the problem.

A Work with a partner. Discuss problems affecting a city you are both interested in. Make a list. Use your own knowledge and experience. If necessary, research the city.

PRESENTATION SKILL Presenting in Pairs

When dividing up material for a pair presentation, you can try different techniques:
- Simply divide the material to present in half.
- Take a "tag-team" approach where you take turns presenting the various points. This can help keep the audience's attention for longer presentations, but avoid switching back and forth too much.
- Assign different parts of the presentation based on who is best qualified to present each part. It's important to consider the strengths of each presenter. A qualified presenter is more confident and will make a better impression on the audience.

B With your partner, choose one of the problems you discussed in exercise A. Discuss the causes of the problem and possible solutions. Use the spider map to organize your ideas.

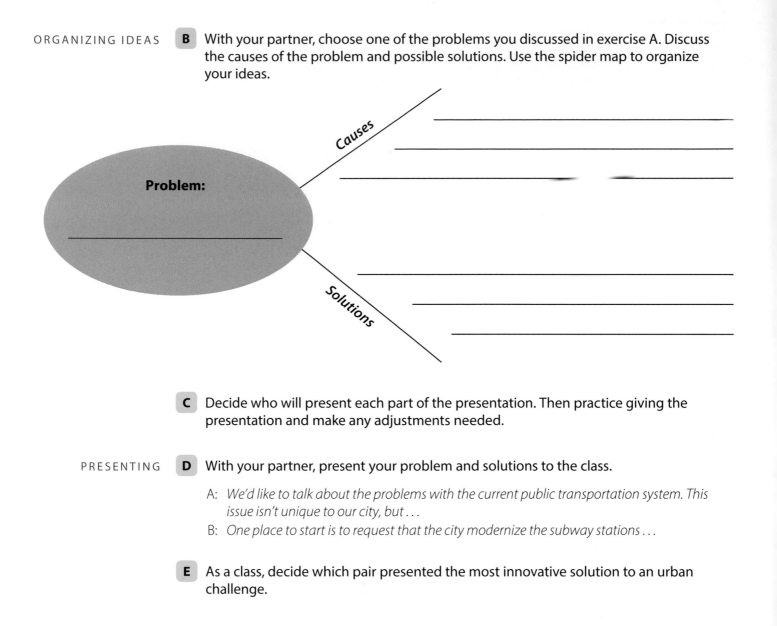

Problem:

Causes

Solutions

C Decide who will present each part of the presentation. Then practice giving the presentation and make any adjustments needed.

D With your partner, present your problem and solutions to the class.

A: *We'd like to talk about the problems with the current public transportation system. This issue isn't unique to our city, but . . .*

B: *One place to start is to request that the city modernize the subway stations . . .*

E As a class, decide which pair presented the most innovative solution to an urban challenge.

REFLECTION

1. What are some useful abbreviations you can use to take notes more quickly?

_____

_____

2. What is the most useful or interesting thing you learned in this unit?

_____

_____

3. Here are the vocabulary words and phrases from the unit. Check (✓) the ones you can use.

☐ affluent
☐ affordable
☐ authorize
☐ be unique to
☐ conform AWL
☐ debatable AWL
☐ dominant AWL

☐ enforce AWL
☐ ethnic AWL
☐ funds AWL
☐ innovative AWL
☐ internalize AWL
☐ maximize AWL
☐ prioritize AWL

☐ rank
☐ regulate AWL
☐ renovation
☐ restrict AWL
☐ scarcity
☐ stroll

PROTECTING THE WILD 2

An innovative program in southern Kenya recruits Lion Guardians among the Maasai to monitor lion movements and prevent conflicts with herders and cattle.

ACADEMIC SKILLS

LISTENING	Activating Prior Knowledge
	Taking Notes during a Q&A
SPEAKING	Responding to an Argument
	Saying and Linking –s Endings
CRITICAL THINKING	Evaluating Arguments in a Debate

THINK AND DISCUSS

1 Where are these men, and what are they doing?
2 What are some reasons that animals become extinct?
3 Who do you think should be responsible for protecting endangered species? Governments? Companies? Citizens?

A Look at the photo and read the caption. Then discuss the questions.

1. Where are the man and the gorilla? What do you think the man's responsibilities are?

2. How does the photograph make you feel? Explain.

B Read the infographic and discuss the questions.

1. What do the 11 animals have in common?

2. What is the Photo Ark? What is its purpose?

OUR WILD FRIENDS

An orphaned mountain gorilla sits with a warden in the gorilla sanctuary of Virunga National Park in the Democratic Republic of the Congo. The orphans in the sanctuary have been the victims of poachers or animal traffickers.

MEET SOME OF THE SPECIES FACING EXTINCTION IN THE WILD

(OF THE 7,000 SPECIES IN THE PHOTO ARK)

Many species are endangered and could disappear in our lifetimes. The National Geographic Photo Ark, led by photographer Joel Sartore, is a long-term project that aims to:

- photograph every species living in the world's zoos and other protected areas
- teach and inspire the public
- help save wildlife by supporting various projects

SOUTH CHINA TIGER

EDWARDS'S PHEASANT

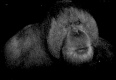

SUMATRAN ORANGUTAN

MITCHELL'S LORIKEET

ARAKAN FOREST TURTLE

ATELOPUS NANAY

NORTHERN WHITE RHINO

BUTTERFLY SPLITFIN

PARTULA SNAILS

RABBS' FROG (EXTINCT)

COLUMBIA BASIN PYGMY RABBIT (EXTINCT)

A Vocabulary

MEANING FROM CONTEXT **A** 🎧 **1.12** Read and listen to the information. Notice each word or phrase in **blue** and think about its meaning.

SAVE THE WHALES!

Of the nearly 90 species of whales and dolphins, nearly all have been affected by human activity.

Are all whales endangered?

Not all, but many. The populations of most species of baleen whales[1], such as blue and humpback whales, have been significantly reduced. Their **status** today is the result of commercial whaling from the 18th to the 20th century. For hundreds of years, they've been sold for meat and oil, and some species were nearly **wiped out**. Although most whale populations have been coming back, five species of baleen whales are still endangered, and the evidence shows that many toothed whales are in danger of dying out. Hunting, **habitat** destruction, and pollution all **threaten** whale populations. In each case, humans **are to blame**.

What kinds of conservation efforts are taking place?

Many **ongoing** conservation strategies are helping whale populations. For example, the International Whaling Commission (IWC) **imposed** a ban on commercial whaling, and the United States has been leading an effort to phase out[2] whale hunting completely. Nevertheless, a number of countries continue to hunt whales.

Can whale populations recover?

Although it may be too late for some species, there are some signs that conservation efforts are working. For example, the California gray whale, which was nearly **extinct**, has made an amazing recovery and is no longer endangered.

How can you help save the whales?

You can help by learning about whales and their habitats. You can donate your time to conservation organizations. Finally, you can **modify** your behavior so that you create as little waste as possible. If we all participate in these efforts, we can help these magnificent animals **thrive**.

[1] **baleen whales** (n): whales that, instead of having teeth, have plates in their mouth that separate food from the water
[2] **phase out** (v): to bring to an end in a gradual manner

North Atlantic right whales were heavily hunted in the 18th and 19th centuries. Their name came from hunters, who said that they were the "right" whale for oil, meat, and other valuable body parts.

B Match each word or phrase with its definition.

1. _____ are to blame (v phr)
2. _____ extinct (adj)
3. _____ habitat (n)
4. _____ imposed (v)
5. _____ modify (v)
6. _____ ongoing (adj)
7. _____ status (n)
8. _____ threaten (v)
9. _____ thrive (v)
10. _____ wiped out (v phr)

a. are responsible for doing something wrong
b. continuing to happen
c. a state or condition at a particular time
d. the natural environment of an animal or plant
e. to grow or develop very well
f. completely eliminated or destroyed
g. to put at risk or in danger
h. no longer existing; died out
i. forced something on, such as a law or punishment
j. to change slightly

VOCABULARY SKILL Two-Part Verbs with *Out*

Two-part verbs, also called phrasal verbs, are common in speaking. Often the two words together have a new meaning. Learn them to help you speak more naturally. In two-part verbs, *out* has three basic meanings.

1. **Outside, or from inside to outside:** *eat out, take out, let out, lock out, leave out*
   Many verbs of motion can be used with *out*: *go out, run out, fly out, walk out*
2. **To distribute:** *send out, hand out, give out, pass out*
3. **To finish or end completely:** *die out, fade out, phase out, wipe out, back out, sign out, wait out*

C Choose the correct verb or verb phrase to complete the sentences.

1. One country (backed / backed out) of the whaling ban agreement at the last minute.
2. The first agreement to regulate whaling was (signed / signed out) in 1946.
3. Whales are good survivors, and very few species have actually (died / died out).
4. When the storm began, our ship headed into port to (wait it / wait it out).
5. British adventurer Tom McClean plans to (cross / cross out) the Atlantic in a whale-shaped boat.
6. A man was (handing / handing out) brochures for a whale-watching tour.
7. This copy of *Moby Dick* is missing pages. Someone (tore them / tore them out).
8. We should also protect dolphins. Let's not (leave them / leave them out).

D Work in a small group. Discuss these questions.

CRITICAL THINKING: REFLECTING

1. Whale-watching tours are popular around the world. Why are people fascinated by whales? If you have seen a whale, what was the experience like?
2. Should bans on hunting whales be imposed on everyone? Explain.
3. How do humans modify animal habitats in ways that can threaten the animals?
4. What are examples of "modifying behavior to create as little waste as possible"?

Listening A Q&A Session about an Extinct Species

BEFORE LISTENING

PREDICTING **A** Work in a small group. Look at the photo and read the caption. Then discuss the questions.

1. What kind of habitat do you think this bird lived in?
2. The dusky seaside sparrow is now extinct. What do you think are some possible causes for its extinction?
3. What types of laws could protect endangered animals?
4. What are some drawbacks of passing laws to protect endangered species?

The dusky seaside sparrow was a bird species of southern Florida.

PREVIEWING **B** 🎧 **1.13** Listen to the first part of a question and answer (Q&A) session and look at the student notes. Notice the use of abbreviations and symbols.

> Dusky Seaside Sparrow
>
> Stat.: Extinct
>
> Former habitat: Merritt Isl., FL
>
> Causes of extinction
>
>   1. Chems used for killing mosqs.
>
>   2. Modified wetlands → no longer good habitat for sparrows

CHECKING PREDICTIONS **C** Look back at the predictions you made in exercise A. Were they correct?

WHILE LISTENING

> **NOTE-TAKING SKILL** Taking Notes during a Q&A
>
> When taking notes during a talk presented in a question and answer (Q&A) format, it is helpful to organize your notes according to the questions and their responses. Number the questions (*Q1, Q2,* etc.). Below each question, write notes on the answer, numbering (*A1, A2,* etc.) and indenting them as needed.
>
>   *Q1: What caused extinction?*
>
>   *A1: Destruction of habitat*

D 🎧 **1.14** Look at the notes for the Q&A session. Notice the format. Then listen and complete the notes *only* for the questions (Q1–Q4).

NOTE TAKING

Dusky Seaside Sparrow (DSS)

Q1: _____

A1: Basic cause: _____
                        1

DSS only on Merritt Isl. in FL. Lots of wetlands & mosquitoes

Chems used _____ mosqs. Chems killed ↑ DSS
                     2

Wtlnds modified. No longr _____ for DSS. Died out
                                3

Q2: _____

A2: Yes. Must protect animals & their _____
                                          4

The 1973 Endangered _____ (ESA) protects both
                          5

Ex: steelhead trout & Columbia Riv. both protected

Q3: _____

A3: ESA diffclt to fully _____
                            6

Ongoing conflict betw. _____ & govt
                            7

Ex: gray wolf

   Once common in N. Am.; 1930s—nearly wiped out

   1973, wolves protected by ESA → ban on _____
                                                          8

   Ranchers want right to shoot wolves that threaten their anmls

Q4: _____

A4: Situation of endangrd animals is _____ now vs. 1973
                                          9

Now >1,400 in U.S. on endangrd list

39 spec. removed—only 14 recovrd, 9 extinct, others = mistake

Meanwhile, _____ more species to be added to list
                10

E 🎧 **1.14** Listen again and complete the notes for the answers (A1–A4). Write no more than two words or a number for each blank.

NOTE TAKING

AFTER LISTENING

F Work with a partner. What are some reasons we should care about the extinction of species?

CRITICAL THINKING: ANALYZING

A Speaking

BRAINSTORMING   **A**   Work in a small group. Look at the list of different habitats. Brainstorm examples of plants and animals that live in each one and the dangers that they may face. Use the expressions in the skill box to suggest ideas. Complete the chart.

Habitat	Plants and Animals	Dangers
polar	polar bear	
desert		
rainforest		
ocean		

B   With your group, have a discussion about the dangers you wrote in exercise A and what the animals might do when faced with such dangers.

▼ A young polar bear leaps between ice floes in the Barents Sea, Svalbard, Norway.

A: *Melting ice can threaten animals in a polar habitat—polar bears, for example.*
B: *I agree. I think it forces the bears to swim long distances when they hunt in the open ocean because there's no ice to rest on.*

GRAMMAR FOR SPEAKING Essential Adjective Clauses

We use adjective clauses, also called relative clauses, to give more information about a noun. The adjective clause usually comes after the noun it is modifying. An adjective clause is introduced by a relative pronoun. *Who, whom,* and *that* are used for people. *Which* and *that* are used for things. In essential adjective clauses, *that* is preferred. *Whose* is used for possessives.

Essential adjective clauses provide information that is necessary to identify a noun. The information is not optional, and commas are *not* used to separate the clause.

> The birds **that are on the fence** are wrens.
> The scientist **who did the research** is available to answer questions.

When the relative pronoun is the subject of the clause, it is followed by a <u>verb</u>.

> We saw a sparrow **that <u>was eating</u>** crumbs on the sidewalk.

When the relative pronoun is the object of the clause, it is followed by a <u>subject + verb</u>. The relative pronoun is optional in this case.

> The birds **<u>(that) we see</u> in our yard a lot** are finches.

Whose + noun is used to indicate possession.

> The birds **whose habitat was destroyed** are at risk of extinction.

C Work with a partner. Combine the sentences into one, adding an adjective clause after the underlined noun.

1. The police initiated an <u>investigation</u>. It led to several arrests.
2. The <u>woman</u> is an advocate for protecting wildlife. She's speaking tonight.
3. I know a <u>man</u>. He keeps two tigers as pets.
4. I think it was a <u>black bear</u>. It was to blame for all the tree damage.
5. There are many <u>people</u>. They care about endangered species.
6. The dodo was a <u>flightless bird</u>. It was wiped out in the 17th century.
7. Irresponsible <u>actions</u> should be fined. They harm wildlife.
8. Greenpeace is an environmental <u>group</u>. Its mission is to protect animal habitats.
9. The <u>wolves</u> are thriving. The government introduced them to this area.
10. The <u>tree</u> was over 200 years old. The environmentalists saved it.

D Complete these sentences with your own ideas. Use essential adjective clauses. Then share your sentences with a partner and explain your ideas.

PERSONALIZING

1. I'm fascinated by animals that _____ .

2. I really admire people who _____ .

3. Let me tell you about the time that _____ .

4. I saw a video that _____ .

5. I know someone whose _____ .

6. The teacher _____ made the students laugh.

PRONUNCIATION Saying and Linking -s Endings

🎧 1.15 The letter *s* at the end of nouns, verbs, and possessives is pronounced in three ways. If you put your hand on your throat and say *zeeeee*, you should feel a vibration. This is a voiced sound. If you put your hand on your throat and say *sssss*, there is no vibration. This is a voiceless sound.

- After voiced consonants and all vowels, *s* is pronounced /z/:
  bir**ds**, mosquit**oes**, chemica**ls**

- After voiceless consonants, *s* is pronounced /s/:
  sto**ps**, resul**ts**, photogra**phs**

- After words ending in *ss, sh, ch, ce, se, ge, x,* or *z, s* is pronounced /əz/ or /ɪz/:
  circumstanc**es**, ranch**es**, wish**es**

When a word ending in *s* is followed by a word that starts with a vowel, the two words are linked.

stop**s a**head   Endangered Specie**s A**ct   wishe**s o**f ranchers

E How is the final *s* pronounced in each word? Check (✓) the correct sound.

	/s/	/z/	/əz/ or /ɪz/			/s/	/z/	/əz/ or /ɪz/
1. hacks	☐	☐	☐		5. fifths	☐	☐	☐
2. lambs	☐	☐	☐		6. sparrows	☐	☐	☐
3. causes	☐	☐	☐		7. inboxes	☐	☐	☐
4. whales	☐	☐	☐		8. tongues	☐	☐	☐

F 🎧 1.16 Listen and check your answers in exercise E. Then listen again and repeat the words you hear.

G 🎧 1.17 Draw a link between the words with a final *s* and the next word with a vowel. Then, with a partner, practice saying the phrases. Listen and check your pronunciation. Then take turns making statements with the phrases.

> *Tourists in cities like to go shopping and visit museums.*

1. tourists in cities
2. animals in movies
3. causes of extinction
4. parks in cities
5. whales and dolphins

6. kids and pets
7. images in ads
8. ponds and lakes
9. habitats in danger
10. species under protection

LESSON TASK Discussing Environmental Impact

A Read the description of the imaginary *Pristine Island*. Why do you think the land birds
are decreasing? Why are the trees endangered? Tell a partner your ideas.

CRITICAL THINKING:
MAKING INFERENCES

> Pristine Island is a small, undeveloped island. It has several beautiful beaches that
> are home to sea turtles. Wandering around the island are groups of deer, and a
> moderate but decreasing number of land birds live there as well. There is also a
> species of endangered trees scattered throughout the island.

B Work in a small group. Imagine that you are in charge of developing Pristine Island for
residences and businesses, and you want to impact wildlife as little as possible. Discuss
how the factors in the chart could impact wildlife. Write notes in the chart.

BRAINSTORMING

Type of Development	Impact on Wildlife
new roads	
tourists on beaches	
residential areas	
high-rise hotels	

A: *I'm concerned that animals could be hit by cars on the new roads.*
B: *That's true. The deer would probably be crossing the roads all day.*
C: *Also, when building roads, we might have to cut down some trees.*

C Work with your group. Discuss solutions to the issues you identified above. Choose
three that you think could be the most effective, and share them with the class.

CRITICAL THINKING:
APPLYING

> *To help minimize the impact of car accidents on deer, we will add deer-crossing signs on
> all major roads.*

> Mugger crocodiles are native to India and surrounding countries and can grow up to 16.4 feet (5 meters) in length.

Hope for the Mugger Crocodile

BEFORE VIEWING

PREDICTING

A Look at the photo and read the caption. What do you think is the biggest problem for mugger crocodiles? Discuss your predictions with your class.

MEANING FROM CONTEXT

B Use the context to choose the correct definition of the **bold** word or phrase in these sentences from the video.

1. Crocs live in wetlands, but most of India's swamps and riversides are now rice fields and farms. So crocs have lost **virtually** all their habitat.
   a. almost   b. not really   c. wholly   d. approximately

2. Man, this place is absolutely **teeming with** crocodiles. I just counted 140 crocodiles. Probably give or take 20 or 30.
   a. working with   b. playing with   c. filled with   d. empty of

3. But when mating season approaches, they're also intensely **territorial**, and any spot with deep water is worth fighting for.
   a. on land   b. global   c. shy   d. protective

4. Contrary to popular legend, muggers are for the most part pretty **laid-back**, sociable animals. In fact, they spend much of their time just basking in the sun.
   a. relaxed   b. happy   c. shy   d. aggressive

WHILE VIEWING

C ▶ 1.3 Watch the beginning of the video. Complete the sentences with words from the box.

habitat	threaten	to blame	captive

1. Human population growth is _____ for animals' problems.

2. Growing human populations _____ crocodiles.

3. Crocodiles have lost their _____ to rice fields and farms.

4. Madras Crocodile Bank has the world's largest _____ population of muggers.

D ▶ 1.4 Watch the next section of the video. Read the statements. Choose T for *True*, F for *False*, or NG for information *Not Given*.

1. The mugger has nearly been wiped out from Iran to Myanmar.   T   F   NG

2. Muggers have opportunities for success in the wild outside Sri Lanka.   T   F   NG

3. Muggers live in pools once used in agriculture.   T   F   NG

4. The muggers seem to be thriving where Whitaker visited.   T   F   NG

5. The park asked Whitaker to find out the status of the muggers.   T   F   NG

6. Whitaker thought finding one small crocodile was a bad sign.   T   F   NG

E With your partner, discuss your answers to exercise A. Were your predictions correct?

F ▶ 1.5 Watch the rest of the video and take notes. Then work with a partner and answer the questions.

1. What kind of conditions were the animals experiencing at the time of Whitaker's visit?
2. Why do animals coming close to the water to drink need to stay alert?
3. Why is Whitaker observing the muggers at night? What does he do as he observes them?
4. Why do the males fight? Are many of them killed?

AFTER VIEWING

G Work in a small group. Discuss the questions.

1. Large crocodiles can be quite dangerous to humans. Why do you think Rom Whitaker works so hard to save them?
2. What are some of the similarities and differences between the situation of these mugger crocodiles and that of the endangered species discussed in the Q&A session you heard in Lesson A?
3. After watching this video, do you think mugger crocodiles can look forward to a bright future in Sri Lanka? Why or why not?

Vocabulary

A 🎧 1.18 Read and listen to the article. Notice each word or phrase in **blue** and think about its meaning.

THE YELLOWSTONE WOLF PROJECT

Wolves were once common throughout North America, but by the mid-1930s, most had been killed. In 1995, wildlife **authorities** in the United States and Canada **initiated** a program of capturing wolves in Canada and freeing them in Yellowstone National Park. This program, known as the Yellowstone Wolf Project, cost only $267,000 in government funds. It was a huge success. Today, the Yellowstone wolf population has recovered and reached a **sustainable** level.

Contrary to the wishes of many farmers and ranchers, wolf populations have also been recovering in other parts of the western United States. As the number of wolves has grown, they have become the focus of bitter **controversy**. It is **undeniable** that wolves occasionally kill sheep, cattle, and other farm animals, and farmers and ranchers naturally feel authorities are **neglecting** their rights.

On the other hand, these efficient **predators** help control populations of the animals they **prey on**, such as elk, moose, and deer. The presence of wolves also brings financial benefits to Yellowstone Park. Tens of thousands of tourists visit annually to see them. These tourists provide money for the **upkeep** of the park. Tourists also contribute about $35 million a year to the area around the park. There are strong feelings on both sides, and the Yellowstone Wolf Project will no doubt continue to be the focus of public debate for years to come.

**Wolves in Yellowstone
National Park, USA**

B Match each word or phrase with its definition.

1. _____ authorities (n)
2. _____ contrary to (adj phr)
3. _____ controversy (n)
4. _____ initiated (v)
5. _____ neglecting (v)
6. _____ predators (n)
7. _____ prey on (v phr)
8. _____ sustainable (adj)
9. _____ undeniable (adj)
10. _____ upkeep (n)

a. maintaining something in good condition

b. animals that kill and eat other animals

c. certain; beyond any doubt or question

d. able to stay at a certain level or in a certain condition

e. not giving something the attention it deserves

f. started a process or action

g. people who have the power to make decisions and to make sure that laws are obeyed

h. to hunt, kill, and eat (as a regular food source)

i. serious and public disagreement

j. different from; opposite

C 🎧 1.19 Read the statements. Then listen to a representative of an environmental organization calling someone to ask for a donation. Write T for *True* or F for *False*.

1. _____ The program to save great whites has been going on for a long time.

2. _____ Great white sharks don't attack humans every year.

3. _____ People think the sharks' natural behavior is to hunt humans.

4. _____ The number of great white sharks is expected to increase over time.

5. _____ Friends of Wildlife assists African officials with policy planning.

6. _____ Friends of Wildlife helps work out conflicts related to animal rights.

7. _____ Friends of Wildlife serves both animals in the wild and in zoos.

8. _____ Friends of Wildlife offers zoos financial support to maintain facilities.

D Work in a small group. Discuss the questions.

1. In many places in the United States, wolves are protected by the Endangered Species Act. If wolf populations have recovered, should they continue to be protected by the law? Explain.
2. If a wolf or another protected predator attacks a farmer's animals, should the farmer have the right to kill the predator? Explain.
3. Do you think the government should pay farmers or ranchers whose animals are killed by wolves or other protected predators? Explain.
4. If an organization like the Friends of Wildlife called you asking for a donation to help great white sharks, how would you react? Explain.

CRITICAL THINKING: REFLECTING

Listening A Debate on Legalized Hunting

BEFORE LISTENING

> **LISTENING SKILL** Activating Prior Knowledge
>
> Studies show that having some prior knowledge about a topic can improve your listening comprehension. In a classroom setting, you can activate your prior knowledge before listening by:
>
> - asking yourself or others *wh-* questions about the topic
> - discussing what you already know about the topic
> - predicting the kind of information the speaker will talk about
> - looking at any accompanying visuals such as photos, charts, or diagrams

PRIOR KNOWLEDGE   **A**   Work in a small group. Discuss the questions.

1. Why do people hunt? What animals do people typically hunt?
2. Have you ever gone hunting? If so, did you like it? If not, would you try it? Explain.
3. What kinds of information do you think the speakers will discuss in the debate?

WHILE LISTENING

PREVIEWING   **B**   🎧 1.20   Listen to the introduction to a student debate about legalized hunting. Are Raoul and Yumi for or against legalized hunting? Complete the sentences.

1. _____ is arguing in favor of legalized hunting.

2. _____ is arguing against legalized hunting.

Hunters and their dogs at the Elkridge Hartford Hunt Club in Maryland, USA

C 🎧 1.21 Listen to the whole debate. Take notes on the speakers' arguments only. (You will listen for the opposing arguments in exercise D.)

1. Yumi's 1st argument: _Hunting helps control the populations of animals such as deer._

   _____

   Raoul's opposing argument: _____

   _____

2. Yumi's 2nd argument: _____

   _____

   Raoul's opposing argument: _____

   _____

3. Raoul's 1st argument: _____

   _____

   Yumi's opposing argument: _____

   _____

4. Raoul's 2nd argument: _____

   _____

   Yumi's opposing argument: _____

   _____

D 🎧 1.21 Listen again. Now take notes on the speakers' opposing arguments.

AFTER LISTENING

E With a partner, compare your notes above. Restate the arguments for and against hunting in your own words.

F Refer back to the debate. Which speaker presented the stronger arguments and made more effective opposing arguments? Explain your opinion to your partner.

B Speaking

> **SPEAKING SKILL** Responding to an Argument
>
> There are specific ways to respond to an argument in a debate or conversation. First, you should acknowledge that you have heard the other speaker's argument. Then you should signal that you have a different point of view, followed by your response, or refutation.
>
> Here are some expressions you can use to respond to an argument.
>
> | | |
> |---|---|
> | *Yes, but . . .* | *That's a good argument, but . . .* |
> | *That's possible, but . . .* | *That may be true, but (on the other hand) . . .* |
> | *OK, but . . .* | *You're right that . . .; however, . . .* |

A 🎧 1.22 In the debate about hunting, the speakers used a number of expressions for responding to and refuting an argument. Listen and fill in the expressions you hear.

1. **Yumi:** So, for example, without hunting, deer populations would grow too large and no longer be sustainable. They'd eat all the available plants and, as a result, many animals would starve because there wouldn't be enough food for them.

   Raoul: _____ I think you're neglecting an important point.

2. **Raoul:** So, instead of allowing humans to hunt, we should allow populations of meat-eating predators to recover.

   Yumi: _____ don't forget that wolves and mountain lions don't just prey on deer and elk.

3. **Raoul:** There was also this case in Shenandoah National Park in Virginia recently where authorities caught a group of hunters who were shooting black bears and selling their body parts for use in medicines.

   Yumi: _____ those kinds of violations occur; _____ , they are rare.

RESPONDING TO AN ARGUMENT

B Read the statements below. Tell a partner whether you agree or disagree with each and why. If you disagree with your partner, use an expression from the skill box above to respond to your partner's argument with an opposing idea.

A: *I agree that humans have always been hunters. Hunting and killing animals is natural for us.*
B: *That may be true, but modern humans can satisfy their desire to hunt through sports, business, or games.*

1. Humans have always been hunters. Hunting and killing animals is natural for us.
2. We should impose a ban on fishing for a few years to allow fish populations to recover.
3. Just as humans have rights, animals have rights, too.
4. The government does not have the right to stop people from hunting on their own land.
5. It doesn't matter that the dusky seaside sparrow became extinct. It doesn't make any difference in our lives.
6. Parents should teach their children about animal rights.

C Work with a partner. Look at the chart about revenues for wildlife protection in the United States. Then answer the questions.

1. How much revenue do states bring in? How much does the federal government bring in? Is this what you would expect? Explain.

2. How much revenue is made from hunting and fishing licenses? How is it used? What is one way the money might be used to improve habitats?

3. What is the source of funds for the Federal Aid in Sport Fish and Wildlife Restoration programs? Give an example of an item that would be taxed with this type of tax.

4. At what age are waterfowl hunters required to purchase duck stamps? Do you agree with this age requirement? Explain.

5. In your own words, summarize the information this chart shows.

REVENUE FOR WILDLIFE PROTECTION

STATES

Hunting and fishing licenses

$1.22 billion

Helps state wildlife agencies acquire, maintain, and improve fish and wildlife habitat through the North American Wetlands Conservation Act and other programs.

Licenses and excise taxes make up about

75%

of state wildlife agencies' revenue.

Excise taxes

$616 million

on fishing and hunting equipment and motor-boat fuels

Helps state agencies buy land and improve fish and wildlife habitat through the Federal Aid in Sport Fish and Wildlife Restoration programs.

FEDERAL

Duck Stamps

$24 million

Required of waterfowl hunters age 16 and older

Purchases wetland habitat for the National Wildlife Refuge System through the Migratory Bird Conservation Fund. Sales since 1934 exceed $700 million, and 5.2 million acres have been preserved.

SOURCES: U.S. FISH AND WILDLIFE SERVICE, CHARITY NAVIGATOR

An Amur Tiger passes through the Big Cat Crossing at the Philadelphia Zoo, Pennsylvania, USA.

FINAL TASK A Debate on Wild Animals in Zoos

> You will evaluate arguments for and against keeping wild animals in zoos. Then you will organize and prepare for a debate on this issue.

CRITICAL THINKING: EVALUATING

A Read the statements. Write F if the argument is *for* keeping animals in zoos and A if it is *against* keeping animals in zoos.

1. _____ Animals do not have rights, so it is acceptable to keep them in zoos.

2. _____ Zoos educate people about how to protect endangered species.

3. _____ In many zoos, animals are kept in small cages and cannot move around.

4. _____ It costs a lot of money to keep animals in zoos.

5. _____ It is fun to see interesting and unusual animals in zoos.

6. _____ Zoos protect animals that are hunted illegally, such as rhinos and elephants.

7. _____ People can be educated about animals without keeping them in zoos.

8. _____ The artificial environment is stressful for many animals. They often stop eating.

RESPONDING TO AN ARGUMENT

B With a partner, take turns responding to the statements in exercise A. Use expressions for responding to an argument from the Speaking Skill box.

A: *Animals do not have rights, so it is acceptable to keep them in zoos.*
B: *Yes, but is it so clear that animals don't have rights? Some people think they do.*

C Your teacher will instruct you to prepare arguments either for or against keeping animals in zoos. Write notes to support your position. Try to predict the arguments the other speaker will make, and think about how you will respond to them.

D Your teacher will pair you with a student who prepared the opposite side of the issue. You will hold a three to five minute debate in front of the class or a small group. The student who speaks in favor of zoos should begin.

REFLECTION

1. What methods of activating prior knowledge work best for you?

_____

_____

2. Did the information you learned in this unit change your mind about protecting the wild? If so, how?

_____

_____

3. Here are the vocabulary words and phrases from the unit. Check (✓) the ones you can use.

☐ authority AWL   ☐ initiate AWL   ☐ sustainable AWL
☐ be to blame   ☐ modify AWL   ☐ threaten
☐ contrary to AWL   ☐ neglect   ☐ thrive
☐ controversy AWL   ☐ ongoing AWL   ☐ undeniable AWL
☐ extinct   ☐ predator   ☐ upkeep
☐ habitat   ☐ prey on   ☐ wipe out
☐ impose AWL   ☐ status AWL

BEAUTY AND APPEARANCE 3

A model on the runway during the Arts University Bournemouth show in London, England.

THINK AND DISCUSS

1 Look at the photo and read the caption. Why do you think people go to fashion shows?
2 How would you describe the items this man is wearing?
3 What surprises or interests you about this photo?

Look at the photo and read the information. Then discuss the questions.

1. Why do you think the man is getting a shave? Is this a common ritual in your country?

2. Do you agree with the top reasons for trying to look good? Do you think the gender differences are accurate?

3. Do you think the reasons for trying to look good change with age? With culture?

4. What other reasons are there for trying to look good?

LOOKING GOOD

How much of a person's beauty is based on physical appearance? On personality? How much depends on what a person wears? Is there a universal standard of beauty, or do these standards vary from country to country? One certainty is that looking good matters, and rituals like the one in the photo can be found everywhere.

Top three reasons for trying to look good*

To feel good about myself

60%

♂ 52%   67% ♀

To make a good impression on people I meet for the first time

44%

♂ 44%   45% ♀

To set a good example for my children

40%

♂ 39%   41% ♀

Weekly time spent on personal grooming*

4.0 h

♂ 3.2 h   4.9 h ♀

*Average across 22 countries

Ali Marili gives a man a shave in his barbershop in Kilis, Turkey. Marili's father opened the shop in 1942, and his son uses the same traditional methods today.

A Vocabulary

A 🎧 **1.23** Read and listen to the article. Notice each word in **blue** and think about its meaning.

HIGH-FASHION MODELING

In the world of high-fashion modeling, you don't see the variations in body type that you find with **random** people on the street. Designers have traditionally shown a **distinct** preference for tall and thin runway models to show off their latest creations. However, images of extremely thin models as seen in fashion shows and magazines can be **alarming** for some people. Some models have a height-to-weight **ratio** that is unhealthy. For example, a model might be around five feet nine inches (175 centimeters) tall but weigh only 110 pounds (50 kilograms).

The modeling business is slowly **evolving**, and the type of model that designers prefer is changing, too. The high-fashion modeling profession is no longer **exclusively** for the thinnest of the thin. The good news is that in recent years, healthy-looking models have also been seen strolling down runways. In some countries—Australia, for example—the government has even asked fashion designers and magazines to stop hiring **excessively** thin models for fashion shows and photo shoots. Now, designers **envision** people with various body types wearing their clothing. This informs their designs and is reflected in the models we are starting to see. As a result, how people **perceive** fashion models and their opinion of what **constitutes** beauty are starting to change.

A model walks down a runway at a fashion show.

B Write each word in **blue** from exercise A next to its definition.

1. _envision_ (v) to have or form a mental picture
2. _evolving_ (v) gradually changing and developing
3. _exclusively_ (adv) only
4. _ratio_ (n) a proportion, e.g., 2:1
5. _excessively_ (adv) more than is necessary, normal, or desirable
6. _constitutes_ (v) composes or forms
7. _alarming_ (adj) shocking or frightening
8. _random_ (adj) chosen without a method or plan
9. _distinct_ (adj) clear
10. _perceive_ (v) to recognize; be aware of

1. random ✓
2. distinct ✓
3. alarming ✓
4. ~~ratio~~ ratio ✓
5. evolving ✓
6. exclusively ✓
7. excessively ✓
8. envision ✓
9. ~~pre~~ perceive ✓
10. constitutes ✓

C Complete the sentences with the correct form (noun, verb, adjective, or adverb) of the word in parentheses. If necessary, use a dictionary.

1. Jia was _____ when she discovered a gray hair on her head. (alarming)

2. That black hat looks _____ better on you than the blue one. (distinct)

3. The designer said the dress wasn't as stylish as what she _____ . (envision)

4. There has been an _____ of workplace fashion from formal to casual. (evolve)

5. Experts warn that the _____ use of makeup can be quite unhealthy. (excessively)

6. Members of our shopping club receive _____ discounts. (exclusively)

7. There is a general _____ that Paris is the world capital of fashion. (perceive)

8. The winners were _____ selected from the audience. (random)

D Work with a partner. Choose the word that forms a collocation with the vocabulary word in **bold** and the underlined words.

1. I never plan what I'm going to wear. I just <u>choose</u> my clothes (at / for) **random**.
2. <u>The</u> **ratio** (for / of) women <u>to</u> men in my class is 2 to 1.
3. Men's shirts <u>are</u> **distinct** (to / from) women's as the buttons are on opposite sides.
4. These beauty products <u>are</u> **exclusively** (for / to) our loyal customers.
5. The increase in extreme dieting is an **alarming** (trend / movement).
6. His small business gradually **evolved** (to / into) a great fashion company.
7. Men who wear neckties <u>are</u> **perceived** (in / as) being professional.
8. Those new fashions <u>are</u> **excessively** (beautiful / expensive).

E Work with a partner. Take turns using the collocations in exercise D to say sentences.

> *I don't think it's a good idea to choose your college major at random.*

F Work in a small group. Discuss the questions.

CRITICAL THINKING: REFLECTING

1. If you asked a random teenager on the street what constitutes beauty, what might he or she say? What celebrities might the teen envision?
2. If you knew someone who was excessively concerned with physical appearance, what could you say to convince him or her that attractiveness is not exclusively physical?
3. Are there any modern trends that you find alarming? Explain.
4. Society's perception of beauty always seems to be evolving, at least in certain ways. What evidence can you give of this?
5. What makes a person look distinctive?

Listening A News Report on Perceptions of Beauty

BEFORE LISTENING

CRITICAL THINKING:
EVALUATING

A With a partner, discuss the questions.

1. Look at the two rows of photos. These photos were shown to people who participated in a study on beauty. In each row, select the photo that you think shows the most beautiful face. Do you and your partner agree?
2. Look at the photos again. According to researchers, most people would choose Photo 4 and Photo 9 as the most beautiful faces. Why do you think most people chose these photos?

Row A

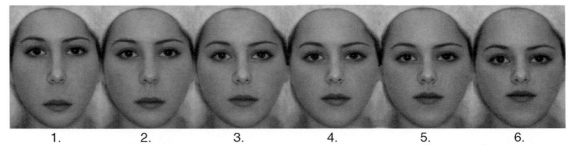

1.   2.   3.   4.   5.   6.

Row B

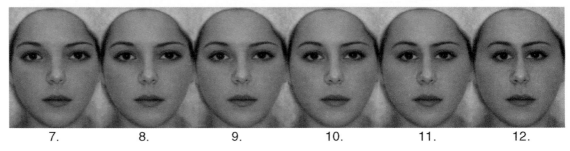

7.   8.   9.   10.   11.   12.

WHILE LISTENING

LISTENING FOR
MAIN IDEAS

B [🎧 1.24] [▶ 1.6] Listen to a news report. Match each scientist or group of scientists to their research result.

Scientists	Research Results
1. _____ Judith Langlois	a. Men's ideas about beauty and attractiveness evolved over thousands of years.
2. _____ Pamela M. Pallett/ Stephen Link/Kang Lee	b. Symmetry is a key part of what makes a face beautiful.
3. _____ Victor Johnston/David Perrett	c. There is a "golden ratio" for the ideal distance between the eyes, the mouth, and the edge of the face.
4. _____ Don Symons	d. Men prefer large eyes, full lips, and a small nose and chin.

Using an outline as you listen can help you organize main ideas and details. A formal outline looks like the outline in exercise C below. Notice how the outline shows the structure of the talk, with roman numerals for main ideas, capital letters for supporting ideas, and numbers for details.

C 🎧 1.24 Listen again and take notes to complete the outline. Write one word only in each blank.

NOTE TAKING

I.   Intro: What is beauty?

    A.   Does each person perceive beauty differently?

    B.   Does social/cultrl _____ influence ideas?
                        1

II. Studies on _____
                  2

    A.   Langlois

        1.   ppl think _____–looking faces are beautfl
                            3

        2.   symmetrical faces are beautfl

            a.   far from average & symmetrical = _____ to observers
                                            4

    B.   Pallett, Link & Lee—discovered " _____ ratio"
                                    5

        1.   ideal dist. btwn eyes, mouth & edge of face

        2.   dist. fr eyes to mouth = 36% _____ of face
                                  6

    C.   Johnston & Perrett—men's prefs

        1.   lg. eyes, full lips, sm. nose & _____
                                7

        2.   Symons—lg. eyes/lips = health & hlthy babies

    D.   not all anthroplgsts agree about one _____ of beauty
                                          8

        1.   diff cultrs have diff ideas about beauty

        2.   crossed eyes, _____ & tattooed lips —all beaut.
                            9

III. Conclusion: Beauty not exclusively in eye of beholder

    A.   some aspects of beauty are _____ , e.g., "gldn ratio"
                                10

    B.   ppl fr. same cultr see beauty in similar ways

AFTER LISTENING

D Work in a small group. Discuss the questions.

PERSONALIZING

1. Do you agree or disagree that "beauty is in the eye of the beholder"? Explain.
2. Scientists believe that a beautiful face is a symmetrical face. What other features make a face beautiful to you?
3. The report said that perceptions of beauty vary from culture to culture. What are some examples of how your perception of beauty might vary from those in other cultures?

Speaking

A 🎧 **1.25** Read and listen to the article. Then look at the bar graph. What is the graph about?

THE GROWING POPULARITY OF COSMETIC SURGERY

If you think the risks of cosmetic surgery are alarming, there's good news! Cosmetic procedures are evolving; many are not excessively dangerous, and some are quite safe. You may be able to get the new look you envision with nonsurgical procedures like tissue fillers and laser treatments, which now constitute 82 percent of cosmetic procedures in the United States. Once exclusively for the rich and famous, cosmetic procedures are being chosen by more people every year.

There is a distinct difference in the way people in different cultures perceive beauty, but cosmetic surgery is a common choice in many parts of the world. The graph Top Markets for Cosmetic Procedures compares 20 countries by procedures per capita[1], total number of procedures, and the ratio of surgical to nonsurgical procedures.

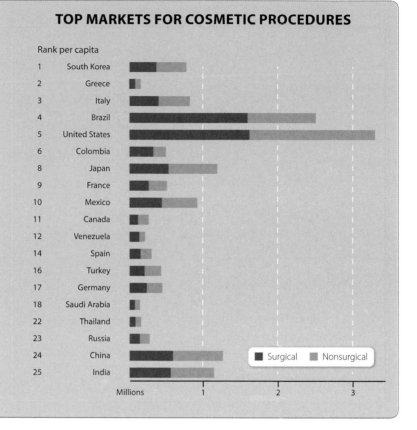

TOP MARKETS FOR COSMETIC PROCEDURES

[1] **per capita** (adj): per person relative to the total population

---

CRITICAL THINKING   Interpreting a Bar Graph

To understand a bar graph, it's important to study the following features:

- **the title:** tells you what the graph is about
- **labels:** tell you what the bars or numbers represent
- **the scale:** tells you the unit of measurement
- **color coding/key:** shows you what different colors mean

CRITICAL THINKING:
INTERPRETING A
BAR GRAPH

B Work with a partner. Answer the questions about the bar graph above.

1. What is the title of the graph?
2. Look at the labels. What do the bars represent?
3. How many countries have more than a million cosmetic procedures?
4. Look at the color coding and the key. What do the colors represent?
5. Which country has the highest number of cosmetic procedures per capita? Which has the lowest?
6. What do you find interesting or surprising about the information in the graph?

C Work with a partner. Discuss the questions.

1. Is it a positive trend that cosmetic procedures are now more affordable? Explain.
2. How has technology contributed to the evolution of cosmetic surgery?
3. Do you think the risks of cosmetic surgery are alarming? Explain.
4. What are some ways to stay young and healthy looking that avoid the need for cosmetic procedures?

SPEAKING SKILL Paraphrasing

When you paraphrase, you express something you said in a different way. Paraphrasing allows you to restate, in a clearer way, information that may be new or difficult for listeners to understand.

> *It's said that beauty lies in the eye of the beholder, yet the opposite seems to be true.* **What I mean by that is people within a culture usually have similar ideas about beauty.**

Here are some expressions you can use to paraphrase information.

I mean . . .	*Let me put it another way.*
In other words, . . .	*To put it another way, . . .*
That is (to say), . . .	*What I mean by that is . . .*

D 🎧 1.26 In the news report, the speaker used a number of expressions to paraphrase. Read the sentences aloud using one of the expressions from the skill box. Then listen and write the expressions that were actually used.

1. An oft-quoted expression is, "Beauty is only skin deep." _____ , someone can be beautiful on the outside but be mean or unpleasant on the inside.

2. Another famous saying is, "Beauty is in the eye of the beholder." _____ , each person's idea of beauty is different.

3. In addition, her research shows that a beautiful face is a symmetrical face. _____ , if both sides of the face are exactly the same, we consider a person beautiful.

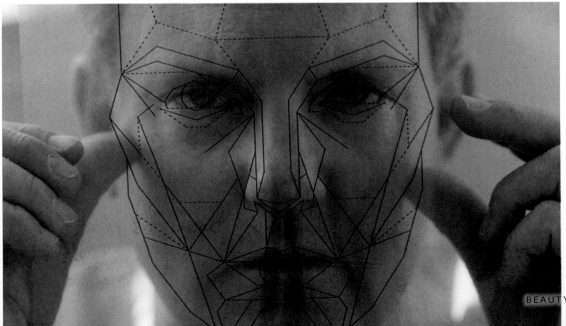

◀ **Cosmetic surgeon Dr. Marquardt uses a grid to ensure facial symmetry for his patients.**

People who smile are often perceived as more attractive.

CRITICAL THINKING:
INTERPRETING

E Read these quotations about beauty. In your own words, write what each means.

1. Beauty is not in the face; beauty is a light in the heart. —Kahlil Gibran

   _____

   _____

2. It matters more what's in a woman's face than what's on it. —Claudette Colbert

   _____

   _____

3. I've never seen a smiling face that was not beautiful. —Author Unknown

   _____

   _____

4. Time is a great healer but a poor beautician.[1] —Lucille S. Harper

   _____

   _____

   _____

   [1] **beautician (n):** a person who cuts hair and performs other beauty-related tasks for people

PARAPHRASING

F Work with a partner. Take turns reading the quotations in exercise E. Explain each quotation to your partner using a paraphrasing expression from the Speaking Skill box.

LESSON TASK Conducting a Survey

A You are going to conduct a survey about beauty and fashion. Choose four of the questions below for your survey and write two new questions of your own.

> ### SURVEY QUESTIONS
>
> - Is it better to be beautiful, intelligent, or wealthy? Why do you think so?
> - Who do you think is the most beautiful woman alive today? Who is the most handsome man alive today?
> - What is the minimum age at which people should be allowed to have cosmetic surgery?
> - What is the most unusual item of clothing you own?
> - What do you spend more money on: clothing and beauty supplies, food, or electronics?
> - Are there any fashions today that you think are strange?
>
> - _____
>
> - _____

> ### EVERYDAY LANGUAGE Conducting a Survey
>
> When you conduct a survey, always be sure to ask politely and to thank your respondent.
>
> _Hello! Would you mind answering a few survey questions for me?_
> _Thank you. Now let's move on to the next question._
> _That's all the questions I have for you today. Thank you for participating in the survey. I really appreciate it!_

B Interview three classmates. Ask each classmate your survey questions. Use the expressions in the Everyday Language box. Take notes on each person's answers.

A: _Is it better to be beautiful, intelligent, or wealthy? Why do you think so?_
B: _Oh, it's definitely better to be intelligent, because beauty is in the eye of the beholder, but intelligence isn't based on people's perceptions._
A: _Interesting. Thank you. Now let's move on to the next question. . ._

C Work in a small group. Share your survey results. What is interesting or surprising about the information you heard? How would you answer each question in the survey? Discuss your thoughts with your group.

CRITICAL THINKING: APPLYING

> _The people that I surveyed think being intelligent is more important than being beautiful or wealthy. I agree with that._

Skin Mask

A model poses next to a silicone mask of her own face.

BEFORE VIEWING

A Write each word or phrase from the video next to its definition. If necessary, use a dictionary.

a touch of	conform	master	mold	silicone	special effects

1. _____ (n) a rubber-like material

2. _____ (n) a hollow form into which materials are put to shape objects

3. _____ (v) to be similar in form, pattern, or shape

4. _____ (n) sights and sounds that seem real on TV, the radio, and in movies

5. _____ (n phr) a small amount of something

6. _____ (adj) main; primary

PREDICTING **B** Look at the photo above and read the caption. This is the skin mask you will see in the video, which was modeled after a real person's face. How do you think the mold was made? Discuss with a partner.

WHILE VIEWING

UNDERSTANDING MAIN IDEAS **C** ▶ 1.7 Watch the video. Check (✓) the two procedures that are shown.

1. ☐ how the material silicone is made
2. ☐ how silicone is used to make a mold
3. ☐ how to choose a model to make a mask
4. ☐ how to make a lifelike mask from a mold
5. ☐ how a lifelike mask is used in special effects

D ▶ **1.7** Watch the video again. Put the steps for making a skin mask in the correct order from 1 to 10.

a. __1__ A cap is placed over the model's hair.

b. _____ A master mold is prepared.

c. _____ Artists paint her face in quick-drying silicone.

d. _____ Makeup, eyebrows, and lashes are added to the skin mask.

e. _____ Soft silicone is mixed with chemicals, creating a natural color.

f. _____ The artists create a series of positive and negative masks.

g. _____ The hardened material comes off, followed by the newly created mold.

h. _____ The mixture is injected into the master mold.

i. _____ The model's face is wrapped in plaster bandages.

j. _____ Vaseline is brushed over her eyebrows and lashes.

AFTER VIEWING

E Work with a partner. Take turns reading the statements from the video. Rephrase them using paraphrasing expressions.

1. "She has to sit motionless for about an hour as the artists brush the icy cold silicone onto her face."
2. "Then the model's face is wrapped in plaster bandages, rather like a living mummy."
3. "A touch of makeup helps bring the skin to life."
4. "The completed mask has all the aspects of real human skin. It has more than just the look. It has the feel."

F Work with a partner. Discuss the questions.

1. Cassandra jokes, "Who said modeling was easy?" What does she mean?
2. Explain how you think special-effects artists choose models to make their skin masks.
3. In Lesson A, you learned that standards of beauty are both universal and cultural. In Lesson B, you will learn about unusual fashions. For fashion to be unusual, it has to differ from standards. What are some fashion standards in your country that are universal? What are some that are cultural?

◀ **The positive cast on the right was made from the negative mold on the left.**

B Vocabulary

MEANING FROM
CONTEXT

A 🎧 1.27 Read and listen to a conversation. Notice each word or phrase in **blue** and think about its meaning.

Customer: Excuse me. What are these shoes made of?

Clerk: They're from an eco-fashion manufacturer that **integrates** natural materials and recycled ones. About half of their materials **are derived from** recycled plastic and metal. As it says on the label, they believe in "the **constructive** use of the waste society produces."

Customer: That's nice. But they're very unusual, aren't they? They look more like a piece of art that you would **exhibit** in a museum than shoes. I mean, they're like something an artist might **daydream** about but that nobody would ever wear in real life.

Clerk: Actually, they're very popular. I bought a pair myself, and they're **unquestionably** the most comfortable pair of shoes I've ever owned.

Customer: Really? Well, comfortable is good, but I do a lot of walking, so I'm not sure they'd be very **practical** for me. I mean, they'd probably fall apart after a week.

Clerk: Not at all. The combination of natural and recycled materials makes them **substantially** stronger than most shoes. Have a seat . . . Now, if you'll just **insert** your right foot in here . . .

Customer: Oh, this is nice! They are comfortable, aren't they? You know, I wasn't going to buy them, but you're very **persuasive**. I think I'll take a pair!

B Write each word or phrase in **blue** from exercise A next to its definition.

1. _____ (v) to lose oneself in pleasant thoughts while awake

2. _____ (v) combines different parts into a united whole

3. _____ (adv) in a large or significant way

4. _____ (v phr) are obtained from a specified source

5. _____ (adj) able to convince people to do or believe something

6. _____ (adv) certainly; beyond doubt

7. _____ (v) to put into

8. _____ (adj) promoting improvement

9. _____ (adj) useful; capable of being used

10. _____ (v) to place on public display

C Discuss the questions with a partner.

1. Have you ever received constructive criticism? If yes, what was it?
2. What kinds of exhibitions are you most interested in?
3. What do you sometimes daydream about?
4. What is an example of a piece of clothing that is not practical?
5. What is a situation that requires you to be persuasive?

VOCABULARY SKILL Suffix *–ive*

The suffix *–ive* is added to certain verbs and nouns to make adjectives. It generally means "doing or tending to do" the action of the word it is formed from.

> *persuasive* = persuading, tending to persuade
> *attractive* = attracting, tending to attract

When adding *–ive* to a verb, sometimes other changes need to be made.

Example	Rule
affirm → affirm**ative**	ends in *m* or *n*: add *–ative/-itive*
innovat**e** → innovat**ive**	ends in consonant + *e*: drop *e* and
defin**e** → defin**itive**	add *–ive/–ative/-itive*
persua**de** → persua**sive**	irregular form
repe**at** → repe**titive**	irregular form

Check a dictionary if you are not sure of the form.

D Use a word from the box and the suffix *–ive* to complete these opinions about fashion. Use a dictionary to help you.

> addict   alternate   construct   decorate   excess   exclude   impress   innovate

1. I think shopping for clothes is _____—once I start, I can't stop!
2. I think it's more important to look _____ than to feel comfortable.
3. I prefer plain, dark colors and not a lot of _____ designs such as stripes, or flower and animal patterns.
4. I'm always open to criticism about the way I dress, as long as it's _____.
5. I'm into _____ fashion. I think it's boring to look like everyone else.
6. I've seen people wearing a ring on every finger, but I think that's _____.
7. That designer is _____; his clothes are really new and different.
8. Many of the stores in this area are _____; only the very wealthy shop here.

Listening A Conversation about Unusual Fashions

BEFORE LISTENING

PREDICTING **A** Look at the photos. What do you think these fashion items are? Discuss your ideas with a partner.

1. _____

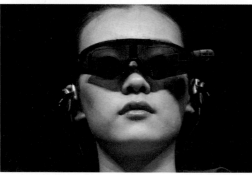

2. _____

3. _____

WHILE LISTENING

LISTENING FOR
MAIN IDEAS
B ∩ 1.28 Listen to a conversation between a teenager and her parents. Look back at the photos. Next to each photo, write the name or a brief description of the item.

> **LISTENING SKILL** Listening for Specific Information
>
> Sometimes you need to listen for specific information. When you need to answer a question (during a test, for example), listening to every word can cause you to miss the information you need. Instead, underline and note the key terms related to the information you need. Then listen for those key terms and related words and phrases.

C 🎧 1.28 Read the questions. Notice the underlined key terms in question 1. For questions 2–4, work with a partner to identify and underline the key terms. Then listen again and write your answers, using the underlined terms to guide your listening.

1. <u>Where</u> was Danish clothing designer <u>Alex Soza</u> when he got the <u>idea</u> for the <u>antigravity jacket</u>? _____

2. When was Kevlar developed? _____

3. How much stronger than steel is spider silk? _____

4. Who provides funds so Ana's friend can develop wearable technology?

_____

D 🎧 1.28 Listen again and complete the outline. Write one word only in each blank.

I. Antigravity jacket

   A. part _____ , part jacket
                     1

   B. designer isn't about being _____
                                 2

II. Kevlar: man-made fiber → cloth stronger than steel

   A. used to make _____-proof vests for police
                     3

   B. used to make ropes for _____
                          4

III. BioSteel: a super-strong fiber

   A. made by inserting spider-silk gene into _____
                             5

   B. may be used to pull things up to _____
                         6

IV. Wearable electronics—integrate _____ & electrnx
                                       7

   A. Ex.: a jacket w/phone in _____
                         8

   B. Ex: GPS sneakers—to track _____ kids & hikers
                           9

AFTER LISTENING

E Work with a partner. Discuss the questions.

1. Can you envision any uses for an antigravity jacket, now or in the future?
2. Goats and spiders are used in the production of BioSteel. Do you think it's acceptable to use animals for the purpose of creating new textiles? Explain.
3. Are there any other uses of GPS sneakers, besides tracking lost people?
4. Do you think wearable electronics are a good idea? Why or why not?
5. Which do you think is more profitable: the fashion industry or the electronics industry? Explain.

B Speaking

A Work with a partner. Take turns making a statement about one of the devices below. Your partner uses intonation to ask for clarification and you respond.

A: *I had no idea that I walked so many miles each week until I got a Fitbit.*
B: *A Fitbit?*
A: *Yeah, a Fitbit. It's a device you wear on your wrist that keeps track of . . .*

Device	Description
Fitbit	a device worn on the wrist that counts the number of steps you take, distance walked, and calories burned
Alexa	a voice-operated personal assistant in an electronic device that can answer questions and do things for you
Ringly	a ring that buzzes when you get a notification on your smartphone from apps like UBER, Slack, Twitter, etc.
Oculus Rift	a helmet that covers your eyes and allows you to "move around" in a virtual world, usually to play 3-D computer games

B Complete the tag questions. Then ask and answer the questions with a partner, using an appropriate response and intonation.

TAG QUESTIONS

1. Alex Soza is an imaginative clothing designer, _____

2. We've already discussed eco-fashion, _____

3. You'd like to learn more about fashion trends, _____

4. You're not going to wear a wool sweater today, _____

5. It's not possible to make fabric from plastic bottles, _____

6. Ana went to the fashion show with her parents, _____

7. You wouldn't wear real animal fur, _____

8. You hadn't heard about Kevlar vests before, _____

FINAL TASK A Presentation about Fashion Trends

You will give a group presentation about fashion trends in a particular country.

A Work in a small group. First, read the questions in the chart below that will guide your presentation. Then brainstorm fashion trends in a particular city or country, and decide on the location you want to report on. Write it at the top of the chart.

BRAINSTORMING

B On your own, research fashion and style trends in your location. Take notes in the chart to help you organize your ideas. Include ideas for visuals.

CRITICAL THINKING: APPLYING

Location: _____	Ideas for visuals: _____, _____
What types of fabrics are popular?	
What clothing fashions are "in"?	
How do people wear their hair?	
What types of shoes do people prefer?	
What accessories do people like to wear?	
Your own question: _____	

▲ **Young men by Umeda Station in Osaka, Japan**

PRESENTATION SKILL Preparing Visuals for Display

When preparing visuals for a presentation, high-tech options like projectors and slides are nice, but low-tech options like posters and handouts can be just as effective. Remember that the main point of visuals is to add interest and enhance your message. When preparing visuals, ask yourself:

- Is the size of the lettering large enough for everyone to see?
- Is the language clear, correct, brief, and easy to understand?
- Will everyone be able to see the photos and graphics clearly?

ORGANIZING IDEAS **C** In your group, share your notes from exercise B. Prepare a new set of notes in outline form to use during your group's presentation as well as any appropriate visuals. Decide who will present each section and which visuals they will use.

PRESENTING **D** Give your presentation. Afterwards, join with another group. Discuss each group's strengths and give any constructive feedback.

REFLECTION

1. In what situations do you need to paraphrase? What expressions can you use to paraphrase information?

   _____

   _____

2. What did you learn about beauty, appearance, or clothes that you will apply to your life?

   _____

   _____

3. Here are the vocabulary words and phrases from the unit. Check (✓) the ones you can use.

   ☐ alarming
   ☐ constitute AWL
   ☐ constructive AWL
   ☐ daydream
   ☐ be derived from AWL
   ☐ distinct AWL

   ☐ envision
   ☐ evolve AWL
   ☐ excessively
   ☐ exclusively AWL
   ☐ exhibit AWL
   ☐ insert AWL
   ☐ integrate AWL

   ☐ perceive AWL
   ☐ persuasive
   ☐ practical
   ☐ random AWL
   ☐ ratio AWL
   ☐ substantially
   ☐ unquestionably

GOING GLOBAL 4

Visual artist Chris Milk hosts the largest collective viewing of virtual reality during his TED Talk in Vancouver, Canada, 2016.

THINK AND DISCUSS

1 What do you think these people are seeing or experiencing?

2 How do you think a virtual reality experience is different from usual viewing?

Look at the photo and read the information. Then discuss the questions.

1. What type of new technology is shown in the photo? How is it useful?
2. What are some other new workplace technologies, and how are they changing the work world?
3. Look at The Future of Work 2020. Rank the drivers from strongest to weakest, in your opinion.
4. Which key skills do you think are most relevant for each driver?

Dmitry Grishin, CEO of Mail.ru, the Russian Internet giant, holding a virtual meeting with his telepresence robots

WORK SKILLS FOR THE FUTURE

The Future of Work 2020

Drivers of Change in the Workplace

| Smart machines and systems | People living longer | Big data | New media | Knowledge sharing | Globally connected world |

Key Skills Needed in the Future Workplace

Creative thinking · Social intelligence · Knowledge of multiple disciplines · Media literacy · Managing mental overload · Computational thinking · Cross-cultural under-standing · Virtual collaboration

A Vocabulary

MEANING FROM CONTEXT

A 🎧 **2.2** Read and listen to the article. Notice each word or phrase in **blue** and think about its meaning.

GLOBAL EMPLOYMENT TRENDS

Globalization is producing enormous changes in **labor** markets, changes that are creating both winners and losers in the workplace. Here are two areas of change that **pertain to** both employers and employees.

- Advanced technologies, a key **component** of globalization, are more **widespread** than ever before. New developments in technology will continue to **facilitate** tasks in business **sectors** such as architecture and engineering. It is not, however, a **promising** trend for office workers or the administrative sector, where jobs will **inevitably** be lost.
- The globalization of communication means more opportunities to learn via remote sources. Accessing information from global sources can increase a person's career **competence** and earning power. Companies who value their employees and hope to **retain**

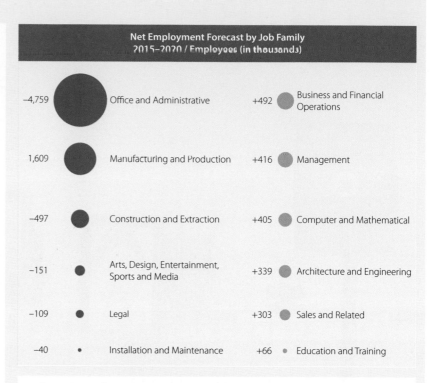

Net Employment Forecast by Job Family
2015–2020 / Employees (in thousands)

–4,759	Office and Administrative	+492	Business and Financial Operations
1,609	Manufacturing and Production	+416	Management
–497	Construction and Extraction	+405	Computer and Mathematical
–151	Arts, Design, Entertainment, Sports and Media	+339	Architecture and Engineering
–109	Legal	+303	Sales and Related
–40	Installation and Maintenance	+66	Education and Training

them in today's competitive global environment must support and fund learning opportunities for ambitious and motivated workers—or risk losing them!

B Match each word or phrase from exercise A with its definition.

1. _____ competence (n)
2. _____ component (n)
3. _____ facilitate (v)
4. _____ inevitably (adv)
5. _____ labor (n)
6. _____ pertain to (v phr)
7. _____ promising (adj)
8. _____ retain (v)
9. _____ sector (n)
10. _____ widespread (adj)

a. area of a society or economy
b. to relate, belong, or apply to
c. showing signs of future success
d. to keep
e. work or employment
f. the ability to do something well
g. certainly, necessarily
h. to make something easier or more efficient
i. existing or happening over a large area
j. a part of a larger whole

C Work in a small group. Look at the information in exercise A. Discuss the questions.

CRITICAL THINKING: ANALYZING

1. For which sectors is the future promising? For which is globalization having a negative effect? Are any of the predictions surprising? Explain.

2. Choose four of the sectors and discuss how globalization might be expanding or shrinking the labor force in each.

VOCABULARY SKILL Using Collocations

Collocations are combinations of words that are frequently used together. Two common patterns are:

Noun + Noun (The first noun acts like an adjective.)

labor markets   *business sector*   *earning power*

Adjective + Noun

private sector   *advanced technologies*   *remote control*

D Complete each global career tip with the correct collocation.

1. Just knowing your _____ isn't enough these days. Learn a second one.

   a. natural language   b. native language   c. national language

2. Do your own Internet research to keep up with _____ in your chosen field.

   a. major trends   b. upper trends   c. considerable trends

3. Take a trip overseas during _____ to explore employment options.

   a. spring break   b. spring pause   c. spring intermission

4. Don't forget that companies often fill their _____ with local talent.

   a. superior positions   b. senior positions   c. elder positions

5. If you hope to work in the _____, do a leadership training program.

   a. managing sector   b. manager sector   c. management sector

6. If you have an _____, look for a position abroad.

   a. adventurous spirit   b. adventurous energy   c. adventurous body

7. Develop the ability to adapt to other cultures, as it's part of a global career

   _____.

   a. skill series   b. skill collection   c. skill set

8. Join online discussions related to your _____ of expertise or interest.

   a. specific region   b. specific field   c. specific environment

---

E Work in a group. Discuss the career tips above. Then use the collocations to make your own career tips.

CRITICAL THINKING: APPLYING

> *Don't worry if you don't speak English as well as your native language. A lot of successful international businesspeople are still perfecting their English!*

A Listening A Lecture about Succeeding in Business

BEFORE LISTENING

PRIOR KNOWLEDGE **A** Work in a small group. Discuss these questions.

1. What does it take to be successful in today's globalized business world?

2. You are going to hear a lecture about four skills, called "competences", needed to succeed in business today. Look at the skills and discuss what you think each means.
   - personal competence
   - social competence
   - business competence
   - cultural competence

WHILE LISTENING

> **LISTENING SKILL** Listening for Advantages
>
> When introducing new ideas, speakers often point out the advantages of those ideas. Listen for the following ways speakers express advantages.
>
> - a clear statement of the advantage
>   > *The advantage/benefit (of) ... is ...*
>   > *... is useful/beneficial/important because ...*
>   > *... is essential for ...*
> - a question before introducing an advantage
>   > *Why is ... useful/beneficial/important?*
> - an explanation of what the advantage allows us to do or what it makes possible
>   > *... allows/helps us/you (to) ...*
>   > *... makes it possible to ...*

▼ **Doing business across different cultures requires a high level of cultural competence.**

NOTE-TAKING SKILL Using Columns

To organize two corresponding sets of information, you can use two columns. Write the main ideas in the left-hand column. Then add a column to the right for the supporting ideas or details that pertain to those main ideas. Using arrows or lines between the corresponding information can make it easier to see and remember the connections between the main ideas and the supporting details.

B 🎧 2.3 ▶ 1.8 Listen to the lecture and follow along with the notes in the first column.   LISTENING FOR DETAILS

Succeeding in Business

Competences | **Advantages**

Personal competence

1. understanding yourself → helps you use time and _____ correctly
   ₁
2. emotional intelligence → facilitates _____
   ₂
3. be realistic but optimistic → helps you be positive when things go wrong

Social competence

1. practical trust → helps you trust ppl to _____ done
   ₃
2. constructive impatience → sends message: do things _____
   ₄
3. connective teaching → makes poss. for others to teach _____
   ₅

Business competence

1. managing chaos → allows you to deal w/ _____ in bus.
   ₆
2. fluency with technology → makes avail. latest e-bus. _____
   ₇
3. developing leadership → helps bus. succeed & _____ better
   ₈

Cultural competence

1. understanding your culture → allows you to value strengths & _____
   ₉
2. international curiosity → allows you to look beyond yr _____ for opps.
   ₁₀
3. bridge building → allows creation of connections across cultrs

C 🎧 2.3 Listen again and complete the second column of notes in exercise B. Write no more than two words in each blank.   NOTE TAKING

AFTER LISTENING

D Work with a partner. Discuss these questions.   PERSONALIZING

1. Which of the competences that the lecturer spoke about is an area of strength for you? If possible, give an example.

2. Which of the competences would you like to develop? Explain.

A Speaking

> **SPEAKING SKILL** Defining Terms
>
> When giving a presentation, you may sometimes use terms that are related to a specific field. Your listeners may not be familiar with these terms, and their meaning may differ from the dictionary definitions. In these cases, you should define the terms using language that your audience will understand. Here are some expressions you can use:
>
> | | |
> |---|---|
> | *The term ... refers to/means ...* | *By ..., I mean ...* |
> | *This means ...* | *... is defined as ...* |
>
> You can also define a term by simply pausing after the term and giving a definition.

A 🎧 **2.4** Work with a partner. Take turns reading the sentences aloud using expressions from the skill box. Then listen and fill in the expressions the speaker uses.

1. _____ emotional intelligence, _____ understanding your own emotions and those of others.

2. _____ *social competence* _____ the skills required to engage with and get the best out of other people.

3. The third component of social competence is known as *connective teaching*. _____ being just as eager to learn from others as you are to pass on your knowledge to them.

4. Cultural competence _____ an understanding of cultural differences and how to make use of that knowledge.

B Match each term related to globalization on the left with its definition on the right.

1. _____ coca-colonization	a.	the distance food is transported from producer to consumer
2. _____ postnationalism	b.	the globalization of American culture through U.S. products
3. _____ food miles	c.	inequality in access to computers and the Internet
4. _____ worldlang	d.	an active user of social media and the Internet
5. _____ netizen	e.	the process by which nations become global entities
6. _____ digital divide	f.	a new language created from several modern languages

DEFINING TERMS **C** Work with a partner. Practice saying sentences to introduce and then define the terms in exercise B. Use expressions for defining terms from the Speaking Skill box.

> *One aspect of globalization that isn't always welcome is coca-colonization. By coca-colonization, I mean the globalization of American culture through U.S. products.*

D Work in a small group. Discuss the advantages and/or disadvantages of the six aspects of globalization. Take notes below. Write an advantage and disadvantage for each.

CRITICAL THINKING: EVALUATING

Aspects of Globalization		Advantages	Disadvantages
1. coca-colonization	→	_____	_____
2. postnationalism	→	_____	_____
3. food miles	→	_____	_____
4. worldlang	→	_____	_____
5. netizen	→	_____	_____
6. digital divide	→	_____	_____

E Consider a job you are interested in and how globalization might impact it. Complete the tasks.

CRITICAL THINKING: APPLYING

1. Write a job you are interested in. _____

2. Look below at the graphic from the beginning of the unit. How do the Drivers and Key Skills relate to the job you chose? Take notes. Then discuss your ideas with a partner.

   • Drivers relevant to the job: _____
   _____

   • Key Skills relevant to the job: _____
   _____

   • Which skills are your strengths and which are your weaknesses?

   Strengths: _____

   Weaknesses: _____

   • Work with a partner. Discuss steps you could take to be better prepared for this job.

Drivers of Change in the Workplace

Smart machines and systems   People living longer   Big data   New media   Knowledge sharing   Globally connected world

Key Skills Needed in the Future Workplace

Creative thinking   Social intelligence   Knowledge of multiple disciplines   Media literacy   Managing mental overload   Computational thinking   Cross-cultural under-standing   Virtual collaboration

GRAMMAR FOR SPEAKING Gerund Phrases

A gerund phrase is a type of noun phrase. Gerund phrases begin with a gerund (the base form of a verb plus -ing) and include one or more modifiers and additional objects. They are used as the subject or subject complement of a sentence, object of a verb, or object of a preposition.

> **Being realistic but at the same time optimistic** allows us to stay positive—even when things go wrong.
>
> The first component of personal competence is **understanding yourself**.
>
> You should not avoid **making difficult decisions**.
>
> Social competence is essential for **bringing together groups of talented people**.

F Put the words and phrases in the correct order to create sentences with gerund phrases about career skills. More than one answer may be possible.

1. to think critically / is / for problem solving / being able / essential

   _____

2. are vital / accessing current information / Internet search skills / for

   _____

3. huge amounts of data / facilitate / analyzing / Big Data skills

   _____

4. a high level of / working with others successfully / emotional intelligence / requires

   _____

5. decisions / a fundamental skill / of leaders / is / making

   _____

6. many employers / is / solve problems effectively / look for / a skill / being able to

   _____

7. change / is / to welcome / a key skill / being able

   _____

8. a foreign language / toward becoming / a global citizen / is / learning / an important step

   _____

CRITICAL THINKING:
RANKING

G Work in a small group. Look at the career skills. Add two more to the list. Then discuss how important they are, and number them from 1 (most useful) to 10 (least useful).

_____ a. analyzing data
_____ b. being able to think critically
_____ c. decision-making
_____ d. researching information online
_____ e. solving problems effectively

_____ f. speaking a foreign language
_____ g. welcoming change
_____ h. working with others
_____ i. _____
_____ j. _____

LESSON TASK Role-Playing a Job Interview

A Work with a partner. You are going to role-play a job interview. Look at the list of interview questions and add one more question about work experience.

> ### INTERVIEW QUESTIONS
> 1. Can you tell me a little about yourself?
> 2. What are your greatest strengths?
> 3. What is your greatest weakness?
> 4. Describe a stressful workplace situation you experienced. How did you handle it?
> 5. What is your approach to working successfully in a team?
> 6. This position requires working with people from different cultural backgrounds. What skills or qualifications do you have to work cross-culturally?
> 7. _____
>   _____

B On your own, study the interview questions and prepare your answers. Make notes to use during the interview. Use any work, school, or life experience you've had, information from this lesson, and your imagination, as necessary.

CRITICAL THINKING: APPLYING

> ### EVERYDAY LANGUAGE Asking about Experiences
>
> *Can you tell me about a time that/when you … ?*
> *Have you ever had the chance/opportunity to … ?*
> *Have you ever had any experience with … ?*

▼ **The Hongkong and Shanghai Banking Company (HSBC) is a globally focused company with headquarters in Hong Kong and branches throughout the world.**

C With your partner, role-play an interview between a hiring manager at an international company and an applicant. Ask the interview questions from exercise A, as well as any follow-up questions as appropriate. Use expressions from the Everyday Language box. Then switch roles and repeat.

Video

Sherpa Lives

A Sherpa replaces rope on Ama Dablam Mountain in the Himalayas.

BEFORE VIEWING

A Work in a small group. Look at the photo and discuss the questions.

1. Where do you think the Sherpa live? What might the climate be like?

2. The Sherpa people are famous for the work they do. What do you think they do?

3. In Lesson A, you learned about some of the ways globalization is affecting job markets and workers. How do you think globalization is affecting the lives and work of the Sherpa people?

WHILE VIEWING

NOTE TAKING **B** ▶ 1.9 Watch the introduction of the video, given by mountain climber and National Geographic Explorer Conrad Anker. Complete the notes. Write no more than two words or a number in each blank.

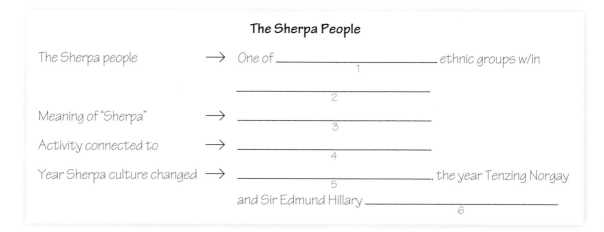

The Sherpa People

The Sherpa people → One of _____ ethnic groups w/in
                              1
_____
          2

Meaning of "Sherpa" → _____
                                3

Activity connected to → _____
                                  4

Year Sherpa culture changed → _____, the year Tenzing Norgay
                                          5
and Sir Edmund Hillary _____
                                  6

C ▶ **1.10** Watch the entire video. Match each idea with the speaker who expresses it.

1. _____ Karma Tsering
2. _____ Conrad Anker
3. _____ Max Lowe
4. _____ Kancha Sherpa
5. _____ Mahendra Kathet

a. Sherpa education, healthcare, and clothing have all improved.
b. Sherpa can earn enough money, although life feels hurried.
c. Sherpa society has become much more connected than before.
d. Many Sherpa people are ambitious and seek success abroad.
e. Sherpas learned a modern skill thanks to a foreigner's gift.

D ▶ **1.10** Watch the video again and choose the correct answer.

1. Sir Edmund Hillary rewarded his Sherpa guides with watches as _____ .
   a. payment   b. a bonus   c. a prize

2. In terms of health care, the Sherpa now have _____ and medical clinics.
   a. an eye doctor   b. a dentist   c. a pharmacy

3. The only issue Kancha Sherpa is concerned about is _____ .
   a. making money   b. dealing with tourists   c. global warming

4. Some believe that people are losing the ability to focus on _____ .
   a. true happiness   b. the tourist trade   c. mountain climbing

5. An increase in food _____ has led to healthier diets.
   a. diversity   b. production   c. education

6. You can now use a cell phone _____ Mount Everest.
   a. at the top of   b. from anywhere on   c. at the base camp of

AFTER VIEWING

CRITICAL THINKING   Evaluating

When you evaluate, you make a judgment based on criteria. To evaluate situations or concepts, make sure you have a good understanding of the criteria you are using. This will allow you to explain your evaluation more clearly to other people. Highlight your evaluation criteria by beginning with one of these expressions:

In terms of [diet],...   *With regard to [culture],...*   *As far as [education] goes,...*

E Work in a small group. Use the criteria below to evaluate this statement: *Since 1953, Sherpa life has changed for the better.*

physical well-being   technological level   traditions and culture

B Vocabulary

A 🎧 **2.5** Listen and check (✓) the words you already know. Use a dictionary to help you with any new words.

☐ **anticipate** (v)   ☐ **emerging** (adj)   ☐ **influential** (adj)   ☐ **portable** (adj)
☐ **application** (n)   ☐ **enrich** (v)   ☐ **mass** (adj)   ☐ **prominent** (adj)
☐ **collaborate** (v)   ☐ **implication** (n)

CRITICAL THINKING:
ANALYZING

B Read the definition of *augment*. Then read the "Revealed World" section in the article below. What do you think *augmented reality* means? Discuss your ideas with a partner.

augment (v): to make something larger, stronger, or more effective by adding to it

C 🎧 **2.6** Complete the article with words from exercise A. Use the correct form of the words. Then listen and check your answers.

THE WORLD OF AUGMENTED REALITY

Augmented reality is one of the most promising and _____ global trends
1
of recent years. This much-talked-about _____
2
technology is most often used to _____ the reality
3
we see through a cell phone or other _____ device with fun or useful information, images, sounds, or videos.
4
Some _____ of augmented reality that are already being widely used include
5
apps that highlight and display information about restaurants, historic sites, museum exhibits, or where you parked your car. A variety of outdoor games use the technology to allow players to _____ as they hunt for digital objects. Among such games,
6
Pokémon Go is the most _____ example; it has introduced augmented
7
reality to a _____ audience. The augmented reality experience is also available
8
through special eyewear or headsets, and soon even contact lenses. As we look toward the future, we _____ many more uses for this promising technology with
9
_____ for nearly every aspect of life in the years to come.
10

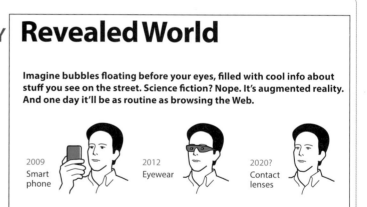

Revealed World

Imagine bubbles floating before your eyes, filled with cool info about stuff you see on the street. Science fiction? Nope. It's augmented reality. And one day it'll be as routine as browsing the Web.

2009 Smart phone

2012 Eyewear

2020? Contact lenses

D Complete the chart with the correct form of each word. Use a dictionary to help you.

	Noun	Verb	Adjective
1.		collaborate	
2.	implication		
3.			influential
4.		anticipate	
5.		X	prominent
6.		emerge	

E Work with a partner. Discuss these questions.

1. Look at the photo below and read the caption. What is another way that augmented reality could enrich a museum experience?

2. Would you prefer to access the Internet via glasses or a headset? Explain.

3. Do you think that augmented reality will continue to generate mass interest? What future uses for this emerging technology do you anticipate?

4. Do all uses of augmented reality enrich our lives? Or are there any negative implications of the mass use of this technology? Explain.

CRITICAL THINKING: EVALUATING

▼ **Augmented reality adds another level of information to museum exhibits. Dinosaur bones get a layer of flesh and the ability to move around at the Royal Ontario Museum, Canada.**

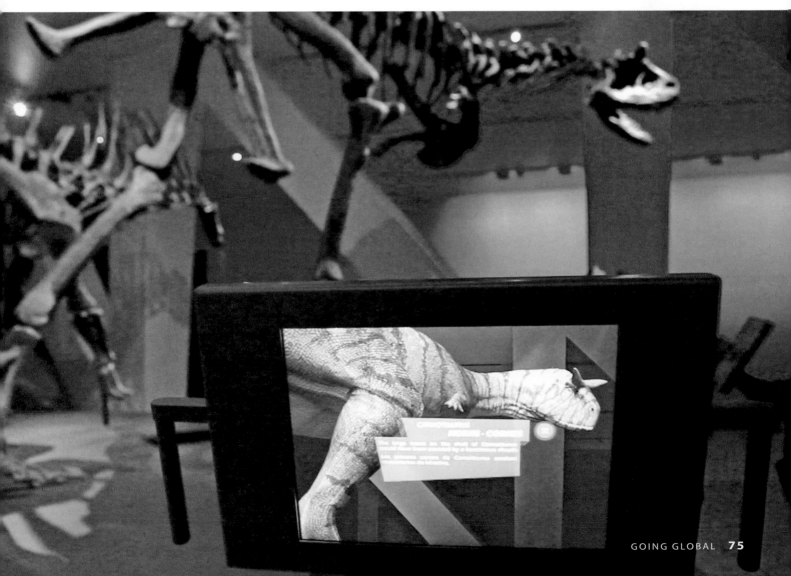

B Listening A Podcast about Augmented Reality

BEFORE LISTENING

CRITICAL THINKING:
INTERPRETING
VISUALS

A Work with a partner. Discuss these questions.

1. Where might you see an image like the one below?
2. What kinds of information are available in the image?

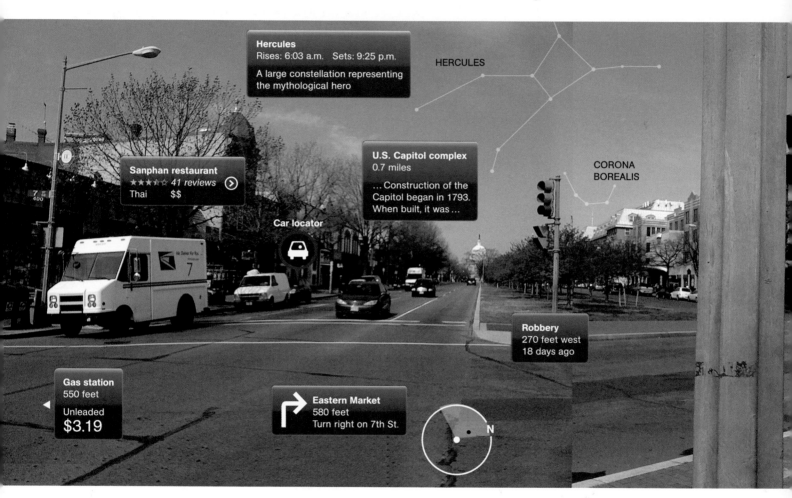

WHILE LISTENING

LISTENING FOR
MAIN IDEAS

B 🎧 **2.7** Listen to a podcast about augmented reality (AR). Check (✓) the two main ideas the speakers discuss.

1. ☐ AR is a useful technology with many different applications.

2. ☐ AR's popularity has contributed to the widespread use of portable devices.

3. ☐ AR is useful when deciding which pieces of furniture to purchase.

4. ☐ AR facilitates the globalization of culture through popular games.

5. ☐ Pokémon Go's popularity has unquestionably benefited local economies.

C 🎧 **2.7** Listen again and complete the outline. Write no more than two words in each blank.

I. Intro to AR—an emerging trend in tech

   A. Combines info/images w/the _____
                                1

   B. Later, AR will integrate sounds

II. AR has importnt implications for globalization of bus.

   A. Potential to enrich _____
                          2

   B. Could imitate facial _____ & glances
                       3

III. More ppl using AR → more affordable

   A. In industry, machines marked w/ _____
                           4

   B. Shopping for furniture—see how looks in room

IV. Pokémon GO

   A. More _____ than Facebook/Twitter in 1 yr
               5

   B. How to play

      1. Look for animated _____ (i.e., Pokémon)
                      6

      2. Goal: capture them in your _____
                          7

   C. Reasons for success

      1. Pokémon was already a _____ brand
                       8

      2. Ppl felt better walking around outside

      3. Chances for _____ other ppl
                    9

   D. The business side

      1. Has pwr to make areas or _____
                        10

      2. Hunters may want to buy snacks, drinks, etc.

AFTER LISTENING

D Work in a small group. Discuss these questions. Use your notes from exercise C to help you.

1. What is an application of AR that would improve your own life? Explain.

2. Some believe that games that are played worldwide, such as Pokémon GO, have contributed to the globalization of culture. Others see them as global fads that have no significant impact. What is your view?

3. What are some of the benefits of the globalization of culture? What are some of the drawbacks?

Speaking

PRONUNCIATION Saying Parentheticals

🎧 2.8 We sometimes use parenthetical expressions to help clarify our ideas. We separate them with a short pause before and after. The intonation of these expressions begins a bit lower than the phrase before the interruption and rises slightly at the end. This prepares the listener for the continuation of the interrupted sentence.

*Augmented reality, **or AR as it's often called**, has been a prominent trend in recent years . . .*

*They can join meetings by phone, **which is great**, but it's not the same as being there.*

A 🎧 2.9 Underline the parenthetical expression in each sentence. Then listen and check your work. With a partner, practice saying these sentences, using correct intonation and pauses with the parentheticals.

1. That car service, though convenient and affordable, is taking jobs away from taxi drivers everywhere.

2. Pokémon GO is, at least for now, a wildly popular augmented reality game.

3. Wearable technology, despite all the advertising, hasn't had the mass appeal we'd anticipated.

4. Bollywood-style dance classes, believe it or not, are a growing trend in many places.

5. Digital art that is created for use on the Internet is sometimes, in my opinion, extremely stunning.

6. Robots and other machines, although they are undeniably useful, are causing some people to lose their jobs.

7. People born between 1982 and 2004, sometimes called "millennials," are skilled at using social media to collaborate.

8. The increase in injuries to teens, which few anticipated, is linked to the global extreme sports trend.

B Work with a partner. Make five statements about topics from popular culture (movies, TV, music, sports, fashion, technology, etc.) using the parenthetical expressions in the box below or ones of your own. Use correct intonation and pauses.

A: *Robert Downey, Jr., I think you'll agree, is a really great actor.*
B: *Oh, definitely. He was in the* Iron Man *movies, which I love, and in* Spiderman.

I think you'll agree	though I've never tried it	believe it or not
in my opinion	which I love	as far as I'm concerned

C Work in a small group. Read about four emerging global trends. Then discuss the benefits and drawbacks these trends could have on people, businesses, or organizations.

CRITICAL THINKING: ANALYZING

A: *Synthetic food would inevitably save the lives of millions of animals.*
B: *That's true, but would it be healthy to eat? It could have some negative effects on people who eat it, couldn't it?*

1. **Synthetic food:** Plant-based meat replacements and meat grown in laboratories without harming animals will be coming to grocery stores.

2. **Virtual reality (VR):** You will be able to watch live shows and concerts and feel as if you're actually there without leaving your living room.

3. **Self-driving cars:** Companies like Tesla and Uber are creating systems that will eliminate the need for drivers and reduce the number of road accidents.

4. **Artificial art:** Computers are already writing songs and will soon be creating movies, paintings, novels, and poetry.

FINAL TASK Evaluating a Social Media Platform

> You are going to research a social media platform, evaluate its importance for globalization, and present your findings to your group.

A Work in a small group. Look at the bar graph and discuss these questions.

CRITICAL THINKING: INTERPRETING A GRAPH

1. How are the social media platforms ranked in the chart?
2. What do the different bar colors represent?
3. Which of the platforms have you heard of? Which have you used?

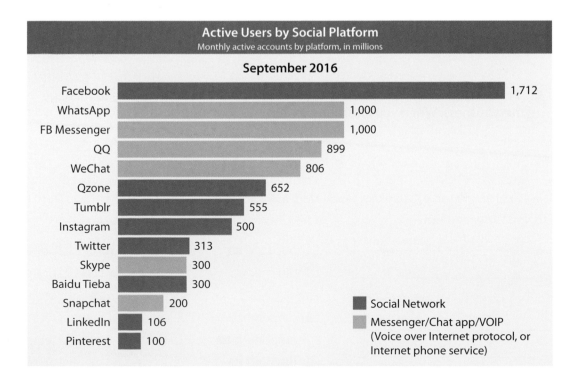

Active Users by Social Platform
Monthly active accounts by platform, in millions

September 2016

Facebook	1,712
WhatsApp	1,000
FB Messenger	1,000
QQ	899
WeChat	806
Qzone	652
Tumblr	555
Instagram	500
Twitter	313
Skype	300
Baidu Tieba	300
Snapchat	200
LinkedIn	106
Pinterest	100

■ Social Network
■ Messenger/Chat app/VOIP (Voice over Internet protocol, or Internet phone service)

B Choose a platform from the graph in exercise A or another to research. Then prepare a presentation using the outline below.

I. Introduction

    A. A brief description of the platform

    B. A brief history of the platform

II. The Business Side

    A. How does it make money?

    B. Who are its competitors?

    C. How does it compare with its competitors? What are the similarities and differences?

III. Globalization

    A. Where is it most popular?

    B. How does the platform facilitate globalization?

IV. The Future

    A. Is the platform currently becoming more or less popular?

    B. How will the platform likely change in the future?

PRESENTATION SKILL Managing Nervousness

It is normal to be a little nervous at the beginning of a presentation. Because the first impression you make on your audience is important, learn to manage any nervousness. First of all, remember to breathe and be as natural as you can. Make an effort to speak slowly and calmly. Memorizing the first few sentences you plan to say can sometimes help. Soon you will feel more comfortable and confident.

PRESENTING **C** Present your platform to your group. Notice which strategy you use to manage nervousness. When you finish, answer any questions.

REFLECTION

1. What information that you learned in this unit is likely to be the most useful to you? Why and how?

    _____

    _____

2. What trend in the unit did you find the most interesting?

    _____

    _____

3. Here are the vocabulary words and phrases from the unit. Check (✓) the ones you can use.

☐ anticipate AWL   ☐ facilitate AWL   ☐ portable

☐ application   ☐ implication AWL   ☐ prominent

☐ collaborate   ☐ inevitably AWL   ☐ promising

☐ competence   ☐ influential   ☐ retain AWL

☐ component AWL   ☐ labor AWL   ☐ sector AWL

☐ emerging AWL   ☐ mass   ☐ widespread AWL

☐ enrich   ☐ pertain to

MIGRATION

5

A migrating herd of pronghorn deer crawls under a fence in Wyoming, USA.

THINK AND DISCUSS

1 Migration is when animals (or people) move from one place to another. Where do you think the deer in the photo are going?

2 What does the photo suggest about the relationship between human development and animal migration?

3 What are reasons people might move from one place to another?

EXPLORE THE THEME

Look at the map and read the information. Then discuss the questions.

1. What route is Paul Salopek taking on his journey, and how is he traveling?
2. What do you think were some reasons that early humans left Africa?
3. Why do you think Salopek is taking this journey?

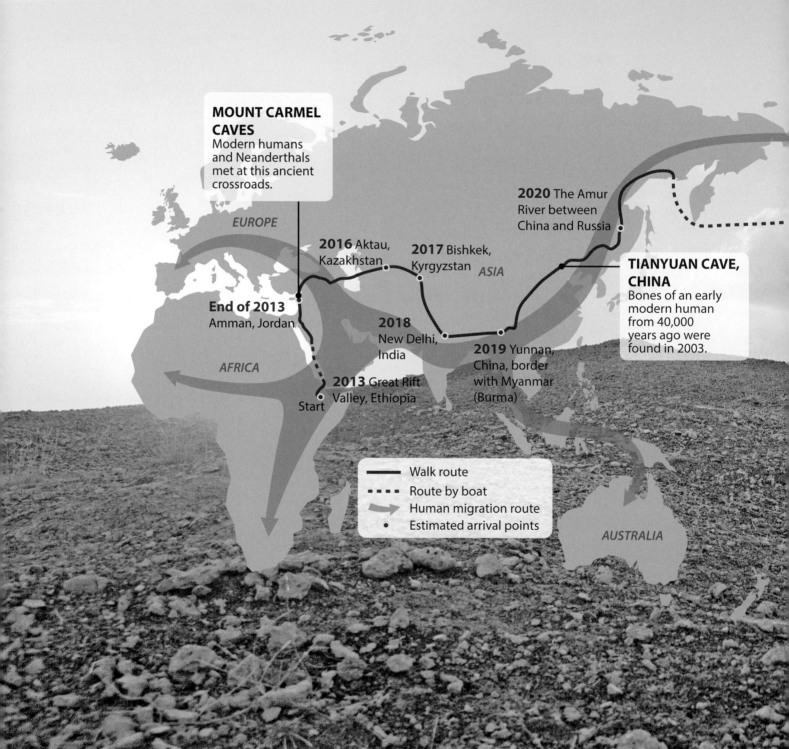

MOUNT CARMEL CAVES
Modern humans and Neanderthals met at this ancient crossroads.

EUROPE

2016 Aktau, Kazakhstan

2017 Bishkek, Kyrgyzstan

ASIA

2020 The Amur River between China and Russia

TIANYUAN CAVE, CHINA
Bones of an early modern human from 40,000 years ago were found in 2003.

End of 2013
Amman, Jordan

2018
New Delhi, India

AFRICA

2013 Great Rift Valley, Ethiopia
Start

2019 Yunnan, China, border with Myanmar (Burma)

──── Walk route

- - - - Route by boat

➤ Human migration route

• Estimated arrival points

AUSTRALIA

THE LONGEST WALK

Evidence suggests that *Homo sapiens* set out to discover regions of Earth some 100 to 125,000 years ago, traveling from Ethiopia's Great Rift Valley to the farthest tip of South America. To retrace their steps, writer Paul Salopek has begun his own global journey, a 21,000-mile trek that touches four continents. Calling the project the *Out of Eden Walk*, Salopek is using the latest fossil and genetic findings to plan his route. His reports from the trail are posted regularly at outofedenwalk.org.

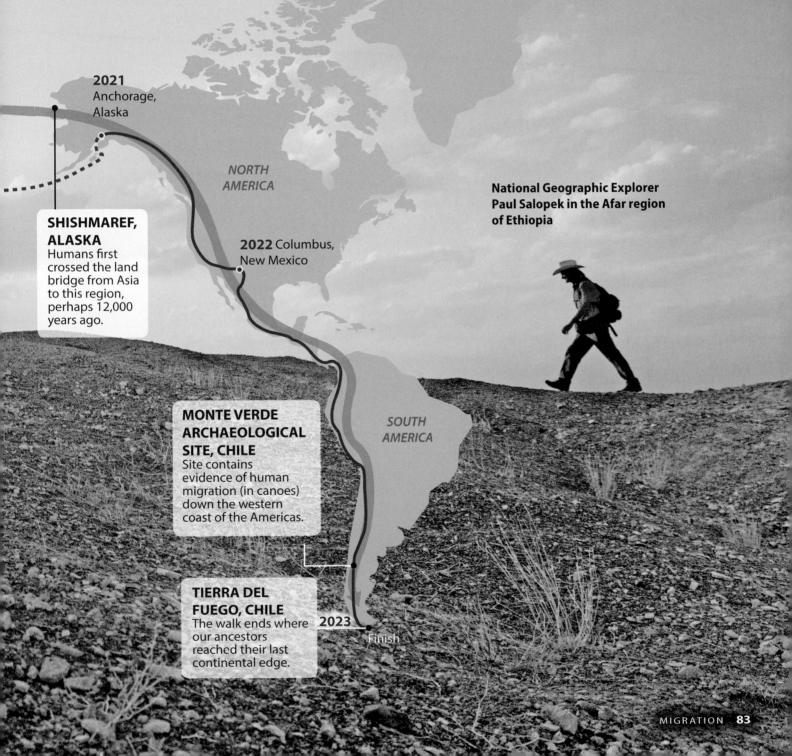

2021
Anchorage, Alaska

NORTH AMERICA

SHISHMAREF, ALASKA
Humans first crossed the land bridge from Asia to this region, perhaps 12,000 years ago.

2022 Columbus, New Mexico

National Geographic Explorer Paul Salopek in the Afar region of Ethiopia

MONTE VERDE ARCHAEOLOGICAL SITE, CHILE
Site contains evidence of human migration (in canoes) down the western coast of the Americas.

SOUTH AMERICA

TIERRA DEL FUEGO, CHILE
The walk ends where our ancestors reached their last continental edge.

2023
Finish

A Vocabulary

MEANING FROM CONTEXT

A 🎧 **2.10** Look at the map. Then read and listen to the information about migration. Notice each word in **blue** and think about its meaning.

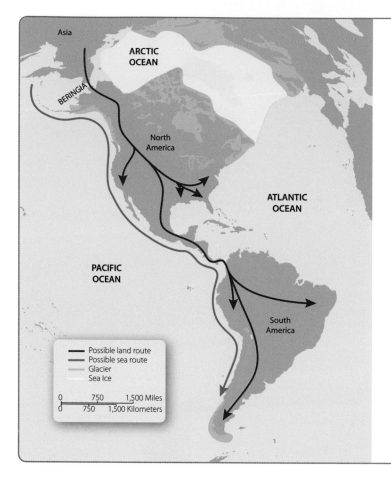

PATHS TO A NEW WORLD

No one is sure how or when the first people got to the Americas. However, recent **notable** discoveries and DNA analyses have changed our **perspective** on the first human migrations into the Americas. **Archaeologists** have found evidence suggesting that a group of perhaps fewer than 5,000 individuals **ventured** from Asia into the Americas over 15,000 years ago. This group, they believe, traveled an **immense** distance along the western coastlines of North and South America. **Subsequently**, after melting glaciers[1] had opened an interior path, a second group **migrated** from Asia following a land route. They aimed to explore and settle the central areas of the Americas. **Genetic** studies have confirmed the **hypothesis** that modern American Indians are indeed the **descendants** of people from Asia.

[1]**glacier** (n): an extremely large mass of ice

B Write each word in **blue** from exercise A next to its definition.

1. _____ (n) a possible explanation suggested by evidence

2. _____ (adv) later or afterwards

3. _____ (n) point of view

4. _____ (n) blood relatives in future generations

5. _____ (v) went into a place that might be dangerous

6. _____ (adj) extremely large or great in amount or scale

7. _____ (adj) related to characteristics of the body that are passed from generation to generation

8. _____ (n) scientists who study ancient cultures through the tools, buildings, and relics of ancient peoples

9. _____ (adj) important, interesting, or remarkable

10. _____ (v) moved from one area to another

C Work in a small group. Discuss the questions and explain your answers.

1. What is a notable discovery of the 21st century?
2. What is a good way to change a person's perspective?
3. Have you ever ventured somewhere unusual or off the beaten track? If you haven't, would you like to?
4. What can you describe as *immense*?
5. Look at the map in exercise A. On which ocean did the 5,000 people who migrated from Asia travel? About what distance did they travel in the Americas?

VOCABULARY SKILL Suffixes *–ant* and *–ist*

The suffix *–ant* is added to some verbs to mean a person who performs the action of the verb.

apply → applic**ant**   descend → descend**ant**

The suffix *–ist* is added to some verbs or nouns to refer to a person who performs an action, uses an instrument or device, or works in a certain field.

type → typ**ist**   archaeology → archaeolog**ist**

D Write a word ending in *–ant* or *–ist* that matches the definition. Use the underlined words and a dictionary to help you.

1. _____ someone who <u>participates</u> in an activity

2. _____ someone who works in the field of <u>biology</u>

3. _____ a person who studies the <u>future</u> and makes predictions

4. _____ a person who <u>migrates</u> from one place to another

5. _____ a person who draws <u>cartoons</u> for a living

6. _____ a person who <u>defends</u> himself or herself in court

7. _____ a scientist who does <u>genetic</u> research

8. _____ a person who <u>inhabits</u> a certain region

E Work in a small group. Discuss the questions.

CRITICAL THINKING: REFLECTING

1. Geneticists have discovered that information is written in our DNA. What sort of information has genetic research uncovered? What can it tell us about ourselves and our families?
2. Notable discoveries, such as the discovery of the ancient civilization of the Egyptians that thrived over 5,000 years ago, have changed the way we understand the past. Would you be interested in becoming an archaeologist and doing this kind of research? Explain.
3. A *time capsule* is a container filled with items that we hope will one day be found by others. If you were going to create a time capsule, what items would you include to best represent your culture today? Explain your choices.

A Listening A Podcast about Ancient Migration

BEFORE LISTENING

A sculpted model of a female Neanderthal

PREDICTING **A** Work with a partner. Look at the photo and caption. Then predict the answers to these questions.

1. Scientists believe that the Neanderthal were a species of ancient humans that became extinct many thousands of years ago. In which regions of the earth do you think Neanderthals lived?
2. What do you think happened when modern humans moved into an area that had already been settled by Neanderthals?
3. Do you think there is any Neanderthal DNA in modern humans?

WHILE LISTENING

CHECKING PREDICTIONS **B** 🎧 2.11 ▶ 1.11 Listen to the podcast. Were your predictions in exercise A correct?

> **CRITICAL THINKING** Distinguishing Fact from Theory
>
> Distinguishing between fact and theory is an important skill because while facts usually remain true, theories may change. In science, facts are situations that can be observed again and again. Theories provide explanations based on facts. To distinguish between the two, it can be helpful to ask whether the information is an observation (fact) or an explanation (theory).

C 🎧 **2.12** Listen to an excerpt from the podcast and write *Theory* or *Fact*.

CRITICAL THINKING:
DISTINGUISHING
FACT FROM THEORY

1. _____ Every once in a while, a baby is born with a slight difference in its DNA.

2. _____ All humans are related to one woman who lived about 150,000 years ago.

3. _____ Over one hundred thousand years ago, humans began migrating out of Africa.

4. _____ Scientists have found the remains of ancient humans in Australia.

5. _____ Humans were already living in Europe 30,000 years ago.

6. _____ Some Neanderthals were absorbed into the modern human family.

NOTE-TAKING SKILL Using a Time Line

When studying a topic that is organized chronologically, a time line can be the clearest and most efficient way to organize your notes. Time lines usually run from left to right, but setting up a time line diagonally or vertically can create more space for events and their descriptions.

D 🎧 **2.13** Listen to an excerpt from the podcast. As you listen, complete the time line about human migration. Write no more than two words or a number.

NOTE TAKING

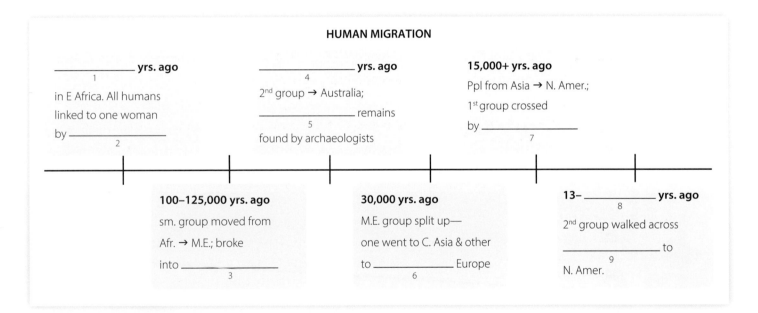

HUMAN MIGRATION

_____ yrs. ago
1
in E Africa. All humans linked to one woman by _____
2

_____ yrs. ago
4
2nd group → Australia;
_____ remains
5
found by archaeologists

15,000+ yrs. ago
Ppl from Asia → N. Amer.;
1st group crossed
by _____
7

100–125,000 yrs. ago
sm. group moved from
Afr. → M.E.; broke
into _____
3

30,000 yrs. ago
M.E. group split up—
one went to C. Asia & other
to _____ Europe
6

13– _____ yrs. ago
8
2nd group walked across
_____ to
9
N. Amer.

AFTER LISTENING

E Work with a partner. Take turns completing the tasks.

CRITICAL THINKING:
REFLECTING

1. From memory, retell the story of the journey of modern humans that you heard. If you need help, refer to the time line in exercise D.

2. The information you heard follows the story of modern humans up until about 12,000 years ago when they had reached every continent except Antarctica. There have been many other migrations of people since then. Think of an example of a migration of people in the past or present. Explain the circumstances and the reasons for it to your partner. Include any facts you know and theories you have.

Speaking

SPEAKING SKILL Approximating

We often need to express approximate numbers, such as amounts, dates, or times.

*I'm leaving work in **about 10 minutes**. I'll see you **around 7:00**.*

Here are some expressions you can use to mean *around* or *about*:

something like	*or thereabouts*	*-ish*	*approximately*
more or less	*roughly*	*an estimated*	*or so*

These expressions are similar in meaning to *nearly* or *equal to*:

up to	*almost*	*not quite*

And these expressions can be used to mean *not less than* or *over* (a certain value):

at least	*more than*

A 🎧 **2.14** The podcast about migration included a number of expressions for approximating. With a partner, read the sentences aloud, using expressions for approximating. Then listen and write the expressions used.

1. Based on genetic evidence, scientists now think that all humans are related to one woman who lived _____ 150,000 years ago in East Africa.

2. It was 50,000 years ago _____ that some of these humans reached Australia, where archaeologists have found ancient human remains.

3. One group reached Central Asia _____ 30,000 years ago.

4. The first group crossed _____ 15,000 years ago using a sea route, keeping close to the shore as they continued down the west coast of North and South America.

Early modern humans hunt during the ice age.

B Work with a partner. Ask each other these questions. Answer using expressions for approximating.

PERSONALIZING

1. How much money would you be willing to spend on a car?
2. How much time off do you get in a year?
3. How long have you been studying English?
4. How much money do you spend per month on entertainment?
5. Think of a childhood friend. How long has it been since you last saw him or her?
6. How long has it been since you last used social media?
7. What percentage of Neanderthal DNA do you think you might have?
8. How long do you think you will be studying English?

GRAMMAR FOR SPEAKING Modals of Past Possibility

To make guesses and inferences about the past, use *could have*, *may (not) have*, or *might (not) have* and a past participle.

> Modern humans entering Central Asia **could have run into** Neanderthals.
> That group **might not have been** larger than a thousand people.

In short responses that are guesses, do not use the past participle.

> A: *Did they come from the Middle East?*
> B: *They* **may have**.

When *be* is the main verb, keep the past participle in the answer.

> A: *Were the Neanderthals absorbed into the modern human family?*
> B: *Scientists think some* **might have been**.

If you feel very certain something wasn't true or didn't happen, use *could not have*.

> There **couldn't have been** 10,000 people in the group that left Africa.

C Work with a partner. Read the situations and make guesses about past possibilities for each situation. Use modals of past possibility.

CRITICAL THINKING: MAKING INFERENCES

1. Samantha walked halfway to the bus stop this morning, then suddenly turned around and walked back to her house. Why did she turn around?
2. Yesterday, Ali had to go to the bank after playing basketball. Why did he go there?
3. Last week, Gabriela was offered her dream job, but she decided to turn it down. Why didn't she accept the job?
4. The lights went out in Dian's home last night. Why did they go off?
5. In the 20th century, millions of people immigrated to the United States. Why did they do this?
6. Peter got a text and then excused himself from the meeting. Why did he do this?
7. Chi failed her math test even though she had studied. Why did she fail?
8. The bookstore in our town had to close down recently. Why did it close?

D Work in a small group. Read the scenarios. Then answer the questions by making inferences using modals of past possibility.

1. Archaeologists working at a site in Oklahoma, USA, that is about 10,750 years old found evidence of early humans living there. Arrows with stone heads were found, but the nearest source of this particular stone was in Texas, at least 265 miles (426 km) away. The bones of bison, large grazing animals of North America, were also found at the site. No metal has ever been found at the site, and none was found in Oklahoma. What do these facts tell us about the early human society there?

2. It is known that Neanderthals lived in Europe and Asia when modern humans first arrived roughly 30,000 years ago. Although researchers have found a small amount of Neanderthal DNA in studies of modern humans, there isn't very much. What happened to the Neanderthals, and why?

E With your group, look at the photo. Use past modals to make inferences about who drew them, how they were drawn, how humans lived at that time, why they made these drawings, and so on.

A: *The pictures of animals may have been drawn by the first modern humans.*
B: *No, they couldn't have been. Modern humans hadn't arrived in Europe yet.*
C: *Neanderthals at that time might have been more skilled at drawing than modern humans.*

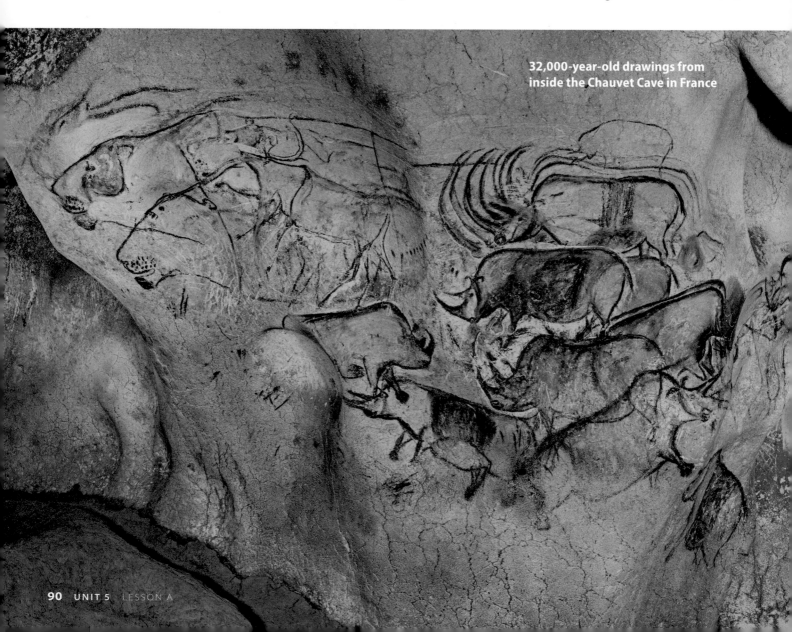

32,000-year-old drawings from inside the Chauvet Cave in France

LESSON TASK Discussing Family Origins

A Where did your family members come from originally? If they left that place, where did they go? Complete the chart with information about your family. If you are not sure about something, write a question mark.

ORGANIZING IDEAS

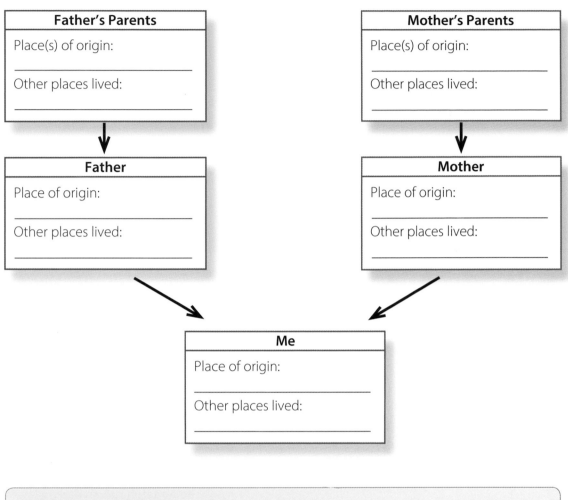

Father's Parents

Place(s) of origin:
_____

Other places lived:
_____

Mother's Parents

Place(s) of origin:
_____

Other places lived:
_____

Father

Place of origin:
_____

Other places lived:
_____

Mother

Place of origin:
_____

Other places lived:
_____

Me

Place of origin:
_____

Other places lived:
_____

EVERYDAY LANGUAGE Showing Surprise

Informal:	*You're kidding (me).*	*That's incredible.*
	Are you serious?	*No way.*
Formal:	*That's really (quite) surprising.*	*That's hard to believe.*
	I never would have guessed.	*I was surprised to learn that… .*

B Work in a small group. Use the information from exercise A to talk about your family. Say where your family members are from and where they have lived. If you are not sure, make a guess. Use expressions of surprise where appropriate.

A: *I was born in Chicago, and my parents were born in Holland. They came to the U.S. in 1967 or so. I'm not sure about my mother's parents. I think they may have migrated from Poland.*

B: *You're kidding. That's where my grandmother is from.*

Wildebeest, zebra, and
European storks in Serengeti
National Park, Tanzania

Wildebeest
Migration

BEFORE VIEWING

A Look at the map and answer the questions.

1. Which two countries does the wildebeest
migration travel through?

_____ _____

2. Use the key to follow the migration of the
wildebeest throughout the year. Where are the wildebeest today?

_____

**Serengeti National Park
Migration:**

1. Jan-Feb-Mar-April	4. Aug-Sep
2. May	5. Oct
3. June-July	6. Nov-Dec

KENYA

TANZANIA

Ikorongo Game
Reserve

Grumeti
Game
Reserve

Loliondo
Game
Controlled
Area

Maswa
Game
Reserve

NCAA

Ndutu

B Match each word in **bold** from the video with its definition.

1. _____ the **calves** can run

2. _____ **carcasses** are left behind

3. _____ wildebeest **grazed** these plains

4. _____ the migrating **herds** arrive

5. _____ **sniff** the air

6. _____ what **triggers** the migration

a. ate grass or other growing plants

b. large groups of animals of one kind

c. young wildebeest

d. the bodies of a dead animals

e. causes an event to happen

f. to smell

WHILE VIEWING

C ▶ 1.12 Watch the video. Does the speaker make these points? Check (✓) the correct answer(s).

UNDERSTANDING MAIN IDEAS

	Yes	No
1. The wildebeest make a massive round-trip journey each year.	☐	☐
2. The migration begins when the herd leader sniffs the air.	☐	☐
3. Not all the animals that begin the migration will make it back.	☐	☐
4. Harsh weather conditions are the main threat to the wildebeest.	☐	☐
5. The journey back begins right after the animals have given birth.	☐	☐

D ▶ 1.12 Watch the video again. Complete the notes. Write no more than three words or a number for each.

NOTE TAKING

> ### Wildebeest Migration
>
> - 2 mil. animals travel almost _____ 1 _____ miles
> - Wildebeest grazed plains more than _____ 2 _____ yrs. ago
> - At beg. of yr., all wldbst give _____ 3 _____ in same mo.
>   - Calves can run _____ 4 _____ their mothers w/in 2 days
> - Nobody knows what _____ 5 _____
> - ~200K of _____ 6 _____ wldbst die of starvation, disease, exhaustion
>   - Others die from preds.; cat tries to separate calf from _____ 7 _____
> - Kenya's Maasai Mara: _____ 8 _____ create huge area of watered _____ 9 _____
> - In Nov., wldbst head south again to the _____ 10 _____

AFTER VIEWING

E Work with a partner. Discuss the questions.

CRITICAL THINKING: EVALUATING

1. In the video, you heard that "no one knows what triggers the migration." What are some possible explanations for why the wildebeest start their migration?
2. Recently, the government of Tanzania wanted to build a highway across the Serengeti National Park. The road would have cut across the migration routes of the wildebeest. What arguments could be made against building this highway? What arguments could be made in favor of building it?
3. How do you think human and animal migrations are similar? How are they different?
4. Every year a great animal migration in Tanzania attracts nearly 200,000 tourists to the area. Would you also call this movement of humans a migration? Explain.

Vocabulary

A 🎧 **2.15** Look at the map and the map key of the Greater Yellowstone Ecosystem. Then read and listen to the description. Notice each word or phrase in **blue** and think about its meaning.

THE GREATER YELLOWSTONE ECOSYSTEM

Yellowstone National Park is a nearly 35,000-square-mile wilderness recreation area in western United States. Yellowstone features canyons, rivers, forests, hot springs, and geysers. It is home to hundreds of animal species, including bears, wolves, bison, elk, and antelope.

Wildlife within Yellowstone National Park itself is protected by **legislation**, but the **ecology** of the park—the plants and animals—extends beyond its borders, where the area is divided among federal, state, private, and **tribal** lands. Conflicting interests create nearly **overwhelming** challenges that conservation managers must **confront** as they **monitor** animal movement in and around the park.

On privately owned land, wildlife habitat is **diminishing**. Development often **interferes** with animal migration, and ancient migration routes are being **displaced**. However, some private land is being protected. Billionaire[1] Ted Turner is **dedicated to** helping wildlife; his Flying D Ranch protects some 113,000 acres of wildlife habitat.

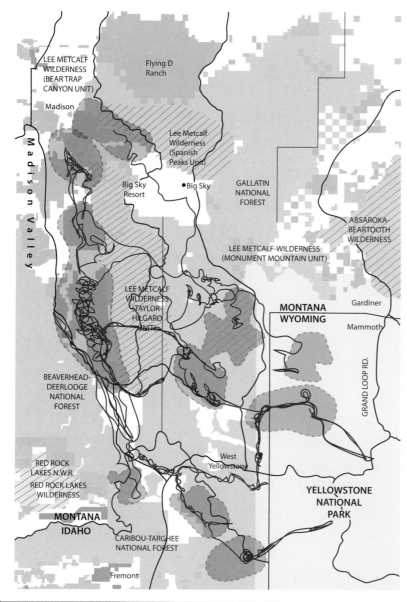

Landownership

- ☐ National Park Service
- ▨ Wilderness
- ☐ U.S. Forest Service
- ☐ Private Protected
- ☐ Fish and Wildlife Service
- ▨ Bureau of Land Management
- ☐ Tribal
- ☐ State and Local Government
- ☐ Private
- ■ Other

Madison Valley Elk Herd

- ■ Summer Range
- ■ Winter Range
- — Migration Route

Lines represent seasonal migrations between summer and winter ranges for 11 elk in the Madison Valley herd. GPS collars collected data on their locations every 30 minutes.

[1] **billionaire** (n): a person with more than one billion (1,000,000,000) dollars

B Match each word or phrase with its definition.

1. _____ confront (v)
2. _____ dedicated to (adj)
3. _____ diminish (v)
4. _____ displace (v)
5. _____ ecology (n)
6. _____ interfere (v)
7. _____ legislation (n)
8. _____ monitor (v)
9. _____ overwhelming (adj)
10. _____ tribal (adj)

a. a habitat, its living things, and their relationships
b. to deal with or face (a problem or challenge)
c. more than can be managed or dealt with
d. to block or get in the way of an activity or goal
e. to follow, check, or observe
f. to get smaller in size, number, importance, etc.
g. belonging or related to a group of native people
h. to force to move from a home or habitat
i. a law or laws
j. very involved in and supportive of

C Work with a partner. Look at the map in exercise A and answer the questions.

CRITICAL THINKING:
INTERPRETING A MAP

1. How was information about the movements of elk obtained?
2. Do the elk spend the winter inside or outside Yellowstone National Park?
3. Do any elk migration routes go through the Flying D Ranch?
4. Who owns the land between Big Sky and the Big Sky Resort?
5. Is there any private protected land in Madison Valley?

D Work in a small group. Read these statements by people living in the Greater Yellowstone Ecosystem. Which landownership group(s) on the map in exercise A might each person belong to?

CRITICAL THINKING:
EVALUATING

1. It is of the greatest importance to protect the ecology of the area and live in harmony with nature here as our ancestors did.
2. We need stricter legislation to keep people from interfering with living things in the rivers, streams, and forests.
3. If I don't displace animals from time to time, I won't be able to develop my land. This isn't state land, after all. It's my property.
4. We're dedicated to confronting the problem of diminishing predator populations and believe introducing more bears and wolves into the area is a great solution.
5. A herd of migrating elk can be overwhelming for a town. It's my job to see that they get the resources they need to deal with it.

◀ **Herd of elk in summer in Yellowstone, USA**

Listening A Conversation about the Serengeti

BEFORE LISTENING

PRIOR KNOWLEDGE **A** Work in a small group. Discuss the questions.

1. What have you learned about the Serengeti National Park in Tanzania and Kenya? Discuss what makes the Serengeti interesting and a popular tourist destination.
2. Think about Yellowstone National Park and the conservation challenges it faces. Could the Serengeti National Park in Tanzania face similar challenges? Explain.

WHILE LISTENING

LISTENING FOR MAIN IDEAS **B** 🎧 2.16 Listen to the conversation. Choose the correct answers.

1. The size of the Serengeti Mara ecosystem has (increased / diminished).
2. The human populations in Kenya and Tanzania have been (increasing / decreasing).
3. Offers of money from tourism companies (have / haven't) persuaded the Robandans to move from their village.
4. Animal populations in the Serengeti Mara ecosystem are (at risk / maintaining their numbers).

LISTENING FOR DETAILS **C** 🎧 2.16 Listen again. Choose T for *True*, F for *False*, or NG for information *Not Given*.

1. In 1950, the authorities felt the animals were a higher priority than the Ikoma people.	T	F	NG
2. Everyone who eats bush meat in Tanzania is punished for it.	T	F	NG
3. An ecotourism group has invested a lot of money to protect the ecology of the Serengeti.	T	F	NG
4. The tourism companies are planning to force the Robandans to move.	T	F	NG
5. Brandon suggests that the tourism companies are only concerned with money.	T	F	NG
6. Ashley is going to go on a trip soon.	T	F	NG

> ### LISTENING SKILL Listening for Clarification
>
> In conversation, speakers often clarify what they have said so that their intended meaning is clear.
>
> Some expressions that signal clarification are:
>
> | | |
> |---|---|
> | *For the most part yes, although…* | *Well, yes/yeah, …, but…* |
> | *Yes/Yeah, partly. But…* | *Well, you're right that…, but…* |
> | *That's true, but…* | *Of course, but…* |
>
> If you listen for what comes after these expressions, you will better understand the speaker's meaning.

D 🎧 2.17 Read these sentences expressing what Ashley thought before Brandon added a clarification. Then listen to excerpts from their discussion and write the clarification that Brandon provided.

LISTENING FOR CLARIFICATION

1. Brandon spent his vacation in Tanzania.

   _____

2. The wildebeest migration takes place in the Serengeti National Park.

   _____

3. 16,700 square kilometers is a huge amount of land to set aside for wildlife.

   _____

4. Hunting, selling, and eating bush meat must be under control because it's illegal.

   _____

5. The ecotourism company Brandon mentions is only interested in making money.

   _____

AFTER LISTENING

E Discuss the questions with a partner.

CRITICAL THINKING: SYNTHESIZING

1. In your own words, how would you explain the conflict between the needs of the animals and the needs of people of the Serengeti Mara ecosystem?
2. If you were villagers from Robanda, would you accept the offer of money to move off the land? What would you gain, and what would you lose from your decision?
3. What if, instead of persuading the Ikoma to leave, the tourism companies invited them to be partners in the business? How would the two groups cooperate to give visitors a great experience of the Serengeti? What difficulties might interfere with this collaboration?

Lions in Serengeti National Park, Tanzania

B Speaking

PRONUNCIATION Linking with *You* or *Your*

🎧 2.18 We often link a word that ends in the sound /t/, /d/, or /z/ with *you* or *your*. Those sounds are softened and change as follows:

- /t/ sounds like /tʃ/   *I see what you mean.*
- /d/ sounds like /dʒ/   *I'm glad you had your camera.*
- /z/ sounds like /ʒ/   *How was your trip?*

A Mark the linked words in each sentence and check (✓) the pronunciation.

	/tʃ/	/dʒ/	/ʒ/
1. Would you like me to take your coat?	☐	☐	☐
2. I'm not sure what you said.	☐	☐	☐
3. Are you sure he's your tour guide?	☐	☐	☐
4. Why didn't you call me sooner?	☐	☐	☐
5. I forgot to feed your bird.	☐	☐	☐
6. Why did you leave the door open?	☐	☐	☐

B 🎧 2.19 Listen and check your answers to exercise A. Then listen again and repeat the sentences.

C Work with a partner. Take turns asking and answering these questions. Be sure that you correctly link *you* and *your*.

1. Would you like to go to Tanzania? Why would you or wouldn't you like to go?
2. Is there another migration, human or animal, that you would like to learn more about? Why did you choose that particular migration?
3. If you had the power, would you give tribal peoples special privileges in national parks? What privileges would you give them?
4. Would you believe me if I told you I'm totally dedicated to learning English? Why would you or wouldn't you believe me?
5. When did you last forget your phone somewhere? What did you do?
6. Think about your life last year. Did you have any notable experiences? Did you have any overwhelming ones?
7. Where would you go to put your English to the test? Why would you choose that place?

D 🎧 2.20 Work with a partner. Listen to a wildlife expert explain some of the ways animals find their way when they migrate. Then discuss with your partner whether each statement below is a theory or a fact. Write *Theory* or *Fact*.

CRITICAL THINKING: DISTINGUISHING FACT FROM THEORY

1. _____ Animals migrate mostly for reasons related to basic needs.
2. _____ Some birds use the sun to find their way as they migrate.
3. _____ Some birds use star patterns to choose the direction to travel.
4. _____ Sea turtles use energy patterns to find their way.
5. _____ Many animals use features of the landscape to find their way.
6. _____ Migration directions may be found in the DNA of some animals.

E Work with a partner. Discuss the questions.

CRITICAL THINKING: APPLYING

1. Think of some migrating animals you know about. Describe their migration and the method(s) you think they use to find their way.
2. What are some of the problems migrating animals encounter along the way? Talk about animals that migrate by land, water, and air.
3. How can humans help to solve the problems animals encounter while migrating and allow them to migrate freely and unharmed?

FINAL TASK A Pair Presentation on Animal Migration

> You are going to research information on a migrating animal. Then you will give a pair presentation to the class with the information you researched.

A Work with a partner. Choose a migrating animal that is not in this unit to research. Then follow the steps on the next page.

Monarch butterflies in the Sierra Chincua Sanctuary, Mexico

1. Research basic facts about the animal you chose, including information such as:
   - physical description
   - how long it lives
   - its habitat and range
   - threats it faces

2. Research information about its migration, such as:
   - the migration path
   - the timing of the migration
   - events related to the migration
   - theories and/or facts that explain the migration and how the animals are able to find their way

3. Find a picture of the animal for your presentation.

4. Create a time line of the migration to use as a visual aid for your presentation.

PRESENTATION SKILL Handling Audience Questions

Questions from the audience can be unpredictable. Here's how to handle them:

- Start by saying "Good question!" to be polite and show interest.
- Repeat the question in your own words. This gives you a little extra time, helps you understand the question, and helps the audience understand it.
- Answer the question as clearly as possible. (If you don't know the answer, say something like "I'm afraid I don't have that information right now. I'll have to get back to you later on that." Then research the question and follow up with the person who asked it.)
- Finish by checking if your answer was understood by asking, "Does that make sense?" or "Is that clear?"

ORGANIZING IDEAS **B** With your partner, organize your presentation (using an outline, numbered notes, index cards, etc.). Decide which parts each of you will present. Then practice giving your presentation, including handling audience questions.

PRESENTING **C** Present the information to the class. Answer any questions from your audience. Use the suggestions in the skill box for handling audience questions.

REFLECTION

1. Which information that you learned in this unit is likely to be the most useful to you? Why and how?

   _____

   _____

2. Which aspect of human or animal migration in this unit did you find the most interesting? Explain.

   _____

   _____

3. Here are the vocabulary words and phrases from the unit. Check (✓) the ones you can use.

   ☐ archaeologist   ☐ genetic   ☐ notable
   ☐ confront   ☐ hypothesis AWL   ☐ overwhelming
   ☐ dedicated to   ☐ immense   ☐ perspective AWL
   ☐ descendant   ☐ interfere   ☐ subsequently AWL
   ☐ diminish AWL   ☐ legislation AWL   ☐ tribal
   ☐ displace AWL   ☐ migrate AWL   ☐ venture
   ☐ ecology   ☐ monitor AWL

TRADITION AND PROGRESS 6

A Wanapum girl and
her horse in central
Washington, USA

THINK AND DISCUSS

1 What cultural values are evident in this photo?
Does your culture share any of these values?
2 What does the word *progress* mean to you?
3 What traditions are important to you?

EXPLORE THE THEME

Look at the photos and read the information. Then answer the questions.

1. What traditional peoples and ways of life are represented by each photo?

2. Do you think the Kyrgyz, the Suri, and the Amish people engage in traditional activities by choice or by necessity? Explain.

3. What might these people prefer about their traditional ways of life?

PAST MEETS PRESENT

Amish traveling in a horse-drawn buggy in Lancaster County, Pennsylvania, USA

Kyrgyz herders checking their cell phones in Afghanistan

In Jujuy, a remote province in northwest Argentina, a woman wears a feathered costume to represent the nandu, or sacred bird of the Suris, an indigenous group of this area.

Is modernization universal? Are traditional lifestyles becoming obsolete? Can modern and traditional ways of life coexist? For some cultures, the answers to these questions are critical to their existence. Ultimately, there is no way of stopping progress and its impact on cultures and traditions nearly everywhere.

A Vocabulary

MEANING FROM CONTEXT

A 🎧 2.21 Read and listen to the article. Notice each word or phrase in **blue** and think about its meaning.

PRESERVING ANCIENT TRADITIONS: THE HADZA

Hunting and gathering food is a survival strategy that scientists believe humans began to **employ** some 1.8 million years ago. Then around 10,000 years ago, a major **transition** occurred: people learned how to grow crops and domesticate[1] animals. However, there is a group of people in an **isolated** region of northern Tanzania that rejects the agricultural way of life. They still **insist on** hunting animals and gathering food. This group, the Hadza people, has lived in the Great Rift Valley for 10,000 years, and the **preservation** of their ancient ways is a priority for them.

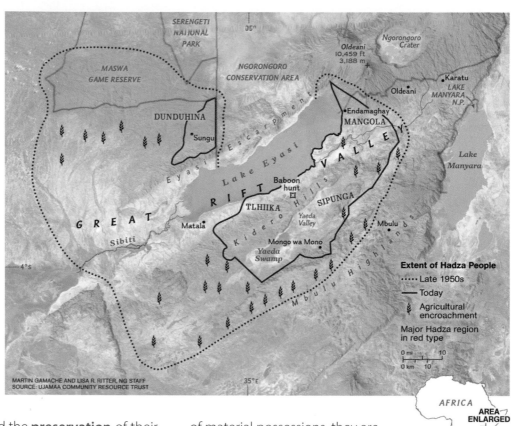

MARTIN GAMACHE AND LISA R. RITTER, NG STAFF
SOURCE: UJAMAA COMMUNITY RESOURCE TRUST

The Hadza are nomads[2] who gather food from plants that grow naturally and move according to the travel patterns of the animals they hunt. They are **accustomed to** living in temporary huts made of branches and dried grass that they can quickly and easily **assemble**. It is an interesting **contradiction** that, although the Hadza have very little in the way of material possessions, they are happy to share everything they have with others. This **principle**, however, is not followed by local farmers, who have converted 75 percent of the Hadza's traditional homeland to farmland since the 1950s. If the modern world continues to interfere with the Hadza as they try to **pursue** their ancient way of life, that way of life may disappear forever.

---

[1] **domesticate** (v): to bring wild animals under control and use them to produce food or as pets
[2] **nomad** (n): a person who has no permanent home, but moves constantly in search of water and food

B Match each word or phrase with its definition.

1. _____ employ (v)
2. _____ transition (n)
3. _____ isolated (adj)
4. _____ insist on (v ph)
5. _____ preservation (n)
6. _____ accustomed to (adj ph)
7. _____ assemble (v)
8. _____ contradiction (n)
9. _____ principle (n)
10. _____ pursue (v)

a. keeping something as it is and protecting it
b. a situation containing two opposite truths
c. used to; familiar with; in the habit of
d. a change from one state to another
e. to use
f. a guiding rule or idea
g. remote and difficult to reach
h. to follow or carry out (an activity, plan, policy, etc.)
i. to build or put together
j. to continue to say or do something despite criticism

C Work with a partner. Discuss the questions.

1. What are some methods employed to conserve water?
2. What is a principle that you insist on following?
3. What is something that you had trouble assembling? Explain.
4. When is it acceptable to contradict someone?
5. What career are you pursuing?

VOCABULARY SKILL Collocations: Verb/Adjective + Preposition

Some verbs and adjectives are followed by prepositions. When you learn a new adjective or verb, be sure to note which preposition it usually occurs with.

Verb + Preposition

insist on, participate in, approve of, object to, interfere with/in

Adjective + Preposition

accustomed to, responsible for, terrified of, content with, involved with/in

There are no easy rules that specify which preposition to use with verbs and adjectives. If you're not sure, check a dictionary.

D Choose the correct preposition for each collocation. Use a dictionary or ask your teacher if you are not sure.

1. The Hadza are not shy (about / for) giving interviews, and a great deal of information that pertains (on / to) Hadza customs and ways of thinking has been discovered that way.
2. For example, contrary (from / to) popular opinion, the Hadza are not opposed (to / against) development but rather (for / to) land use that is not sustainable.
3. Fewer and fewer cultures are isolated (from / with) the world.
4. Recent studies have shown that Hadza DNA is distinct (from / to) that of their neighbors.
5. Some people in Tanzania interfere (with / to) the ancient traditions of the Hadza.

Listening A Student Presentation about Bhutan

BEFORE LISTENING

PREVIEWING **A** Look at the images and read the information. Then answer the questions.

1. Where is Bhutan located? What do you know about it?
2. Describe the image on Bhutan's flag. What do you think it means?
3. Bhutan is trying to measure its *Gross National Happiness*. What do you think this phrase means?

The flag of Bhutan

Bhutan Fast Facts

Population: 793,897

Capital: Thimphu

Area: 14,824 square miles
(38,394 square kilometers)

WHILE LISTENING

LISTENING FOR
MAIN IDEAS
B 🎧 2.22 ▶ 1.13 Listen and check (✓) the three main topics presented by the speaker.

1. ☐ the circumstances surrounding the decision to open Bhutan up to the world
2. ☐ how Bhutan opened itself up in reaction to external political events
3. ☐ a new approach to development devised by the king of Bhutan
4. ☐ policies to facilitate more rapid and efficient economic development
5. ☐ the rise of a movie industry in Bhutan
6. ☐ social and cultural changes since the Gross National Happiness policy was implemented

LISTENING FOR
DETAILS
C 🎧 2.22 Listen again. Choose T for *True*, F for *False*, or NG for information *Not Given*.

1. The policy of remaining cut off from the world was to blame for problems in public education.   T   F   NG
2. The king of Bhutan can take back his absolute power if he decides it is necessary.   T   F   NG

3. Bhutan is trying to make its agricultural methods more efficient to maximize exports.　　T　F　NG

4. The government of Bhutan has placed certain restrictions on what the media is allowed to broadcast.　　T　F　NG

5. Movies examining how Bhutanese culture is evolving are very popular in Bhutan.　　T　F　NG

NOTE-TAKING SKILL Using an Idea Map

An idea map can provide a clear visual overview of a topic and connections between ideas. It is a useful note-taking format for a topic that has a clear structure.

Place the main topic at the top of the idea map. Directly connected to the main topic are sub-topics; details are then connected to the sub-topics.

D 🎧 2.23 Listen to an excerpt from the presentation. Complete the idea map with information from the presentation. Write only one word for each answer.

NOTE TAKING

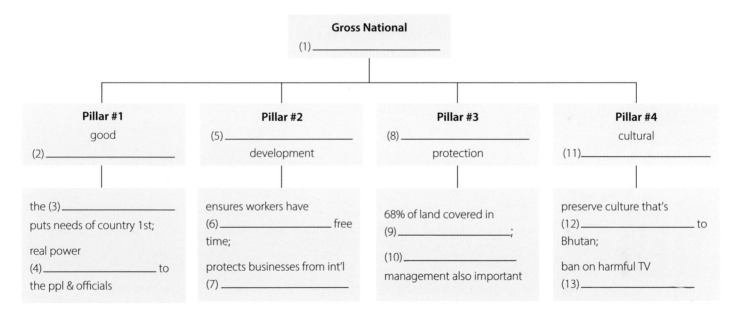

Gross National
(1) _____

Pillar #1	Pillar #2	Pillar #3	Pillar #4
good	(5) _____	(8) _____	cultural
(2) _____	development	protection	(11) _____

| the (3) _____ puts needs of country 1st; real power (4) _____ to the ppl & officials | ensures workers have (6) _____ free time; protects businesses from int'l (7) _____ | 68% of land covered in (9) _____; (10) _____ management also important | preserve culture that's (12) _____ to Bhutan; ban on harmful TV (13) _____ |

AFTER LISTENING

E Work in a small group. For each pillar of Gross National Happiness in the idea map, brainstorm additional ideas that Bhutan could try. Write your ideas in your notebook. Then share your best ideas with the class.

CRITICAL THINKING: SYNTHESIZING

> *For good government, I think they could try keeping the taxes low.*

Speaking

SPEAKING SKILL Using Rhetorical Questions

Rhetorical questions are questions that a speaker asks for dramatic effect or to make a point, not to get an answer. Here are three types of rhetorical questions:

1. Questions that encourage your audience to think about something:

   There were no cars or trucks, no phones, and no postal service. **Can you imagine what life must have been like?**

2. Questions that invite your audience to agree with you, such as tag questions:

   Gross domestic product is one way to evaluate a country's success. But it's not really related to the happiness of the people, **is it?**

3. Questions you think your audience would like to ask that you then answer:

   So, what is meant by good government? *Well, the king puts the needs of the country first.*

A 🎧 **2.24** Work with a partner. Read the excerpts from the presentation, adding a rhetorical question to each. Then listen and write the questions the speaker used.

1. Bhutan is known as *Druk Yul,* which in English is . . . land of the thunder dragon.
   _____ I imagine a brilliantly colored dragon jumping from mountain to mountain and making an incredible noise!

2. _____ Well, part of it is taking into consideration the contributions that families make to the society and to the economy.

3. And I think Gross National Happiness is the right approach. It helps to make sure that we don't lose our beautiful environment and the best parts of our ancient culture.

   _____

B Are the rhetorical questions above type 1, 2, or 3? Write the correct number.

Question 1: _____   Question 2: _____   Question 3: _____

USING RHETORICAL QUESTIONS

C For each item, write a rhetorical question of the type indicated. Then read your questions to a partner.

1. The king of Bhutan had absolute power over his people. That means his power was unlimited, and the people had to do anything he said without question.
   (Type 1) _____

2. Just a short time ago, Bhutan didn't even have electricity. Today, young Bhutanese are addicted to video games, smartphones, social media, and Pokémon Go.
   (Type 2) _____

3. (Type 3) _____
   Well, it's a way of measuring economic growth that also takes happiness into consideration.

PRONUNCIATION Stress in Adjective-Noun Combinations

🎧 **2.25** There are two different stress patterns for adjective-noun combinations. When the adjective describes the noun, emphasize the noun. This is the more common pattern.

> I have a <u>light</u> **schedule** this week.
> He wore a <u>blue</u> **shirt**.

When the two words form a compound noun that is a fixed expression with a specific meaning, emphasize the adjective. These compound nouns are sometimes written as one word, as in *mailbox*.

> There were no **light** <u>bulbs</u> in Bhutan.
> People started wearing **blue** <u>jeans</u>.

D 🎧 **2.26** Listen to each sentence and check (✓) the correct meaning of the adjective-noun combination it contains.

1. a. ☐ a teacher of the English language b. ☐ a teacher who is English
2. a. ☐ juice made from oranges b. ☐ orange-colored juice, maybe mango
3. a. ☐ the house painted white b. ☐ the White House, Washington, D.C.
4. a. ☐ a difficult drive by car b. ☐ a piece of computer equipment
5. a. ☐ bluebirds (a species of bird) b. ☐ birds with blue-colored feathers
6. a. ☐ lights positioned up high b. ☐ important moments
7. a. ☐ a jacket that is yellow b. ☐ a yellow jacket (a species of insect)
8. a. ☐ a right whale (a species of whale) b. ☐ the correct whale

E Work with a partner. Use the adjective-noun combinations below to make sentences. Say them to your partner. Your partner will tell you the meaning she hears.

English teacher	orange juice	white house/White House	hard drive
bluebirds/blue birds	yellow jacket	highlights/high lights	right whale

◂ **A traditional dancer at the Paro festival, Paro, Bhutan**

Taktshang, or "Tiger's Nest," monastery in Bhutan

GRAMMAR FOR SPEAKING Verb + Object + Infinitive

Certain verbs can be followed by an object + <u>infinitive</u>.

Mobile phones **allow people** <u>**to communicate**</u> *more easily than ever before.*
We **invited English teachers** <u>**to teach**</u> *in our schools.*

To form the negative of the infinitive, insert *not* before it:

The king **ordered the Bhutanese people** <u>**not to have connections**</u> *with other countries.*

These are some of the verbs that can be followed by an object + infinitive.

advise	*ask*	*force*	*invite*	*permit*	*remind*	*tell*
allow	*encourage*	*help*	*order*	*persuade*	*require*	*warn*

F Put the words and phrases in the correct order to create sentences about Bhutan.

1. Bhutan / its citizens / to take / for / encourages / responsibility /the environment

   _____

2. sustainable / asks / The government / to work / companies / in / way / a

   _____

3. The government / companies / to cut down / has ordered / not / trees for export

   _____

4. The king / invites / to implement / other countries / of Bhutan / GNH strategies

   _____

5. Bhutan / to obtain / all visiting tourists / requires / a tourist visa

   _____

CRITICAL THINKING:
APPLYING

G Work in a small group. Imagine you govern a country. What rules would you create in these areas? Use verbs from the skill box and the object + infinitive pattern.

restaurants	transportation	employment	pet ownership	education

LESSON TASK Conducting an Interview

A Work with a partner. Take turns completing the interview. Follow these steps.

CRITICAL THINKING: APPLYING

1. Each of you choose a country (or a large city) where you have lived.
2. Take turns interviewing each other to determine the Gross National Happiness of that place. Ask the questions and record your partner's answers in the chart.
3. Ask your partner to explain his or her answers and ask follow-up questions about anything you don't understand.

Gross National Happiness in _____	Yes	No
Pillar 1: Good Government		
1. Is the state of the transportation system satisfactory?		
2. Is the public education system adequate?		
Pillar 2: Sustainable Development		
1. Do most jobs provide enough time off?		
2. Do most jobs pay workers enough to live comfortably?		
Pillar 3: Environmental Protection		
1. Are levels of pollution, noise, and traffic acceptable?		
2. Are there parks or natural areas available to the public?		
Pillar 4: Cultural Preservation		
1. Do people try to maintain traditions along with new practices?		
2. Do young people value and respect the older generations?		

EVERYDAY LANGUAGE Acknowledging an Error

I made a mistake.   *I'm wrong.*

I should have checked more carefully.   *My mistake.*

I wasn't thinking properly.   *You're right.*

B Share the responses to your Gross National Happiness interview with the class. Then discuss these questions as a class.

1. Which countries or cities have the highest level of GNH and which have the lowest, based on the interview results?
2. Are any of the answers surprising to you?
3. What was the most challenging aspect of conducting an interview? What would you do differently if you interviewed another person?

Greg Anderson and David Harrison, National Geographic Explorers and linguists on the Enduring Voices Project, interview two men in Thungri village, Arunachal Pradesh.

Preserving Endangered Languages

BEFORE VIEWING

PREDICTING **A** Read the information about the Enduring Voices Project. Then discuss the questions.

1. How many of the world's 7,000 languages do you think are in danger of extinction?
2. What do you think is the main cause of language extinction?

> **THE ENDURING VOICES PROJECT** The Enduring Voices Project documents and works to preserve endangered languages. They have created online Talking Dictionaries using recordings of native speakers from small language communities.

MEANING FROM CONTEXT **B** Read the sentences with words from the video. Guess the meaning of the underlined words. Then write each word next to its definition.

- A <u>savvy</u> shopper takes advantage of sales, coupons, and other promotions.
- When a city wants to <u>revitalize</u> a neighborhood, it often adds a public green space.
- Adjusting to a new career includes learning the specific <u>lexicon</u> of the job.
- Scientific researchers gain <u>insight</u> into cures for diseases by doing experiments.
- American Indians are the <u>indigenous</u> people of North America.

1. _____ (n) the vocabulary of a particular field or sector

2. _____ (n) the ability to see or know the truth about something

3. _____ (adj) born in or native to a place

4. _____ (adj) smart, knowledgeable

5. _____ (v) to give new life or energy to something

WHILE VIEWING

C ▶ 1.14 Watch the video. Check (✓) the statement that is the main message of the video.

UNDERSTANDING MAIN IDEAS

☐ Talking Dictionaries are rapidly modernizing small languages around the world.

☐ The best way to preserve a language is by insisting that its young people speak it.

☐ The Enduring Voices Project helps preserve languages with Talking Dictionaries.

☐ Siletz Dee-ni, Matukar Panau, and Tuvan are isolated, small language communities.

☐ The Enduring Voices Project and the AAAS are concerned about language extinction.

D ▶ 1.14 Watch the video again. Complete this summary with words from the video. Write only one word for each answer.

UNDERSTANDING DETAILS

There are 7,000 languages in the world, and _____ of them may
_____(1)_____

_____ in this century. Languages go extinct mostly because of
_____(2)_____

_____ pressure and _____ that devalue small languages. The goal
_____(3)_____ _____(4)_____

of Talking Dictionaries is to give some small languages a first-ever _____ on the
_____(5)_____

Internet. The Talking Dictionaries for three languages are highlighted: Siletz Dee-ni language,

Matukar Panau, and Tuvan. The Siletz Nation is using the dictionary as a _____
_____(6)_____

to revitalize their language. The speakers of Matukar Panau wanted to see their language

on the _____ , which shows that their language is just as good as any other. The
_____(7)_____

Tuvan Talking Dictionary was also launched as an iPhone _____ . Since linguistic
_____(8)_____

diversity is such an important part of our _____ heritage, indigenous communities,
_____(9)_____

along with scientists, are responding to the crisis of language _____ .
_____(10)_____

E Look back at your answers to exercise A. Were your predictions correct? Tell a partner.

CHECKING PREDICTIONS

AFTER VIEWING

F Work with a partner. Discuss the questions.

CRITICAL THINKING: EVALUATING

1. The risk of language extinction is higher in isolated communities. Does isolation benefit languages in any way? Why or why not?
2. Can small languages with Talking Dictionaries avoid extinction? Why or why not?
3. When a culture transitions from traditional to modern life, what else is at risk of extinction besides its language?
4. If you were going to create a Talking Dictionary for your language, which words would you start with? Explain.

Vocabulary

A 🎧 3.2 Read and listen to the article. Notice each word in **blue**.

REVITALIZING A SWEET TRADITION

While traveling through eastern Turkey in 2008, National Geographic Explorer Catherine de Medici Jaffee was fascinated by the people, culture, and beauty of the area, and especially by the ancient tradition of beekeeping. The great **diversity** of the flowers that grow there gives honey many different flavors. But she also noticed that the local women who relied on honey for their **livelihood** were having trouble earning enough money despite the obvious **merits** of their product. The **hardship** they were experiencing inspired Jaffee to **undertake** a project that would **ultimately** become Balyolu (which means "honey path" in Turkish), "the world's very first honey-tasting **heritage** trail."

Jaffee recalls, "For the next four years, I began planning how I would make it back to the region to work with local communities to bring something like this to life." She obtained the **consent** of local beekeepers to guide tourists to their villages to taste their honey, traveling along ancient footpaths once used by nomads. To further **replicate** the lifestyle of nomads, Balyolu invited visitors to sleep in yurts, traditional round portable tents. Thus, Balyolu was able to provide a better business model to help the community **flourish**. Asked about her favorite experience, Jaffee replied, "My favorite experiences are watching different beekeepers over the years grow and change with their bees. Visiting the same families over and over, I get to become closer to their lives and their hives[1] like a member of a special tribe."

[1] **hive** (or **beehive**) (n): a natural or man-made structure that bees live in

B Write each word in **blue** from exercise A next to its definition.

1. _____ (v) to start doing a task and take responsibility for it
2. _____ (v) to have success and develop quickly and strongly
3. _____ (n) a wide range of different things
4. _____ (adv) finally; after a long and often complicated series of events
5. _____ (v) to create a copy of an object or experience
6. _____ (n) a way of making money or obtaining the necessities of life
7. _____ (n) permission from another person to do something
8. _____ (n) a difficult life situation usually due to lack of money
9. _____ (n) advantages, benefits, or other good points
10. _____ (n) tradition, passed from generation to generation

C Complete the chart with the correct form of each word. Use a dictionary to help you.

	Noun	Verb	Adjective
1.	consent		
2.	diversity		
3.		flourish	
4.	merit		
5.		replicate	
6.		undertake	

D Match the words with their synonyms. Use a dictionary to help you if needed.

1. _____ consent
2. _____ diversity
3. _____ flourish
4. _____ hardship
5. _____ heritage
6. _____ livelihood
7. _____ merit
8. _____ replicate
9. _____ ultimately
10. _____ undertake

a. to thrive
b. tradition
c. to reproduce
d. to start
e. in the end
f. variety
g. approval
h. challenge
i. occupation
j. positive quality

E Complete the sentences with your own ideas and discuss with a partner.   PERSONALIZING

1. People flourish when _____

    _____

2. The part of my heritage I appreciate most is _____

    _____

3. One benefit of hardship is _____

    _____

4. A respected livelihood in my country is _____

    _____

5. Diversity is important because _____

    _____

6. One merit of studying alone is _____

    _____

7. My parents would never give their consent for me to _____

    _____

8. Ultimately, my goal _____

Listening A Discussion about American Indian Lands

BEFORE LISTENING

PREDICTING **A** You will hear a discussion about American Indian lands. Choose the answers you think are correct.

1. How many American Indian reservations are there in the United States?
   a. nearly 100   b. over 300   c. over 500

2. How many American Indian tribes are there in the United States?
   a. nearly 100   b. over 300   c. over 500

3. What percentage of the land area of the United States do reservations occupy?
   a. about 0.5 percent   b. around 2 percent   c. close to 5 percent

WHILE LISTENING

CHECKING
PREDICTIONS
B 🎧 **3.3** Listen to the students' discussion. Take notes on the numbers mentioned at the beginning of the discussion. Were your answers in exercise A correct?

LISTENING SKILL Listening for a Correction

Speakers will sometimes say something, realize that what they've said was incorrect, and then correct themselves. Before a correction, you may hear "Sorry" or an admission of the error such as "You're right." Then the speaker will go on to correct the mistake with expressions such as:

What I mean/meant (to say) is/was . . .	*I mean/meant . . .*
What I'm trying to say is . . .	*Let me rephrase that.*
What I want/wanted to say is/was . . .	*Let me try again.*

▶ **Valerie Stanley, a Pomo Indian, in Intertribal Park, an Indian-run wilderness area in California, USA**

C 🎧 **3.4** Read these statements from the discussion. Then listen to the excerpts and correct each statement so it reflects what the speakers meant to say.

LISTENING FOR DETAILS

1. Oh, you mean the one about Native American tribes?

2. For example, I was surprised to learn that there are over 500 American Indian reservations in the United States.

3. And the land is important to them.

4. The first one was in Mexico, wasn't it?

5. I think it was the InterTribal Sinkyone Wilderness State Park.

D 🎧 **3.5** Listen to an excerpt from the discussion and complete the idea map. Write no more than one word or number in each blank. Take your own notes on the Big Cypress Swamp.

NOTE TAKING

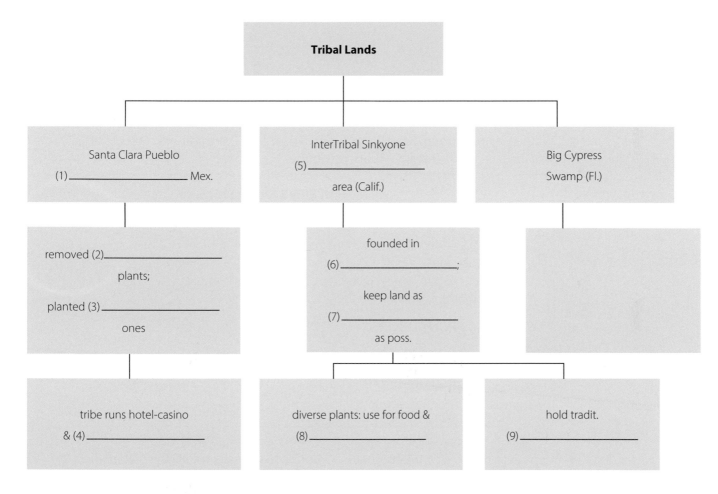

Tribal Lands

Santa Clara Pueblo
(1) _____ Mex.

InterTribal Sinkyone
(5) _____
area (Calif.)

Big Cypress
Swamp (Fl.)

removed (2) _____
plants;
planted (3) _____
ones

founded in
(6) _____;
keep land as
(7) _____
as poss.

tribe runs hotel-casino
& (4) _____

diverse plants: use for food &
(8) _____

hold tradit.
(9) _____

AFTER LISTENING

E Work with a partner. Discuss the questions.

CRITICAL THINKING: ANALYZING

1. What is your attitude toward nature?
2. Today fewer than half of American Indians live on reservations. Why do you think that is?

Speaking

► **Lanterns decorate a door for Chinese New Year Spring Festival, Beijing, China.**

A Work in a small group. Read about some New Year's Eve traditions. Discuss which ones you have heard of and any others you know.

NEW YEAR'S EVE TRADITIONS

LUCKY FOOD

 Food traditions often represent good luck and happiness in the new year. In the Netherlands, people bring in the new year by eating ring-shaped treats; in Spain, it's custom to eat twelve grapes at midnight, and in Switzerland, it's a tradition to drop ice cream on the floor.

SYMBOLIC FRONT DOORS

 Doors also hold special significance for the new year. In China, a red front door signifies happiness and good luck. In Greece, an onion hanging on the front door symbolizes rebirth. In Turkey, sprinkling salt in front of your door brings peace and abundance.

B Complete the chart with information about a New Year's tradition you know.

New Year's Eve Tradition in _____	
Location	
Decorations	
Food and Drink	
Activity/Ritual	

C Work with a partner. Discuss how your celebrations are similar and different.

> **CRITICAL THINKING**   Thinking Outside the Box
>
> Thinking outside the box means to look beyond the normal or traditional way of doing things. It is a good way to come up with alternative approaches to situations. When thinking outside the box, don't be afraid to express your ideas–even ones that are out of the ordinary and unconventional. By not judging your ideas as they occur to you, you keep your thoughts flowing, which can lead to some innovative thinking.

D Work in a small group. Suggest new traditions for New Year's Eve celebrations that are interesting, fun, or symbolic. Note your best ideas.

CRITICAL THINKING: THINKING OUTSIDE THE BOX

Suggestions for New Year's Celebration	
Location	
Decorations	
Food and Drink	
Activity/Ritual	

FINAL TASK   Presenting a Tradition

> You are going to work with a partner to give a presentation on a current tradition other than a New Year's tradition. You may choose a completely new tradition, or an older one that has been modernized. You can do research if necessary.

A Work with a partner. Brainstorm current traditions that you are both interested in. Some examples are holidays, festivals, or traditions related to family, school, food, clothing, sports, or a life event (e.g., wedding, birthday, or graduation). Then decide on the tradition that you will present.

BRAINSTORMING

B Consider these points to help you research and organize your presentation:

- If it is a completely new tradition, describe how it began, its purpose, and how it is carried out.
- If it is an older tradition that has been modernized, provide background on the original tradition, how it has changed, and the reason for the change.
- Look for images or video that you might be able to use in your presentation. These may help you decide which details to include in your presentation.

ORGANIZING IDEAS **C** In your notebook, use an idea map to organize your ideas. Include the information from exercise B. Decide which parts each person will present.

D Add one or two rhetorical questions, as appropriate, for dramatic effect or to emphasize important points. If possible, create or obtain a visual related to the tradition to use in your presentation.

E Take turns rehearsing your presentation with your partner. After each turn, give each other feedback on how to improve.

PRESENTATION SKILL Speaking with Confidence

When speaking in front of a group, it is important to appear confident. This will give the impression that you know your topic well and that you believe in what you are saying. There are several things that you can do to feel more confident.

- Organize your notes well and practice your presentation at least once.
- Always have good posture and face the audience.
- Use hand gestures, eye contact, and body language, and smile when you can.
- Finally, remember to pause between sentences and to speak slowly and clearly.

PRESENTING **F** Give your presentation in front of the class, focusing on strategies for speaking with confidence.

REFLECTION

1. What information that you learned in this unit is likely to be the most useful to you? Why and how?

_____

_____

2. What information about different cultures are you likely to remember from this unit?

_____

_____

3. Here are the vocabulary words and phrases from the unit. Check (✔) the ones you can use.

☐ accustomed to   ☐ hardship   ☐ principle AWL

☐ assemble AWL   ☐ heritage   ☐ pursue AWL

☐ consent AWL   ☐ insist on   ☐ replicate

☐ contradiction AWL   ☐ isolated AWL   ☐ transition AWL

☐ diversity AWL   ☐ livelihood   ☐ ultimately AWL

☐ employ   ☐ merit   ☐ undertake AWL

☐ flourish   ☐ preservation

MONEY IN OUR LIVES 7

A bride and groom are showered with money at their wedding in the Egyptian Nile Delta province of al-Minufiyah.

THINK AND DISCUSS

1 Look at the photo and read the caption. Does anything about it surprise you?

2 Why do you think money is a typical gift for a couple on their wedding day?

Look at the photo and the chart. Then discuss these questions.

1. What are the people in the photo spending money on?
2. Look at the chart. Which five areas spend the highest percentage of household budget on food?
3. Which categories do areas spend the lowest percentage of household budget on? Why do you think that is?
4. If your area is in the graph, does it accurately reflect your spending? If it isn't, which area's spending pattern is most similar to yours or your family's?

A cafe in New Orleans, Louisiana, USA

MONEY—HOW DO WE SPEND IT?

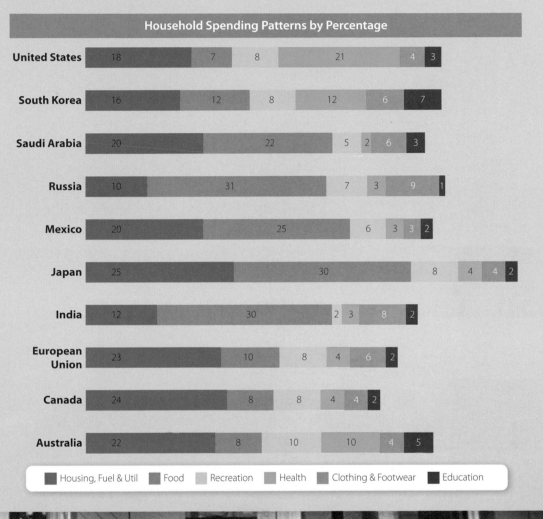

Household Spending Patterns by Percentage

Country	Housing, Fuel & Util	Food	Recreation	Health	Clothing & Footwear	Education
United States	18	7	8	21	4	3
South Korea	16	12	8	12	6	7
Saudi Arabia	20	22	5	2	6	3
Russia	10	31	7	3	9	1
Mexico	20	25	6	3	3	2
Japan	25	30	8	4	4	2
India	12	30	2	3	8	2
European Union	23	10	8	4	6	2
Canada	24	8	8	4	4	2
Australia	22	8	10	10	4	5

A Vocabulary

MEANING FROM CONTEXT

A 🎧 **3.6** Read and listen to the survey from a study on money. Notice each word or phrase in **blue** and think about its meaning. Then choose your answers.

SURVEY: YOUR VIEWS ON MONEY	Yes	No
1. Do you **associate** a high salary with happiness?	☐	☐
2. Does how much money you have frequently **determine** what you can or can't do?	☐	☐
3. Do you find more **fulfillment** doing activities that require money than ones that don't?	☐	☐
4. Do you believe that saving money is a **virtue**?	☐	☐
5. Does spending money contribute to your sense of **well-being**?	☐	☐
6. Is it important to use your money to **impact** others' lives for the better?	☐	☐
7. Does having more money increase your sense of **security**?	☐	☐
8. Does having money **promote** independence?	☐	☐
9. Do you **engage in** financial planning for the future?	☐	☐
10. Do you have an optimistic **outlook** regarding your financial future?	☐	☐

B Write each word or phrase in **blue** from exercise A next to its definition.

1. _____ (v) to do (an activity)

2. _____ (v) to decide; to influence

3. _____ (v) to connect in the mind

4. _____ (v) to have a direct effect on

5. _____ (n) a point of view; an attitude

6. _____ (n) safety; protection from harm

7. _____ (n) a feeling of achievement or satisfaction

8. _____ (n) a positive personal characteristic

9. _____ (v) to help or encourage something to happen

10. _____ (n) a state of happiness and health

C Work with a partner. Compare and discuss your answers in exercise A.

VOCABULARY SKILL Choosing the Right Definition

Many English words have more than one definition. When looking up words with multiple definitions, carefully examine the context for clues to the meaning.

For example, read the sentence and three possible definitions.

*I don't **associate** with my old coworkers anymore.*

>   1. (v) to connect ideas in one's mind
>   2. (v) to join as a friend or companion
>   3. (v) to connect logically

Because the meaning is clearly not related to things only in the mind or connections of logic, we know the correct definition must be number two.

D Choose the best definition for the **bold** word in each sentence.

1. I'd say her greatest **virtue** is patience.
   a. (n) a positive personal characteristic (I teach my son the virtue of honesty.)
   b. (n) an advantage or benefit (The virtue of toast is that it's easy to make.)
   c. (n) moral excellence (His mother is a model of virtue.)

2. Strict **security** is planned for the concert.
   a. (n) safety; protection from harm (The kitten sought security behind its mother.)
   b. (n) measures taken to protect a place (They are tightening security at the airport.)
   c. (n) a certificate proving investment (Securities are traded on Wall Street.)

3. The size of a piece of chicken **determines** its cooking time.
   a. (v) to choose or resolve to do (He'll do better once he determines to improve.)
   b. (v) to discover after investigation (Tests will determine the cause of his illness.)
   c. (v) to decide; to influence (Years of service determine salary.)

4. The new president was able to **restore** confidence in the economy.
   a. (v) to repair and renovate (She's an expert in restoring paintings.)
   b. (v) to cause to possess again (The money must be restored to its owner.)
   c. (v) to cause to exist again (The revolution restored democracy.)

5. The economic **outlook** right now is relatively poor.
   a. (n) a forecast or prediction (The political outlook is rather unclear.)
   b. (n) a view (That hotel has a spectacular outlook on the lake.)
   c. (n) a point of view; an attitude (I try to keep a positive outlook on life.)

E Complete the statements. Then discuss your answers with a partner.

1. The three factors that impact a person's well-being the most are _____

   _____

2. I believe the most important virtue a person could have is _____

   _____

3. Engaging in activities such as _____ promotes _____

   _____

A Listening An Interview about Money and Happiness

BEFORE LISTENING

CRITICAL THINKING:
RANKING

A Read the phrases. How happy does each situation make you? Rank them from 1 (the happiest) to 6 (the least happy).

_____ having money in the bank

_____ earning money

_____ spending money on items you want

_____ receiving money as a gift

_____ giving money to other people

_____ spending money on travel

WHILE LISTENING

LISTENING FOR
MAIN IDEAS

B 🎧 3.7 Listen to the interview. Then choose the correct answers.

1. What does a recent study by psychologist Elizabeth Dunn show?
   a. Spending money brings us more happiness than saving money.
   b. Possessions determine our happiness level more than experiences do.
   c. Spending money on others makes you happier than spending it on yourself.

2. What common error do people make when they try to buy happiness with money?
   a. They hesitate to buy the things that will really make them happy.
   b. They think major purchases such as houses will make them happy.
   c. They don't spend freely enough when buying meaningful items.

3. What question did researchers Leaf Van Boven and Tom Gilovich want to answer?
   a. Do people feel happier possessing money or material goods?
   b. Does spending money on things increase people's sense of well-being?
   c. Which makes people happier: spending money on experiences or on items?

▼ **There are approximately 180 currencies recognized by the United Nations.**

4. What did Angus Deaton and Daniel Kahneman's study reveal?
   a. Making more than a certain amount of money doesn't affect happiness much.
   b. Making more than a certain amount of money causes unhappiness.
   c. Making more than a certain amount of money results in greater happiness.

NOTE-TAKING SKILL Summarizing

A summary is a shortened version of a passage. It contains the main ideas and some important details. Summarizing teaches you to distinguish between important and less important information, and writing a summary can improve your memory of information you read, listen to, or watch. When you summarize:

- start with a phrase or sentence describing the topic of the summary
- leave out unnecessary information and information that is repeated
- express ideas in as few words as possible, and combine ideas when possible

C 🎧 **3.7** Listen to the interview again. Complete the summaries of the three studies described by Dr. Simmons. Write no more than two words in each blank.

LISTENING FOR DETAILS

Study 1: A study by E. Dunn at the University of British Columbia determined that

_____ away brings a greater sense of well-being than spending it on
1

oneself. Dunn gave money to two groups. Members of the first group spent money on

_____; members of the other spent it on _____.
2   3

Afterwards, the people were _____. The group that spent money on
4

others was found to be _____.
5

Study 2: L. Van Boven and T. Gilovich looked at the value of spending money on

_____ versus material things. The scientists used _____
6   7

to ask how people felt about each. They discovered that spending money on

_____ made people happier than spending it on _____.
8   9

The reason is that experiences are more _____ and contribute to
10

_____ relationships.
11

Study 3: Economist A. Deaton and _____ D. Kahneman wanted to know
12

whether more money means _____. They analyzed surveys filled out
13

by _____ of people. They found that once a person earns $75,000/year,
14

making more money doesn't _____ his or her happiness level.
15

AFTER LISTENING

D In a group, discuss which option in each pair would result in more happiness according to the research studies you heard. Use *According to . . .* to start your sentences. Then discuss your opinions.

CRITICAL THINKING: SYNTHESIZING

- buying yourself a $1,000 coat/giving $1,000 to a charity
- taking a trip around the world/making an initial payment on a new house
- an easy job that pays $30,000 per year/a stressful job that pays $75,000 per year

A Speaking

> **SPEAKING SKILL** Referencing Research Studies
>
> Referencing research is a good way to support your message. When referring to studies, you can leave out the details and make a general reference instead. This is useful when there are too many studies to mention, when you can't remember the exact studies but know they exist, or when such details are unimportant. Here are some expressions you can use to reference research.
>
> *Research has proven/determined/demonstrated (that)...*
> *(A number of/Various) studies show/have shown/suggest (that)...*
> *Statistics show (that)...*
> *According to (various) studies...*

A 🎧 **3.8** Work with a partner. Take turns reading the excerpts from the interview about money and happiness. Use expressions from the Speaking Skill box. Then listen and complete each excerpt with the expression used.

1. But, you know, buying a home is a big financial commitment ... and, in fact, people often go deep into debt to buy one. Actually, _____statistics show_____ that owning your home brings no more happiness than renting.

2. People say that "the best things in life are free," which implies that money doesn't matter to happiness. But we all know that's not really true. _____Research has proven_____ that debt has a negative effect on happiness, while savings and financial security tend to increase it.

3. What's important to remember is this: _____Various studies show_____ that happiness isn't about how much money you have. It's what you do with the money that can promote happiness ...

REFERENCING
RESEARCH STUDIES

B With your partner, role-play a conversation between a college student and a student advisor using the information in the chart below. The advisor gives advice using expressions from the Speaking Skill box. Then switch roles.

Student's Questions	Research for Advisor's Answers
Should I get a part-time job on campus?	Working more than 15 hours a week lowers grades.
Should I apply for a credit card?	Credit cards make people spend more.
Should I quit school and work full time?	People with more education make more money.
Should I get financial advice from other students?	Young people don't always understand money.
Should I blame myself for not saving money?	Two-thirds of college students have little or no savings.

CRITICAL THINKING   Interpreting Visuals

Information in visuals is often coded according to color, shape, and/or size. Use the coding to interpret the information correctly. If the meaning of the visual coding isn't clear, look for a "key" that explains the coding system.

C   Work with a partner. Study the chart. Then answer the questions below.

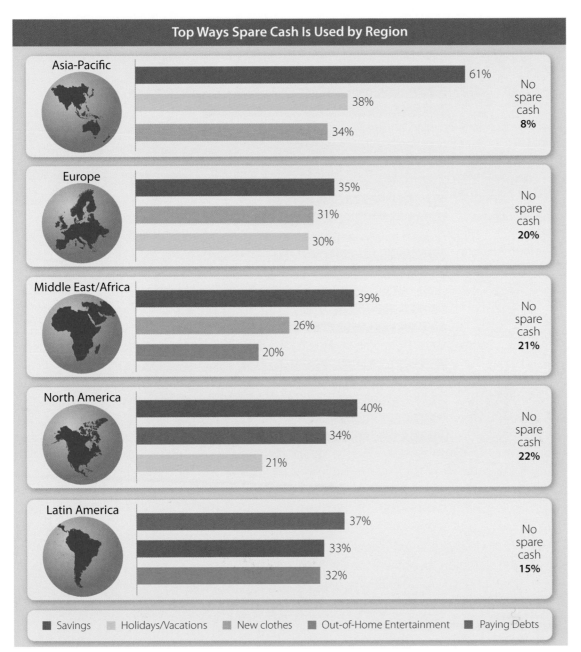

Top Ways Spare Cash Is Used by Region

Asia-Pacific — 61% / 38% / 34% — No spare cash **8%**

Europe — 35% / 31% / 30% — No spare cash **20%**

Middle East/Africa — 39% / 26% / 20% — No spare cash **21%**

North America — 40% / 34% / 21% — No spare cash **22%**

Latin America — 37% / 33% / 32% — No spare cash **15%**

■ Savings   ■ Holidays/Vacations   ■ New clothes   ■ Out-of-Home Entertainment   ■ Paying Debts

1. What do the different colors and bar lengths represent?
2. In which region do people tend to save the most?
3. In which regions do people use their spare cash to pay debts?
4. What conclusion(s) can you draw from this information?

1. Asia-Pacific has the highest percentage of spare cash contributed to savings

D Work with a partner. Study the graph. Then answer the questions below.

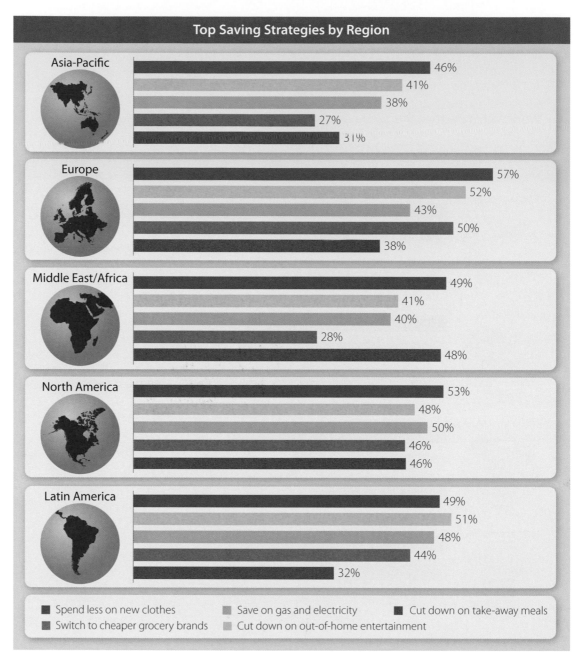

Top Saving Strategies by Region

Asia-Pacific
46%
41%
38%
27%
31%

Europe
57%
52%
43%
50%
38%

Middle East/Africa
49%
41%
40%
28%
48%

North America
53%
48%
50%
46%
46%

Latin America
49%
51%
48%
44%
32%

- Spend less on new clothes
- Save on gas and electricity
- Cut down on take-away meals
- Switch to cheaper grocery brands
- Cut down on out-of-home entertainment

1. What do the different colors and bar lengths represent?
2. Which region saves the most in each category?
3. Does the data for your region reflect your reality? Explain.

E Work in a small group. Discuss these questions.

1. Which of the five strategies for saving money would be easiest for you to implement? Which would be the most difficult?
2. What other strategies for saving money can you think of?

LESSON TASK Discussing Purchases and Happiness

A Write five of the most expensive items, services, or experiences that you have ever purchased. Then rank them in order of most expensive (1) to least expensive (5).

Purchase	Expense Rank	Happiness Rank

> **EVERYDAY LANGUAGE** Asking and Answering Personal Questions
>
> Asking
>
> Can/May I ask you (about) . . . ?   Would you mind if I asked you (about) . . . ?
>
> Would you mind telling me (about) . . . ?   Is it all right/OK if I ask (about) . . . ?
>
> Answering
>
> You certainly may./Of course.   No, I don't/wouldn't mind.
>
> Actually, I'd rather not talk about that.   Sure./Of course.

B Work with a partner. Take turns sharing the items on your list and asking and answering questions about them. Find out if the items made your partner happy and why or why not. Use the expressions in the Everyday Language box.

A: *Do you mind if I ask you how expensive your watch was?*
B: *No, I don't mind. It was about $300. It's a Swiss watch.*
A: *Can I ask if it makes you happy?*

C Now go back to exercise A and rank your purchases in order of the happiness they gave you (1 = most happiness, 5 = least happiness).

CRITICAL THINKING: RANKING

D With your partner, discuss the questions.

1. How did your purchase lists and your happiness rankings compare? Describe the similarities or differences between you and your partner.
2. Does any of the research from the three studies discussed in the interview on money and happiness support your list and ranking? Explain.
3. Considering your purchase list and happiness ranking, what conclusions can you make about what brings you personal fulfillment? Explain.

CRITICAL THINKING: ANALYZING

Bitcoin: The New Way to Pay

BEFORE VIEWING

PREDICTING **A** Work in a small group. Discuss these questions. Predict answers if you are not sure.

1. What is virtual money, and how can people get it?
2. Can virtual money buy real-life objects and experiences?
3. Is virtual money regulated by a real-life bank?

B Match each word from the video to its definition. Use a dictionary to help you.

1. _____ back up (v)   a. computer program instructions

2. _____ code (n)   b. limited in number

3. _____ engrave (v)   c. to cut or carve a design into something

4. _____ finite (adj)   d. to dig up, remove (from the earth)

5. _____ mine (v)   e. to support, help

WHILE VIEWING

C ▶ **1.15** Watch the video. Which statement is the main idea?

UNDERSTANDING MAIN IDEAS

1. Bitcoins are like gold—they are difficult to find, and their value changes daily.
2. Bitcoin is a valuable digital currency, but it has problems like all forms of money.
3. A major Bitcoin owner created a Web series about it to promote its use.
4. The use and security of Bitcoins are limited because they're not supported by a bank.

D Look back at your answers to exercise A. Were your predictions correct?

E ▶ **1.15** Watch the video again and complete the summary. Write no more than three words in each blank.

UNDERSTANDING DETAILS

BITCOIN IN A NUTSHELL

Bitcoin is an Internet currency that gets its value from _____.
                                                                    1
There are two ways you can get Bitcoins: _____ like virtual
                                                            2
gold or _____ another Bitcoin user. However, there is only a
              3
_____ amount of them online. People use Bitcoin to make big and
        4
small purchases; there's _____ to how much you can spend online
                              5
with Bitcoin. There's a risk in using Bitcoin because there's no central banking system
_____. While it's been associated with hacking and illegal activities,
        6
most crimes are committed _____.
                                    7

AFTER VIEWING

F Work in a small group. Discuss these questions.

CRITICAL THINKING: REFLECTING

1. How would you explain what Bitcoin is to a friend?
2. How do you usually pay for things such as food, phone and Internet service, eating out, rent, etc.?
3. Have you ever used Bitcoin? If not, would you ever? Explain.
4. What might be some of the benefits and drawbacks of using Bitcoin?
5. Do you think it would be fair for the creator of Bitcoin, who was anonymous, to use Bitcoin for personal financial gain? Why or why not?
6. Bitcoin is one form of cashless payment, which is becoming more and more popular. What do you think about the future of cash in your country?

Vocabulary

A 🎧 **3.9** Read and listen to the personal finance tips. Notice each word or phrase in **blue** and think about its meaning.

NINE PERSONAL FINANCE TIPS

1. Don't trust yourself to remember to pay your bills on time. Instead, set up a bill pay **reminder** on your bank's website.

2. If your company offers direct deposit, **deposit** a percentage of your pay into a savings account. You'll be less tempted to spend money you never see.

3. Banking fees (monthly maintenance fees, ATM fees, foreign **transaction** fees) can add up. Consider opening an account with an online bank to save on fees.

4. **Allocate** at least 20 percent of your pay to financial priorities such as paying off debt and building your retirement **nest egg**.

5. It's possible to **overdo** saving money in the bank. If you have more than six months' savings in your account, then think about investing.

6. Pay attention to **seemingly** small daily expenses because they add up. Just giving up caffè lattes could save you hundreds every month.

7. College students: Be sure to apply for financial **aid** even if you think you won't get any. Last year, over a million students missed out on free money for school by not filling out the forms.

8. College graduates: Pay off your student loans quickly to avoid paying added **interest**. Making more than the minimum payment will help.

9. Don't **withdraw** money from retirement accounts unless absolutely necessary. It can mean paying high penalties. Instead, keep a separate fund for emergencies.

B Write the correct word or phrase in **blue** from exercise A to complete each definition.

1. _____ is the fee you pay for borrowing money.

2. When you _____ a sum of money, you put it into a bank account.

3. A(n) _____ is an exchange of goods, services, or funds.

4. If you _____ money from a bank account, you take it out.

5. If you _____ something, you dedicate it to a particular person or purpose.

6. A(n) _____ is something that makes you not forget another thing.

7. _____ is assistance in the form of money, equipment, or services.

8. A(n) _____ is a sum of money saved for the future.

9. If something is _____ true, it appears to be true.

10. If you _____ an activity, you do it excessively.

C Work with a partner. Look back at the financial tips in exercise A. Tell your partner which tips you follow or have followed and how well they work or worked.

CRITICAL THINKING: REFLECTING

D Look at the pie chart. Then create a pie chart about your own spending. Share your chart with a partner. How are you similar to or different from the typical American?

ORGANIZING IDEAS

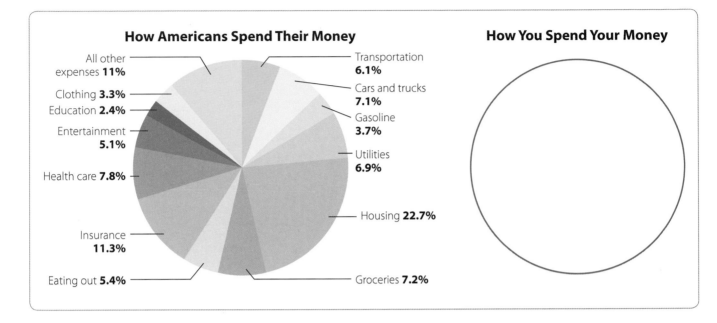

How Americans Spend Their Money

- All other expenses **11%**
- Clothing **3.3%**
- Education **2.4%**
- Entertainment **5.1%**
- Health care **7.8%**
- Insurance **11.3%**
- Eating out **5.4%**
- Transportation **6.1%**
- Cars and trucks **7.1%**
- Gasoline **3.7%**
- Utilities **6.9%**
- Housing **22.7%**
- Groceries **7.2%**

How You Spend Your Money

E Look at your pie chart. How could you better manage your money? Write five personal finance tips. Use vocabulary from exercise A. Then share your best tip with the class.

PERSONALIZING

Listening A Conversation about Money

BEFORE LISTENING

PRIOR KNOWLEDGE **A** Read about three types of payment cards and discuss the questions with a partner.

> **THREE TYPES OF PAYMENT CARDS**
>
> **Debit Cards:** Debit cards are directly connected to the money in your bank account. When you use your debit card, money is immediately withdrawn from your account.
>
> **Credit Cards:** When you use a credit card, you are borrowing money. The credit card company makes the payment for you, and you must pay the money back, usually with interest. If you don't make your payments on time, you can be charged late fees.
>
> **Stored-Value Cards:** Stored-value cards have electronic money stored right on the card. Anyone can use these cards, not just the person who originally bought the card. Examples are prepaid phone cards and gift cards.

1. Which of these payment cards do you use? When do you use them?
2. What other methods of payment do you regularly use?

WHILE LISTENING

LISTENING FOR
MAIN IDEAS

B 🎧 3.10 Listen to the conversation. Choose the two main topics the speakers discuss.

1. the decreasing number of ATMs available in the city
2. the degree of safety of electronic transactions
3. when each method of payment was first used
4. the top reasons that credit cards are widely used
5. an alternative system for lending and borrowing money

A small business owner in Ghana, West Africa, was able to start her own business through micro loans.

C ⌒ **3.10** Listen again. Then read the statements. Choose T for *True*, F for *False*, or NG for information *Not Given*.

LISTENING FOR
DETAILS

1. The restaurant where they are doesn't accept debit cards. T F NG
2. Both women feel that credit cards tempt them to spend too much. T F NG
3. The man has probably lost a stored-value card in the past. T F NG
4. Peer-to-peer lending services are offered by local banks. T F NG
5. Peer-to-peer lending services allow international loans. T F NG
6. The man has lent money through peer-to-peer lending. T F NG

LISTENING SKILL Listening for Shifts in Topic

While talking about a topic, speakers sometimes remember a related topic that they want to mention. Recognizing when a speaker is shifting topics will help you follow the talk or discussion. Here are some expressions that signal a shift in topic:

Speaking of [topic], . . .   *Incidentally,* . . .
Speaking of which, . . .   *By the way,* . . .
That reminds me, . . .

D ⌒ **3.11** Listen to excerpts from the conversation. Match the expressions with the topics they introduce.

LISTENING FOR
SHIFTS IN TOPIC

Expressions	Topics
1. _____ Speaking of which, . . .	a. credit cards coming before debit cards
2. _____ By the way, . . .	b. peer-to-peer lending
3. _____ Incidentally, . . .	c. using credit cards
4. _____ That reminds me, . . .	d. the service being slow
5. _____ Speaking of helping people, . . .	e. taking out a car loan

AFTER LISTENING

E Work with a partner. Look at the topics in the box. Discuss the impact (if any) that each has had on your financial well-being. What changes would you like to make with how you use any of these? Explain.

CRITICAL THINKING:
REFLECTING

cash	ATM machines	direct deposit	credit cards
debit cards	stored-value cards	peer-to-peer lending	interest

B Speaking

PRONUNCIATION Linking Vowel Sounds

🎧 **3.12** When one word ends in a vowel sound and the next word begins with a vowel sound, we often add a slight *w* or *y* sound between the words.

1. Add a *w* sound when the first word ends in these sounds:
   /u/ overd**o** _it   /oʊ/ g**o** _online   /aʊ/ h**ow** _about

2. Add a *y* sound when the first word ends in these sounds:
   /i/ th**e** _amount   /eɪ/ w**eigh** _it   /aɪ/ l**ie** _about   /ɔɪ/ enj**oy** _it

A 🎧 **3.13** Insert a *y* or *w* sound under each link. Then listen to check your answers.

1. I like the_idea of building affordable housing units.
2. The financial data are too_inaccurate to use.
3. The boss needs to_authorize your monthly_expense report.
4. I can see_it's going to be_immensely profitable.
5. The changes to_our financial situation worry me_a little.
6. She advised me to_engage in financial planning early_on.
7. It's so_easy to go_into debt when you spend excessively.
8. The trial of the_affluent doctor became a media event.

GRAMMAR FOR SPEAKING Connectors of Concession

Connectors of concession (*though, even though*, etc.) introduce information that is in contrast or contrary to what the listener might expect. Look at the underlined information introduced by the connectors of concession. Note how it contrasts with the information in the main clause.

> I don't want my nest egg stolen **even though** it's not that big.
> **Though** they're really useful, I find credit cards dangerous.

Use the connectors *although, even though*, or *though* in dependent clauses.

> **Although** the dollar amount is small, microloans can buy a lot.
> **Even though** credit cards are convenient, I prefer to pay with cash.

Use the connectors *even so, nonetheless*, or *nevertheless* in independent clauses:

> I don't have a big nest egg. **Even so**, I want to keep what I have!
> The restaurant only accepts cash. **Nevertheless**, it's always busy at lunchtime.

B Work with a partner. Match the sentences that go together. Then take turns connecting the sentences with connectors of concession. Discuss which sentences you think are true and say why.

1. _____ It's fun to daydream about being rich.

2. _____ The cost of living is rising at an alarming rate.

3. _____ You may or may not be able to make more money.

4. _____ It's important to determine your budget ahead of time.

a. There are inevitably unplanned expenses to deal with.
b. Money doesn't guarantee one's happiness or well-being.
c. The increase has yet to impact the majority of the population.
d. Better use of the money you have can increase your happiness.

FINAL TASK A Role-Play about Financial Advice

You will role-play a meeting between a financial advisor and a client to discuss ways that the client can save money. Then you will prepare and present a budget.

A Work with a partner. Read the roles and decide who will play each one.

Role #1: Financial Advisor
You are a financial professional. Discuss the client's budget with him or her, ask questions, and offer suggestions for reducing expenses and debt.

Role #2: Client
You recently moved into a new home, and now your expenses are more than your income. Explain the problem and ask about ways to reduce your expenses and debt.

B Study the client's monthly budget and prepare suggestions for reducing expenses and debt to fit a monthly income of $2,800. Use these questions to guide you.

Financial Advisor	Client
• Which expenses cannot be changed?	• Which expenses can be changed?
• Which items should the client allocate less money to? How much less?	• Of those expenses, which items are priorities for you?
• Which items should the client allocate more money to? How much more?	• Which items are you willing to spend less on? How much less?
• Which loan should be paid back first?	

Monthly Expenses		Debts		New Budget
Rent:	$1,040	Student loan balance: $10,500 (2% interest for 15 years)		
Food:	$300			
Heat and electricity:	$150			
Gas for car:	$120	Car loan balance: $4,600 (4% interest for 4 years)		
Entertainment:	$425			
Health insurance:	$450			
Charity donation:	$100			
Credit card payment:	$400	Credit card balance: $1,290 (18% interest per year)		
Student loan payment:	$100			
Car loan payment:	$140			
Total Expenses:	**$3,225**	**Total Debt:**	**$16,390**	**New Total Expenses:**

C Role-play a meeting between the financial advisor and client. Share your suggestions and come to an agreement on a budget so that the client's expenses are less than his or her income. Also include a plan for how to repay the client's debt.

D Decide on which parts of the budget you and your partner will each be responsible for presenting. Then present your budget to another pair of students.

REFLECTION

1. What skill in this unit do you think will be most useful to you?

_____

_____

2. What is the most useful information related to money that you learned in this unit?

_____

_____

3. Here are the vocabulary words and phrases from the unit. Check (✔) the ones you can use.

☐ aid AWL	☐ impact AWL	☐ security AWL
☐ allocate AWL	☐ interest	☐ seemingly
☐ associate	☐ nest egg	☐ transaction
☐ deposit	☐ outlook	☐ virtue
☐ determine	☐ overdo	☐ well-being
☐ engage in	☐ promote AWL	☐ withdraw
☐ fulfillment	☐ reminder	

HEALTH AND TECHNOLOGY 8

Students react while watching a robot practice surgical techniques at a hospital in Pennsylvania, USA.

ACADEMIC SKILLS

LISTENING Listening for Assessments
Using a T-Chart
SPEAKING Emphasizing Important Information
Dropped Syllables
CRITICAL THINKING Synthesizing Information

THINK AND DISCUSS

1 Look at the photo and read the caption. What are the advantages and disadvantages of robots performing surgery?

2 In what other ways is technology being used in health care?

141

Look at the photo and read the information. Then discuss the questions.

1. What are the devices shown in the photo and what are they used for?

2. What other functions do you think these devices could have?

3. What kinds of information related to the environment, health, or fitness can be monitored by technology?

INNOVATIONS IN MEDICINE

Innovation and advances in medical technology are at the heart of modern medicine and have led to life-changing treatments and cures for patients around the world. Technology is also transforming the way health care information is accessed and communicated. It has impacted everything from better diagnostic, therapeutic, and surgical procedures to preventative medicine and disease management. It has also allowed individuals to take a more active role in monitoring their own health through the development of personal health and fitness trackers and apps. The Pollen-robots shown here are one of the latest innovations in health and technology.

Employees of Japanese weather forecasting company Weathernews display the "Pollen-robot" in Tokyo. These pollen-detecting robots will be set up at 1,000 points across Japan to observe pollen levels and send reports back to the company. This information will help people with allergies and breathing problems avoid unhealthy areas.

A Vocabulary

A 🎧 **3.14** Read and listen to this information from a health management company. Notice each word or phrase in **blue** and think about its meaning.

HEALTH DATA: MAKE USE OF IT!

The use of technology to manage personal health is growing **by leaps and bounds**! It's easy to wear a cool **gadget** to help you **keep track of** your activity, blood pressure, or body weight. And many of us surf the Web for health tips. There is a great deal of health information available, but studies show that most people are **reluctant** to take advantage of it. Many people have a **tendency** to put off taking care of their health, and often wait until a serious problem comes up to **consult** a doctor. With our service, we keep all of your information strictly **confidential**. We analyze your data and send you health reminders. In addition, if you have a problem, we have health professionals who can discuss a possible **diagnosis** and **clarify** any issues. Remember, prevention is **comparatively** cheap when you think of the alternative! Let us help you manage your health data today!

B Match each word or phrase with its definition.

1. _____ by leaps and bounds (adv phr)
2. _____ gadget (n)
3. _____ keep track of (v)
4. _____ reluctant (adj)
5. _____ tendency (n)
6. _____ consult (v)
7. _____ confidential (adj)
8. _____ diagnosis (n)
9. _____ clarify (v)
10. _____ comparatively (adv)

a. to monitor
b. to make something easier to understand; to explain
c. in relation to something else; relatively
d. a habit of acting or thinking in a certain way
e. meant to be kept secret or private
f. a medical assessment of a disease or condition
g. with rapid progress; at a rapid pace
h. unwilling; not enthusiastic
i. to seek advice or information from; to refer to
j. a small and useful device or tool

C Discuss the questions with a partner.

1. How do you keep track of your finances?
2. Have you ever been reluctant to try something new? Explain.
3. What kinds of things do you have a tendency to put off doing?
4. In what situations do you consult a dictionary? A grammar book?
5. What is something that you keep confidential?

D 🎧 3.15 Work with a partner. Listen to part of a conversation between a manager of a health club and a member. Complete the statements with words from exercise B.

1. At first, Jessica feels _____ about participating in the survey.

2. Jessica is concerned that her information won't be kept _____.

3. Jessica feels her fitness has improved _____.

4. When Jessica joined, she received a _____ to track her activity.

5. She doesn't usually _____ her workouts.

6. Jessica thinks the monthly fee is _____ higher than other clubs' fees.

7. Jessica has a _____ to work late, so she likes the health club's late hours.

8. Mike offers to _____ the contract for Jessica when she finishes the survey.

9. Jessica went to the wellness center to _____ with a doctor about her back.

10. The doctor's _____ was that Jessica had strained her back.

VOCABULARY SKILL Using Synonyms

Synonyms are words with the same meaning or very similar meanings. Learning synonyms enables you to use a greater variety of words and avoid sounding repetitious. It is important to be aware of any differences in meaning and usage between synonyms. For example, *tall* and *high* are synonyms, but we say *tall building* or *person* but *high mountain* or *ceiling*. You can find examples of usage in a dictionary, or by searching online.

E Choose the word or phrase that best completes each sentence. Choose both choices if they are both appropriate. Use a dictionary or other resource to help you.

1. The best therapy for your elbow is to move it back and forth (by leaps and bounds / at a rapid pace).

2. All construction workers on this site must wear a helmet and a (tool / gadget) belt.

3. Where are your keys? Why is it so hard for you to (keep track of / monitor) them?

4. I buy the store brand medicine because it's (comparatively / relatively) inexpensive.

5. He said he's (slow / reluctant) to go, but I still think we can convince him.

6. If your blood pressure is still too high, you should (consult / refer to) a doctor.

7. If you are concerned about your information being kept (private / confidential), we can assure you that our servers follow the highest levels of security.

8. My art teacher told me his general (diagnosis / assessment) of my painting.

9. In my family, excellent health and long life seem to be genetic (tendencies / habits).

10. Our meeting was helpful and (clarified / explained) my understanding of the problem.

11. This is a (confidential / private) club—you can only join if invited by a member.

12. Companies, from Apple to small startups, are creating (gadgets / devices) that monitor and track health data.

A Listening A Lecture about Big Data in Health Care

BEFORE LISTENING

PRIOR KNOWLEDGE **A** Work in a small group. Discuss the questions.

1. What kind of medical data about patients do doctors need?
2. Do you think health data should be kept confidential? Explain.
3. What do you think the term *big data* means?

WHILE LISTENING

B 🎧 3.16 Listen to the first part of the lecture. Was your understanding of big data correct?

LISTENING FOR MAIN IDEAS **C** 🎧 3.17 ▶ 1.16 Listen to the lecture. Which of these points does the lecturer make? Put a check (✓) in the correct column.

	Yes	No
1. Advertisers are reluctant to use big data because of consumer concerns.	☐	☐
2. Until recently, health care data has had a tendency to be unreliable.	☐	☐
3. Health care data has focused on collection and storage rather than analysis.	☐	☐
4. It is predicted that artificial intelligence will one day replace doctors.	☐	☐
5. Big data can enhance patient health even after patients leave the hospital.	☐	☐

> **NOTE-TAKING SKILL** Using a T-Chart
>
> A T-chart can be an effective note-taking tool when a lecture or presentation deals with two sides of a topic (e.g., advantages and disadvantages, challenges and solutions, causes and effects). Placing these aspects on the same line on either side of a chart creates a visually clear arrangement that helps both comprehension and memory.

▶ **Students visit Corporea, an interactive museum in Naples, Italy, devoted entirely to the subject of health, science and biomedical technologies, and prevention.**

D 🎧 3.18 Listen again to part of the lecture. As you listen, complete the notes related to challenges in the left column. Then listen again, and complete the notes related to solutions in the right column. Write no more than two words in each blank.

Big Data and Health Care	
Challenges	**Solutions**
Patients have tendency to be ⎯⎯⎯⎯ 1 ⎯⎯⎯⎯ when reporting their health data	Collect ⎯⎯⎯⎯ 8 ⎯⎯⎯⎯ only, from dr. appts, lab tests, devices
Patients afraid data won't be kept ⎯⎯⎯⎯ 2 ⎯⎯⎯⎯	Dev. of better & better ⎯⎯⎯⎯ 9 ⎯⎯⎯⎯ technlgy
Medical data useless unless in a form that doctors ⎯⎯⎯⎯ 3 ⎯⎯⎯⎯	Pittsburgh Health Data Alliance's profiles give docs info in form that's easy ⎯⎯⎯⎯ 10 ⎯⎯⎯⎯
The amount of patient data is becoming ⎯⎯⎯⎯ 4 ⎯⎯⎯⎯	Use artificial intell. (AI) to ⎯⎯⎯⎯ 11 ⎯⎯⎯⎯ & interpret data
Even ideas suggested by ⎯⎯⎯⎯ 5 ⎯⎯⎯⎯ can't be trusted	These new ideas must be tested in studies supervised ⎯⎯⎯⎯ 12 ⎯⎯⎯⎯
Some patients are ⎯⎯⎯⎯ 6 ⎯⎯⎯⎯ or unable to follow doc's orders	Big data being used to determine who these ⎯⎯⎯⎯ 13 ⎯⎯⎯⎯
Traditionally, it's been difficult to ⎯⎯⎯⎯ 7 ⎯⎯⎯⎯ in follow-up care	New ⎯⎯⎯⎯ 14 ⎯⎯⎯⎯ keep track of patient location, meds, sleep, psych. state

AFTER LISTENING

E Work in a small group. Discuss the questions.

1. The speaker says that for big data to be useful, it needs to be analyzed and distributed to the "right people." Who are the "right people" to receive big data in this context?
2. The speaker says, "We haven't yet reached the point where a computer can replace a doctor." Does his lecture imply that will happen someday? Explain.
3. What does the speaker imply about patients' use of new apps when he says, "And while it has traditionally been difficult to monitor patients in follow-up care, new apps keep track of where they are, whether they're taking their medicine, how well they're sleeping, and even their psychological state after they've left the hospital"?

Speaking

SPEAKING SKILL Emphasizing Important Information

When you want to make a point and be sure that your listeners don't miss it, you need to emphasize that point. You can use these expressions to emphasize important information.

It's important to note/remember/keep in mind that . . .

We need to remember/keep in mind that . . .

Let me point out/stress/highlight that . . .

I'd like to emphasize/point out/stress that . . .

A **3.19** Listen to the excerpts from the lecture. Write the information the speaker emphasizes. With a partner, discuss why this information is important.

1. _____

_____

2. _____

_____

3. _____

_____

B With a partner, discuss the positive and negative implications of institutions having unlimited access to data about a person's health, diet, and daily activities. Write your ideas in the T-chart. Then share your ideas with another pair.

Full Access to Data	
Positive Implications	**Negative Implications**

GRAMMAR FOR SPEAKING Noun Clauses with *That*

A noun clause functions as a noun in a sentence. *That* can introduce a noun clause, but is often omitted in speaking. Noun clauses can come:

After *be* + certain adjectives, such as *sure, concerned, interesting, true,* and *worried.*

> I'm *sure* <u>(that) we'll see a lot more collaboration in the future</u>.
> It's *true* <u>(that) advertisers use big data about people's shopping habits</u>.

After verbs related to thinking, such as *agree, keep in mind, realize,* and *worry.*

> Many people *agree* <u>(that) big data has immense potential</u>.

C 🎧 **3.20** Listen to Dr. Stafford's answer to a student's question after the lecture. Match each main clause with the noun clause the doctor uses.

1. _____ This leads some people to worry

    a. that there are more opportunities for their data to be unprotected.

2. _____ ... some people are worried

    b. that these new methods of recording and sharing health data will also require new security measures.

3. _____ It is obvious

    c. that the wireless networks used by health institutes could present security issues.

D With a partner, take turns creating sentences. Combine main clauses from the first column with noun clauses in the second to express your opinions on information from the lecture. Explain your reasons.

I (don't) agree	(that) health care professionals should trust big data.
I (don't) think	(that) AI can be trusted to analyze big data.
I (don't) feel	(that) drug companies should share their data with each other.
I am (not) sure	(that) big data has immense potential to treat and monitor patients.

A doctor examines a child's throat via smart phone held by a nurse in a digital medical consultation.

E Form a small group and discuss the situation below. Was the company's decision the right one? Explain.

> Two equally qualified candidates were being considered for one position at a company. The company used big data to determine that one of the candidates could suffer from a serious health problem in the future. This candidate was not offered the job.

CRITICAL THINKING Synthesizing Information

When we synthesize information, we make connections among different ideas. For example, in academic classes, you will be asked to combine information from multiple sources such as a reading and a lecture to gain a deeper understanding of a topic.

F With a partner, synthesize the information you learned in Lesson A about health care and the use of big data. Create a T-chart and list the pros and cons. Discuss your ideas and give examples.

Dubai has launched a smart city initiative to explore energy, environment, infrastructure, and mobility. Its goal: to be the world's happiest and smartest city.

LESSON TASK Assessing a City's Health

A Work in a small group. Read this definition of a healthy city. Discuss whether your city or town fits the description.

> The World Health Organization defines a healthy city as one that is continually creating and improving physical and social environments in order to support personal health. A healthy city enables residents to support each other in daily activities and to reach their maximum potential.

B With your group, discuss how a city you know is doing in the areas listed below. Then decide on the area that is most important to improve.

- air / water / noise pollution
- parks / green space
- sports / exercise facilities
- public transportation cost / availability

- stress at home / in the workplace
- food prices / quality
- health care costs / availability / quality
- unhealthy lifestyles

EVERYDAY LANGUAGE   Evaluating Ideas

Positive Evaluation: *I'd say that (idea) has a lot of potential.*
I think that (idea) could/might work.
That (idea) sounds good/That sounds like a good idea.

Uncertain Evaluation: *I'm not sure how well that (idea) would work.*
I don't know if that's the best way to do it/go.
That might not be the best solution/plan/idea.

C With your group, brainstorm methods of improving the area you chose in exercise B. Use expressions for evaluating ideas.

A: *One way to improve public transportation is to bring in experts to analyze the situation.*
B: *That sounds like a good idea. What's another idea?*

D Choose one person to report your ideas to the class.

Bikers squeeze between cars and buses in Tokyo, Japan.

Biking in the City

BEFORE VIEWING

PRIOR KNOWLEDGE

A You are going to watch a video about a small study that is collecting health data from bicyclists in the city. Discuss the questions with a partner.

1. In Lesson A, you learned about big data and health. What kinds of data would help the well-being of bicyclists riding in cities?
2. Are you concerned about the health effects of air pollution on the streets of your city or town?
3. Is biking in polluted city air better or worse for your health than just staying home?

B Match each word from the video with its definition. Use a dictionary as needed.

1. _____ deploy (v)   a. to produce or send out (a sound, signal, etc.)

2. _____ emit (v)   b. a bit of material as small as or smaller than a piece of dust

3. _____ optimize (v)   c. to put something into use

4. _____ particle (n)   d. how near a thing or place is to another

5. _____ proximity (n)   e. to make the best or most effective use of

WHILE VIEWING

C ▶ 1.17 Watch the video. Read the statements. Choose T for *True*, F for *False*, or NG for information *Not Given*.

UNDERSTANDING MAIN IDEAS

1. The health study is attempting to clarify a question about exercising in close proximity to traffic.   T   F   NG

2. Pollution from vehicles on the road is increasing.   T   F   NG

3. Participants wear clothing and gadgets that take measurements.   T   F   NG

4. Information collected about participants is kept confidential.   T   F   NG

5. Pollution and smoking can lead to a similar disease diagnosis.   T   F   NG

6. The researchers' goal is to create an app that bicyclists can consult for the quietest route.   T   F   NG

D ▶ 1.17 Preview the questions. Then watch the video again. Take notes as you watch. Write no more than three words for each answer.

UNDERSTANDING DETAILS

1. What does the study want to find new ways of measuring? _____

2. How frequently does the blood pressure monitor take a measurement?

   _____

3. What device do the participants use to log their location? _____

4. How long do the researchers have to prove the success of their study?

   _____

5. When particles of pollution are breathed in, where in the body do they go?

   _____

6. The planned app would balance less pollution with what other factor?

   _____

AFTER VIEWING

E Work with a partner. Think about the study in the video and answer the questions.

1. What was the research question that inspired the study?
2. How was the research carried out?
3. What will the researchers do after this study is completed?
4. In Lesson B, you will learn about various devices related to health maintenance. Would you use a pollution tracking app? Why or why not?

B Vocabulary

MEANING FROM CONTEXT **A** 🎧 **3.21** Read and listen to this email. Notice each word or phrase in **blue** and think about its meaning.

From: Human Resources

To: All employees

Subject: Technology and Service Upgrades

Plans to update our office technologies and services are moving forward! Below is a list of suggestions for equipment upgrades and new services that we would like your feedback on. Please rank them from 1 to 10 (1 = most important, 10 = least important) and send this form back to HR at your earliest convenience.

_____ Replace standard keyboards and mouse devices with ergonomic[1] ones to reduce and prevent injuries caused by **repetitive** movements.

_____ Supply employees with monitors that **detect** steps taken, calories burned, activity level, etc.

_____ Provide "smart chairs" that monitor worker **posture** and sitting time.

_____ Equip desks with emotion monitors that **notify** employees of high levels of stress and anxiety.

_____ Provide wearable gadgets to **track** blood pressure, blood sugar levels, heart rate, temperature, etc.

_____ Install apps on office computers to provide information about the **nutritional** value of different foods.

_____ Institute game breaks with fitness videos to fight the negative effects of **sedentary** time.

_____ Give employees sleep monitors to use at home to check for sleep-related health issues that can impact **productivity** at the office.

_____ Equip computers with anti-glare[2] screen protectors and provide special eyewear for employees who are **prone to** eye strain.

_____ Set up a technology hotline to take questions on using new technology and services and to help **resolve** any issues that employees may have.

[1] **ergonomic** (adj): designed for health and comfort
[2] **glare** (n): light that is very bright and difficult to look at

B Write each word or phrase in **blue** from exercise A next to its definition.

1. _____ (n) the position in which you stand or sit

2. _____ (adj) sitting down a lot and getting little physical exercise

3. _____ (v) to inform someone about something

4. _____ (adj) having a tendency, usually negative

5. _____ (n) effectiveness of workers at getting things done

6. _____ (adj) related to the health benefits of food and drink

7. _____ (v) to regularly check the value or position of something

8. _____ (v) to find a solution to a problem or difficulty

9. _____ (v) to find or discover by investigating

10. _____ (adj) occurring again and again, sometimes in a boring way

C Choose the word that forms a correct collocation with the word in **bold**. Use a dictionary or other resource to help you.

USING COLLOCATIONS

1. People who use computers a lot are prone to **repetitive** (stress / tension) injuries.

2. I avoid working in an office because I don't want a **sedentary** (livelihood / lifestyle).

3. Eating foods with a high **nutritional** (value / amount) will improve your health.

4. A healthy diet, exercise, and sleep can **resolve** many (issues / topics) with one's health.

5. All the hospitals were **notified** (on / of) the new data privacy legislation.

6. What are the legal implications of so much **tracking** (of / to) personal data?

7. The new workflow is the reason for our team's (increased / multiplied) **productivity**.

8. I keep track of my calories because I (am / have) **prone** to overdoing it whenever I eat out.

9. Marco had (poor / serious) **posture** until he bought an ergonomic chair.

10. The gadget was so small that it (escaped / exited) **detection** by the authorities.

D Work with a partner. Imagine you work at the company in exercise A. Discuss the importance of the suggestions to you and rank them from 1 to 10.

CRITICAL THINKING: RANKING

E Work with a partner. Use the vocabulary words to describe or make suggestions to improve your own work, school, or home life.

PERSONALIZING

> *I want an app that notifies me whenever I make a mistake in English!*

B Listening A Podcast about Fitness Gadgets

BEFORE LISTENING

PRIOR KNOWLEDGE **A** Work with a partner. Think of three gadgets, apps, or websites related to fitness that you have owned or know about. What functions do they perform? How do they work? Write them in the chart.

Gadget	Function

WHILE LISTENING

LISTENING FOR MAIN IDEAS **B** 🎧 3.22 Listen to a podcast reviewing five gadgets related to health and fitness. Check (✓) the ones that Tyler and Hannah would recommend to their listeners.

Gadget	Recommended by Tyler	Recommended by Hannah
FitterYet		
Smarty Sleep Mask		
Sun Disc 3		
e-Beverage System		
BestPosture		

An athlete gets ready for a run with her fitness smartwatch.

When reviewing products or services, people often make positive or negative assessments. Listening for assessments allows you to understand what the speaker perceives to be the pros and cons of the topic of discussion.

Positive Assessments	Negative Assessments
What I like about it is (that) …	*What I don't like about it is (that)* …
I'm impressed with …	*I'm not impressed with* …
On the plus side/positive side/upside, …	*On the minus side/negative side/ downside,* …
A/One (big/major/significant/important) advantage/benefit is (that) …	*A/One (big/major/significant/important) disadvantage/drawback is (that)* …

C 🎧 3.22 Listen again. What features of the gadgets were positively or negatively assessed by the speakers? Take notes in the chart.

LISTENING FOR DETAILS

Gadget	Pros	Cons
FitterYet	– accurately tracks how far you walk – inexpensive	– big and unattractive
Smarty Sleep Mask		
Sun Disc 3		
e-Beverage System		
BestPosture		

AFTER LISTENING

D Work in a small group. Discuss the questions.

PERSONALIZING

1. Of the gadgets you heard about, which ones would you be interested in using? Which ones don't interest you?
2. Do you think fitness gadgets are a passing trend or are they here to stay? Explain.

Speaking

PRONUNCIATION Dropped Syllables

🎧 **3.23** We sometimes drop a vowel sound in words with three syllables or more. In these words, the vowel sound that comes after a stressed syllable is dropped.

> Maybe it's unattractive, but then, it's not a piece of **jew~~e~~lry**, is it?
>
> I was very **int~~e~~rested** in trying this one out because I have a tendency to burn.
>
> It also analyzes the nutritional profile of the **bev~~e~~rage** you're drinking.
>
> It's a **myst~~e~~ry** to me how it works …

A 🎧 **3.24** One or two words in each sentence has a syllable where the vowel sound can be dropped. Cross out the vowels that are dropped. Then listen to check your answers.

1. The laboratory was open during renovation.
2. I was able to internalize what I learned in my mathematics class.
3. I find it easy to conform to the corporate culture.
4. I think it's undeniable that broccoli improves one's memory.
5. To me, vegetable juice is just cold soup.
6. The drop in sales was disastrous for our restaurant.
7. We're planning to initiate several new projects every year.
8. Did you know that I actually daydream about chocolate?
9. My family takes a two-week vacation each year.
10. Success in business is always a collaborative effort.

B 🎧 **3.25** Practice saying the following words that are often pronounced with a dropped syllable. Then listen and check your pronunciation.

1. average
2. deliberately
3. elementary
4. desperate
5. federal
6. different
7. preference
8. reference
9. temperature
10. traveler

C Work with a partner. Make your own sentences using words with dropped syllables from this page. Say them with and without dropping the syllables, and ask your partner if he or she can hear the difference.

> I deliberately try to avoid being sedentary on the weekends.

D Work in a small group. Look at the graphic and discuss the questions.

1. Where do people prefer to attach health/fitness gadgets? Why do you think that is?
2. What might be the advantage of a device worn in contact lenses?
3. Where would you prefer to wear a health/fitness gadget?

Where Would You Wear A Health/Fitness Gadget?

4% Contact lenses

6% Around chest

3% Tattooed on skin

29% Attached to clothing

10% Upper arm

12% Set in jewelry

28% Wrist

12% Glasses

18% Attached to shoe

12% Earbuds/ headphones

15% Set in clothing

FINAL TASK Presenting on a Health Tech Product

> You will give an individual presentation on a health/fitness technology product.

A Research a health/fitness tech product that has some product reviews available.

B Use these questions to guide your research:

- Is there a story behind the invention?
- What company makes it?
- Is there anything interesting or notable about it?
- What does the device look like and how is it used?
- Where do you wear it?
- What kinds of information does it track?
- What features does it offer?
- Are there any competing brands?

C Analyze online reviews of the product. As you read the reviews, take notes in a T-chart on the positive and negative assessments.

ORGANIZING IDEAS **D** Organize your notes for the presentation. Highlight the important information. Review the expressions for emphasizing important information in the Speaking Skill box, and the expressions for making assessments in the Listening Skill box. Choose an appropriate picture of the product, and prepare a T-chart of the pros and cons to use as visuals or handouts.

PRESENTATION SKILL Engaging Your Audience

Here are some suggestions to help you engage your audience.
- At the beginning of your presentation, ask some questions that can be answered by a show of hands.
- As appropriate during your presentation, ask for one or more volunteers to assist you or to provide an example for a point.
- Focus on how the points you are making can benefit your audience. When you do, check if they agree.
- Use rhetorical questions to encourage your audience to think about something, to invite them to agree with you, or to ask questions you think your audience would like to ask.

E Prepare questions to engage your audience and plan where in your presentation you will ask them. Then with a partner, practice giving your presentations. Provide feedback and modify your presentation based on your partner's feedback.

PRESENTING **F** Give your presentation to the class. Invite audience questions at the end of your presentation.

REFLECTION

1. What skill in this unit do you think will be most useful to you? In what way?

   _____

   _____

2. Which technological gadget in this unit interested you most? Why?

   _____

   _____

3. Here are the vocabulary words and phrases from the unit. Check (✓) the ones you can use.

☐ by leaps and bounds	☐ gadget	☐ reluctant AWL
☐ clarify AWL	☐ keep track of	☐ repetitive
☐ comparatively	☐ notify	☐ resolve AWL
☐ confidential	☐ nutritional	☐ sedentary
☐ consult AWL	☐ posture	☐ tendency
☐ detect AWL	☐ productivity	☐ track
☐ diagnosis	☐ prone to	

THE MYSTERIOUS MIND 9

Colored 3D computed angiogram of the blood vessels in the left hemisphere of a 27-year-old's brain

ACADEMIC SKILLS

LISTENING	Recognizing Appositives
	Highlighting Conclusions
SPEAKING	Expressing Causal Relationships
	Reduced Function Words
CRITICAL THINKING	Evaluating Conclusions

THINK AND DISCUSS

1 How do humans show intelligence?
2 Besides humans, what animals do you think are intelligent? Why?
3 How good is your memory? Explain.

EXPLORE THE THEME

Look at the images and read the text. Then discuss these questions.

1. What would be an advantage of having a fully developed frontal lobe?
2. Which parts do you think are probably the most developed in a professional athlete's brain? Why?
3. Think of activities that you are able to do well. Which areas of your brain do you think are the most developed?

THE AMAZING MIND

The brain consists of six major parts, each responsible for certain functions. A comprehensive list of all the functions would fill a book. However, to gain a better understanding of this remarkable organ, it is useful to look at where some essential functions are located. Keep in mind, though, that the parts of your brain don't work in isolation. Rather, they work together through an intricate network of nerves to communicate to all parts of your body.

Frontal Lobe

Reasoning • Speaking • Problem solving

Temporal Lobe

Memory • Recognizing faces • Generating emotions

Brain Stem

Breathing • Heartbeat • Body temperature

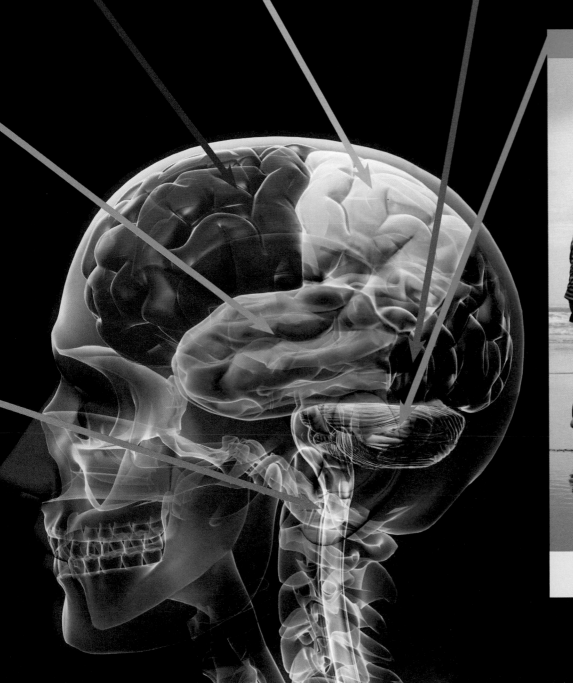

Parietal Lobe

Sensation • Reading • Body orientation

Occipital Lobe

Vision • Color perception • Light perception

Cerebellum

Balance • Coordination •
Fine muscle control

Vocabulary

A 🎧 **4.2** Read and listen to the information. Notice each word or phrase in **blue** and think about its meaning.

WHAT DOES IT MEAN TO BE INTELLIGENT?

Traditionally, a person who could solve problems, use **logic**, or think critically was considered smart. However, that understanding has changed over time, thanks in part to the work of Professor Howard Gardner of Harvard University. In the 1980s, Gardner made the surprising claim that there are at least seven "intelligences," **namely** logical, linguistic, visual/spatial, musical, kinesthetic, interpersonal, and intrapersonal—in other words, there are "multiple intelligences." Which intelligences do *you* have?

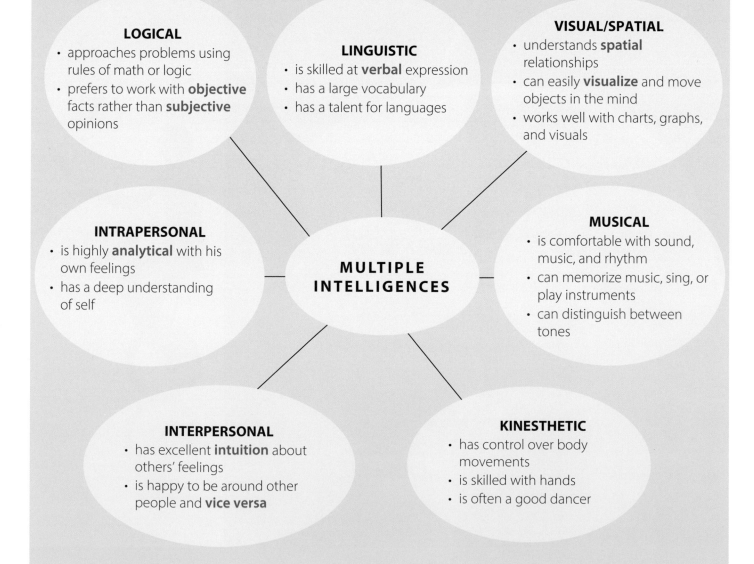

LOGICAL
- approaches problems using rules of math or logic
- prefers to work with **objective** facts rather than **subjective** opinions

LINGUISTIC
- is skilled at **verbal** expression
- has a large vocabulary
- has a talent for languages

VISUAL/SPATIAL
- understands **spatial** relationships
- can easily **visualize** and move objects in the mind
- works well with charts, graphs, and visuals

INTRAPERSONAL
- is highly **analytical** with his own feelings
- has a deep understanding of self

MULTIPLE INTELLIGENCES

MUSICAL
- is comfortable with sound, music, and rhythm
- can memorize music, sing, or play instruments
- can distinguish between tones

INTERPERSONAL
- has excellent **intuition** about others' feelings
- is happy to be around other people and **vice versa**

KINESTHETIC
- has control over body movements
- is skilled with hands
- is often a good dancer

B Complete each sentence with the correct word or phrase in **blue** from exercise A.

1. _____ information is true from a scientific point of view.

2. "_____" is used to say that the reverse of a statement is also true.

3. "_____" describes things related to size, shape, area, and position.

4. If you are a(n) _____ person, you think about things in a logical way.

5. "_____" is a word that introduces specific information or examples.

6. If you _____ something, you form a picture of it in your mind.

7. Something that is _____ is based on personal opinions and feelings.

8. Something that is _____ has to do with words and language.

9. Our _____ tells us something is true though we have no proof that it is.

10. _____ is a thought process based on good judgment and common sense.

VOCABULARY SKILL Suffixes *–al*, *–tial*, and *–ical*

The suffixes *–al*, *–tial*, and *–ical* are used to create adjectives from nouns.

- With many nouns, the suffix *–al* is added directly with no changes in spelling.
  logic → logic**al**   nutrition → nutrition**al**   verb → verb**al**

- With some nouns, adding *–al* involves slight changes in spelling.
  controvers**y** → controvers**ial**   trib**e** → trib**al**   benefi**t** → benefi**cial**

- Nouns ending in *–ce* often take the suffix *–tial* in their adjective form.
  confiden**ce** → confiden**tial**   referen**ce** → referen**tial**   spa**ce** → spa**tial**

- Some adjectives are formed by adding the suffix *–ical* with other spelling changes.
  analy**sis** → analy**tical**   hypothe**sis** → hypothe**tical**   ecolog**y** → ecolog**ical**

C Complete each question with the correct form of the word in parentheses. Use the suffix *–al*, *–tial*, or *–ical*. Use a dictionary as needed.

1. Which of your _____ (education) experiences has been most useful to you?

2. Do you have a _____ (math) mind?

3. Which of your teachers has been the most _____ (influence) in your life?

4. Do you prefer books that are _____ (history) or ones that are
   _____ (biography)?

5. What is one _____ (practice) strategy you use when preparing for a test?

D Work with a partner. Take turns asking and answering the questions from exercise C.   PERSONALIZING

Listening A Podcast on the Brain and Intelligence

BEFORE LISTENING

PRIOR KNOWLEDGE **A** Work in a small group. Look at the photo. What do you know about the two sides of the brain? Discuss with your group and write down your ideas.

WHILE LISTENING

LISTENING FOR MAIN IDEAS **B** 🎧 4.3 ▶ 1.18 Listen to the podcast. Does the speaker make these points? Check (✓) *Yes* or *No*.

	Yes	No
1. Experiments have shown differences in the two halves of the brain.	☐	☐
2. The experiments of early brain researchers were not scientific.	☐	☐
3. People have drawn incorrect conclusions about the brain in the past.	☐	☐
4. Right-brained and left-brained personalities are scientific facts.	☐	☐
5. Modern brain science has cleared up some confusion about the brain.	☐	☐

NOTE-TAKING SKILL Highlighting Conclusions

The details of scientific experiments are not usually as important as the conclusions. When you take notes, highlight or underline the conclusions so that they stand out. Later, it will be simple to review these key pieces of information. Here are some expressions to listen for.

> . . . it can be concluded that . . .
> . . . we came to/reached/arrived at/drew the conclusion that . . .
> It is clear that . . .

🎧 4.4 ▶ 1.19 **Listen to the main portion of the podcast. Complete the notes with no more than two words in each blank, and underline the conclusions.**   NOTE TAKING

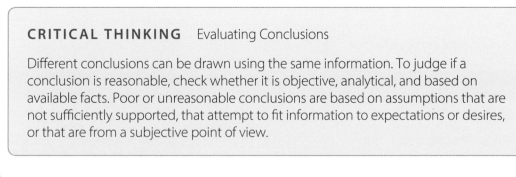

1861, France, P. P. Broca

   Examined brain damage that affected _____ 1

   Discovered damage was on left side of brain

   Seemed obvious that _____ 2 problms = result of L-brain damage

1960s, California, R. Sperry

   Expermnts on patients whose R&L-brains were surgically _____ 3

   Exper. #1: Patients saw words on R of screen easily, but didn't see on L

   Concl. L-brain is dominant in _____ 4

   Exper. #2: Patients arrange shapes & patterns on objects to match cards

   Easy w/their _____ 5 hand, diffclt w/their

   _____ 6 hand

   Concl: spatial abilities are in the _____ 7

Psychology & Education

   L-brain has language, & lang. is brain's most imp. capability

   Concl: L-brain is the _____ 8

   Educational ideas: brain-balancing activities

      Sit up straight and do _____ 9 problems (to help L-brain)

      Lie down and draw _____ 10 (to help R-brain)

Modern Brain Science

   Electrical actvty exists in _____ 11 halves of brain during all thinking

   Clear that the _____ 12 of brain always work together

AFTER LISTENING

> **CRITICAL THINKING**   Evaluating Conclusions
>
> Different conclusions can be drawn using the same information. To judge if a conclusion is reasonable, check whether it is objective, analytical, and based on available facts. Poor or unreasonable conclusions are based on assumptions that are not sufficiently supported, that attempt to fit information to expectations or desires, or that are from a subjective point of view.

D Work in a small group. Look back at the conclusions you underlined in exercise C. Discuss why they seem reasonable or unreasonable.   CRITICAL THINKING: EVALUATING CONCLUSIONS

A Speaking

A 🎧 **4.5** Listen to three excerpts from the podcast about the brain. Match the statements about cause and effect. Underline the cause in each statement.

1. _____ It seemed obvious that the speech problems

2. _____ Unfortunately, the fascinating scientific discoveries of Broca, Sperry, and others

3. _____ The influence of the right-brain/left-brain model on those in the education field

a. led to some less-than-scientific conclusions about the brain in the fields of psychology and education.
b. was responsible for the idea that "brain-balancing" activities could strengthen the less dominant side of the brain.
c. were a direct result of the damage.

EXPRESSING CAUSAL
RELATIONSHIPS

B Work in a small group. Discuss possible causes and effects for each of these topics related to psychology, and write them in the chart.

> *A self-confident personality is usually a result of having successful or positive experiences. I think it can lead to more leadership opportunities.*

Topics	Causes	Effects
1. A self-confident personality		
2. Computer game addiction		
3. A positive outlook on life		
4. Stress in the workplace		
5. Strong social connections		

A baby listens to music with headphones.

C Look at this list of popular ideas related to psychology and the mind. Do you think they are probably true or probably false, or are you unsure? Mark T for *Probably True*, F for *Probably False*, and U for *Unsure*.

CRITICAL THINKING: EVALUATING

1. Playing classical music to babies increases their level of intelligence.   T   F   U

2. Human beings normally use only 10 percent of their brain.   T   F   U

3. People with opposite personalities find each other attractive.   T   F   U

4. When the moon is full, there is an increase in crime and crazy behavior.   T   F   U

5. Repeating new words is the most effective way to learn them.   T   F   U

6. If you let yourself occasionally show a little anger, you will avoid getting very angry.   T   F   U

D Work in a small group. Compare and discuss your answers from exercise C.

E Now read the explanations below and check your answers from exercise C. With your group, discuss any facts that surprise you.

1. Two recent studies determined that playing classical music to babies produces no clear measurable effect on their intelligence.
2. Although the entire brain isn't used all the time, modern brain imaging techniques have shown that all parts of the brain are regularly active and no part is left unused.
3. Research has shown that people are more often attracted to people with whom they share various similarities.
4. Physics tells us that the pull of the moon has almost no effect on our brains, and studies show that there is no more crime during full moons than at other times.
5. Research has shown that effective vocabulary learning is the result of encountering new vocabulary in various meaningful ways, and not the result of simple repetition.
6. Recent scientific studies show that people who allow themselves to show their anger actually become angrier, which leads to negative consequences.

F Work with a partner. Read about four psychological experiments. Then discuss the question below each.

1. Participants are shown a short video of six people passing basketballs back and forth. Three of the people are wearing white, and three are wearing black. The participants are asked to count the number of passes between the people wearing white. At one point during the video, a person dressed in a gorilla costume walks through the people passing basketballs.
   Question: How do you think the participants reacted?

2. In a subway station in Washington, D.C., world-famous violinist Joshua Bell played his 3.5 million-dollar violin during rush hour for people walking by. He had recently played in Boston at $100 a ticket, but in the station he put his open violin case in front of him to collect donations.
   Question: What do you think happened?

3. In a 150-seat movie theater, all the seats except two in the middle are taken by people who look like members of a motorcycle gang. They are, in fact, paid actors. A real couple walks into the theater. The experiment is repeated with several couples.
   Question: What do you think most couples did?

4. Three groups of people were given simple word problems. Group 1 had words like *polite, patient*, and *courtesy*. Group 2 had words like *bother, disturb*, and *bold*. A third group had random words. They were then told to go talk with the experimenter, but they found him deep in conversation with someone.
   Question: How do you think the behavior of the people in the groups differed?

G 🎧 **4.6** Now listen to the results of the experiments and take notes. What conclusion can you make about human psychology based on each experiment? Discuss your ideas with the class.

LESSON TASK Discussing Learning Styles

A Psychology tells us that different people prefer to learn in different ways. Look at these seven learning styles. Which styles do you prefer? Check (✓) Y for *Yes*, N for *No*, or NS for *Not Sure*.

Learning Style	Description	Preferred		
visual	prefer to take in information by seeing it	☐ Y	☐ N	☐ NS
audio	receive information best through sound	☐ Y	☐ N	☐ NS
verbal	focus best on words—written, spoken, or recorded	☐ Y	☐ N	☐ NS
physical	eager to get the body in action when learning	☐ Y	☐ N	☐ NS
logical	like numbers, rules, logic, and solving problems	☐ Y	☐ N	☐ NS
social	prefer group work and interacting with others	☐ Y	☐ N	☐ NS
solitary	focused and productive in individual activities	☐ Y	☐ N	☐ NS

B Work in a small group. Compare your learning style preferences from exercise A.

▲ **Students creating a robotic arm**

> **EVERYDAY LANGUAGE**   Making Recommendations
>
> *I (would) recommend (that) . . .*   *It would be a good idea to . . .*
> *I think (that) . . .*   *. . . would/could/might be a good idea.*
> *Why don't you/we . . . ?*   *I suggest (that) . . .*

C Work in a group. For each group member, discuss ideas for studying effectively. Consider their preferred learning styles from exercise A. Use expressions for making recommendations. Take notes in the chart on the suggestions made for you.

CRITICAL THINKING: SYNTHESIZING

A: *Since Sung-min is a visual learner, I think studying grammar charts would be a good idea.*
B: *Yes, and for vocabulary, flash cards with pictures might be good.*

Subject Area	Study Suggestions
Grammar	
Vocabulary Building	
Listening and/or Speaking	
Reading and/or Writing	

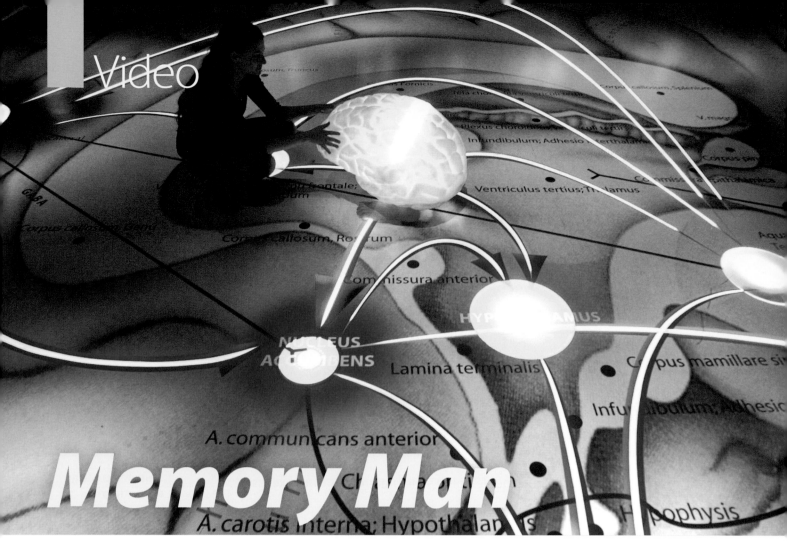

Video

Memory Man

▲ **An exhibit of neurobiological memory processes at the Deutsches Hygiene Museum, Dresden, Germany**

BEFORE VIEWING

A Work with a partner. Discuss the questions.

1. What kinds of things are easy for you to remember? Difficult?
2. How far back can you remember? Describe your earliest memory.
3. What are some techniques you use when you need to remember something?

WHILE VIEWING

UNDERSTANDING
MAIN IDEAS

B ▶ 1.20 Watch the video about an amazing man named Gianni Golfera. Are these points made in the video? Check (✓) *Yes* or *No*.

	Yes	No
1. Gianni Golfera's memory attracts popular and scientific attention.	☐	☐
2. Some people question whether Golfera's memory abilities are real.	☐	☐
3. Scientists are working to discover a genetic component to memory.	☐	☐
4. Golfera's great memory skill is due in part to his own efforts.	☐	☐
5. Doctors can improve memory by making changes to the brain.	☐	☐

C ▶ 1.20 Watch the video again. Complete the facts about Gianni Golfera. Write one word or a number for each answer.

1. Gianni Golfera can remember _____ numbers and repeat them forward and backward.

2. Gianni has memorized over 250 _____ .

3. Gianni can remember every _____ of every day of his life.

4. Dr. Malgaroli will compare the Golfera family's _____ with those of other families.

5. Researchers are investigating how memory and learning _____ the brain.

6. Dr. Malgaroli says that remembering well is just a matter of _____ .

7. Gianni has been training his brain since he was _____ years old.

8. Gianni has memorized a series of _____ books.

9. For Gianni, working to improve his memory is like a _____ job.

10. Despite his obvious gift, Gianni has a relatively _____ life.

AFTER VIEWING

D Look at this list of strategies for improving memory. Rank them according to how effective you think they would be for you, from 1 (most effective) to 5 (least effective). Then share your ranking with a partner.

_____ Eat memory-enhancing foods, such as avocado, berries, coconut, oily fish, nuts, and dark chocolate, frequently.

_____ Strengthen your memory by not using a GPS for directions, learning a new language, trying an online brain-training game, or starting a new hobby.

_____ Get physical exercise to clear your mind and provide oxygen to your brain, and do mind-body exercises such as yoga, which has a proven positive impact on memory.

_____ Live a healthy lifestyle that improves memory by getting eight hours of sleep, socializing with friends regularly, and avoiding junk food and unhealthy snacks.

_____ Use memory techniques such as making words from the first letters of the words you need to remember, making lists, and drawing mind maps to connect ideas.

E Work with a partner. Discuss these questions.

1. Sometimes something you see, taste, touch, hear, or smell causes you to have a certain memory. From your experience, which of the senses (sight, hearing, taste, smell, and touch) do you think is linked most closely to memory? Explain.

2. After watching the video, are you inspired to improve your memory? If so, would you like to try one of the strategies from exercise D? Which one(s)?

B Vocabulary

A 🎧 **4.7** Listen and check (✓) the words or phrases you already know. Use a dictionary to help you with any new words.

☐ **deepen** (v)	☐ **ethical** (adj)	☐ **inferior** (adj)	☐ **innate** (adj)
☐ **obsolete** (adj)	☐ **radical** (adj)	☐ **stemmed from** (v phr)	☐ **superior** (adj)
☐ **norm** (n)	☐ **unprecedented** (adj)		

MEANING FROM CONTEXT

B 🎧 **4.8** Read the blog post and fill in each blank with the correct word or phrase from exercise A. Then listen and check your answers.

THE ANIMAL MIND

Do animals think and feel like we do? Are they similar to or completely different from humans? In the early 20th century, British psychologist C. L. Morgan claimed that animal behavior could only be interpreted in terms of lower mental faculties.[1] This guideline _____ the ideas that 17th century thinkers had about the animal mind. At that time, the _____ was to see animals as living machines. The French philosopher Nicolas Malebranche wrote that animals "eat without pleasure, cry without pain, grow without knowing it: they desire nothing, fear nothing, know nothing." For Malebranche, the animal mind seemed _____ to the human mind in every way.

Today there has been a(n) _____ change in the way scientists view the animal mind, and the ideas of Malebranche have become _____. No longer are all animal behaviors regarded as _____; examples of learning in birds, dolphins, and apes have proven that point of view to be false. On the contrary, there have been _____ discoveries of language abilities in parrots and apes. In one experiment, a kind of memory competition between humans and apes, apes demonstrated _____ memory skills by defeating their human opponents. In addition, evidence of empathy[2] among animals has been observed in the wild. As scientists' understanding of the animal mind continues to _____, it is becoming clear that various characteristics once thought to be uniquely human actually are not. This is leading some to ask serious _____ questions about the treatment of animals and their rights in the human-dominated world.

[1] **faculty** (n): power, capability
[2] **empathy** (n): the ability to share another person's feelings and emotions as if they were your own

A blue and yellow macaw performs a trick at the KL Bird Park in Kuala Lumpur, Malaysia.

C Match each word or phrase with its <u>opposite</u> meaning.

1. _____ unprecedented
2. _____ superior
3. _____ norm
4. _____ stem from
5. _____ radical
6. _____ ethical
7. _____ inferior
8. _____ obsolete
9. _____ deepen
10. _____ innate

a. a strange or unusual situation
b. of lower status or importance
c. having happened before
d. dishonest; immoral
e. decrease; weaken; lighten
f. of higher status or importance
g. current and up-to-date
h. acquired or learned
i. modest or balanced
j. cause; produce

D Work with a partner. Discuss the questions.

CRITICAL THINKING: ANALYZING

1. What are some examples of innate abilities in humans or animals?
2. In what ways might some animal minds be superior to human minds?
3. What are some of the benefits of pet ownership?
4. In 2004, the city of Reggio Emilia in Italy passed unprecedented regulations that made it illegal to boil lobsters alive, to keep goldfish in glass bowls, or for amusement parks to give customers live rabbits as prizes. What is your opinion of these regulations?

Listening A Conversation about Memory

BEFORE LISTENING

PREDICTING **A** You are going to listen to a conversation about memory. Guess the meanings of two terms you will hear discussed.

1. What is *superior autobiographic memory*?

   _____

2. What is the *method of loci* used for? (*Loci* means *locations* or *places*.)

   _____

WHILE LISTENING

CHECKING
PREDICTIONS
B 🎧 **4.9** Listen to the conversation and check if your predictions were correct.

> **LISTENING SKILL** Recognizing Appositives
>
> An appositive is a noun or noun phrase that identifies or gives more information about another noun or noun phrase. An appositive usually follows the noun or noun phrase it modifies.
>
> > Have you ever heard of "superior autobiographical memory," **an incredibly accurate memory for past events**?
>
> The slight pause a speaker makes before an appositive can help you identify it.

C 🎧 **4.10** Listen to excerpts from the conversation. Write the appositives you hear in these sentences. Then underline the noun/noun phrase that it identifies.

1. Oh, wait. I saw a TV show about that, _____.

2. Oh, and I know the meaning stems from two ancient Greek words, _____

   _____

3. You could try this approach to remembering things that began in ancient Greece,

   _____

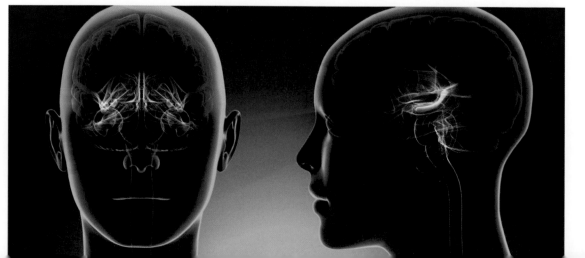

▶ **The hippocampus is a part of the brain that is vital for memory creation.**

D 4.11 Preview the questions. Then listen again to part of the conversation. Take notes as you listen. Write no more than three words or a number for each answer.

LISTENING FOR DETAILS

1. What institution were the researchers studying superior autobiographic memory from? _____

2. How many people with superior autobiographic memory did the researchers find?

   _____

3. What career did one person with superior autobiographical memory have?

   _____

4. What was different about some parts of the brains of people with superior autobiographical memory? _____

5. In what year did Dr. Scoville's famous operation take place?

   _____

6. What was the major negative result of the operation for the patient?

   _____

E 4.12 Listen to the last part of the conversation. Complete the outline with information from the conversation. Write no more than three words in each blank.

NOTE TAKING

I. The method of loci

   A. Began in ancient Greece; a way to remember _____
      1

   B. How it works
      a. Picture a path that _____ .
         2
      b. Look at a list of words and _____ for each.
         3
      c. Put those _____ @ places along the path.
         4
      d. Later, you _____ walking along the path.
         5
      e. The images will _____ the words.
         6

AFTER LISTENING

F Work with a partner. Discuss these questions.

1. Trying to help, Dr. Scoville permanently damaged his patient's memory. However, as a result, scientists learned a great deal about the brain. Do you think Dr. Scoville's actions were ethical?

2. Try to remember the Lesson A or Lesson B vocabulary words using the method of loci. Your partner will try to remember the other list. Check the vocabulary lists as you recite the words to each other.

Speaking

PRONUNCIATION Reduced Function Words

🎧 **4.13** Function words are words that show grammatical relationships in a sentence. They include: auxiliary verbs, prepositions, pronouns, conjunctions, and articles.

Function words are not usually stressed. Often, the vowel sounds are reduced to a schwa sound (/ə /), and certain consonants may be dropped. Notice the pronunciation of the underlined function words.

Prepositions:	*We went to the center of town for the lesson.*
Pronouns / Possessive Adjectives:	*Did you give him his award for winning your memory contest?*
Auxiliary Verbs:	*The test will be hard. Can we study together?*
	She couldn't have seen the answers.
Conjunctions:	*My memory is better than my brother's and sister's.*
Articles:	*Give me the test again. I have an hour.*

A 🎧 **4.14** Underline the function words that you think are reduced in these sentences from the conversation. Then listen and repeat to check your answers.

1. People with superior autobiographical memory can remember virtually everything that's ever happened to them.
2. It's a part of the brain that's really important for memory function.
3. I have a huge history exam next week, and I have to memorize a ton of information.
4. Having a good memory isn't an innate skill, you know.
5. In your mind, you need to visualize a path that you know well, like the way to school.

B Practice the conversation with a partner. Reduce the function words. Then switch roles.

A: Hey, how have you been?
B: Um, I've been a little depressed. Can you tell?
A: Yeah, I knew something or other was wrong. You know, I know a great doctor. Do you want his number? I highly recommend him!
B: No, it's something that will pass. It always happens in January and February.
A: Oh, the *winter blues*! That's what my mom calls them, anyway. She sits under a special lamp for half an hour a day and says it's better than medicine.
B: Really? Can I have her email? I want to ask her about her lamp so I can get one, too.

GRAMMAR FOR SPEAKING Subject-Verb Agreement with Quantifiers

When using quantifiers with a noun, be sure to check for subject-verb agreement.

- With *all*, *a lot*, *some*, *a few*, *both*, and *most* + *of* + a plural count noun, use a plural verb.

    And **some** of the **methods** <u>work</u> surprisingly well.

    All of the **questions** <u>were</u> incredibly difficult.

- With *one*, *none*, *each*, *neither*, and *every one* + *of* + a plural count noun, use a singular verb.

    Anyway, **one** of the most famous **case studies** <u>was</u> in 1953, in Connecticut.

C Work with a partner. Take turns using quantifiers from the Grammar for Speaking box to make sentences with the following topics.

> *Some of the parrots I've seen on YouTube videos speak surprisingly well.*

abilities that animals have	methods for memory improvement	my parents
learning styles		my friends
standardized English tests	the people I know	my memories
the lessons in this unit	the students in the class	

FINAL TASK Speaking about a "Life Hack"

You are going to research and give a speech about three psychological "life hacks," or strategies we use to manage our time and daily lives in a more efficient way.

A Work with a partner. Read the information and discuss how useful you think this psychological life hack is.

CRITICAL THINKING: EVALUATING

LIFE HACK

At the supermarket, we all want to choose the fastest line. If you are like most people, you would get in line behind three people with 10 items each instead of someone with a cart containing 50 items—but you would be wrong! Research shows that each individual takes about 41 seconds while each item takes only three seconds. The total time is the individual time plus the time for each item.

3 shoppers with 10 items each = (41 sec. $\times$ 3) + (10 items $\times$ 3 sec. $\times$ 3) = 213 seconds

1 shopper with 50 items = 41 sec. + (50 items $\times$ 3 sec.) = 191 seconds

So next time, don't be afraid to get behind a shopper with a full cart!

B Look online and make a list of four to six psychological life hacks that sound interesting. Then work in a small group and share your lists. Choose three life hacks that you would like to research for your speech.

C Research your three life hacks. For each, take notes on the information below.

- a description of the life hack
- the problem it is designed to solve (if any) and/or who it might benefit
- an explanation of how the hack is implemented
- an explanation of why it works (include a psychological explanation, if appropriate)
- whether you have tried it or would like to try it, and why

PRESENTATION SKILL Using Gestures

Gestures can be very useful in a presentation. Keep your hands and body mainly in a neutral position until you want to make a gesture. Here are some ways to gesture:

- Use your hands and fingers to show size, speed, location, or numbers
- Raise or lower your shoulders to express doubt or sadness, raise or open your arms to show strength or openness, and use your face to show a variety of expressions
- Raise your hand and say, "Raise your hand if . . ." to get your audience involved

---

D With a partner, practice your speech. Remember to use gestures. Give each other feedback on your speeches and on any gestures used, and adjust your speech as needed.

PRESENTING **E** Give your speech to your group. When you finish, invite and answer questions from the group.

REFLECTION

1. Which language skill in this unit do you think will be most useful to you? In what situation(s)?

   _____

   _____

2. What did you learn about the mind, the brain, or memory that you didn't know before?

   _____

   _____

3. Here are the vocabulary words and phrases from the unit. Check (✓) the ones you can use.

   ☐ analytical AWL   ☐ namely   ☐ subjective
   ☐ deepen   ☐ norm AWL   ☐ superior
   ☐ ethical AWL   ☐ objective AWL ☐ unprecedented AWL
   ☐ inferior   ☐ obsolete   ☐ verbal
   ☐ innate   ☐ radical AWL   ☐ vice versa
   ☐ intuition   ☐ spatial   ☐ visualize AWL
   ☐ logic AWL   ☐ stem from

THE FUTURE OF FOOD 10

A drought-tolerant tomato photographed with sand illustrates the research of Dan Chitwood. Chitwood grows these tomatoes by crossing standard tomato plants with wild tomato plants from the Atacama Desert, the driest place on earth.

ACADEMIC SKILLS

LISTENING   Listening for Suggestions
           The Cornell Method
SPEAKING   Referring to Group Opinions
           Reduced Auxiliary Phrases
CRITICAL THINKING   Categorizing

THINK AND DISCUSS

1 How do you choose the food you buy? What types of things do you think about before you buy food? What are some things you always buy? Never buy?

2 What do you think it means when we say food is genetically modified?

Look at the photo and read the information. Then discuss the questions.

1. What is the goal of the Svalbard Global Seed Bank?

2. Why might a remote location have been chosen for this seed bank?

3. What does *doomsday* mean, and why do you think this name was given to the seed bank?

4. Name some crops that you would like to see saved in a seed bank. Why are they important?

SAVING FOR THE FUTURE

WHAT: The Svalbard Global Seed Vault, called the "Doomsday Seed Vault" by some, was created to preserve samples of seeds from around the world. More than two billion seeds can be stored in the vault in case of natural or man-made disaster.

HOW: The climate and the thick rock surrounding the vault will ensure that even without electricity the samples will remain frozen.

WHEN: Building started June 19, 2006.

WHERE: It's north of the Arctic Circle on the island of Spitsbergen in the Arctic Ocean, 621 miles (1,000 km) north of mainland Norway. It is the northernmost part of the Kingdom of Norway.

WHY: It's being built to protect the earth's crop diversity.

American agriculturalist Cary Fowler holds vials of peas at the Svalbard Global Seed Bank in Longyearbyen, Svalbard, Norway.

Vocabulary

A 🎧 **4.15** Read and listen to the article about the world's food supply. Notice each word or phrase in **blue** and think about its meaning.

WHY PUT SEEDS IN A BANK?

**Cary Fowler inside
the seed bank**

The world population is now over seven billion people and growing, and the pressure on world food suppliers is more **intense** than ever. Many large farms now **cultivate** only a small number of crops such as corn, wheat, or rice over vast areas. This type of agriculture is known as monoculture. While experts acknowledge how well it maximizes harvests, **skeptics** say that this benefit is **offset** by its negative effects.

One serious **drawback** of monoculture is the effect it has on the number of vegetable varieties grown by farmers. The diversity of crops has greatly diminished since the beginning of the 10th century, and many crop species no longer exist. We are moving toward a risky situation in which global agriculture relies on too few crops. If existing crop species get diseases against which they have no **resistance**, they could be wiped out. This would be **detrimental** to the world's food supply.

To save vegetable varieties from extinction, many experts **advocate** for the preservation of seeds **by means of** "seed banks." There are farmers and scientists who devote themselves to setting up such facilities. At last count, there were about 1,400 seed banks around the world. The seeds inside these seed banks could be **invaluable** in the future.

B Write each word or phrase in **blue** from exercise A next to its definition.

1. _____ (prep phr) with the use of (a tool, method, idea, etc.)

2. _____ (v) to act to balance another action or effect

3. _____ (adj) high in energy or degree

4. _____ (adj) extremely useful

5. _____ (adj) having a harmful or damaging effect

6. _____ (n) people who doubt things that others believe

7. _____ (n) the act of fighting against something

8. _____ (v) to prepare land and grow crops there

9. _____ (v) to publicly recommend something

10. _____ (n) a negative or unwanted aspect or feature

VOCABULARY SKILL Investigating Authentic Language

One way to investigate authentic examples of words and phrases is to do an Internet search. If you put multiple words in quotation marks, search engines will return many examples of the exact phrase. Another way to find authentic examples is to use online concordancers. Concordancers also reveal word collocations.

C Read these sample lines from a concordancer and answer the questions.

```
government resources proved invaluable to private sector corporations
stoves that have proven invaluable for preparing food that is sub
thank John, whose efforts were invaluable to bringing this project to a
```

1. What verb is a strong collocation with *invaluable*? _____

2. What prepositions are used after *invaluable*? _____

```
the problem had a clearly detrimental effect on the remaining part
against its potentially detrimental impact on sources of clean
that has a particularly detrimental effect in areas that have been
```

3. What adverbs are used with *detrimental*? _____

4. What noun is a strong collocation with *detrimental*? _____

```
which exposed a serious drawback of the envisioned plan, namely
investors of a potential drawback to leaving funds in an account
covered yet another serious drawback to the strategy of planting crop
```

5. What prepositions are used after *drawback*? _____

6. What adjective is a strong collocation with *drawback*? _____

```
sufficient period to build up resistance to recently developed pesticide
disease has shown unusual resistance to treatment with conventional
which continues to show resistance to GM corn varieties designed
```

7. What preposition is a strong collocation with *resistance*? _____

8. What verb is a strong collocation with *resistance*? _____

D Complete the statements. Use a dictionary or a concordancer to help you. Discuss your answers with a partner.

PERSONALIZING

1. I tend to be a skeptic _____.

2. I generally advocate _____.

3. A drawback _____ is _____.

4. _____ has a detrimental _____ on my studies.

5. _____ has been invaluable _____.

Listening A Lecture about GM Foods

BEFORE LISTENING

PRIOR KNOWLEDGE **A** Work in a small group. In what ways are specific crops and animals (for food) altered by genetic modifications? Discuss your ideas and take notes in the chart.

Plants	Animals
Apples are altered to last longer.	Cows are altered to produce more milk.

WHILE LISTENING

LISTENING FOR MAIN IDEAS **B** 🎧 4.16 ▶ 1.21 Listen to a lecture about genetically modified (GM) foods. Which points does the speaker make? Put a check (✓) in the correct column.

	Yes	No
1. There is controversy around the issue of genetically modified foods.	☐	☐
2. The government has acted in response to concerns about GM foods.	☐	☐
3. The dangers of GM foods mentioned have been scientifically proven.	☐	☐
4. There have been some promising developments in GM food research.	☐	☐
5. The professor feels that GM foods are a little too risky.	☐	☐

NOTE-TAKING SKILL The Cornell Method

The Cornell method of note taking, invented by an education professor at Cornell University, is a three-step note-taking method.

Step 1: Take detailed notes as you listen.

Step 2: After listening, write main points or questions for the different parts of your notes in a column to the left of your notes.

Step 3: Write a short summary of the notes at the bottom of your paper.

The advantage of the Cornell method is that it keeps your notes organized and turns them into an efficient study sheet.

▶ **These two Coho salmon are 18 months old, but one was genetically modified to be larger than the other.**

⌂ 4.16 Listen again and complete the notes section below. Write only one word or number for each answer. You will complete the summary section in exercise D.

GM Foods

Main Points	Notes
What are GM foods?	Foods made from animals & plants with modified _____ 1 Ex: Rat gene into _____ = vit. C 2
Concerns about GM foods	Weeds pick up resist. to weed _____ → "super weeds" 3 Detrimental effects of GM plants on _____ & animals 4 Mixing GM plants w/conventional ones could impact gene _____ 5 If insects become _____ to GM crops → super pests 6
Eating GM foods	GM _____ sold in U.S. & planted in Argentina, Canada, 7 China, S. Africa, Australia, Germany & Spain GM salmon declared safe in _____ but didn't sell 8 GM animals may be in markets w/in next _____ yrs. 9
Golden rice	Golden rice = rice w/beta-carotene, needed to produce vitamin A 100–140 mil _____ suffer from lack of vitamin A 10 _____ say it may not raise vit. A levels in pop. 11
Benefits of GM foods	↑ food production; crops w/_____ to pests & disease; 12 ways to cultivate crops on ↓ quality land

Summary

The _____ of any animal and plant can be mixed and matched to create
1
useful _____. Although there are _____ about the
2   3
dangers of GM plants, such as super weeds and gene flow, we are already eating them.
_____ for various GM animals is taking longer but will likely happen. A type
4
of _____ was declared safe, but it wasn't _____. The
5   6
_____ of GM foods include more food, _____ crops, and
7   8
useable farmable land.

AFTER LISTENING

Now complete the summary section in the lecture notes in exercise C with the words and phrases in the box.

approval	resistant	GM salmon	characteristics
benefits	concerns	genes	popular

A Speaking

You can support an opinion with the opinion of a knowledgeable group. You do not have to name a specific person or organization. Instead you refer to the group in general.

Many scientists *are optimistic about the technology and feel that GM foods could be the key to significant advances in agriculture and health.*

Researchers *haven't been able to demonstrate that GM crops are detrimental to human health or to the environment.*

Groups (often used with *some, many*, etc.):

advocates (of/for …)	*experts (on …)*	*journalists*	*doctors*
proponents (of …)	*critics (of …)*	*scientists*	*researchers*

Verbs/Verb phrases:

be pessimistic	*be certain*	*agree*	*admit*	*feel*
be concerned	*point out*	*think*	*insist*	*fear*
be optimistic	*believe*	*claim*	*warn*	*say*

CRITICAL THINKING:
EVALUATING

A Work in a small group. The lecturer refers to general advocates and critics of GM foods. Discuss which specific people, groups of people, and organizations might belong to each general group and why. List your ideas in the chart.

Advocates	Critics
Farmers with low-quality farmland	Organic farmers

B Work with a partner. Role-play a conversation at a grocery store between roommates. Take turns suggesting the grocery items in the chart below, referring to a positive then a negative group opinion. You can also make other suggestions using your own ideas.

A: *How about we get some of this fruit juice? It looks really fresh.*
B: *I'm not sure. Some experts say it can have as much sugar as soda.*
A: *Yeah, some juice does. But doctors point out that it contains a lot of vitamins.*

Grocery Item	Positives	Negatives
fruit juice	contains a lot of vitamins	can have as much sugar as soda
tomatoes	may fight some kinds of cancer	tomato farm workers not always well paid
GM salmon	completely safe to eat	likely to escape into the environment
beef	high in protein	raising beef may harm the environment
organic apples	fight tooth decay	go bad faster than conventional apples

C Work with a partner. Read about three methods of breeding and modifying crops. Then, discuss the benefits and drawbacks of each.

Breeding Better Crops

Genetic modification gets the public attention—and the controversy—but plant breeders today have numerous tools for creating crops with new traits[1]. The goal: continually increasing yields[2] in an increasingly challenging climate.

Traditional Breeding	Interspecies Crosses	Genetic Modification
Desired traits are identified in separate individuals of the same species, which are then bred to combine those traits in a new hybrid[3] variety.	Breeders can also cross different species. Modern wheat comes from such hybridizations, some of which happened naturally.	Genes identified in one species can be transferred directly to an unrelated species, giving it an entirely new trait—resistance to a pest, say, or to a weed killer.

[1] **trait** (n): a genetic characteristic
[2] **yield** (n): the amount of food produced by crops
[3] **hybrid** (adj): bred by combining two different species

▼ **Javier Alcantar tends to corn crops at the Monsanto test field in California, where the crop is from genetically modified seed.**

CRITICAL THINKING:
CATEGORIZING

D Read about these crops and animals. Decide if each was created by traditional breeding (TB), interspecies cross (IC), or genetic modification (GM). Write the appropriate abbreviation. You will use each one twice.

1. _____ The tangelo fruit is a cross between a grapefruit and a tangerine. It has characteristics of both species and is extremely popular.

2. _____ GloFish® are brightly colored red, green, and orange fish sold as pets. They were created by inserting genes from a colorful jellyfish into black and white zebra fish.

3. _____ Since the 1930s, the yield of corn plants has greatly increased because farmers have bred the most productive plants of that species in each generation.

4. _____ To wipe out dangerous mosquito populations, scientists "programmed" their genes to make them die before becoming adults. The young bred from "programmed" and wild mosquitoes also die early.

5. _____ Wheat has been improving for over 10,000 years because farmers have selected the healthiest and largest plants to pass on their genetic characteristics to future generations.

6. _____ When the wild South American strawberry was bred with the North American strawberry, the result was the pineberry, a fruit that looks like a white strawberry but tastes like a pineapple.

E Work with a partner. Compare and explain the reasons for your answers in exercise D.

GloFish® were genetically engineered to glow in order to help scientists study pollution.

LESSON TASK Role-playing a Town Hall Meeting

A Work with a partner. Prepare to role-play a question-and-answer (Q&A) session at a town hall meeting (a public meeting where people can ask officials questions). Choose a role and read the information.

Role #1: Leader of a Farmers' Association

You are the leader of a farmers' association in a country that uses traditional farming methods. Recent problems of drought, crop disease, and insect pests have caused farmers to consider using GM crops. You are attending a town hall meeting to ask an official from GM Industries, a company that wants to supply GM crops to your country, about the concerns of the farmers.

Notes for Questions
- GM crops harmful to animals and humans?
- Insects develop resistance to GM crops, become more difficult to control?
- Genes from GM plants flow to other plant populations, create "super weeds"?
- GM crop seed too expensive?

Role #2: Spokesperson for GM Industries

You are a spokesperson for GM products in this country and believe they will dramatically improve the situation of its farmers. You are participating in a town hall meeting to answer questions and reduce fears that local farmers have about using GM crops.

Notes for Answers
- GM crops tested for safety more than other crops
- Insect resistance to GM crops can occur; will teach how to avoid
- Information about gene flow and "super weeds" scarce, being studied
- Initial cost of GM crop seed is more, but yields, quality, reliability are higher

---

EVERYDAY LANGUAGE Inviting Responses

Once you present an idea, you often want others to respond. Use these phrases.

> *What do you say to that?*
> *Can/How do you respond to that issue/claim/concern?*
> *What's your response to that issue/claim/concern?*
> *Can you address that/those issue(s)/claim(s)/concern(s)?*

B Role-play the town hall Q&A with your partner. Try not to read your notes as you speak. Invite responses using the expressions above, and refer to group opinions as appropriate.

CRITICAL THINKING:
APPLYING

A: *Critics of GM crop companies say that you always put profits ahead of people. What do you say to that?*

B: *I understand your concern, but GM Industries is different. That's why we're having this meeting—we're here to show you that we care about farmers.*

Farming the Open Ocean

A fish farm in Colon, Panama

Panama

BEFORE VIEWING

A Read the information about fish farming. Then answer the questions with a partner.

> **FISH FARMS** About half of the world's seafood comes from fish farms, and in 15 years that amount will rise to about two-thirds. Unfortunately, fish farms have problems due to: diseases created by crowded, stressful conditions; pollution caused by drugs and chemicals put in the water to fight those diseases; and too much waste in the area. In open-ocean fish farms, however, increased space reduces stress on the fish, and the constant movement of water keeps the area clean.

1. The video you are going to watch is about Open Blue, the world's largest open-ocean fish farm. What are some similarities and differences between farming crops and farming fish?

2. Open Blue fish farm is located in Panama. Why do you think Open Blue is located there?

WHILE VIEWING

UNDERSTANDING
MAIN IDEAS

B ▶ 1.22 Watch the video. Which of these points does Brian O'Hanlon make? Put a check (✓) in the correct column.

	Yes	No
1. The open ocean provides a clean environment for fish farming.	☐	☐
2. The techniques used in open-ocean farming are still evolving.	☐	☐
3. O'Hanlon plans to manufacture open-ocean farming equipment.	☐	☐
4. Cobia are the most suitable type of fish to farm in the open ocean.	☐	☐
5. O'Hanlon hopes to expand his fish farming business in the future.	☐	☐

C ▶ 1.22 Watch the video again. Complete this summary. Write one word only in each blank.

OPEN BLUE SEA FARMS

The open ocean is pristine and not impacted by _____ -based activities,
                                                              1
so the fish produced there are very clean. Brian O'Hanlon is the _____
                                                                              2
of Open Blue Sea Farms. Panama offers efficiency of transportation for bringing in raw

_____ and transporting finished products to the _____ .
       3   4

The busy fish farm is 7.5 to 8 miles out in the ocean. It has mooring grid structures

that are one-kilometer long with fish pens inside. One harvest of fish is 20 to 25

_____ . The process is still _____ intensive, but they are
       5   6

working on streamlining and automating it. Farming the ocean has greater potential for

_____ than farming on land because it's three-dimensional. They farm cobia,
       7

a fast-growing fish. O'Hanlon sees the open ocean as a huge _____ in
                                                                         8

the future.

D ▶ 1.22 Watch the video again. Complete each sentence with a word or phrase from the box.

by means of	detrimental	intense
cultivating	drawback	invaluable

1. The _____ effects of pollution don't affect the open ocean very much.

2. The _____ activity over the fish farm makes it look like a little town.

3. One current _____ to fish farming work is that it requires a lot of labor.

4. The potential for farming the ocean is much greater than for _____ land.

5. The fish are kept from escaping _____ enormous pens made of netting.

6. The fast-growing cobia have clearly been _____ to Open Blue's success.

AFTER VIEWING

E Work with a partner. Discuss the questions.

1. Is open-ocean fish farming a good alternative to traditional fish farming? Explain.

2. Sometimes a solution to a specific problem may have unintended consequences. What might be some unintended consequences of open-ocean fish farming?

B Vocabulary

A 🎧 **4.17** Listen and check (✓) the words and phrases you already know.

☐ **ample** (adj) ☐ **call for** (v) ☐ **coincided** (v) ☐ **exceed** (v)
☐ **inadequate** (adj) ☐ **opt** (v) ☐ **output** (n) ☐ **root** (n)
☐ **scenario** (n) ☐ **surge** (n)

MEANING FROM
CONTEXT

B 🎧 **4.18** Read the article and fill in each blank with the correct form of a word or phrase from exercise A. Then listen and check your answers.

The Next "Green Revolution"

The increase in agricultural _____ of the late 1900s is sometimes referred

1
to as the "Green Revolution." During this period, four important farming technologies
_____, bringing immense benefits. They are:

2

- irrigation, a technology that brings water to crops;

- chemical pesticides to help kill or control insects;

- fertilizers, which give plants what they need to grow;

- smaller plants that produce as much food as larger plants.

Unfortunately, we can no longer depend on agricultural production rates to continue to
increase as they have in the past. This puts us in a dangerous situation. The _____

3
of the problem is the rising global population, which threatens to _____ nine

4
billion by the year 2050. Many are now _____ a second "Green Revolution" that

5
will help the world avoid a future nightmare _____ with excessively high food

6
prices, _____ food supplies, and their disastrous consequences.

7

On the other hand, many experts remain optimistic that another _____

8
in agricultural productivity will occur if farmers _____ to use GM crops and

9
sustainable farming methods. Only time will tell if this second "Green Revolution" can
ensure _____ food for future generations.

10

▼ **Urban farm on
rooftop in New
York City, USA**

C Match the words and phrases with their synonyms. Use a dictionary if needed.

1. _____ ample   a. coexist
2. _____ call for   b. go beyond
3. _____ coincide   c. insufficient
4. _____ exceed   d. abundant
5. _____ inadequate   e. yield
6. _____ opt   f. rise
7. _____ output   g. situation
8. _____ root   h. demand
9. _____ scenario   i. choose
10. _____ surge   j. cause

D Choose the correct collocation for the word or phrase in **bold**. Use a dictionary or concordancer to help you.

1. The funds for the seed program were (darkly / emptily / hopelessly) **inadequate**.
2. The **root** (to / of / for) the extinction was the modification of the birds' habitat.
3. The winner shouted, "This **calls for** (celebrating / a celebration / celebrations)!"
4. After the fire, the diversity of plants will return given **ample** (period / age / time).
5. The merits of the plants **exceeded** (confidence / expectations / hypotheses).
6. A flood wiping out the crops would be a worst (model / state / case) **scenario**.
7. The warm, wet spring ultimately caused a **surge** (up / at / in) the insect population.
8. The tribal ceremonies **coincide** (with / as / to) the beginning of the corn harvest.
9. Multiple storms were the reason for the (low / bare / cheap) **output** of farms that year.
10. The farmer **opted** (on / for / to) a variety of rice with exceptional resistance to disease.

E With a partner, make sentences about food issues with collocations from exercise D.

> *The choice of restaurants in my neighborhood is hopelessly inadequate.*

F Work with a partner. Discuss the questions.   PERSONALIZING

1. When shopping for vegetables, do you opt for organic varieties? Explain.
2. In your opinion, what is the root of the world hunger issue?
3. Have you ever had a restaurant experience when the food, the service, or something else was inadequate? How about an experience that exceeded your expectations?

Listening A Conversation about Food Prices

BEFORE LISTENING

PRIOR KNOWLEDGE

A Work with a partner. Discuss the questions.

1. Study the bar chart below. What are some possible reasons for the difference between the percentage of income spent on food in the United States and Singapore and the other countries shown?
2. What percentage of your income do you or your family spend on food? Is the percentage increasing or decreasing? Explain.
3. What are some reasons for changes in food prices?

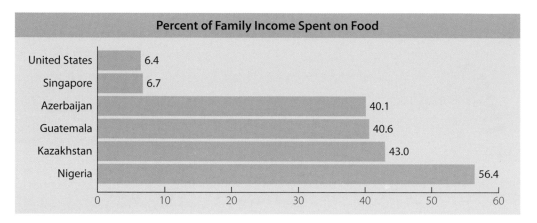

Percent of Family Income Spent on Food

Country	Percent
United States	6.4
Singapore	6.7
Azerbaijan	40.1
Guatemala	40.6
Kazakhstan	43.0
Nigeria	56.4

WHILE LISTENING

LISTENING FOR
MAIN IDEAS

B 🎧 4.19 Listen to a conversation about food issues. Then read the statements. Choose T for *True*, F for *False*, or NG for information *Not Given*.

1. Emily says there are multiple factors affecting food prices.	T	F	NG
2. Economic success in certain countries is affecting food prices.	T	F	NG
3. The habit of eating meat and dairy pushes grain prices down.	T	F	NG
4. Governments are planning food aid for parts of Africa and Asia.	T	F	NG
5. Lucas feels the current food shortages are a hopeless situation.	T	F	NG

LISTENING SKILL Listening for Suggestions

Sometimes speakers make suggestions about changes they would like to see happen in the world around them but don't mention who will actually make the change. To recognize these kinds of suggestions, listen for:

• the pronouns *they, somebody, someone* + *should, have/has to, need(s) to* + verb
• negative questions with *Why don't they . . . ?* or *Why doesn't somebody/someone . . . ?*
• the passive voice of *should, have to, need to,* without an agent (e.g., *This problem really needs to be solved.*)

C 🎧 **4.20** Listen to four excerpts. For each, write the problem and suggestion you hear.

1. _____

_____

2. _____

_____

3. _____

_____

4. _____

_____

D 🎧 **4.19** Preview the questions. Then listen again to the conversation. Take notes as you listen. Write no more than three words or a number for each answer.

LISTENING FOR DETAILS

1. What does Emily believe is the basic cause of rising food prices?

_____

2. About how much cultivatable farmland has been lost in the past 40 years?

_____

3. What kinds of foods do middle classes tend to eat more of?

_____

4. What amount of meat can be produced with 3.2 kilograms of grain?

_____

5. About what percent of their calories do humans derive from grain?

_____

6. What have some governments called for to ensure people have enough food to eat?

_____

7. Which continents may see large areas become deserts in the future?

_____

8. Where do scientists suggest increasing the quantity of food grown?

_____

AFTER LISTENING

E Work in a small group. Discuss the questions.

CRTICAL THINKING: ANALYZING

1. What are some specific trends in food prices that you've noticed? What changes in the availability of food have you noticed?
2. Where are the vegetables and fruits you eat grown? Where is the meat raised? Do you expect the supplies to remain steady in the future? Explain.
3. How has your diet changed over the years? Have your food choices been affected by your income or lifestyle?

B Speaking

A Work in a small group. Imagine you are advisors to the president of a small island nation. The president has sent you a letter asking for advice. Read the letter and prepare as many suggestions as you can. Use subjunctive verbs in *that* clauses.

> *It is crucial that we stop using monoculture and increase crop diversity!*

To My Trusted Advisors:

Please advise me on how to deal with the following issues:

- Agricultural output is low due to insect pests and plant diseases.
- We need to let the world know about our delicious agricultural products.
- The amount of seafood caught around the island is diminishing every year.
- Tourists have been complaining about the quality of island restaurants.
- Islanders are suffering from health problems due to poor nutrition.
- There is a scarcity of young people who want to pursue farming as a career.

I look forward to hearing your invaluable suggestions.

▼ **Blueberries displayed at an organic farmers market in Maine, USA**

PRONUNCIATION Reduced Auxiliary Phrases

4.21 Auxiliary verbs, such as modals or other helping verbs, are commonly reduced. The vowels in these unstressed words reduce to schwa (/ə/), and certain consonant sounds are changed or dropped. Listen to these examples.

have to → /ˈhæftə/	should have → /ˈʃʊdəv/	must have → /ˈmʌstəv/
has to → /ˈhæstə/	would have → /ˈwʊdəv/	may have → /ˈmeɪyəv/
want to → /ˈwʌnə/	could have → /ˈkʊdəv/	might have → /ˈmaɪdəv/
going to → /ˈgʌnə/	shouldn't have → /ˈʃʊdnəv/	
ought to → /ˈɔdə/	wouldn't have → /ˈwʊdnəv/	
supposed to → /səˈpoʊstə/	couldn't have → /ˈkʊdnəv/	

Note: In casual speech, the /v/ sound is often dropped from *have*. For example, *should have* sounds like *shoulda* (/ˈʃʊdə/).

B **4.22** Read the sentences. Underline the auxiliary phrases. Then listen and repeat the sentences. Notice the reduced phrases.

1. I could have told you it was going to rain.
2. They must have raised the price again.
3. I'll have to get some next time.
4. I could have told you that.
5. Someone really has to do something about it.
6. I would have brought home lamb for dinner.
7. And I certainly wouldn't have had any trouble buying rice!
8. We're going to be in trouble.

C With a partner, practice the conversation using reduced auxiliary phrases. Then switch roles and repeat.

A: Did you check out the farmers' market on Sunday? The vegetables were amazing.
B: I didn't know about it. But I couldn't have gone anyway. I was studying for a test.
A: How did you do on the test?
B: I could have done better, but I was tired. I shouldn't have stayed up so late.
A: You know what might have helped? Blueberries from the farmers' market.
B: Blueberries? I don't know how those would have helped.
A: Well, they're supposed to be really good for the brain.
B: Really? You should have told me that before the test. I love blueberries!

FINAL TASK Making a Formal Proposal

You and your group members are part of a government-appointed team assigned to create a program to address a particular food or nutrition issue. This will require identifying a population with unmet nutritional or other food-related needs, finding solutions to meet those needs, and preparing a proposal to submit to the appropriate government agency for approval.

A Work in a small group. Look at the chart and decide the population you will target and the types of assistance you will provide. Check your choices.

Populations in Need	Types of Assistance
Elderly in community living settings	Funds to purchase food
Elderly living alone	Food giveaways and distribution
Limited-income families/individuals	Kitchen appliances and tools
Homeless families/individuals	Assistance with food-related transportation
Schoolchildren	Assistance with food preparation
People with mobility/transportation issues	Organizing farmers' markets
Other:	Other:

BRAINSTORMING   **B** Read the four sections that your proposal should include. With your group, brainstorm ideas and prepare the information needed for each section.

1. **Provide an overview:** Give a brief description of your program.
2. **Describe the problem:** What need(s) is your program attempting to meet? What type(s) of assistance will you provide? Who is the target population?
3. **Describe the solution:** What will you do to meet the need(s)? How will you accomplish this? What problems do you expect to face? How will you solve them?
4. **Describe the resources needed:** What resources will you need—money, people, other materials? How will these resources be used?

C With your group, prepare a presentation of your proposal to an appropriate government agency. Decide who will present each section. Include statements using the subjunctive, and support your ideas with others' opinions as appropriate. Practice your presentation as needed.

PRESENTING   **D** Present your proposal to the class. After each group has presented, discuss what was the strongest point in each proposal.

REFLECTION

1. Which skill in the unit do you think you will be able to use in the future?

   _____

   _____

2. What aspects of the modern food industry do you see differently after finishing this unit?

   _____

   _____

3. Here are the vocabulary words and phrases from the unit. Check (✓) the ones you can use.

☐ advocate AWL	☐ drawback	☐ output AWL
☐ ample	☐ exceed AWL	☐ resistance
☐ by means of	☐ inadequate AWL	☐ root
☐ call for	☐ intense AWL	☐ scenario AWL
☐ coincide AWL	☐ invaluable	☐ skeptic
☐ cultivate	☐ offset AWL	☐ surge
☐ detrimental	☐ opt	

Independent Student Handbook

Table of Contents

LISTENING SKILLS

Predicting

Speakers giving formal talks usually begin by introducing themselves and their topic. Listen carefully to the introduction of the topic so that you can predict what the talk will be about.

Strategies:

- Use visual information including titles on the board or on presentation slides.
- Think about what you already know about the topic.
- Ask yourself questions that you think the speaker might answer.
- Listen for specific phrases that indicate an introduction (e.g., *My topic is…*).

Listening for Main Ideas

It is important to be able to tell the difference between a speaker's main ideas and supporting details. It is more common for teachers to test understanding of main ideas than of specific details.

Strategies:

- Listen carefully to the introduction. Speakers often state the main idea in the introduction.
- Listen for rhetorical questions, or questions that the speaker asks, and then answers. Often the answer is the statement of the main idea.
- Notice words and phrases that the speaker repeats. Repetition often signals main ideas.

Listening for Details (Examples)

A speaker often provides examples that support a main idea. A good example can help you understand and remember the main idea better.

Strategies:

- Listen for specific phrases that introduce examples.
- Listen for general statements. Examples often follow general statements.

Listening for Details (Cause and Effect)

Speakers often give reasons or list causes and/or effects to support their ideas.

Strategies:

- Notice nouns that might signal causes/reasons (e.g., *factors, influences, causes, reasons*) or effects/results (e.g., *effects, results, outcomes, consequences*).
- Notice verbs that might signal causes/reasons (e.g., *contribute to, affect, influence, determine, produce, result in*) or effects/results (often these are passive, e.g., *is affected by*).

Understanding the Structure of a Presentation

An organized speaker uses expressions to alert the audience to important information that will follow. Recognizing signal words and phrases will help you understand how a presentation is organized and the relationship between ideas.

Introduction

A good introduction identifies the topic and gives an idea of how the lecture or presentation will be organized. Here are some expressions to introduce a topic:

I'll be talking about . . .   *My topic is* . . .

There are basically two groups . . .   *There are three reasons* . . .

Body

In the body of a lecture, speakers usually expand upon the topic. They often use phrases that signal the order of events or subtopics and their relationship to each other. Here are some expressions to help listeners follow the body of a lecture:

The first/next/final (point/reason) is . . .   *First/Next/Finally, let's look at* . . .

Another reason is . . .   *However,* . . .

Conclusion

In the conclusion of a lecture, speakers often summarize what they have said. They may also make predictions or suggestions. Sometimes they ask a question in the conclusion to get the audience to think more about the topic. Here are some expressions to give a conclusion:

In conclusion, . . .   *In summary,* . . .

As you can see. . .   *To review, + (restatement of main points)*

Understanding Meaning from Context

When you are not familiar with a word that a speaker says, you can sometimes guess the meaning of the word or fill in the gaps using the context or situation itself.

Strategies:

- Don't panic. You don't always understand every word of what a speaker says in your first language, either.
- Use context clues to fill in the blanks. What did you understand just before or just after the missing part? What did the speaker probably say?
- Listen for words and phrases that signal a definition or explanation (e.g., *What that means is* . . .).

Recognizing a Speaker's Bias

Speakers often have an opinion about the topic they are discussing. It's important for you to know if they are objective or subjective about the topic. Objective speakers do not express an opinion. Subjective speakers have a bias or a strong feeling about the topic.

Strategies:

- Notice words like adjectives, adverbs, and modals that the speaker uses (e.g., *ideal, horribly, should, shouldn't*). These suggest that the speaker has a bias.
- Listen to the speaker's voice. Does he or she sound excited, angry, or bored?
- Notice if the speaker gives more weight or attention to one point of view over another.
- Listen for words that signal opinions (e.g., *I think…*).

NOTE-TAKING SKILLS

Taking notes is a personalized skill. It is important to develop a note-taking system that works for you. However, there are some common strategies to improve your note taking.

Before You Listen

Focus

Try to clear your mind before the speaker begins so you can pay attention. If possible, review previous notes or think about what you already know about the topic.

Predict

If you know the topic of the talk, think about what you might hear.

Listen

Take Notes by Hand

Research suggests that taking notes by hand rather than on a computer is more effective. Taking notes by hand requires you to summarize, rephrase, and synthesize information. This helps you *encode* the information, or put it into a form that you can understand and remember.

Listen for Signal Words and Phrases

Speakers often use signal words and phrases (e.g., *Today we're going to talk about…*) to organize their ideas and show relationships between them. Listening for signal words and phrases can help you decide what information to write in your notes.

Condense (Shorten) Information

- As you listen, focus on the most important ideas. The speaker will usually repeat, define, explain, and/or give examples of these ideas. Take notes on these ideas.

    Speaker: *The Itaipu Dam provides about 20% of the electricity used in Brazil and about 75% of the electricity used in Paraguay. That electricity goes to millions of homes and businesses, so it's good for the economy of both countries.*

    Notes: Itaipu Dam → electricity: Brazil 20%, Paraguay 75%

- Don't write full sentences. Write only key words (nouns, verbs, adjectives, and adverbs), phrases, or short sentences.

    Full sentence: *Teachers are normally at the top of the list of happiest jobs.*

    Notes: teachers happiest

- Leave out information that is obvious.

    Full sentence: *Photographer Annie Griffiths is famous for her beautiful photographs. She travels all over the world to take photos.*

    Notes: *A. Griffiths famous for photos; travels world*

- Write numbers and statistics using numerals. (9 bil; 35%)
- Use abbreviations (e.g., *ft., min., yr*) and symbols (=, ≠, >, <, %, →)
- Use indenting. Write main ideas on the left side of the paper. Indent details.

    Benefits of eating ugly foods
       Save $
          10-20% on ugly fruits & vegs. at market

- Write details under key terms to help you remember them.
- Write the definitions of important new words.

After You Listen

- Review your notes soon after the lecture or presentation. Add any details you missed.
- Clarify anything you don't understand in your notes with a classmate or teacher.
- Add or highlight main ideas. Cross out details that aren't important or necessary.
- Rewrite anything that is hard to read or understand. Rewrite your notes in an outline or other graphic organizer to organize the information more clearly.
- Use arrows, boxes, diagrams, or other visual cues to show relationships between ideas.

ORGANIZING INFORMATION

You can use a graphic organizer to take notes while you are listening, or to organize your notes after you listen. Here are some examples of graphic organizers:

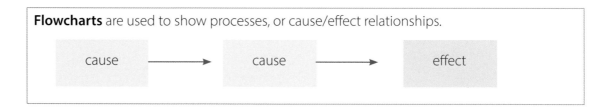

Flowcharts are used to show processes, or cause/effect relationships.

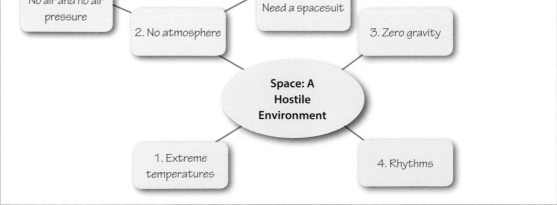

Mind maps show the connection between concepts. The main idea is usually in the center with supporting ideas and details around it.

Outlines show the relationship between main ideas and details.

To use an outline for taking notes, write the main ideas at the left margin of your paper. Below the main ideas, indent and write the supporting ideas and details. You may do this as you listen, or go back and rewrite your notes as an outline later.

> **I. Introduction:** How to feed the world
>
> **II. Steps**
>
> Step One: Stop deforestation
>
> a. stop burning rainforests
>
> b. grow crops on land size of South America

T-charts compare two topics.

Climate Change in Greenland	
Benefits	**Drawbacks**
shorter winters	rising sea levels

Timelines show a sequence of events.

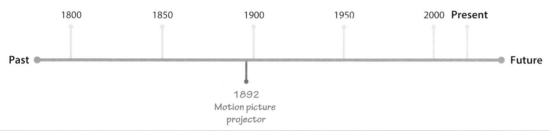

Venn diagrams compare and contrast two or more topics. The overlapping areas show similarities.

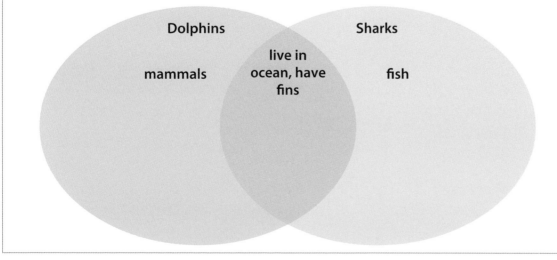

SPEAKING: COMMON PHRASES

Phrases for Expressing Yourself	
Expressing Opinions	**Expressing Likes and Dislikes**
I think…	*I like…*
I believe…	*I prefer…*
I'm sure…	*I love…*
In my opinion/view…	*I can't stand…*
If you ask me,…	*I hate…*
Personally,…	*I really don't like…*
To me,…	*I don't care for…*
Giving Facts	**Giving Tips or Suggestions**
There is evidence/proof…	*Imperatives (e.g., Try to get more sleep.)*
Experts claim/argue…	*You/We should/shouldn't…*
Studies show…	*You/We ought to…*
Researchers found…	*It's (not) a good idea to…*
The record shows…	*I suggest (that)…*
	Let's…
	How about… + (noun/gerund)
	What about… + (noun/gerund)
	Why don't we/you…
	You/We could…
Agreeing	**Disagreeing**
I agree.	*I disagree.*
True.	*I'm not so sure about that.*
Good point.	*I don't know.*
Exactly.	*That's a good point, but I don't agree.*
Absolutely.	*I see what you mean, but I think that…*
I was just about to say that.	
Definitely.	
Right!	

Phrases for Interacting with Others

Clarifying/Checking Your Understanding

So are you saying that…?
So what you mean is…?
What do you mean?
How's that?
How so?
I'm not sure I understand/follow.
Do you mean…?
I'm not sure what you mean.

Asking for Clarification/Confirming Understanding

Sorry, I didn't catch that. Could you repeat it?
I'm not sure I understand the question.
I'm not sure I understand what you mean.
Sorry, I'm not following you.
Are you saying that…?
If I understand correctly, you're saying that…
Oh, now I get it. You're talking about…, right?

Checking Others' Understanding

Does that make sense?
Do you understand?
Do you see what I mean?
Is that clear?
Are you following/with me?
Do you have any questions?

Asking for Opinions

What do you think?
We haven't heard from you in a while.
Do you have anything to add?
What are your thoughts?
How do you feel?
What's your opinion?

Taking Turns

Can/May I say something?
Could I add something?
Can I just say…?
May I continue?
Can I finish what I was saying?
Did you finish your thought?
Let me finish.
Let's get back to…

Interrupting Politely

Excuse me.
Pardon me.
Forgive me for interrupting…
I hate to interrupt but…
Can I stop you for a second?

Asking for Repetition

Could you say that again?
I'm sorry?
I didn't catch what you said.
I'm sorry. I missed that. What did you say?
Could you repeat that please?

Showing Interest

I see.	*Good for you.*
Really?	*Seriously?*
Um-hmm.	*No kidding!*
Wow.	*And? (Then what?)*
That's funny / amazing / incredible / awful!	

SPEAKING: PHRASES FOR PRESENTING

Introduction

Introducing a Topic

I'm going to talk about…	*Today we're going to talk about…*
My topic is…	*So we're going to show you…*
I'm going to present…	*Now/Right/So/Well, (pause), let's look at…*
I plan to discuss…	*There are three groups/reasons/effects/ factors…*
Let's start with…	*There are four steps in this process.*

Body

Listing or Sequencing

First/First of all/The first (noun)/To start/To begin,…

Second/Secondly/The second/Next/Another/ Also/Then/In addition,…

Last/The last/Finally,…

There are many/several/three types/kinds of/ ways…

Signaling Problems/Solutions

One problem/issue/challenge is…

One solution/answer/response is…

Giving Reasons or Causes

Because + (clause): Because the climate is changing…

Because of + (noun phrase): Because of climate change…

Due to + (noun phrase)…

Since + (clause)

The reason that I like hip-hop is…

One reason that people listen to music is…

One factor is + (noun phrase)

The main reason that…

Giving Results or Effects

so + (clause): so I went to the symphony

Therefore, + (sentence): Therefore, I went to the symphony.

As a result, + (sentence)

Consequently, + (sentence)

…causes + (noun phrase)

…leads to + (noun phrase)

…had an impact/effect on + (noun phrase)

If…then…

Giving Examples

The first example is…

Here's an example of what I mean…

For instance,…

For example,…

Let me give you an example…

…such as…

…like…

Repeating and Rephrasing

What you need to know is…

I'll say this again…

So again, let me repeat…

The most important point is…

Signaling Additional Examples or Ideas	Signaling to Stop Taking Notes
Not only…but	*You don't need this for the test.*
Besides…	*This information is in your books/on your handout/on the website.*
Not only do…, but also	*You don't have to write all this down.*
Identifying a Side Track	**Returning to a Previous Topic**
This is off-topic,…	*Getting back to our previous discussion,…*
On a different subject,…	*To return to our earlier topic…*
As an aside, …	*OK, getting back on topic…*
That reminds me…	*So to return to what we were saying,…*
Signaling a Definition	**Talking about Visuals**
Which means…	*This graph/infographic/diagram shows/explains…*
What that means is…	*The line/box/image represents…*
Or…	*The main point of this visual is…*
In other words,…	*You can see…*
Another way to say that is…	*From this we can see…*
That is…	
That is to say…	

Conclusion	
Concluding	
Well/So, that's how I see it.	*To sum up,*
In conclusion,	*As you can see,…*
In summary,	*At the end,…*
	To review, (+ restatement of main points)

PRESENTATION STRATEGIES

You will often have to give individual or group presentations in your class. The strategies below will help you to prepare, present, and reflect on your presentations.

Prepare

As you prepare your presentation:

Consider Your Topic

- **Choose a topic you feel passionate about.** If you are passionate about your topic, your audience will be more interested and excited about your topic, too. Focus on one major idea that you can bring to life. The best ideas are the ones your audience wants to experience.

Consider Your Purpose

- **Have a strong start.** Use an effective hook, such as a quote, an interesting example, a rhetorical question, or a powerful image to get your audience's attention. Include one sentence that explains what you will do in your presentation and why.
- **Stay focused.** Make sure your details and examples support your main points. Avoid sidetracks or unnecessary information that takes you away from your topic.
- **Use visuals that relate to your ideas.** Drawings, photos, video clips, infographics, charts, maps, slides, and physical objects can get your audience's attention and explain ideas effectively. For example, a photo or map of a location you mention can help your audience picture a place they have never been. Slides with only key words and phrases can help emphasize your main points. Visuals should be bright, clear, and simple.
- **Have a strong conclusion.** A strong conclusion should serve the same purpose as a strong start—to get your audience's attention and make them think. Good conclusions often refer back to the introduction, or beginning of the presentation. For example, if you ask a question in the beginning, you can answer it in the conclusion. Remember to restate your main points, and add a conclusion device such as a question, a call to action, or a quote.

Consider your Audience

- **Use familiar concepts.** Think about the people in your audience. Ask yourself these questions: Where are they from? How old are they? What is their background? What do they already know about my topic? What information do I need to explain? Use language and concepts they will understand.
- **Share a personal story.** Consider presenting information that will get an emotional reaction; for example, information that will make your audience feel surprised, curious, worried, or upset. This will help your audience relate to you and your topic.
- **Be authentic (be yourself!).** Write your presentation yourself. Use words that you know and are comfortable using.

Rehearse

- **Make an outline** to help you organize your ideas.
- **Write notes on notecards.** Do not write full sentences, just key words and phrases to help you remember important ideas. Mark the words you should stress and places to pause.
- **Review pronunciation.** Check the pronunciation of words you are uncertain about with a classmate, a teacher, or in a dictionary. Note and practice the pronunciation of difficult words.
- **Memorize the introduction and conclusion.** Rehearse your presentation several times. Practice saying it out loud to yourself (perhaps in front of a mirror or video recorder) and in front of others.
- **Ask for feedback.** Note and revise information that doesn't flow smoothly based on feedback and on your own performance in rehearsal. If specific words or phrases are still a problem, rephrase them.

Present

As you present:

- **Pay attention to your pacing** (how fast or slowly you speak). Remember to speak slowly and clearly. Pause to allow your audience to process information.
- **Speak at a volume loud enough to be heard** by everyone in the audience, but not too loud. Ask the audience if your volume is OK at the beginning of your talk.

- **Vary your intonation.** Don't speak in the same tone throughout the talk. Your audience will be more interested if your voice rises and falls, speeds up and slows down to match the ideas you are talking about.
- **Be friendly and relaxed with your audience**—remember to smile!
- **Show enthusiasm for your topic.** Use humor if appropriate.
- **Have a relaxed body posture.** Don't stand with your arms folded, or look down at your notes. Use gestures when helpful to emphasize your points.
- **Don't read directly from your notes.** Use them to help you remember ideas.
- **Don't look at or read from your visuals too much.** Use them to support your ideas.
- **Make frequent eye contact** with the entire audience.

Reflect

As you reflect on your presentation:

- **Consider what you think went well** during your presentation and what areas you can improve upon.
- **Get feedback** from your classmates and teacher. How do their comments relate to your own thoughts about your presentation? Did they notice things you didn't? How can you use their feedback in your next presentation?

PRESENTATION OUTLINE

When you are planning a presentation, you may find it helpful to use an outline. If it is a group presentation, the outline can provide an easy way to divide the content. For example, one student can do the introduction, another student the first idea in the body, and so on.

1. Introduction

Topic: _____

Hook: _____

Statement of main idea: _____

2. Body

First step/example/reason: _____

Supporting details: _____ _____ _____

Second step/example/reason: _____

Supporting details: _____ _____ _____

Third step/example/reason: _____

Supporting details: _____ _____ _____

3. Conclusion

Main points to summarize: _____ _____

Suggestions/Predictions: _____ _____

Closing comments/summary: _____ _____

PRONUNCIATION GUIDE

Sounds and Symbols

Vowels

Symbol	Key Words
/ɑ/	hot, stop
/æ/	cat, ran
/aɪ/	fine, nice
/i/	eat, need
/ɪ/	sit, him
/eɪ/	name, say
/ɛ/	get, bed
/ʌ/	cup, what
/ə/	about, lesson
/u/	boot, new
/ʊ/	book, could
/oʊ/	go, road
/ɔ/	law, walk
/aʊ/	house, now
/ɔɪ/	toy, coin

Consonants

Symbol	Key Word	Symbol	Key Word
/b/	boy	/t/	tea
/d/	day	/tʃ/	cheap
/dʒ/	job, bridge	/v/	vote
/f/	face	/w/	we
/g/	go	/y/	yes
/h/	hat	/z/	zoo
/k/	key, car		
/l/	love	/ð/	they
/m/	my	/θ/	think
/n/	nine	/ʃ/	shoe
/ŋ/	sing	/ʒ/	measure
/p/	pen		
/r/	right		
/s/	see		

Source: *The Newbury House Dictionary plus Grammar Reference,* Fifth Edition, National Geographic Learning/ Cengage Learning, 2014.

Rhythm

The rhythm of English involves stress and pausing.

Stress

- English words are based on syllables—units of sound that include one vowel sound.
- In every word in English, one syllable has the primary stress.
- In English, speakers group words that go together based on the meaning and context of the sentence. These groups of words are called *thought groups*. In each thought group, one word is stressed more than the others—the stress is placed on the syllable with the primary stress in this word.
- In general, new ideas and information are stressed.

Pausing

- Pauses in English can be divided into two groups: long and short pauses.
- English speakers use long pauses to mark the conclusion of a thought, items in a list, or choices given.
- Short pauses are used in between thought groups to break up the ideas in sentences into smaller, more manageable chunks of information.

English speakers use intonation, or pitch (the rise and fall of their voice), to help express meaning. For example, speakers usually use a rising intonation at the end of *yes/no* questions, and a falling intonation at the end of *wh-* questions and statements.

VOCABULARY BUILDING STRATEGIES

Vocabulary learning is an on-going process. The strategies below will help you learn and remember new vocabulary words.

Guessing Meaning from Context

You can often guess the meaning of an unfamiliar word by looking at or listening to the words and sentences around it. Speakers usually know when a word is unfamiliar to the audience, or is essential to understanding the main ideas, and often provide clues to its meaning.

- Repetition: A speaker may use the same key word or phrase, or use another form of the same word.
- Restatement or synonym: A speaker may give a synonym to explain the meaning of a word, using phrases such as *in other words, also called, or…, also known as.*
- Antonyms: A speaker may define a word by explaining what it is NOT. The speaker may say *Unlike A/In contrast to A, B is…*
- Definition: Listen for signals such as *which means* or *is defined as.* Definitions can also be signaled by a pause.
- Examples: A speaker may provide examples that can help you figure out what something is. For example, **Mascots** *are a very popular marketing tool. You've seen them on commercials and in ads on social media –* **cute, brightly colored creatures that help sell a product**.

Understanding Word Families: Stems, Prefixes, and Suffixes

Use your understanding of stems, prefixes, and suffixes to recognize unfamiliar words and to expand your vocabulary. The stem is the root part of the word, which provides the main meaning. A prefix comes before the stem and usually modifies meaning (e.g., adding *re-* to a word means "again" or "back"). A suffix comes after the stem and usually changes the part of speech (e.g., adding *-ion, -tion,* or *-ation* to a verb changes it to a noun). Words that share the same stem or root belong to the same word family (e.g., *event, eventful, uneventful, uneventfully*).

Word Stem	Meaning	Example
ann, enn	year	anniversary, millennium
chron(o)	time	chronological, synchronize
flex, flect	bend	flexible, reflection
graph	draw, write	graphics, paragraph
lab	work	labor, collaborate
mob, mot, mov	move	automobile, motivate, mover
port	carry	transport, import
sect	cut	sector, bisect

Prefix	Meaning	Example
dis-	not, opposite of	disappear, disadvantages
in-, im-, il-, ir-	not	inconsistent, immature, illegal, irresponsible
inter-	between	Internet, international
mis-	bad, badly, incorrectly	misunderstand, misjudge
pre-	before	prehistoric, preheat
re-	again; back	repeat; return
trans-	across, beyond	transfer, translate
un-	not	uncooked, unfair

Suffix	Meaning	Example
-able, -ible	worth, ability	believable, impossible
-en	to cause to become; made of	lengthen, strengthen; golden
-er, -or	one who	teacher, director
-ful	full of	beautiful, successful
-ify, -fy	to make or become	simplify, satisfy
-ion, -tion, -ation	condition, action	occasion, education, foundation
-ize	cause	modernize, summarize
-ly	in the manner of	carefully, happily
-ment	condition or result	assignment, statement
-ness	state of being	happiness, sadness

Using a Dictionary

Here are some tips for using a dictionary:

- When you see or hear a new word, try to guess its part of speech (noun, verb, adjective, etc.) and meaning, then look it up in a dictionary.

- Some words have multiple meanings. Look up a new word in the dictionary and try to choose the correct meaning for the context. Then see if it makes sense within the context.

- When you look up a word, look at all the definitions to see if there is a basic core meaning. This will help you understand the word when it is used in a different context. Also look at all the related words, or words in the same family. This can help you expand your vocabulary. For example, the core meaning of *structure* involves something built or put together.

> **structure** /ˈstrʌktʃər/ *n.* **1** [C] a building of any kind: *A new structure is being built on the corner.* **2** [C] any architectural object of any kind: *The Eiffel Tower is a famous Parisian structure.* **3** [U] the way parts are put together or organized: *the structure of a song||a business's structure*
> *–v.* [T] **-tured, -turing, -tures** to put together or organize parts of s.t.: *We are structuring a plan to hire new teachers.*
> *-adj.* **structural.**

Source: *The Newbury House Dictionary plus Grammar Reference*, Fifth Edition, National Geographic Learning/Cengage Learning, 2014

Multi-Word Units

You can improve your fluency if you learn and use vocabulary as multi-word units: idioms (*go the extra mile*), collocations (*wide range*), and fixed expressions (*in other words*). Some multi-word units can only be understood as a chunk—the individual words do not add up to the same overall meaning. Keep track of multi-word units in a notebook or on notecards.

Vocabulary Note Cards

You can expand your vocabulary by using vocabulary note cards or a vocabulary building app. Write the word, expression, or sentence that you want to learn on one side. On the other, draw a four-square grid and write the following information in the squares: definition; translation (in your first language); sample sentence; synonyms. Choose words that are high frequency or on the academic word list. If you have looked a word up a few times, you should make a card for it.

definition:	first language translation:
sample sentence:	synonyms:

Organize the cards in review sets so you can practice them. Don't put words that are similar in spelling or meaning in the same review set as you may get them mixed up. Go through the cards and test yourself on the words or expressions. You can also practice with a partner.

VOCABULARY INDEX

Word	Page	CEFR† Level	Word	Page	CEFR† Level	Word	Page	CEFR† Level
accustomed to	104	C1	descendant	84	C2	innate	174	C2
advocate	184	C2	detect	154	C1	innovative	4	C1
affluent	14	C1	determine	124	C1	insert	54	C1
affordable	4	C1	detrimental	184	C2	insist on	104	C1
aid	134	C1	diagnosis	144	C2	integrate	54	C1
alarming	44	C1	diminish	94	C1	intense	184	C1
allocate	134	C1	displace	94	C1	interest	134	C1
ample	194	C1	distinct	44	C1	interfere	94	C1
analytical	164	C1	diversity	114	C1	internalize/	14	off-list
anticipate	74	C1	dominant	14	C1	internalise		
application	74	C2	drawback	184	C1	intuition	164	C2
archaeologist	84	C1	ecology	94	C1	invaluable	184	C1
assemble	104	C2	emerging	74	C1	isolated	104	C1
associate	124	C1	employ	104	C1	keep track of	144	C1
authority	34	C1	enforce	14	C1	labor / labour	64	C1
authorize /	4	C1	engage in	124	C2	legislation	94	C2
authorise			enrich	74	C1	livelihood	114	off-list
be derived from	54	C1	envision	44	C1	logic	164	C1
be to blame	24	C1	ethical	174	C2	mass	74	C1
be unique to	14	C1	ethnic	14	C1	maximize /	4	C2
by leaps and	144	C2	evolve	44	C1	maximise		
bounds			exceed	194	C1	merit	114	C1
by means of	184	C1	excessively	44	off-list	migrate	84	C1
call for	194	C2	exclusively	44	C1	modify	24	C1
clarify	144	C1	exhibit	54	C1	monitor	94	C1
coincide	194	C2	extinct	24	C1	namely	164	C1
collaborate	74	C1	facilitate	64	C1	neglect	34	C1
comparatively	144	C1	flourish	114	C2	nest egg	134	C2
competence	64	C1	fulfillment /	124	C2	norm	174	C1
component	64	C1	fulfilment			notable	84	C1
confidential	144	C1	funds	4	C1	notify	154	C1
conform	14	off-list	gadget	144	C1	nutritional	154	C1
confront	94	C2	genetic	84	C1	objective	164	B2
consent	114	C1	habitat	24	C1	obsolete	174	C1
constitute	44	C1	hardship	114	C1	offset	184	C2
constructive	54	C1	heritage	114	C2	ongoing	24	C2
consult	144	C1	hypothesis	84	C2	opt	194	C1
contradiction	104	C2	immense	84	C1	outlook	124	C2
contrary (to)	34	C1	impact	124	C1	output	194	C2
controversy	34	C1	implication	74	C1	overdo	134	C1
cultivate	184	C1	impose	24	C1	overwhelming	94	C1
daydream	54	C1	inadequate	194	C1	perceive	44	C1
debatable	14	off-list	inevitably	64	C1	perspective	84	C1
dedicated (to)	94	C1	inferior	174	C1	persuasive	54	C1
deepen	174	C1	influential	74	C1	pertain (to)	64	off-list
deposit	134	C1	initiate	34	C2	portable	74	C1

Word	Page	CEFR† Level	Word	Page	CEFR† Level	Word	Page	CEFR† Level
posture	154	C1	replicate	114	off-list	tendency	144	C1
practical	54	C1	resistance	184	C2	threaten	24	C1
predator	34	C1	resolve	154	C1	thrive	24	C1
preservation	104	C1	restrict	14	C1	track	154	C2
prey on	34	off-list	retain	64	C2	transaction	134	C1
principle	104	C2	root	194	C1	transition	104	C2
prioritize / prioritise	4	off-list	scarcity	4	C2	tribal	94	C2
			scenario	194	C2	ultimately	114	C1
productivity	154	C1	sector	64	C1	undeniable	34	C1
prominent	74	C2	security	124	C1	undertake	114	C1
promising	64	C1	sedentary	154	C2	unprecedented	174	C2
promote	124	C1	seemingly	134	C1	unquestionably	54	C1
prone to	154	C2	skeptic / sceptic	184	off-list	upkeep	34	C2
pursue	104	C1	spatial	164	off-list	venture	84	C2
radical	174	C1	status	24	C1	verbal	164	C2
random	44	C1	stem from	174	C1	vice versa	164	C1
rank	14	C1	stroll	4	C1	virtue	124	C2
ratio	44	C1	subjective	164	C1	visualize / visualise	164	off-list
regulate	4	C1	subsequently	84	C1			
reluctant	144	C1	substantially	54	C1	well-being	124	C1
reminder	134	C1	superior	174	C1	widespread	64	C1
renovation	4	C1	surge	194	C1	wipe out	24	C2
repetitive	154	C1	sustainable	34	C1	withdraw	134	C1

†The Common European Framework of Reference for Languages (CEFR) is an international standard for describing language proficiency. Pathways Level 4 is intended for students at CEFR level C1. The target vocabulary is at the following CEFR levels:

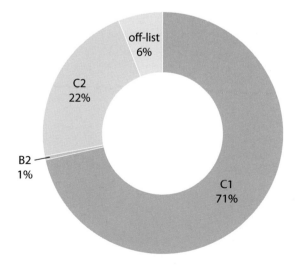

off-list 6%
C2 22%
B2 1%
C1 71%

*These words are on the Academic Word List (AWL). The AWL is a list of the 570 highest-frequency academic word families that regularly appear in academic texts. The AWL was compiled by researcher Averil Coxhead based on her analysis of a 3.5-million-word corpus (Coxhead, 2000).

RUBRICS

UNIT 1   Lesson B Lesson Task

Check (✓) if the presenter did the following:	Name		
1. described a problem affecting a city and its causes	☐	☐	☐
2. proposed possible solutions to the problem	☐	☐	☐
3. used signal phrases to introduce additional aspects of the topic	☐	☐	☐
4. divided the presentation appropriately	☐	☐	☐
5. spoke clearly and at an appropriate pace	☐	☐	☐
6. used appropriate vocabulary	☐	☐	☐
OVERALL RATING Note: 1 = lowest; 5 = highest	1 2 3 4 5	1 2 3 4 5	1 2 3 4 5
Notes:			

UNIT 2   Lesson B Final Task

Check (✓) if the presenters did the following:	Name		
1. provided appropriate support in favor of or against the argument	☐	☐	☐
2. responded to arguments appropriately	☐	☐	☐
3. debated for three to five minutes	☐	☐	☐
4. spoke clearly and at an appropriate pace	☐	☐	☐
5. used appropriate vocabulary	☐	☐	☐
OVERALL RATING Note: 1 = lowest; 5 = highest	1 2 3 4 5	1 2 3 4 5	1 2 3 4 5
Notes:			

UNIT 3   Lesson B Final Task

Check (✓) if the presenter did the following:	Name		
	_____	_____	_____
1. described fashion trends in a particular location in detail	☐	☐	☐
2. displayed appropriate visuals	☐	☐	☐
3. organized the presentation appropriately	☐	☐	☐
4. paraphrased new or difficult information	☐	☐	☐
5. spoke clearly and at an appropriate pace	☐	☐	☐
6. used appropriate vocabulary	☐	☐	☐
OVERALL RATING Note: 1 = lowest; 5 = highest	1 2 3 4 5	1 2 3 4 5	1 2 3 4 5
Notes:			

UNIT 4   Lesson B Lesson Task

Check (✓) if the presenters did the following:	Name		
	_____	_____	_____
1. described a social media platform and its history	☐	☐	☐
2. discussed the advantages of the platform and how it compares to others	☐	☐	☐
3. evaluated the platform in terms of its effect on globalization and its future prospects	☐	☐	☐
4. clarified terms/ideas with definitions	☐	☐	☐
5. spoke slowly and confidently	☐	☐	☐
6. used appropriate vocabulary	☐	☐	☐
OVERALL RATING Note: 1 = lowest; 5 = highest	1 2 3 4 5	1 2 3 4 5	1 2 3 4 5
Notes:			

UNIT 5   Lesson B Final Task

Check (✓) if the presenters did the following:	Name		
	_____	_____	_____
1. explained the animal migration clearly	☐	☐	☐
2. displayed a time line of the animal migration	☐	☐	☐
3. handled audience questions appropriately	☐	☐	☐
4. spoke clearly and at an appropriate pace	☐	☐	☐
5. used appropriate vocabulary	☐	☐	☐
OVERALL RATING Note: 1 = lowest; 5 = highest	1 2 3 4 5	1 2 3 4 5	1 2 3 4 5
Notes:			

UNIT 6   Lesson B Final Task

Check (✓) if the presenters did the following:	Name		
	_____	_____	_____
1. described a current tradition in detail	☐	☐	☐
2. organized ideas effectively	☐	☐	☐
3. used rhetorical questions appropriately	☐	☐	☐
4. used strategies to appear confident when speaking	☐	☐	☐
5. used appropriate vocabulary	☐	☐	☐
OVERALL RATING Note: 1 = lowest; 5 = highest	1 2 3 4 5	1 2 3 4 5	1 2 3 4 5
Notes:			

UNIT 7   Lesson B Final Task

Check (✓) if the presenter did the following:	Name		
	_____	_____	_____
1. presented a balanced budget	☐	☐	☐
2. described a plan to repay the client's debt	☐	☐	☐
3. used appropriate connectors to organize ideas	☐	☐	☐
4. spoke clearly and at an appropriate pace	☐	☐	☐
5. used appropriate vocabulary	☐	☐	☐
OVERALL RATING Note: 1 = lowest; 5 = highest	1 2 3 4 5	1 2 3 4 5	1 2 3 4 5
Notes:			

UNIT 8   Lesson B Final Task

Check (✓) if the presenter did the following:	Name		
	_____	_____	_____
1. described a health/fitness technology product	☐	☐	☐
2. emphasized important information	☐	☐	☐
3. discussed the positive and negative assessments of the product	☐	☐	☐
4. presented a pros and cons chart for the product	☐	☐	☐
5. used questions to engage the audience	☐	☐	☐
6. used appropriate vocabulary	☐	☐	☐
OVERALL RATING Note: 1 = lowest; 5 = highest	1 2 3 4 5	1 2 3 4 5	1 2 3 4 5
Notes:			

UNIT 9   Lesson B Final Task

Check (✓) if the presenters did the following:	Name		
	_____	_____	_____
1. described three life hacks, the problems they solve, and/or who they benefit	☐	☐	☐
2. discussed his/her personal experience with and/or opinions of the life hacks	☐	☐	☐
3. used appropriate gestures	☐	☐	☐
4. spoke clearly and at an appropriate pace	☐	☐	☐
5. used appropriate vocabulary	☐	☐	☐
OVERALL RATING Note: 1 = lowest; 5 = highest	1 2 3 4 5	1 2 3 4 5	1 2 3 4 5
Notes:			

UNIT 10   Lesson B Final Task

Check (✓) if the presenters did the following:	Name		
	_____	_____	_____
1. explained how the program solves a problem	☐	☐	☐
2. described the resources needed to implement the program	☐	☐	☐
3. supported ideas with others' opinions when appropriate	☐	☐	☐
4. spoke clearly and at an appropriate pace	☐	☐	☐
5. used appropriate vocabulary	☐	☐	☐
OVERALL RATING Note: 1 = lowest; 5 = highest	1 2 3 4 5	1 2 3 4 5	1 2 3 4 5
Notes:			

ACKNOWLEDGEMENTS

The Authors and Publisher would like to acknowledge the teachers around the world who participated in the development of the second edition of *Pathways*.

A special thanks to our Advisory Board for their valuable input during the development of this series.

ADVISORY BOARD

Mahmoud Al Hosni, Modern College of Business and Science, Muscat; **Safaa Al-Salim**, Kuwait University, Kuwait City; **Laila AlQadhi**, Kuwait University, Kuwait City; **Julie Bird**, RMIT University Vietnam, Ho Chi Minh City; **Elizabeth Bowles**, Virginia Tech Language and Culture Institute, Blacksburg, VA; **Rachel Bricker**, Arizona State University, Tempe, AZ; **James Broadbridge**, J.F. Oberlin University, Tokyo; **Marina Broeder**, Mission College, Santa Clara, CA; **Shawn Campbell**, Hangzhou High School, Hangzhou; **Trevor Carty**, James Cook University, Singapore; **Jindarat De Vleeschauwer**, Chiang Mai University, Chiang Mai; **Wai-Si El Hassan**, Prince Mohammad Bin Fahd University, Dhahran; **Jennifer Farnell**, University of Bridgeport, Bridgeport, CT; **Rasha Gazzaz**, King Abdulaziz University, Jeddah; **Keith Graziadei**, Santa Monica College, Santa Monica, CA; **Janet Harclerode**, Santa Monica Community College, Santa Monica, CA; **Anna Hasper**, TeacherTrain, Dubai; **Phoebe Kamel Yacob Hindi**, Abu Dhabi Vocational Education and Training Institute, Abu Dhabi; **Kuei-ping Hsu**, National Tsing Hua University, Hsinchu; **Greg Jewell**, Drexel University, Philadelphia, PA; **Adisra Katib**, Chulalongkorn University Language Institute, Bangkok; **Wayne Kennedy**, LaGuardia Community College, Long Island City, NY; **Beth Koo**, Central Piedmont Community College, Charlotte, NC; **Denise Kray**, Bridge School, Denver, CO; **Chantal Kruger**, ILA Vietnam, Ho Chi Minh City; **William P. Kyzner**, Fuyang AP Center, Fuyang; **Becky Lawrence**, Massachusetts International Academy, Marlborough, MA; **Deborah McGraw**, Syracuse University, Syracuse, NY; **Mary Moore**, University of Puerto Rico, San Juan; **Raymond Purdy**, ELS Language Centers, Princeton, NJ; **Anouchka Rachelson**, Miami Dade College, Miami, FL; **Fathimah Razman**, Universiti Utara Malaysia, Sintok; **Phil Rice**, University of Delaware ELI, Newark, DE; **Scott Rousseau**, American University of Sharjah, Sharjah; **Verna Santos-Nafrada**, King Saud University, Riyadh; **Eugene Sidwell**, American Intercon Institute, Phnom Penh; **Gemma Thorp**, Monash University English Language Centre, Melbourne; **Matt Thurston**, University of Central Lancashire, Preston; **Christine Tierney**, Houston Community College, Houston, TX; **Jet Robredillo Tonogbanua**, FPT University, Hanoi.

GLOBAL REVIEWERS

ASIA

Antonia Cavcic, Asia University, Tokyo; **Soyhan Egitim**, Tokyo University of Science, Tokyo; **Caroline Handley**, Asia University, Tokyo; **Patrizia Hayashi**, Meikai University, Urayasu; **Greg Holloway**, University of Kitakyushu, Kitakyushu; **Anne C. Ihata**, Musashino University, Tokyo; **Kathryn Mabe**, Asia University, Tokyo; **Frederick Navarro Bacala**, Yokohama City University, Yokohama; **Tyson Rode**, Meikai University, Urayasu; **Scott Shelton-Strong**, Asia University, Tokyo; **Brooks Slaybaugh**, Yokohama City University, Yokohama; **Susanto Sugiharto**, Sutomo Senior High School, Medan; **Andrew Zitzmann**, University of Kitakyushu, Kitakyushu

LATIN AMERICA AND THE CARIBBEAN

Raul Billini, ProLingua, Dominican Republic; **Alejandro Garcia**, Collegio Marcelina, Mexico; **Humberto Guevara**, Tec de Monterrey, Campus Monterrey, Mexico; **Romina Olga Planas**, Centro Cultural Paraguayo Americano, Paraguay; **Carlos Rico-Troncoso**, Pontificia Universidad Javeriana, Colombia; **Ialê Schetty**, Enjoy English, Brazil; **Aline Simoes**, Way To Go Private English, Brazil; **Paulo Cezar Lira Torres**, APenglish, Brazil; **Rosa Enilda Vasquez**, Swisher Dominicana, Dominican Republic; **Terry Whitty**, LDN Language School, Brazil.

MIDDLE EAST AND NORTH AFRICA

Susan Daniels, Kuwait University, Kuwait; **Mahmoud Mohammadi Khomeini**, Sokhane Ashna Language School, Iran; **Müge Lenbet**, Koç University, Turkey; **Robert Anthony Lowman**, Prince Mohammad bin Fahd University, Saudi Arabia; **Simon Mackay**, Prince Mohammad bin Fahd University, Saudi Arabia.

USA AND CANADA

Frank Abbot, Houston Community College, Houston, TX; **Hossein Aksari**, Bilingual Education Institute and Houston Community College, Houston, TX; **Sudie Allen-Henn**, North Seattle College, Seattle, WA; **Sharon Allie**, Santa Monica Community College, Santa Monica, CA; **Jerry Archer**, Oregon State University, Corvallis, OR; **Nicole Ashton**, Central Piedmont Community College, Charlotte, NC; **Barbara Barrett**, University of Miami, Coral Gables, FL; **Maria Bazan-Myrick**, Houston Community College, Houston, TX; **Rebecca Beal**, Colleges of Marin, Kentfield, CA; **Marlene Beck**, Eastern Michigan University, Ypsilanti, MI; **Michelle Bell**, University of Southern California, Los Angeles, CA; **Linda Bolet**, Houston Community College, Houston, TX; **Jenna Bollinger**, Eastern Michigan University, Ypsilanti, MI; **Monica Boney**, Houston Community College, Houston, TX; **Nanette Bouvier**, Rutgers University – Newark, Newark, NJ; **Nancy Boyer**, Golden West College, Huntington Beach, CA; **Lia Brenneman**, University of Florida English Language Institute, Gainesville, FL; **Colleen Brice**, Grand Valley State University, Allendale, MI; **Kristen Brown**, Massachusetts International Academy, Marlborough, MA; **Philip Brown**, Houston Community

College, Houston, TX; **Dongmei Cao**, San Jose City College, San Jose, CA; **Molly Cheney**, University of Washington, Seattle, WA; **Emily Clark**, The University of Kansas, Lawrence, KS; **Luke Coffelt**, International English Center, Boulder, CO; **William C Cole-French**, MCPHS University, Boston, MA; **Charles Colson**, English Language Institute at Sam Houston State University, Huntsville, TX; **Lucy Condon**, Bilingual Education Institute, Houston, TX; **Janice Crouch**, Internexus Indiana, Indianapolis, IN; **Charlene Dandrow**, Virginia Tech Language and Culture Institute, Blacksburg, VA; **Loretta Davis**, Coastline Community College, Westminster, CA; **Marta Dmytrenko-Ahrabian**, Wayne State University, Detroit, MI; **Bonnie Duhart**, Houston Community College, Houston, TX; **Karen Eichhorn**, International English Center, Boulder, CO; **Tracey Ellis**, Santa Monica Community College, Santa Monica, CA; **Jennifer Evans**, University of Washington, Seattle, WA; **Marla Ewart**, Bilingual Education Institute, Houston, TX; **Rhoda Fagerland**, St. Cloud State University, St. Cloud, MN; **Kelly Montijo Fink**, Kirkwood Community College, Cedar Rapids, IA; **Celeste Flowers**, University of Central Arkansas, Conway, AR; **Kurtis Foster**, Missouri State University, Springfield, MO; **Rachel Garcia**, Bilingual Education Institute, Houston, TX; **Thomas Germain**, University of Colorado Boulder, Boulder, CO; **Claire Gimble**, Virginia International University, Fairfax, VA; **Marilyn Glazer-Weisner**, Middlesex Community College, Lowell, MA; **Amber Goodall**, South Piedmont Community College, Charlotte, NC; **Katya Goussakova**, Seminole State College of Florida, Sanford, FL; **Jane Granado**, Texas State University, San Marcos, TX; **Therea Hampton**, Mercer County Community College, West Windsor Township, NJ; **Jane Hanson**, University of Nebraska – Lincoln, Lincoln, NE; **Lauren Heather**, University of Texas at San Antonio, San Antonio, TX; **Jannette Hermina**, Saginaw Valley State University, Saginaw, MI; **Gail Hernandez**, College of Staten Island, Staten Island, NY; **Beverly Hobbs**, Clark University, Worcester, MA; **Kristin Homuth**, Language Center International, Southfield, MI; **Tim Hooker**, Campbellsville University, Campbellsville, KY; **Raylene Houck**, Idaho State University, Pocatello, ID; **Karen L. Howling**, University of Bridgeport, Bridgeport, CT; **Sharon Jaffe**, Santa Monica Community College, Santa Monica, CA; **Andrea Kahn**, Santa Monica Community College, Santa Monica, CA; **Eden Bradshaw Kaiser**, Massachusetts International Academy, Marlborough, MA; **Mandy Kama**, Georgetown University, Washington, D.C.; **Andrea Kaminski**, University of Michigan – Dearborn, Dearborn, MI; **Phoebe Kang**, Brock University, Ontario; **Eileen Kramer**, Boston University CELOP, Brookline, MA; **Rachel Lachance**, University of New Hampshire, Durham, NH; **Janet Langon**, Glendale Community College, Glendale, CA; **Frances Le Grand**, University of Houston, Houston, TX; **Esther Lee**, California State University, Fullerton, CA; **Helen S. Mays Lefal**, American Learning Institute, Dallas, TX; **Oranit Limmaneeprasert**, American River College, Sacramento, CA; **Dhammika Liyanage**, Bilingual Education Institute, Houston, TX; **Emily Lodmer**, Santa Monica Community College, Santa Monica Community College, CA; **Ari Lopez**, American Learning Institute Dallas, TX; **Nichole Lukas**, University of Dayton, Dayton, OH; **Undarmaa Maamuujav**, California State University, Los Angeles, CA; **Diane Mahin**, University of Miami, Coral Gables, FL; **Melanie Majeski**, Naugatuck Valley Community College, Waterbury, CT; **Judy Marasco**, Santa Monica Community College, Santa Monica, CA; **Murray McMahan**, University of Alberta, Alberta; **Deirdre McMurtry**, University of Nebraska Omaha, Omaha, NE; **Suzanne Meyer**, University of Pittsburgh, Pittsburgh, PA; **Cynthia Miller**, Richland College, Dallas, TX; **Sara Miller**, Houston Community College, Houston, TX; **Gwendolyn Miraglia**, Houston Community College, Houston, TX; **Katie Mitchell**, International English Center, Boulder, CO; **Ruth Williams Moore**, University of Colorado Boulder, Boulder, CO; **Kathy Najafi**, Houston Community College, Houston, TX; **Sandra Navarro**, Glendale Community College, Glendale, CA; **Stephanie Ngom**, Boston University, Boston MA; **Barbara Niemczyk**, University of Bridgeport, Bridgeport, CT; **Melody Nightingale**, Santa Monica Community College, Santa Monica, CA; **Alissa Olgun**, California Language Academy, Los Angeles, CA; **Kimberly Oliver**, Austin Community College, Austin, TX; **Steven Olson**, International English Center, Boulder, CO; **Fernanda Ortiz**, University of Arizona, Tucson, AZ; **Joel Ozretich**, University of Washington, Seattle, WA; **Erin Pak**, Schoolcraft College, Livonia, MI; **Geri Pappas**, University of Michigan – Dearborn, Dearborn, MI; **Eleanor Paterson**, Erie Community College, Buffalo, NY; **Sumeeta Patnaik**, Marshall University, Huntington, WV; **Mary Peacock**, Richland College, Dallas, TX; **Kathryn Porter**, University of Houston, Houston, TX; **Eileen Prince**, Prince Language Associates, Newton Highlands, MA; **Marina Ramirez**, Houston Community College, Houston, TX; **Laura Ramm**, Michigan State University, East Lansing, MI; **Chi Rehg**, University of South Florida, Tampa, FL; **Cyndy Reimer**, Douglas College, New Westminster, British Columbia; **Sydney Rice**, Imperial Valley College, Imperial, CA; **Lynnette Robson**, Mercer University, Macon, GA; **Helen E. Roland**, Miami Dade College, Miami, FL; **Maria Paula Carreira Rolim**, Southeast Missouri State University, Cape Girardeau, MO; **Jill Rolston-Yates**, Texas State University, San Marcos, TX; **David Ross**, Houston Community College, Houston, TX; **Rachel Scheiner**, Seattle Central College, Seattle, WA; **John Schmidt**, Texas Intensive English Program, Austin, TX; **Mariah Schueman**, University of Miami, Coral Gables, FL; **Erika Shadburne**, Austin Community College, Austin, TX; **Mahdi Shamsi**, Houston Community College, Houston, TX; **Osha Sky**, Highline College, Des Moines, WA; **William Slade**, University of Texas, Austin, TX; **Takako Smith**, University of Nebraska – Lincoln, Lincoln, NE; **Barbara Smith-Palinkas**, Hillsborough Community College, Tampa, FL; **Paula Snyder**, University of Missouri, Columbia, MO; **Mary; Evelyn Sorrell**, Bilingual Education Institute, Houston TX; **Kristen Stauffer**, International English Center, Boulder, CO; **Christina Stefanik**, The Language Company, Toledo, OH; **Cory Stewart**, University of Houston, Houston, TX; **Laurie Stusser-McNeill**, Highline College, Des Moines, WA; **Tom Sugawara**, University of Washington, Seattle, WA; **Sara Sulko**, University of Missouri, Columbia, MO; **Mark Sullivan**, University of Colorado Boulder, Boulder, CO; **Olivia Szabo**, Boston University, Boston, MA; **Amber Tallent**, University of Nebraska Omaha, Omaha, NE; **Amy Tate**, Rice University, Houston, USA; **Aya C. Tiacoh**, Bilingual Education Institute, Houston, TX; **Troy Tucker**, Florida SouthWestern State College, Fort Myers, FL; **Anne Tyoan**, Savannah College of Art and Design, Savannah, GA; **Michael Vallee**, International English Center, Boulder, CO; **Andrea Vasquez**, University of Southern Maine, Portland, ME; **Jose Vasquez**, University of Texas Rio Grande Valley, Edinburg, TX; **Maureen Vendeville**, Savannah Technical College, Savannah, GA; **Melissa Vervinck**, Oakland University, Rochester, MI; **Adriana Villarreal**, Universided Nacional Autonoma de Mexico, San Antonio, TX; **Summer Webb**, International English Center, Boulder, CO; **Mercedes Wilson-Everett**, Houston Community College, Houston, TX; **Lora Yasen**, Tokyo International University of America, Salem, OR; **Dennis Yommer**, Youngstown State University, Youngstown, OH; **Melojeane (Jolene) Zawilinski**, University of Michigan – Flint, Flint, MI.

CREDITS

Photos

Cover Credit: Guang Niu/Getty Images

1 (t) 2009 TYRONE TURNER/National Geographic Image Collection, **2-3** (c) Kirklandphotos/Getty Images, (t) Cengage Learning, Inc., **5** (b) Alan Tan Photography/Shutterstock.com, **6** (c) ©National Geographic Maps, (bl) Franco Debernardi/Getty Images, **9** (br) Cengage Learning, Inc., (bl) USGS, 010-011 (b) mandritoiu/Shutterstock.com, **12** (t) VCG/Getty Images, **15** (t) DESIGN PICS INC/National Geographic Creative, **16** (cl) ©National Geographic Maps, (b) DESIGN PICS INC/National Geographic Creative, **19** (t) FRANCOIS GUILLOT/Getty Images, **21** (t) ©Brent Stirton/Reportage/Getty Images, **22** (l) AFP/Getty Images, **23** (r) ©Joel Sartore/National Geographic Photo Ark, **24** (b) Francois Gohier/VWPics/Alamy, **26** (tr) Science History Images/Alamy, **28** (b) PAUL NICKLEN/National Geographic Creative, **31** (c) Heather Lucia Snow/Shutterstock, **32** (t) ©Axel Gomille/NPL/Minden Pictures, **34** (b) ROBBIE GEORGE/National Geographic Creative, **36** (b) Edwin Remsberg/Alamy Stock Photo, **39** (b) Charles Mostoller/Reuters, **41** (t) Tristan Fewings/Getty Images, **42-43** (t) Anadolu Agency/Getty Images, **43** (r) Cengage Learning, Inc., **44** (tr) Tim Graham/Alamy Stock Photo, **46** (c) RightsLink, **49** (b) JODI COBB/National Geographic creative, **50** (t) ©Xavier Zimbardo/Getty Images, **52** (t) SARAH LEEN/National Geographic Creative, **53** (b) www.BibleLandPictures.com/Alamy Stock Photo, **54** (tr) Camila Turriani/Alamy Stock Photo, **56** (tl) ©Alex Soza, (cl) Tom Vickers/Newscom/Splash News/Ventura/CA/United States, (cl) Chung Sung-Jun/Getty Images, **60** (t) Alexey Kopytko/Getty Images, 61 (c) ©Marla Aufmuth/TED, **62-63** (c) © Matthew Mahon/Redux Pictures, (c) Daxiao Productions/Shutterstock.com, **66** (b) Grapheast/Alamy Stock Photo, **69** (c) ©National Geographic Maps, (b) ©National Geographic Maps, **71** (b) ©Mark Leong/Redux, 72 (t) ©Aaron Huey/National Geographic Creative, (tl) National Geographic, **74** (cr) Oliver Uberti/National Geographic Magazine, **75** (b) Meldmedia Inc., **76** (c) Oliver Uberti/National Geographic Creative, 81 (c) JOE RIIS/National Geographic Creative, **82-83** (c) Morris Ryan/National Geographic Creative, (c) John Stanmeyer LLC/National Geographic Creative, **84** (tl) Cengage Learning, Inc., **86** (t) MARK THIESSEN/National Geographic, **88** (b) Gregory Manchess/National Geographic Creative, **90** (b) ©Stephen Alvarez/National Geographic Creative, **92** (t) Frans Lanting/National Geographic Creative, (cr) Cengage Learning, Inc., **94** (cl) Martin Gamache/National Geographic Creative, **95** (b) Jonathan Eden/Alamy, **97** (b) MICHAEL NICHOLS/National Geographic Creative, **99** (b) JOEL SARTORE/National Geographic Creative, **101** (c) ERIKA LARSEN/National Geographic Creative, **102** (c) Marco Vernaschi/National Geographic Creative, **103** (c) MATTHIEU PALEY/National Geographic Creative, (t) Chris Minihane/Getty Images, **104** (cr) Martin Gamache/National Geographic, **106** (c) Atlaspix/Shutterstock.com, (cl) Cengage Learning, Inc., **109** (b) ©Jordan Banks/Robert Harding/Aurora Photos, **110** (t) Pete McBride/National Geographic Creative, **114** (tr) ©Catherine Jaffee, **116** (b) Carolyn Cole/Getty Images, **118** (t) John Warburton Lee Photography/Alamy Stock Photo, **121** (c) MOHAMED EL-SHAHED/Getty Images, **122** (t) ©K. David Harrison, **122-123** (c) ©Christian Heeb/laif/Redux, **126** (b) Razvan Ionut Dragomirescu/Alamy Stock Photo, **132** (t) Bloomberg/Getty Images, 135 (b) Blend Images/Alamy Stock Photo, 136 (b) ©James Florio/Redux, **139** (t) David Litschel/Alamy Stock Photo, **141** (c) Steph Chambers/AP Images, **142-143** (c) KAZUHIRO NOGI/Getty Images, **146** (b) KONTROLAB/Getty Images., **149** (b) SEBASTIEN BOZON/Getty Images, **150** (b) Ashraf Jandali/Shutterstock.com, **152** (t) Petri Artturi Asikainen/Getty Images, **154** (bl) Boston Globe/Getty Images, **156** (b) Maridav/Shutterstock.com, **159** (c) Cengage Learning, Inc, **161** (c) Zephyr/Science Source, **162** (tr) Hero Images/Getty Images, (c) DAVID EVANS/National Geographic Creative, (b) NICK CALOYIANIS/National Geographic Creative, **162-163** (c) Digital Storm/Shutterstock.com, **163** (tl) DAVID EVANS/National Geographic Creative, (tr) BRUCE DALE/National Geographic Creative, (cr) Peter Cade/Getty Images, **166** (c) Peshkova/Shutterstock.com, **169** (t) Markus Mainka/Alamy Stock Photo, **171** (t) FatCamera/Getty Images, **172** (t) NORBERT MILLAUER/Getty Images, **175** (t) Joshua Davenport/Alamy Stock Photo, **176** (b) decade3d - anatomy online/Shutterstock.com, **181** (c) ©Craig Cutler/National Geographic Creative, **182-183** (c) JIM RICHARDSON/National Geographic Creative, **184** (tl) JIM RICHARDSON/National Geographic Creative, 186 (b) Jim Richardson/National Geographic Creative, **188-189** (b) Bloomberg/Getty Images, **190** (b) Getty Images/Getty Images, **192** (t) BRIAN J. SKERRY/National Geographic Creative, (cr) Cengage Learning, Inc., **194-195** (b) Richard Levine/Alamy Stock Photo, **198** (b) ©Robbie George/National Geographic Creative.

Maps

2–3 Created by MPS; **6** Mapping Specialists; **16** Mapping Specialists; **69** Adapted from "Interconnectivity," National Geographic Maps, 2014; **82–83** Adapted from "The Longest Walk," National Geographic, December 2013; **84** Adapted from "Early Americans," https://mrgrayhistory.wikispaces.com/UNIT+8+-+EARLY+AMERICAS; **92** Mapping Specialists; Map courtesy of Roy Safaris–Tanzania; **94** Adapted from "Who Owns This Land?" by Martin Gamache and Lauren C. Tierney, National Geographic, May 2016; **104** Adapted from "Extent of Hadza People," Martin Gamache and Lisa R. Ritter, National Geographic, December 2009; Mapping Specialists; **106** Mapping Specialists; **192** Mapping Specialists

Illustrations/Infographics

2–3 "The 10 Most Multicultural Cities In The World," https://theculturetrip.com/north-america/usa/california/articles/the-10-most-multicultural-cities-in-the-world/; "The 10 Most Visited Cities of 2017," http://www.cntraveler.com/galleries/2015-06-03/the-10-most-visited-cities-of-2015-london-bangkok-new-york/10 **9** Adapted from "Can Venice be Saved?" https://sites.google.com/site/unknownglobalhazards/subsidence-in-venice/why-is-subsidence-a-problem; **23** Adapted from "Meet Some of the Species Facing Extinction in the Wild," National Geographic/Joel Sartore, Photo Ark; **39** Adapted from "Saving Wildlife Through Licenses and Taxes," National Geographic, November 2007; **43** Adapted from "Top 3 Reasons for Trying to Look Good and Weekly Time Spent on Personal Grooming," https://blog.gfk.com/2016/01/what-makes-us-want-to-look-good/; **48** Adapted from "Countries with Top Number of Procedures, 2010," National Geographic, December 2012; **63** Adapted from "Future Work Skills 2020," http://www.iftf.org/futureworkskills/; **64** Adapted from "Net Employment Outlook by Job Family, 2015-2020," http://reports.weforum.org/future-of-jobs-2016/employment-trends/; **74** Adapted from "Revealed World," National Geographic, September 2010; **76** "Revealed World," National Geographic, September 2010; **79** Adapted from "Active Users of Key Global Social Platforms," https://wearesocial.com/special-reports/digital-in-2017-global-overview; **123** Adapted from "How Countries Spend Their Money," http://www.economist.com/blogs/graphicdetail/2015/09/daily-chart-9; **129** Adapted from "Top 3 Ways to Spend Spare Cash by Region," http://www.nielsen.com/be/en/insights/news/2015/saving-was-key-for-most-in-q1-but-millennials-outpaced-the-global-averages-for-spending-intentions.html; **130** Adapted from "Top 5 Savings Strategies by Region," http://www.nielsen.com/content/dam/corporate/us/en/images/news-trends/2015-newswire/9080-0729-cci-wire-image.jpg; **135** Adapted from "How Americans Spent Their Money in 2015," http://www.marketwatch.com/story/heres-how-americans-are-spending-their-money-2016-08-31; **159** Adapted from "How would you be interested in wearing/using a sensor device, assuming it was from a brand that you trust, offering a service that interests you?" https://www.mouser.com/images/microsites/wearable-consumer-survey.png; **189** Adapted from "Breeding Better Crops," National Geographic, October 2014; **196** Adatped from "These Countries Spend the Least on Food," and "These Countries Spend the Most on Food," https://www.weforum.org/agenda/2016/12/this-map-shows-how-much-each-country-spends-on-food/

Listening and Text Sources

6–8 "Vanishing Venice" by Cathy Newman, National Geographic, August 2009; "Venice Tourism Debate 2015: Residents Fear Visitors Are Destroying Their City, Demand Authorities Crack Down On Cruise Ships," http://www.ibtimes.com/venice-tourism-debate-2015-residents-fear-visitors-are-destroying-their-city-demand-2063682; "Venice

Matters to History – Ventians Matter to Me," http://news.nationalgeographic.com/news/2015/01/150129-venice-my-town-zwingle-grand-canal-motondoso-piazza-san-marco-vaporetto/; **14** "10 Most Affluent Cities In The World: Macau and Hartford Top The List," http://www.newgeography.com/content/004853-10-most-affluent-cities-world-macau-and-hartford-top-list; "List of countries and dependencies by area," https://en.wikipedia.org/wiki/List_of_countries_and_dependencies_by_area; "Singapore," http://www.averagesalarysurvey.com/singapore; **16-17** "The Singapore Solution," by Mark Jacobson, National Geographic, January 2010; **17** "16 Odd Things that are Illegal in Singapore," http://www.businessinsider.com/things-that-are-illegal-in-singapore-2015-7; "$200 Fine for Anyone Caught Breeding Mozzies," http://www.straitstimes.com/singapore/health/200-fine-for-anyone-caught-breeding-mozzies **24** "Species Guide," http://us.whales.org/species-guide?gclid=Cj0KCQjwn6DMBRC0ARIsAHZtCeON4EPNKq59YzOdMc1XIQ0VABitwoyoKCAzJsrdXKxryetvrdqJvUYaAtpFEALw_wcB; "U.S. Leads New Bid to Phase Out Whale Hunting," http://www.nytimes.com/2010/04/15/science/earth/15whale.html?_r=1&; **25** "International Convention for the Regulation of Whaling," https://en.wikipedia.org/wiki/International_Convention_for_the_Regulation_of_Whaling; "Which Cetacean Species are Extinct?" http://baleinesendirect.org/en/which-cetacean-species-are-extinct/; "British Adventurer Builds Whale-shaped Boat to Sail to Canada," http://www.cbc.ca/radio/asithappens/as-it-happens-wednesday-edition-1.3472671/british-adventurer-builds-whale-shaped-boat-to-sail-to-canada-1.3472704; **26–27** "Last One" by Verlyn Klinkenborg, National Geographic, January 2009; "Listed Species Summary (Boxscore)," http://ecos.fws.gov/ecp0/reports/box-score-report; **34** "Wolf Wars" by Douglas Chadwick, National Geographic, March 2010; **36–38** "Hunters: For the Love of the Land," by Robert M. Poole, National Geographic, November 2007, **40** "New 'Golden' Ratios for Facial Beauty" by Pamela M. Pallett, Stephen Link, and Kang Lee, https://www.ncbi.nlm.nih.gov/pmc/articles/PMC2814183/; **46-47, 49** "The Enigma of Beauty" by Cathy Newman, National Geographic, January 2000; **56-57** "Dreamweavers" by Cathy Newman, National Geographic, January 2003; "Artificial Spider Silk Could Be Used for Armor, More" by Brian Handwerk, National Geographic Daily News, January 14, 2005; **67** "What Skills We Need to Succeed in the World," YouTube, posted by Globalization 101, August 23, 2010; WESO Trends 2017: The Disconnect Between Growth and Employment," http://www.ilo.org/global/about-the-ilo/multimedia/video/institutional-videos/WCMS_541539/lang--en/index.htm; "Decision-making with Emotional Intelligence," https://www.ideasforleaders.com/ideas/decision-making-with-emotional-intelligence; **68** "Globalization Terminology," https://en.wikipedia.org/wiki/Category:Globalization_terminology; **74** "Revealed World" by Tim Folger, National Geographic, September 2010; **76–77** "Is Pokémon Go Taking Over the World?," https://kantanmtblog.com/2016/07/25/is-pokemon-go-taking-over-the-world/; "Pokémon Go Becomes Global Craze as Game Overtakes Twitter for US Users," https://www.theguardian.com/technology/2016/jul/12/pokemon-go-becomes-global-phenomenon-as-number-of-us-users-overtakes-twitter; "Popular Augmented Reality & Pokémon Go! Shows," https://www.mixcloud.com/discover/augmented-reality+pokemon-go/; "Virtual and Augmented Reality Could Take Online Meetings to the Next Level," http://blog.clickmeeting.com/virtual-and-augmented-reality-could-take-online-meetings-to-the-next-level; "Deglobalization is Already Well Underway – Here are 4 Technologies that Will Speed it Up," http://www.mauldineconomics.com/editorial/deglobalization-is-already-well-underwayhere-are-4-technologies-that-will-s; **84** "Tracking the First Americans" by Glenn Hodges, National Geographic, January 2015; **86–88** "The Greatest Journey: The Trail of Our DNA," by James Shreeve, National Geographic, March 2006; "From Africa to Astoria by Way of Everywhere" by James Shreeve, http://ngm.nationalgeographic.com/big-idea/02/queens-genes, August 17, 2009; **94** Adapted from "Who Owns This Land?" by Martin Gamache and Lauren C. Tierney, National Geographic, May 2016; **96–97** "Heartbreak on the Serengeti" by Robert M. Poole, National Geographic, February 2006; **99** "Animal Migration: Facts," idahoptv.org/sciencetrek/topics/animal_migration/facts.cfm; **104** "The Hadza: Tanzania's Hunter-Gatherers" by Michael Finkel; Adapted from "Shifting Ground," National Geographic, December 2009; **106–107** "Bhutan's Enlightened Experiment" by Brook Larmer, National Geographic, March 2008; "The 4 Pillars of GNH," http://www.gnhcentrebhutan.org/what-is-gnh/the-4-pillars-of-gnh/; "The 9 Domains of GNH," http://www.gnhcentrebhutan.org/what-is-gnh/the-9-domains-of-gnh/; "Bhutan to Become Self Sufficient in Vegetables," https://www.positive.news/2012/environment/agriculture/8644/bhutan-sufficient-vegetables/; **114** Adapted from http://www.nationalgeographic.com/explorers/bios/catherine-jaffee/; **116–117** "Reviving Native Lands" by Charles Bowden, National Geographic, August 2010; **118** "New Year Traditions from Around the World; How to Have a Happy New Year," http://www.almanac.com/content/new-year-traditions-around-world; "50 New Year Traditions from Around the World," http://www.lifehack.org/articles/lifestyle/50-new-year-traditions-from-around-the-world.html; **126** "List of Circulating Currencies," https://en.wikipedia.org/wiki/List_of_circulating_currencies; **126–127** "Can You Buy Happiness? Not How You Think . . . New Research," http://happinessbeyondthought.blogspot.com/2014/11/can-you-buy-happiness-not-how-you.html; "So You Think Owning a Home Will Make You Happy? Don't Be Too Sure," http://knowledge.wharton.upenn.edu/article/so-you-think-owning-a-home-will-make-you-happy-dont-be-too-sure/; "Homeownership, the Key to Happiness?" http://www.nytimes.com/2013/07/14/realestate/homeownership-the-key-to-happiness.html; "Can Money Buy You Happiness?" http://www.wsj.com/articles/can-money-buy-happiness-heres-what-science-has-to-say-1415569538; **128** "Millennials and Money," https://www.fasthorseinc.com/blog/2017/01/millennials-money-financial-literacy/; **146–147** "Big Data: A Game Changer in Healthcare," https://www.forbes.com/sites/bernardmarr/2016/05/24/big-data-a-game-changer-in-healthcare/#760e3698525b; "Big Data Coming in Faster Than Biomedical Researchers Can Process It," http://www.npr.org/sections/health-shots/2016/11/28/503035862/big-data-coming-in-faster-than-biomedical-researchers-can-process-it; **149** "The Top Six Challenges of Healthcare Data Management," http://www.ingrammicroadvisor.com/data-center/the-top-six-challenges-of-healthcare-data-management; **154** "Health Technology in the Workplace: Leveraging Technology to Protect and Improve Worker Health," http://healthyworkplaces.berkeley.edu/wellness/health-technology-in-the-workplace-leveraging-technology-to-protect-and-improve-worker-health/; **162–163** "Anatomy of the Brain," https://www.mayfieldclinic.com/PE-AnatBrain.htm; "Human Brain Functions–Functioning of Human Brain with Diagram," http://humanbrainfacts.org/human-brain-functions.php; **164** "Multiple Intelligences," http://www.tecweb.org/styles/gardner.html; "Multiple Intelligences: Definitions & Examples," http://enhancinged.wgbh.org/research/multi/examples.html; **166–167** "Neuromyth 6: The Left Brain/Right Brain Myth," https://www.oecd.org/edu/ceri/neuromyth6.htm; "The Truth about the Left Brain/Right Brain Relationship," http://www.npr.org/sections/13.7/2013/12/02/248089436/the-truth-about-the-left-brain-right-brain-relationship; **169** "Fact or Fiction?: Babies Exposed to Classical Music End Up Smarter," https://www.scientificamerican.com/article/fact-or-fiction-babies-ex/; "Do People Only Use 10 Percent of Their Brains?" https://www.scientificamerican.com/article/do-people-only-use-10-percent-of-their-brains/; "Do Opposites Really Attract? It's Complicated," https://www.psychologytoday.com/blog/head-games/201412/do-opposites-really-attract-its-complicated; "Lunacy and the Full Moon," https://www.scientificamerican.com/article/lunacy-and-the-full-moon/; "A Review on the Current Research on Vocabulary Instruction," https://www2.ed.gov/programs/readingfirst/support/rmcfinal1.pdf; "Venting Anger May do More Harm than Good," http://www.nytimes.com/1983/03/08/science/venting-anger-may-do-more-harm-than-good.html?pagewanted=all; **170** "The Invisible Gorilla," http://theinvisiblegorilla.com/gorilla_experiment.html; "Pearls Before Breakfast: Can One of the Nation's Great Musicians Cut Through the Fog of a D.C. Rush Hour? Let's Find Out," https://www.washingtonpost.com/lifestyle/magazine/pearls-before-breakfast-can-one-of-the-nations-great-musicians-cut-through-the-fog-of-a-dc-rush-hour-lets-find-out/2014/09/23/8a6d46da-4331-11e4-b47c-f5889e061e5f_story.html?utm_term=.6b5690ff6e91; "Why Carlsberg's Toast to Courage Went Viral," http://mashable.com/2012/05/10/carlsberg-viral-video/#8a3EkQ7umuqU; "Stereotypes: Why We Act Without Thinking," http://www.spring.org.uk/2010/03/stereotypes-why-we-act-without-thinking.php; **174** "Animal Minds," http://www.economist.com/news/essays/21676961-inner-lives-animals-are-hard-study-there-evidence-they-may-be-lot-richer-science-once-thought; "Animal Cognition," https://en.wikipedia.org/wiki/Animal_cognition; **176–177** "Remember This" by Joshua Foer, National Geographic, November 2007; **179** "How to Pick the Fastest Line at the Supermarket," https://www.nytimes.com/2016/09/08/business/how-to-pick-the-fastest-line-at-the-supermarket.html; **182** "Arctic Stronghold of World's Seeds Flooded After Permafrost Melts," https://www.theguardian.com/environment/2017/may/19/arctic-stronghold-of-worlds-seeds-flooded-after-permafrost-melts; **184** "Food Ark: How Heirloom Seeds Can Feed the World," by Charles Siebert, National Geographic, July 2011; **184, 186–187** "Food: How Altered?" by Jennifer Ackerman, National Geographic, May 2002; **186–187** "Sen. Donna Nesselbush: Three Quarters of Processed Foods Have Genetically Modified Organisms," http://www.politifact.com/rhode-island/statements/2015/mar/22/donna-nesselbush/sen-donna-nesselbush-three-quarters-processed-food/; "Genetically Modified Animals Will Be on Your Plate in No Time," https://www.wired.com/2015/07/eating-genetically-modified-animals/; "GMO Safety Debate is Over," http://allianceforscience.cornell.edu/blog/mark-lynas/gmo-safety-debate-over; **189** "Breeding Better Crops," National Geographic, October 2014; **190** "Tangelo," https://en.wikipedia.org/wiki/Tangelo; "GloFish," https://en.wikipedia.org/wiki/GloFish; "Plant Breeding: A Success Story to be Continued Thanks to the Advances of Genomics," https://www.ncbi.nlm.nih.gov/pmc/articles/PMC3355770/; "Genetically Modified Animals," http://www.enki-village.com/genetically-modified-animals.html; "The History of Wheat," http://prairiecalifornian.com/history-wheat/; "Pinebery & Pineberries," http://strawberryplants.org/2010/09/pineberry-pineberries/; **194, 196–197** "The End of Plenty: The Global Food Crisis," by Joel K. Bourne, Jr., National Geographic, June 2009; **196–197** "The Global Staple," http://ricepedia.org/rice-as-food/the-global-staple-rice-consumers

INDEX OF EXAM SKILLS AND TASKS

Pathways Listening, Speaking, and Critical Thinking is designed to provide practice for standardized exams, such as IELTS and TOEFL. Many activities in this book practice or focus on the **key exam skills** needed for test success. In addition, a number of activities are designed to be the same as (or similar to) **common question types** found in these tests and to provide effective practice of these questions.

Listening

Key Exam Skills	IELTS	TOEFL	Page(s) / Exercise(s)
Distinguishing facts from theories	X	X	86 LS, 87 C, 99 D
Listening for advantages	X	X	66 LS, 67 C
Listening for clarifying answers	X	X	96 LS, 97 D
Listening for key details or specific information	X	X	56 LS, 56 C, 77 C, 96 C, 107 C, 127 C, 137 C, 167 C, 177 D, 197 D
Listening for main ideas	X	X	7 C, 46 B, 56 B, 76 B, 96 B, 106 B, 126 B, 136 B, 146 C, 156 B, 157 D, 166 B, 186 B, 196 B
Listening for positive or negative views	X	X	157 LS, 157 C
Listening for shifts in topic	X	X	137 LS
Taking notes: using abbreviations	X	X	7 NT, 7 D, 7 E
Taking notes: using a time line or idea map	X	X	87 NT, 87 D, 107 NT, 107 D, 117 D
Taking notes: using a T-chart	X	X	146 NT, 147 D
Understanding the introduction to a lecture	X	X	6 LS, 6 B
Using prior knowledge to listen effectively	X	X	36 LS, 36 A, 66 A, 96 A, 146 A, 156 A, 166 A, 196 A

KEY

EL	Everyday Language
LS	Listening Skill
NT	Note-Taking Skill
PRON	Pronunciation
SS	Speaking Skill

Common Question Types	IELTS	TOEFL	Page(s) / Exercise(s)
Connecting content		X	146 C, 156 B, 166 B, 186 B
Matching	X		46 B, 137 D, 168 A
Multiple choice	X	X	6 B, 126 B
Multiple response		X	6 C, 76 B, 106 B, 136 B
Note completion	X		7 D, 27 D, 27 E, 47 C, 57 D, 67 C, 77 C, 87 D, 107 D, 117 D, 127 C, 147 D, 167 C, 177 E, 187 C, 187 D
Sentence completion	X		17 D
Short answer	X		177 D, 197 D

INDEX OF EXAM SKILLS AND TASKS

Speaking

Key Exam Skills	IELTS	TOEFL	Page(s) / Exercise(s)
Approximating	X	X	88 SS, 89 B
Asking rhetorical questions	X	X	108 SS, 108 C
Brainstorming Ideas	X	X	28 A, 59 A, 107 E, 119 B, 200 B
Citing research or knowledgeable groups	X		128 SS, 128 A, 128 B, 188 SS, 189 B, 191 B
Defining unfamiliar terms	X	X	60 SS, 68 A, 68 C
Discussing personal experiences or feelings	X	X	13 F, 71 C, 98 C, 165 D, 173 E, 195 F, 197 E
Discussing pros and cons	X	X	10 B, 10 C, 69 D
Emphasizing important information	X	X	148 SS, 148 A, 149 C
Expressing opinions and/or reasons	X	X	37 F, 38 B, 55 D, 78 B, 149 E
Expressing probability and possibility	X	X	89 C, 90 E
Linking	X	X	18 PRON, 18 A, 18 B, 18 C, 30 PRON, 30 E, 30 F, 30 G, 98 PRON, 98 A, 98 B, 98 C, 138 PRON, 138 A
Making suggestions or recommendations	X	X	171 EL, 171 C
Paraphrasing	X	X	49 SS, 53 E
Pronouncing reduced words	X	X	178 PRON, 178 A, 178 B, 199 PRON, 199 B, 199 C
Speaking about abstract concepts	X	X	5 D, 10 A, 15 E, 17 E, 19 D, 25 D, 26 A, 27 F, 28 B, 35 C, 45 E, 47 D, 49 C, 53 F, 57 E, 66 A, 77 D, 79 C, 85 E, 105 E, 113 F, 115 E, 117 E, 125 E, 133 F, 157 D, 175 D, 193 E
Speaking about causal relationships	X	X	168 SS, 169 D
Speaking about conditional situations	X	X	10 F, 13 F, 110 G, 127 D
Speaking about familiar, everyday topics	X	X	67 D, 78 B, 80 C, 89 B, 91 A, 91 B, 98 C, 118 A, 118 C, 120 F, 130 F, 131 B, 136 A, 151 B, 155 E, 165 C
Speaking about past actions or situations	X	X	71 B, 71 C
Speaking about problems and solutions	X	X	20 A, 20 D, 30 B, 30 C, 99 E, 180 E
Summarizing information you heard		X	87 E, 97 D, 177 F
Summarizing written or illustrated information	X	X	9 D, 38 C, 48 B, 189 C
Using correct stress	X	X	109 PRON, 109 D, 109 E
Using parentheticals to clarify ideas	X	X	78 PRON, 78 A, 78 B
Using signal phrases to introduce ideas	X	X	8 SS, 8 B

KEY

EL	Everyday Language
LS	Listening Skill
NT	Note-Taking Skill
PRON	Pronunciation
SS	Speaking Skill

Pathways	CEFR	IELTS Band	TOEFL Score
Level 4	**C1**	**6.5–7.0**	**81–100**
Level 3	B2	5.5–6.0	51–80
Level 2	B1–B2	4.5–5.0	31–50
Level 1	A2–B1	0–4.0	0–30
Foundations	A1–A2		